America's
TEST KITCHEN

ALSO BY THE EDITORS AT AMERICA'S TEST KITCHEN

The America's Test Kitchen Family Cookbook
America's Best Lost Recipes
The Best of America's Test Kitchen 2007

THE BEST RECIPE SERIES:
The Best International Recipe
The Best Make-Ahead Recipe
The Best 30-Minute Recipe
The Best Light Recipe
The Cook's Illustrated Guide to Grilling & Barbecue
Best American Side Dishes
The New Best Recipe
Cover & Bake
Steaks, Chops, Roasts & Ribs
Baking Illustrated
Restaurant Favorites at Home
The Best Vegetable Recipes
The Best Italian Classics
The Best American Classics
The Best Soups & Stews

THE TV COMPANION SERIES:
Cooking with America's Test Kitchen
Test Kitchen Favorites
Cooking at Home with America's Test Kitchen
America's Test Kitchen Live!
Inside America's Test Kitchen
Here in America's Test Kitchen
The America's Test Kitchen Cookbook

834 Kitchen Quick Tips

For a full listing of all our books or to order titles:
http://www.cooksillustrated.com
http://www.americastestkitchen.com
or call 800-611-0759

PRAISE FOR OTHER AMERICA'S TEST KITCHEN TITLES

"This tome definitely raises the bar for all-in-one, basic, must-have cookbooks. . . . Kimball and his company have scored another hit." Portland Oregonian on *The America's Test Kitchen Family Cookbook*

"A foolproof, go-to resource for everyday cooking."
Publishers Weekly on *The America's Test Kitchen Family Cookbook*

"A time-saving tome."
The Chicago Tribune on *834 Kitchen Quick Tips*

"For anyone looking for a lighter way of cooking, this book and its 300 recipes would be a most valuable resource." Providence Journal on *The Best Light Recipe*

"Further proof that practice makes perfect, if not transcendent. . . . If an intermediate cook follows the directions exactly, the results will be better than takeout or mom's." The New York Times on *The New Best Recipe*

"Exceptional renditions with thorough instruction…"
Publishers Weekly on *Cooking at Home with America's Test Kitchen*

"Like a mini-cooking school, the detailed instructions and illustrations ensure that even the most inexperienced cook can follow these recipes with success."
Publishers Weekly on *Best American Side Dishes*

"Makes one-dish dinners a reality for average cooks, with honest ingredients and detailed make-ahead instructions." The New York Times on *Cover & Bake*

"*Steaks, Chops, Roasts & Ribs* conquers every question one could have about all things meat."
The San Francisco Chronicle on *Steaks, Chops, Roasts & Ribs*

"The best instructional book on baking this reviewer has seen."
Library Journal (starred review) on *Baking Illustrated*

"A must-have for anyone into our nation's cooking traditions—and a good reference, too."
Los Angeles Daily News on *American Classics*

"If you've always wanted to make real Italian dishes as close to the Italian way as we can make them in America, here's a cookbook that shows you how." Pittsburgh Post-Gazette on *Italian Classics*

"*Cook's Illustrated* to the rescue. . . . *The Best Vegetable Recipes* belongs on every cooking reference shelf. Here's to our health." Pittsburgh Tribune-Review on *The Best Vegetable Recipes*

AMERICA'S TEST KITCHEN
17 Station Street, Brookline, MA 02445

Library of Congress Cataloging-in-Publication Data
The Editors at America's Test Kitchen

THE BEST OF AMERICA'S TEST KITCHEN 2008:
The Year's Best Recipes, Equipment Reviews, and Tastings

1st Edition

Hardcover: $35.00 US/$41.50 CAN
ISBN-13: 978-1-933615-19-6   ISBN-10: 1-933615-19-2
1. Cooking. 1. Title
2007

Manufactured in the United States of America

10 9 8 7 6 5 4 3 2 1

Distributed by America's Test Kitchen
17 Station Street, Brookline, MA 02445

EDITORIAL DIRECTOR: Jack Bishop
EXECUTIVE EDITOR: Elizabeth Carduff
ASSOCIATE EDITORS: Elizabeth Wray Emery and Rachel Toomey
CONTRIBUTING EDITOR: Matthew Card
DESIGN DIRECTOR: Amy Klee
LAYOUT: Chin Wang
DESIGNER: Matthew Warnick
FRONT COVER PHOTOGRAPH: Keller + Keller
COVER STYLING: Marie Piraino
STAFF PHOTOGRAPHER: Daniel J. van Ackere
ADDITIONAL PHOTOGRAPHERS: Keller + Keller and Carl Tremblay
SENIOR PRODUCTION MANAGER: Jessica Lindheimer Quirk
COLOR AND IMAGING SPECIALIST: Andrew Mannone
COPYEDITOR: Evie Righter
PROOFREADER: Jeffrey Schier
INDEXER: Elizabeth Parson

PICTURED ON THE FRONT COVER: Lemon Layer Cake (page 288)

THE BEST OF
America's
TEST KITCHEN

THE YEAR'S BEST RECIPES, EQUIPMENT REVIEWS, AND TASTINGS

2008

BY THE EDITORS AT
AMERICA'S TEST KITCHEN

CONTENTS

INTRODUCTION **1**

STARTERS & SALADS **2**

SOUPS & STEWS **34**

VEGETABLES & SIDE DISHES **56**

EGGS & BREADS **92**

PASTA **122**

MEAT **142**

POULTRY **196**

SEAFOOD **236**

DESSERTS **260**

CONVERSIONS **326**

INDEX **329**

INTRODUCTION

IN THE SMALL VERMONT TOWN WHERE I GREW UP,
I was never surprised to find out that a farmer was also
a fiddler or that the backhoe operator in town was
also an accomplished turkey hunter. One of my favorite old-timers was Cliff McKee, who lived down by
Doug's Gulf gas station and, in his later years, helped
out during the morning shift. If you just stopped by
and said hello as he filled your pickup with regular, you
would never have known that he was born when Teddy
Roosevelt was president and that his family had a farm
up on Red Mountain where they used home remedies
made of calomel and rhubarb. When he got going, Cliff
would talk about the time the colt ran away with the
cutter or the fierce wind that twisted off the doors of
the barn and uprooted the old apple tree. Nobody in
the country is just one thing. They had to know quite a
lot about many things just to get by.

Here at America's Test Kitchen, we are very different from those old-timers. We know how to do only
one thing: Test recipes until we find the best way to
make them. It might be something as commonplace as
Cincinnati Chili or slow-cooker Guinness Beef Stew, or
a fancy Saturday night recipe like Herb-Crusted Beef
Tenderloin. So, unlike most of my country neighbors,
we are not jacks of many trades.

But we do what we do in a variety of different forums.
We test recipes for *Cook's Illustrated* as well as for its
sister magazine, *Cook's Country*. We test recipes for our
many cookbooks as well as for our public television
show, *America's Test Kitchen*. We also test recipes and
rate equipment for our various websites, including
www.cooksillustrated.com.

So if you want an easy way to get a taste of our favorite recipes each year, this volume, *The Best of America's
Test Kitchen*, is the place to go. You get a collection of
recipes, tastings, and testings that represents the best

work we have done in the last 12 months. That might
mean a simple but unusual recipe for Hot Cocoa Mix
from *Cook's Country* (believe it or not, it calls for white
chocolate chips as the secret ingredient) or an updated,
from-scratch version of Strawberry Poke Cake (invented
by the Kraft Company in 1969 as a way to sell more
strawberry Jell-O). For those who want fancier cooking, one of my personal favorites was the Roast Beef
Tenderloin with Caramelized Onion and Mushroom
Stuffing from *Cook's Illustrated*. You will also find out
which brand of extra-virgin olive oil is the best (it hails
from Spain, not Italy), which moderately-priced Dutch
oven will do the job, and which pie plate and pie server
are our favorites. Simple stuff, all of it, but useful.

On a farm, nobody takes anything for granted—not
the weather, the soundness of a horse, or if the tractor is
going to start on a cold morning. In the kitchen, we feel
much the same about recipes. We don't take the ingredients, the cookware, or the methodology for granted.
Everything is up for grabs. This is based on many lifetimes of disappointment with recipes that never turned
out right, no matter how pretty the photos and enthusiastic the text.

So if you want our best work all in one volume, this
is it. We haven't taken anything for granted when developing these recipes, and neither should you. But for
those of you who are not familiar with our test kitchen,
purchasing this volume does require a small leap of faith.
After that, I expect that this recipe collection will have to
prove itself worthy of the cover price and, all things considered, that's a bet that I am happy to make.

CHRISTOPHER KIMBALL
Founder and Editor
Cook's Illustrated and *Cook's Country*
Host, *America's Test Kitchen*

STARTERS
& SALADS

CLASSIC CHEDDAR CHEESE BALL **4**

HOT CHEESE DIP WITH POBLANO
AND CHORIZO **6**

SPICY WHIPPED FETA
WITH ROASTED RED PEPPERS **7**

STUFFED MUSHROOMS
WITH GOAT CHEESE AND HERB STUFFING **9**

CRISPY POLENTA TRIANGLES
WITH HERBED GOAT CHEESE **10**

COCKTAIL CRAB CAKES
WITH RÉMOULADE SAUCE **12**

MINI BEEF AND CHEESE EMPANADAS **14**

THE ULTIMATE SPICY BEEF NACHOS **16**

ZUCCHINI FRITTERS **19**

FRENCH ONION AND BACON TART **20**

GERMAN TART WITH ONION, BACON,
AND CRÈME FRAÎCHE **23**

FRISÉE SALAD WITH BACON
AND POACHED EGG **24**

SPICY ASIAN CUCUMBER SALAD **27**

SOUTHWESTERN CAESAR SALAD **28**

ARUGULA SALAD WITH GRAPES, FENNEL,
GORGONZOLA, AND PECANS **30**

FRESH BASIL VINAIGRETTE **31**

CLASSIC CHEDDAR CHEESE BALL

SERVES 15 TO 20

WHAT MAKES THIS A BEST RECIPE: A great cheese ball is the star of any appetizer spread, though few of them ever taste as good as they look. The attractive herb or nut covering masks a bland, fake-cheese filling tasting more of Cheetos than cheddar. This recipe, however, succeeds because it actually tastes of its namesake: real, honest-to-goodness, tangy cheddar cheese. From soft and smooth to sour and crumbly, cheddar cheese comes in several distinct styles. After trying them all in varying recipes, we found that the powerful flavor of aged extra-sharp cheddar produced the best-tasting ball. Flavor aside, extra-sharp cheddar's crumbly texture wouldn't do on its own, so we combined it with smooth cream cheese and a slightly unexpected ingredient, mayonnaise, which lent the mixture a lush, ultra-smooth texture. While the tangy cheddar provided the main thrust of flavor, we wanted to round out its edges. After trying all manner of seasonings, we settled on small amounts of assertive ingredients like Worcestershire, cayenne, and garlic. Each added a new dimension to the cheddar ball, without taking over or impacting the creamy texture. As for a mixing method, nothing could surpass the ease or effectiveness of a food processor. Within seconds, the mixture was thoroughly and evenly mixed. After a quick turn in the fridge to firm up, our cheese ball was almost ready to go, requiring only a roll in minced fresh chives. With a deep flavor, creamy texture, and inviting appearance (orange cheddar will give the cheese ball a rosy color), this cheese ball tasted as good as it looked.

---

8 ounces extra-sharp cheddar cheese, shredded (2 cups)

8 ounces cream cheese, softened

2 tablespoons mayonnaise

1 tablespoon Worcestershire sauce

1 garlic clove, minced

¼ teaspoon cayenne pepper

½ cup minced fresh chives

1. Process all the ingredients, excluding the chives, in a food processor until smooth, scraping down the sides as necessary, about 1 minute. Transfer the cheese mixture to the center of a large sheet of plastic wrap.

2. Holding the corners of the wrap in one hand and, following the photos, twist the cheese with your other hand to seal the wrap and shape the cheese into a rough ball. (The mixture will be somewhat loose.) Refrigerate until firm, about 3 hours. Once the cheese ball is firm, reshape it as necessary into a smooth sphere. Unwrap the cheese ball and roll it in the chives to cover evenly. Let it sit at room temperature for 15 minutes before serving.

WHAT YOU CAN DO AHEAD OF TIME: The cheese ball can be wrapped tightly in plastic wrap and refrigerated for up to 2 days.

NOTES FROM THE TEST KITCHEN

HOW TO MAKE A CHEESE BALL

We found shaping the soft cheese mixture into a uniformly round ball much easier said than done. After making a mess of several batches, we landed on an easy solution that combined both shaping and storing the cheese ball.

1. Transfer the cheese mixture to the center of a large sheet of plastic wrap.

2. Holding the corners of the wrap in one hand, twist the cheese with your other hand to seal the wrap and shape the cheese into a rough ball.

SPICY WHIPPED FETA
WITH ROASTED RED PEPPERS
MAKES ABOUT 2 CUPS

WHAT MAKES THIS A BEST RECIPE: *Htipiti*, or spicy whipped feta, is a classic Greek *meze* dip, or spread. It is, simply, feta cheese pureed with olive oil and spices, and sometimes roasted red peppers. While we love its strong, dynamic flavors, we most appreciate how easy htipiti is to pull together, requiring just a few seconds in a food processor to whip smooth and a couple of hours in the refrigerator for the flavors to blend and the texture to firm up. It couldn't be more convenient for quick entertaining. After working our way through different types of feta, the only real drama during testing arose around choosing an ingredient to provide the dip's requisite heat. We whipped up batches using fresh green chiles, red pepper flakes, and cayenne pepper, and while each had its merits, we liked the way that the cayenne was evenly incorporated into the dip, and the subtle background heat that it imparted. The feta provided some tanginess (courtesy of the brine in which it is packed), which we enhanced by the addition of a bracing shot of fresh lemon juice. Served with pita chips or a crusty baguette, whipped feta easily sets the stage for any Mediterranean-flavored meal.

- 1 pound feta cheese, rinsed and crumbled (about 4 cups)
- ⅓ cup extra-virgin olive oil, plus extra for serving
- 1 tablespoon fresh lemon juice
- ½ teaspoon cayenne pepper, plus extra for serving
- ¼ teaspoon pepper
- 1 (6-ounce) jar roasted red peppers, drained, rinsed, and patted dry

Process all the ingredients in a food processor until smooth, about 20 seconds. Transfer the mixture to a serving bowl, cover with plastic wrap, and refrigerate until firm, about 2 hours. Drizzle with oil and dust with cayenne before serving.

WHERE THINGS CAN GO WRONG: If your feta is very salty, be sure to rinse it before adding it to the food processor, or the resulting dip will be very salty.

WHAT YOU CAN DO AHEAD OF TIME: The whipped feta can be refrigerated in an airtight container for up to 2 days. Let it come to room temperature before serving.

NOTES FROM THE TEST KITCHEN

CHOOSING FETA CHEESE
We typically use imported Greek feta (available at specialty stores), but wondered if supermarket feta would work just as well. The feta in the supermarket is almost certainly made with pasteurized cow's milk rather than the more traditional sheep's or goat's milk. As we suspected, the Greek feta was preferred for its creaminess and pleasant milky flavor. Much to our surprise, however, the vacuum-sealed supermarket feta fared pretty well in this recipe, aside from being a touch salty. It was moist, creamy, fresh tasting, and tangy—all the qualities one looks for. Coming in a distant third was the feta sold on a Styrofoam tray; this cheese tasted chalky and was nearly flavorless. The bottom line? Look for feta packed in brine. As a general rule, taste feta before using. If it is overly salty, rinse it under cool running water before adding it to a recipe.

THE BEST EXTRA-VIRGIN OLIVE OIL
For most cooked dishes we're perfectly happy reaching for supermarket olive oil, but for other uses, sometimes only a good-quality, extra-virgin olive oil will do. Typically produced in Italy, Greece, and Spain, extra-virgin oils range wildly in price, color, and packaging, so it's hard to know what you're really purchasing. While many things can impact the quality and flavor of olive oil, the type of olive, the harvest (earlier means greener, more bitter, and pungent; later more mild and buttery), and processing are the most important factors. The best-quality oil comes from olives picked at their peak and processed as quickly as possible without heat (which can coax more oil from the olives but at the expense of flavor). The good news is that after tasting 10 popular brands from Italy, Spain, Greece, and the United States, we found all acceptable. Our favorite oils were produced from a blend of olives and, thus, were well rounded—no one element came on too strong. Out of those tasted, we most liked **Columela Extra Virgin Olive Oil** from Spain ($22 for 25.4 ounces) for its fruity flavor and excellent balance.

STUFFED MUSHROOMS

STUFFED MUSHROOMS
WITH GOAT CHEESE AND HERB STUFFING
MAKES 24 MUSHROOMS

WHAT MAKES THIS A BEST RECIPE: A perfect stuffed mushroom combines an earthy, chewy mushroom with a potent, complementary filling and crunchy topping. Few, however, attain such heights and most are usually a sordid coupling of soggy mushroom, boring filling, and insipid topping. This recipe bests the rest by yielding near-perfect stuffed mushrooms. We researched dozens of stuffed mushroom recipes and, while most were duds, we discovered a technique in one recipe that we couldn't pass up. The recipe seasoned and roasted the mushrooms prior to stuffing them, which effectively eliminated much of their excess liquid. We retooled the existing recipe a bit and seasoned the mushrooms with olive oil, lemon juice, salt, and pepper before roasting them gill side up on a wire rack (and finishing for a few minutes gill side down), elevated above the cooking sheet. This approach wicked away extra moisture, yet left the mushrooms moist and tender. Given that we had to roast the mushrooms, we wanted a filling that did not require any additional cooking. After tasting a variety of different options, we settled on a blend of tangy goat cheese and smooth cream cheese, which accented both the flavor and texture of the roasted mushrooms. Fresh herbs, like basil, tarragon, and thyme, and a little minced garlic added big, easy flavor. As for bread crumbs and baking, we unanimously preferred fresh bread crumbs to dry (too crunchy once baked) and a short bake in a very hot oven (450 degrees). The quick burst of heat crisped the topping and tempered the filling without drying out the mushroom caps. Richly flavored and easy to prepare, these stuffed mushrooms would be the hit of any party.

FILLING

- 4 ounces goat cheese, softened
- 2 ounces cream cheese, softened
- 1 tablespoon olive oil
- 1 garlic clove, minced
- 1 tablespoon chopped fresh basil
- 1 tablespoon chopped fresh tarragon
- 2 teaspoons chopped fresh thyme
  Salt and pepper

TOPPING

- 1 slice high-quality white sandwich bread, quartered
- 1 tablespoon chopped fresh parsley
- 2 garlic cloves, minced
- 2 tablespoons olive oil

MUSHROOMS

- 24 large mushrooms, stems removed
- ¼ cup olive oil
- 1 teaspoon fresh lemon juice
  Salt and pepper

1. FOR THE FILLING: Process all the ingredients, including ¼ teaspoon salt and ⅛ teaspoon pepper, in a food processor until smooth. Transfer the mixture to a zipper-lock plastic bag and refrigerate until ready to use.

2. FOR THE TOPPING: Pulse the bread in a food processor to coarse crumbs. Mix the parsley, garlic, and oil in a bowl; stir the crumbs into the oil mixture to coat. Set aside.

3. FOR THE MUSHROOMS: Adjust an oven rack to the middle position and heat the oven to 450 degrees. Line a rimmed baking sheet with foil and set a wire rack inside the baking sheet. Toss the mushrooms with the oil, lemon juice, ¼ teaspoon salt, and ⅛ teaspoon pepper in a bowl. Arrange the mushrooms gill side up on the rack and roast until the juices are released, about 20 minutes. Turn the caps over and roast until the mushrooms are well browned, about 10 minutes.

4. Remove the baking sheet from the oven. Flip the roasted mushrooms gill side up and cool slightly. Snip off one corner from the bag with the filling, then fill the mushrooms following the photos on page 10. Press each cap (stuffing side down) into the bread-crumb topping to coat and arrange (topping side up) on the rack. Bake until the filling is hot and the topping is golden brown, about 10 minutes. Cool 5 minutes before serving.

WHERE THINGS CAN GO WRONG: Because mushrooms shrink so much as they cook, it is important to choose the largest mushrooms you can find.

WHAT YOU CAN DO AHEAD OF TIME: The mushrooms can be roasted and stuffed up to 3 days in advance, but don't top them with bread crumbs until you're ready to heat and serve the mushrooms. Store stuffed mushrooms, stuffing side up, on a paper towel–lined plate in the refrigerator, covered tightly with plastic wrap. The crumb topping can be refrigerated separately in an airtight container for up to 3 days.

NOTES FROM THE TEST KITCHEN

PREPARING AND STUFFING THE MUSHROOMS
For mushroom caps that are large enough to accommodate the filling, it's best to remove the stems with your fingers rather than a paring knife. And for the tidiest appearance, we found it best to pipe the filling into the roasted caps from a zipper-lock bag with one corner snipped off.

1. Grasp the stem where it joins the cap and gently wiggle the stem back and forth until it pops off in one solid piece.

2. Press the filling down into one corner of a zipper-lock bag, twist the bag to squeeze out excess air, then cut one corner off the bag with scissors.

3. Gently squeeze some filling into each mushroom.

CRISPY POLENTA TRIANGLES
WITH HERBED GOAT CHEESE
MAKES 48 BITE-SIZED TRIANGLES

WHAT MAKES THIS A BEST RECIPE: While polenta can take myriad forms and be served in a variety of situations, one of our favorite preparations involves crisp-cooked triangles of garlic-and-rosemary-flavored polenta topped with goat cheese. The interplay of flavor and texture makes it a perfect appetizer, one that can be prepared well ahead of time. While we normally prefer long-cooked traditional polenta to instant polenta (polenta that has been precooked and dried), we found that the differences between the two were very subtle once flavorings were added, so we opted to use quicker, easier instant polenta. Within just 5 minutes of simmering (and a minimum of stirring), the instant polenta was creamy tasting and thick textured, and could easily be poured into a baking dish to cool and firm up. We wanted the polenta to have a rich garlic and rosemary flavor, but stirring raw garlic and minced rosemary into the polenta proved harsh. Stewing the garlic slowly in oil until sweet and mild was much more successful. As for the rosemary, cooking wasn't required; adding it to the warm oil once the garlic was cooked was enough to temper its bite. To achieve the crispest polenta triangles, a very hot oven proved essential. A blistering 500 degrees delivered the best results—in less than half an hour, the polenta triangles were perfectly golden brown on both the top and the bottom and the interior was appealingly tender. When baked on top of the polenta from the start, the goat cheese turned to a grainy mess; adding the cheese halfway through was both messy and dangerous. The perfect solution proved to be spreading the goat cheese and olive oil mixture on the just-baked polenta. There was just enough residual heat to soften the cheese, and tasters loved the temperature contrast between the cheese and the triangles. And while a spoon worked fine for spreading the cheese mixture, we found it neater and far easier to pipe it using a zipper-lock bag.

6 garlic cloves, minced

4 tablespoons olive oil

1½ teaspoons minced fresh rosemary

4 cups water

Salt

1 cup instant polenta

Pepper

8 ounces goat cheese, softened

3 tablespoons minced fresh parsley

1. Cook the garlic and 3 tablespoons of the oil in a small nonstick skillet over low heat, stirring often, until golden and fragrant, about 10 minutes. Off the heat, stir in the rosemary; let cool.

2. Meanwhile, line the bottom of a 13 by 9-inch baking dish with parchment paper and coat lightly with vegetable oil spray. Bring the water to a boil, covered, in a heavy-bottomed 4-quart saucepan over high heat. Reduce the heat to low, stir in 1 teaspoon salt, then pour the polenta into the water in a very slow stream, stirring in a circular motion with a wooden spoon.

3. Reduce the heat to low and cook uncovered, stirring often, until the polenta is soft and smooth, 3 to 5 minutes. Off the heat, stir in the rosemary and garlic mixture and season with salt and pepper to taste. Pour into the prepared baking dish and refrigerate, uncovered, until firm and sliceable, about 1 hour.

4. Mix the goat cheese with the remaining 1 tablespoon oil and parsley; transfer to a small zipper-lock bag.

5. TO SERVE: When the polenta is firm, use the tip of a paring knife to slice it into twenty-four 2 by 2¼-inch rectangles. Slice each rectangle in half on the diagonal into 2 bite-sized triangles.

6. Adjust an oven rack to the lowest position and heat the oven to 500 degrees. Line 2 baking sheets with foil and spray them with vegetable oil spray. Let the goat cheese mixture stand at room temperature to soften (to soften quickly, microwave on 50 percent power for 10 to 20 seconds). Transfer the polenta triangles to the prepared baking sheets (don't crowd the triangles or they won't crisp).

7. Bake the polenta, 1 sheet at a time, until crisp and golden, 20 to 25 minutes. Transfer the hot polenta triangles to a warm serving platter. Snip off one corner of the zipper-lock bag, and pipe about 1 teaspoon of the goat cheese mixture on top of each polenta triangle. Serve warm.

WHERE THINGS CAN GO WRONG: Make sure to let the polenta cool completely before slicing it into triangles, or it will likely fall apart once cut and baked.

WHAT YOU CAN DO AHEAD OF TIME: The polenta can be prepared through step 3, wrapped tightly with plastic wrap, and refrigerated for up to 2 days. The goat cheese mixture (step 4) may also be prepared and refrigerated for up to 2 days in advance. The polenta triangles can be arranged on the baking sheets up to 3 hours before baking in step 7.

NOTES FROM THE TEST KITCHEN

BUYING GOAT CHEESE

The French once cornered the market on goat cheese (or *chèvre*), but that's no longer the case. We conducted a tasting of four domestic and five readily available imported goat cheeses, ranging in price from $11 to nearly $19 per pound. The result? We concluded that American producers have mastered the craft of making goat cheese. All of the domestic cheeses were well liked, but the clear favorite was **Vermont Chèvre** ($16 per pound), from the Vermont Butter and Cheese Company. Reviews of the imported cheeses were mixed. Tasters were enthusiastic about Le Biquet ($19 per pound) from Canada, but many of the French cheeses were described as gamy or muttony, with a chalky, Spackle-like texture. A few adventurous tasters appreciated the assertive flavors of the imported cheeses, but the overall feeling was that the domestic cheeses were cleaner tasting, more balanced, and better suited for use in salads or spreads.

COCKTAIL CRAB CAKES
WITH RÉMOULADE SAUCE
MAKES 24 SMALL CRAB CAKES

WHAT MAKES THIS A BEST RECIPE: Some of us in the test kitchen grew up in the Middle Atlantic States and still have fond memories of the local crab cakes there: lightly seasoned, succulent crabmeat barely bound together and encased in a light, crisp-fried crust. Most recipes, however, don't measure up to that paradigm; instead, the crab is all but buried beneath seasonings and crumbs. This recipe succeeds by leaving the crab well enough alone. Great crab cakes begin with great crabmeat, and, after tasting all the options, we decided that only fresh, lump crabmeat was really worth it (see page 14). If you're going to make crab cakes, it's well worth splurging. To keep the tender meat bound in a discrete cake, recipes add mayonnaise (we added ¼ cup), eggs (we added 1), and all manner of different starches; we liked dried bread crumbs best for their innocuous presence. A scant 1½ teaspoons of Old Bay seasoning, the Baltimore-produced spice blend, a little minced scallion, and some parsley brought out the best in the crabmeat. Flavor aside, there's the matter of cooking the crab cakes. Pan-frying worked great and required a minimum of oil, though despite our best efforts, the crab cakes frequently fell apart as they pan-fried. Extra bread crumbs or mayonnaise didn't really solve anything, but in a serendipitous accident, we found a half-hour chill effectively glued them together. Finally, we had crab cakes as good as those served around the Chesapeake Bay.

RÉMOULADE SAUCE

- ½ **cup mayonnaise**
- ½ **teaspoon capers, drained**
- ½ **teaspoon Dijon mustard**
- 1 **anchovy fillet, chopped coarse**
- 1 **garlic clove, chopped**
- 1½ **teaspoons sweet pickle relish, or 1 gherkin, chopped**
- 1 **teaspoon hot pepper sauce, such as Tabasco**
- 1 **teaspoon fresh lemon juice**
- 1 **teaspoon minced fresh parsley**
  Salt and pepper

CRAB CAKES

- 1 **pound jumbo lump crabmeat, picked over for shells**
- 4 **scallions, green parts only, minced**
- 1 **tablespoon chopped fresh parsley**
- 1½ **teaspoons Old Bay seasoning**
- 2–4 **tablespoons fine dry bread crumbs**
- ¼ **cup mayonnaise**
  Salt and white pepper
- 1 **large egg**
- ½ **cup unbleached all-purpose flour**
- 6 **tablespoons vegetable oil**

1. FOR THE SAUCE: Pulse all of the ingredients except the salt and pepper in a food processor until well combined but not smooth, about ten 1-second pulses. Season with salt and pepper to taste. Transfer to a serving bowl and set aside.

2. FOR THE CRAB CAKES: Gently mix the crabmeat, scallions, parsley, Old Bay, 2 tablespoons of bread crumbs, and mayonnaise in a medium bowl, being careful not to break up the crab lumps. Season with salt and white pepper to taste. Carefully fold in the egg with a rubber spatula until the mixture just clings together. Add more crumbs if necessary.

3. Line a rimmed baking sheet with parchment paper. Using a generous tablespoon, form the mixture into 24 cakes, each 1½ inches in diameter and ½ inch thick. Place each cake on the prepared baking sheet. Cover with plastic wrap and chill at least 30 minutes.

4. Adjust an oven rack to the middle position and heat the oven to 200 degrees. Line a baking sheet with a double thickness of paper towels. Put the flour into a pie dish. Lightly dredge half of the crab cakes, knocking off the excess.

5. Meanwhile, heat 3 tablespoons of the oil in a large, preferably nonstick skillet over medium-high heat until shimmering. Gently place the floured crab cakes in the skillet; pan-fry until the outside is crisp and brown,

1 to 2 minutes. (Flour the remaining cakes while the first batch is browning.) Using a spatula, turn the cakes. Pan-fry until the second side is crisp and brown, 1 to 2 minutes. Transfer to a paper towel–lined baking sheet and place the sheet in the oven.

6. Pour off the fat from the hot skillet and wipe clean with paper towels. Return the skillet to the heat, add the remaining 3 tablespoons oil, and heat until shimmering. Add the remaining cakes and pan-fry as above. Serve hot with the rémoulade sauce.

WHERE THINGS CAN GO WRONG: The moisture content of fresh crabmeat can vary from batch to batch, so it is important to adjust the amount of bread crumbs added accordingly. Start with the lesser amount of crumbs specified in the recipe. If the cakes won't hold together once you have added the egg, add more bread crumbs, 1 tablespoon at a time.

WHAT YOU CAN DO AHEAD OF TIME: The rémoulade sauce can be refrigerated in an airtight container for up to 3 days. The crab cakes can be prepared through step 3 and refrigerated, wrapped tightly in plastic wrap, for up to 24 hours.

NOTES FROM THE TEST KITCHEN

CHOOSING THE RIGHT CRABMEAT

When it comes to dishes in which the crabmeat is the star of the show, we've found there's really only one choice: fresh-picked meat. In a head-to-head taste test of all the available options, we found canned and frozen crabmeat virtually inedible; pasteurized crabmeat was better, though it still paled in comparison to fresh-picked meat. Depending on the region of the country in which you live, or the amount you're willing to pay to have crabmeat shipped, you may have several options from which to choose. Jumbo lump is the highest-quality crabmeat (and the most expensive, too) and, as the name suggests, consists of large lumps of meat. Back-fin costs a little less and may contain smaller pieces of meat mixed with the lumps. Claw meat is the least expensive grade and contains few if any lumps.

MINI BEEF AND CHEESE EMPANADAS
MAKES 48 EMPANADAS

WHAT MAKES THIS A BEST RECIPE: *Empanadas* are Latin-style turnovers filled with all manner of savory and sweet fillings. They make a convenient snack or, when fashioned in small, bite-sized versions, a perfect appetizer that can be prepared well ahead of time and stored at the ready for easy entertaining. While most recipes for empanadas require specialty ingredients and employ unique cooking methods, this one produces authentic flavor with ingredients found in a typical American supermarket and it can be made with appliances found in an average kitchen. Empanada dough is prepared by blending flour and salt with melted fat (lard or vegetable shortening) and kneading it into a malleable paste. Tasters were offput by this style of dough, and instead favored a butter and flour dough prepared like classic pie dough (cutting the fat into the flour, after which ice water is added). Scaling back the amount of butter from the typical ratio ensured the crust wouldn't be too rich. As for the filling, we worked our way through a dozen iterations and settled on a ground-beef base flavored with cumin, clove, and cayenne and sweetened with a bit of sugar and tomato paste. Simmering with a little beef broth rendered the mixture a little saucy, perfect for an empanada filling. Neutral-flavored Monterey Jack cheese melted smoothly and balanced the spiciness of the filling. Baked golden brown, these empanadas looked authentic and tasted right on the mark.

DOUGH

3¾ cups (18¾ ounces) unbleached all-purpose flour, plus extra for dusting the work surface

1 tablespoon sugar

1½ teaspoons salt

12 tablespoons (1½ sticks) unsalted butter, cut into ½-inch cubes and frozen for 10 minutes

1¼ cups ice water

FILLING

- 1 tablespoon olive oil
- 1 onion, minced (about 1 cup)
- 1 tablespoon tomato paste
- 2 garlic cloves, minced
- 1 teaspoon minced fresh oregano or ¼ teaspoon dried
- 1 teaspoon ground cumin
- Pinch ground cloves
- Pinch cayenne pepper
- ½ pound 85 percent lean ground beef
- ¾ cup low-sodium beef broth
- 1 teaspoon sugar
- Salt and pepper
- 2 ounces Monterey Jack cheese, shredded (about ½ cup)

ASSEMBLY

- 1 large egg, beaten

1. FOR THE DOUGH: Process the flour, sugar, and salt together in a food processor until combined, about 6 seconds. Scatter the butter pieces over the flour mixture and pulse until the mixture resembles coarse crumbs with butter bits no larger than small peas, about 16 pulses.

2. Transfer the flour mixture to a large mixing bowl. Working with ¼ cup of water at a time, sprinkle the water over the flour mixture and stir it in using a rubber spatula, pressing the mixture against the side of the bowl to form a dough, until no small bits of flour remain (you may not need to use all of the water).

3. Turn the dough out onto a clean work surface and divide it into 2 equal pieces. Press each dough half into a cohesive ball, then flatten the ball into a 6-inch disk. Wrap each disk in plastic and refrigerate until firm but not hard, about 2 hours.

4. FOR THE FILLING: While the dough rests, heat the oil in a 12-inch nonstick skillet over medium-high heat until just shimmering. Add the onion and cook until softened, 5 to 7 minutes. Stir in the tomato paste, garlic, oregano, cumin, cloves, and cayenne and cook until fragrant, about 30 seconds. Stir in the beef and cook, breaking up the clumps with a wooden spoon, until no longer pink, about 4 minutes.

5. Stir in the broth, reduce the heat to low, and simmer until the mixture is moist but not wet, about 8 minutes. Off the heat, stir in the sugar and season with salt and pepper to taste. Transfer the mixture to a medium bowl, cover with plastic wrap, and refrigerate until completely cool, about 1 hour. Stir in the cheese and continue to chill until needed.

6. TO ASSEMBLE THE EMPANADAS: Line 2 baking sheets with parchment paper. Remove 1 disk of dough from the refrigerator (if refrigerated for longer than 2 hours, let sit at room temperature until malleable). Roll the dough out on a lightly floured work surface into an 18-inch circle about ⅛-inch thick. Using a 3-inch round biscuit cutter, cut out 24 rounds and transfer them to the prepared baking sheet, discarding the dough scraps; wrap the baking sheet with plastic wrap and refrigerate. Repeat with the second disk of dough and the second prepared baking sheet.

7. Working with the first batch of dough rounds, and following the photos on page 16, fill, seal, and shape the empanadas using roughly 1 teaspoon of the chilled filling per empanada. Crimp the edges of the empanadas using a fork, and arrange them on a fresh, parchment-lined baking sheet. Wrap the baking sheet tightly with plastic wrap and refrigerate while making a second batch of empanadas using the remaining dough rounds and filling.

8. Adjust 2 oven racks to the upper-middle and lower-middle positions and heat the oven to 425 degrees. Unwrap the empanadas and brush with the beaten egg. Bake until golden brown, about 20 minutes, switching and rotating the trays halfway through the baking time. Let cool for 5 minutes before serving.

WHERE THINGS CAN GO WRONG: If the empanada dough becomes too warm, it can become very sticky and intractable. The solution, however, is easy: Refrigerate all the dough ingredients for 30 minutes before preparation. And if the dough ever becomes too soft or sticky to work with, simply return it to the refrigerator until firm; a dough scraper also comes in handy here.

WHAT YOU CAN DO AHEAD OF TIME: The prepared empanadas can be covered tightly with plastic wrap and refrigerated for up to 3 days, or frozen for up to 1 month. (After the empanadas are completely frozen, about 8 hours, they can be transferred to a zipper-lock bag to save space in the freezer. Transfer back to parchment-lined baking sheets before baking.) If frozen, increase the baking time by about 5 minutes. The dough and filling may also be prepared and stored separately, wrapped tightly in plastic wrap and refrigerated: the dough for up to 2 days, and the filling for 3 days.

NOTES FROM THE TEST KITCHEN

MAKING EMPANADAS

If improperly folded, the empanadas can pop apart and leak the filling. Here's a foolproof technique:

1. Place 1 teaspoon filling in the center of each dough round and moisten the edges with water, using your finger or a pastry brush.

2. Fold the dough in half over the filling, making a half-moon shape.

3. Pinch the seam along the edge to secure.

4. Using a dinner fork, crimp the sealed edge to secure.

THE ULTIMATE SPICY BEEF NACHOS
SERVES 8

WHAT MAKE THIS A BEST RECIPE: Most of the "ultimate nachos" we've ordered in restaurants come to the table loaded down with bland, greasy beef, dry beans, and cold strings of unmelted cheese smothering tough, soggy chips. They might be an "ultimate" kitchen disaster but are otherwise unremarkable. We like this recipe because the hot, crisp chips are evenly covered with rich, spicy beef, creamy refried beans, gooey melted cheese, and plenty of jalapeños. Beginning with the beef, we found it imperative to use lean, 90 percent ground beef to avoid a greasy texture—and season it boldly with a smoky mixture of chili powder, cumin, and oregano. The further addition of tomato paste, brown sugar, and a canned chipotle chile added a sweet richness and touch of heat, while fresh lime juice brightened it all up. We preferred refried beans to plain beans, but canned refried beans were lackluster in flavor and chalky in texture. Processing the beans with pickled jalapeños and cheese produced a lively, spreadable puree. As for the cheese, it turned out that cheddar (the top choice in many recipes) doesn't melt nearly as well as Monterey Jack. Most of the test kitchen preferred the kick of pepper Jack, but plain Jack worked fine too. As for assembly, most recipes simply dump the chips on a platter and layer on the toppings, but this creates pockets of ingredients and left some chips uncovered. After much trial and error, we learned two tricks for more successful assembly. First, the order of ingredients is important. The beans should be added first, so you can spread them evenly; the beef comes next, so it can adhere to the beans and not roll off the chips; then the cheese goes on, to blanket everything. Second, to prevent all the toppings from being consumed with the top layer of chips, we found it necessary to make two layers of chips and toppings. A couple of additional garnishes, like fresh jalapeños, and a side of fresh salsa, made these, without a doubt, the ultimate nachos.

SALSA

- ½ small red onion
- ¼ cup packed fresh cilantro
- 1 tablespoon fresh lime juice
- 1 garlic clove, peeled
- 2 tablespoons canned pickled jalapeño chile, drained
- ¼ teaspoon salt
- 1 (14.5-ounce) can diced tomatoes, drained

REFRIED BEANS

- ½ cup canned refried beans
- 1 ounce pepper Jack cheese, shredded (about ¼ cup)
- 1 tablespoon chopped canned pickled jalapeño chile

SPICY BEEF

- 2 teaspoons vegetable oil
- 1 small onion, minced
- 3 garlic cloves, minced
- 1 tablespoon chili powder
- 1 teaspoon ground cumin
- ½ teaspoon dried oregano
- 1 teaspoon salt
- 1 pound 90 percent lean ground beef
- 2 tablespoons tomato paste
- 1 teaspoon brown sugar
- 1 medium canned chipotle chile, chopped, plus 1 teaspoon adobo sauce
- ½ cup water
- 2 teaspoons fresh lime juice

ASSEMBLY

- 1 (9½-ounce) bag tortilla chips
- 16 ounces pepper Jack cheese, shredded (about 4 cups)
- 2 jalapeño chiles, sliced into thin rings
  Sour cream (optional)
  Diced avocado (optional)
  Cilantro sprigs (optional)

1. FOR THE SALSA: Pulse the onion, cilantro, lime juice, garlic, jalapeños, and salt in a food processor until roughly chopped, about five 1-second pulses. Add the tomatoes and pulse until chopped, about two 1-second pulses. Transfer the mixture to a fine-mesh strainer and drain briefly; place in a small bowl and set aside.

2. FOR THE BEANS: Pulse all the ingredients in the food processor until smooth. Transfer to a bowl and cover with plastic wrap.

3. FOR THE BEEF: Heat the oil in a large skillet over medium heat until shimmering. Cook the onion, stirring occasionally, until softened, about 4 minutes. Add the garlic, chili powder, cumin, oregano, and salt and cook until fragrant, about 1 minute. Add the beef and cook, breaking the meat into small bits with a wooden spoon and scraping the pan bottom to prevent scorching, until no longer pink, about 5 minutes. Add the tomato paste, sugar, chile, and adobo sauce and cook until the paste begins to darken, about 1 minute. Add the water, bring to a simmer, and cook over medium-low until the mixture is nearly dry, 5 to 7 minutes. Stir in the lime juice and transfer the mixture to a plate lined with several layers of paper towels. Use more paper towels to blot up excess grease.

4. TO ASSEMBLE: Adjust an oven rack to the middle position and heat the oven to 400 degrees. Spread half of the chips on a large, oven-safe serving platter or a 13 by 9-inch baking dish. Dollop half of the bean mixture over the chips, then spread evenly. Scatter half of the beef mixture over the beans, top with 2 cups of the cheese and half of the jalapeños. Repeat with the remaining chips, beans, beef, cheese, and jalapeños. Bake until the cheese is melted and just beginning to brown, 12 to 14 minutes. Top with the salsa and garnish with sour cream, avocado, and cilantro leaves if desired.

WHERE THINGS CAN GO WRONG: To avoid greasy nachos, use 90 percent lean ground beef and blot the cooked beef dry with paper towels.

WHAT YOU CAN DO AHEAD OF TIME: The salsa, refried beans, and spicy beef can be refrigerated in separate airtight containers for up to 1 day.

NOTES FROM THE TEST KITCHEN

PICKING THE PERFECT CHIP
A sturdy chip is a must when making nachos. Tostitos Restaurant Style Chips are our favorite with salsa or guacamole, but are too thin for nachos. **Tostitos Natural Chips**, however, are hearty enough to support plenty of toppings and are our top choice for nachos.

ZUCCHINI FRITTERS

MAKES 12 FRITTERS, SERVING 4 TO 6

WHAT MAKES THIS A BEST RECIPE: Come mid-summer, we are always looking for new and interesting ways to use up the inevitable bumper crop of zucchini. One of our new favorite recipes is Turkish-style zucchini fritters. They are crisp and well seasoned, blessedly free of the blandness and sogginess usually associated with zucchini-based dishes. How did we avoid the pitfalls? We grated the zucchini on the large holes of a box grater, then salted and drained it in a strainer for 10 minutes. A squeeze in paper towels removed even more moisture, resulting in shredded zucchini that is dry to the touch and, when cooked, packed with very concentrated flavor. A little flour and two whole eggs bound the zucchini, without the gumminess of many other fritter recipes. For seasonings, the recipe hews close to traditional Turkish interpretations and relies on scallion and dill, the freshness of which really emphasizes the zucchini's flavor. Lastly, and most interestingly, the recipe includes crumbled feta cheese, so that every bite of the fritters contains a pocket of creamy, tangy, and salty cheese. Pan-fried crisp (no deep frying necessary, making for substantially less oil to purchase and discard), these fritters are one of the best-tasting uses of zucchini we have recently come upon.

2	zucchini (about 1 pound)
1	teaspoon salt
8	ounces feta cheese, crumbled (about 2 cups)
2	scallions, minced
2	tablespoons minced fresh dill
2	large eggs, lightly beaten
1	garlic clove, minced
¼	teaspoon pepper
¼	cup unbleached all-purpose flour
6	tablespoons olive oil
1	lemon, cut into wedges, for serving

1. Adjust an oven rack to the middle position and heat the oven to 200 degrees. Shred the zucchini on the large holes of a box grater or in a food processor fitted with the shredding disk. Toss the shredded zucchini with the salt and let drain in a fine-mesh strainer set over a bowl for 10 minutes. Wrap the zucchini in a clean dish towel and squeeze out the excess liquid.

2. Combine the zucchini, feta, scallions, dill, eggs, garlic, and pepper together in a medium bowl. Sprinkle the flour over the mixture and stir until uniformly incorporated.

3. Heat 3 tablespoons of the oil in a 12-inch nonstick skillet over medium heat until shimmering. Drop 2-tablespoon-sized portions of the batter into the pan, then use the back of a spoon to press the batter into a 2-inch-wide fritter (you should fit about 6 fritters in the pan at a time). Fry until golden brown on both sides, 2 to 3 minutes per side.

4. Transfer the fritters to a paper towel–lined baking sheet and place in the oven to keep warm. Wipe the skillet clean with paper towels. Return the skillet to medium heat, add the remaining 3 tablespoons oil, and repeat with the remaining batter. Serve warm or at room temperature with the lemon wedges.

WHERE THINGS CAN GO WRONG: Be sure to squeeze the zucchini until it is completely dry, or the fritters will fall apart in the skillet. And don't let the squeeze-dried zucchini sit for too long before making the batter, or it will turn brown and the fritters will look unappetizing.

NOTES FROM THE TEST KITCHEN

PREPARING THE ZUCCHINI

1. Using the coarse holes on a box grater, grate the zucchini, peel and all (you can also use a food processor fitted with the shredding disk).

2. Place the grated zucchini in a clean dish towel and wring out as much liquid as possible.

FRENCH ONION AND BACON TART

SERVES 6 TO 8

WHAT MAKES THIS A BEST RECIPE: A classic bistro dish, French onion and bacon tart combines sweet onions, smoky bacon, and smooth custard in a buttery pastry crust—all baked in a slim tart shell. More refined than homey quiche, it elevates the humble onion to a refined plane. We think this recipe is the best onion and bacon tart recipe this side of the Atlantic. There are three main components to the tart: the crust, the onion and bacon filling, and the custard. With the crust, it's not just a matter of making the dough; there's the rolling and fitting the dough to the tart shell. We simplified both steps by developing a dough that was both simple to prepare and could be patted by hand into the tart shell. The secret was completely cutting the butter into the flour mixture using a food processor and adding less than the conventional amount of water. The relatively stiff dough could easily be shaped into the shell and baked up into a flavorful, tender crust that was sturdy enough to hold a heavy filling. As for the filling, after innumerable tests regarding ingredients and temperature, we found that yellow or white onions, halved and sliced crosswise against the onion's fibers, delivered the best flavor and texture and cooking them covered—starting over high heat and dropping to low heat partway through—effectively stewed them in their own juices so that they were remarkably soft and deeply flavored. The bacon was easy: Cut into small pieces and fry until crisp. We were then able to cook the onions in the same skillet in the rendered fat, thereby maximizing the onion flavor. Between the bacon and the bacon fat in which the onions are cooked, the tart was pretty rich, so we found it important to make the custard leaner than we expected. We trimmed an egg and used half-and-half rather than the more traditional heavy cream. The resulting tart was rich without being cloying and as delicious as anything served in Paris.

CRUST

- 1¼ cups (6¼ ounces) unbleached all-purpose flour
- 1 tablespoon sugar
- ½ teaspoon salt
- 8 tablespoons (1 stick) unsalted butter, cut into ½-inch cubes and chilled
- 2–3 tablespoons ice water

FILLING

- 4 slices bacon, halved lengthwise, then cut crosswise into ¼-inch pieces
  Vegetable oil, if needed
- 3 onions, halved and sliced thin (about 3 cups) (see page 24)
- ¾ teaspoon salt
- 1 sprig fresh thyme
- 2 large eggs
- ½ cup half-and-half
- ¼ teaspoon pepper

1. FOR THE CRUST: Spray a 9-inch tart pan with a removable bottom with nonstick cooking spray. Combine the flour, sugar, and salt in a food processor with four 1-second pulses. Scatter the butter pieces over the flour mixture; pulse to cut the butter into the flour until the mixture resembles coarse sand, about fifteen 1-second pulses. Add 2 tablespoons of ice water and process until large clumps form and no powdery bits remain, about 5 seconds, adding up to 1 tablespoon more water if the dough will not form clumps. Transfer the dough to the prepared tart pan. Following the photos, pat the dough into the pan. Lay plastic wrap over the dough and smooth out any bumps or shallow areas. Place the tart shell on a plate and transfer to the freezer for 30 minutes.

2. Adjust an oven rack to the middle position and heat the oven to 375 degrees. Place the frozen tart shell on a baking sheet; lightly spray one side of an 18-inch square extra-wide heavy-duty piece of aluminum foil with nonstick cooking spray. Press the foil greased side down inside the tart shell, folding the excess foil over the edge of the pan. Fill with pie weights and bake until the top edge just starts to color and the surface of the dough under the foil no longer looks wet, about 30 minutes. Remove from the oven and carefully remove the foil and weights by gathering the edges of the foil and pulling it

FRENCH ONION AND BACON TART

up and out. Return the baking sheet with the tart shell to the oven and bake until golden brown, 5 to 10 minutes. Set the baking sheet with the tart shell on a wire rack. Do not turn off the oven.

3. FOR THE FILLING: While the crust is baking, cook the bacon in a 12-inch nonstick skillet over medium heat until browned and crisp, 8 to 10 minutes. Drain the bacon through a mesh strainer set over a small bowl; transfer the bacon to a paper towel–lined plate. Return 2 tablespoons of the bacon fat to the skillet, adding vegetable oil to make up the difference if necessary.

4. Add the onions, salt, and thyme to the skillet. Cover and cook until the onions release their liquid and start to wilt, about 10 minutes. Reduce the heat to low and continue to cook, covered, until the onions are very soft, about 20 minutes, stirring once or twice (if after 15 minutes the onions look wet, remove the lid and continue to cook another 5 minutes). Remove the pan from the heat and let the onions cool 5 minutes.

5. Whisk the eggs, half-and-half, and pepper together in a large bowl. Remove the thyme sprig from the onions and discard. Stir the onions into the egg mixture until just incorporated. Spread the onion mixture over the baked crust (the pan still on the baking sheet) and sprinkle the bacon evenly on top.

6. Return the baking sheet with the tart to the oven and bake until the center of the tart feels firm to the touch, 20 to 25 minutes. Cool on a wire rack at least 10 minutes. When ready to serve, remove the tart pan ring; gently slide a thin-bladed spatula between the tart pan bottom and crust to loosen, then slide the tart onto a serving plate. Cut into wedges and serve.

WHERE THINGS CAN GO WRONG: Either yellow or white onions work well in this recipe, but stay away from sweet onions, such as Vidalias, which will make the tart watery.

WHAT YOU CAN DO AHEAD OF TIME: The dough for the crust can be prepared through step 1, wrapped tightly in plastic wrap, and frozen for up to 1 month.

NOTES FROM THE TEST KITCHEN

HOW TO PREPARE THE CRUST
While there are many methods of coercing dough into a tart pan, we found this was the simplest and quickest method to ensure an even crust—and no rolling pin is required.

1. Sprinkle walnut-sized clumps of dough evenly into the prepared tart pan.

2. Working outward from the center, press the dough into an even layer, sealing any cracks.

3. Working around the edge, press the dough firmly into the corners of the pan with your index finger.

4. Go around the edge once more, pressing the dough up the sides and into the fluted ridges.

5. Use your thumb to level off the top edge. Use this dough to patch any holes.

GERMAN TART
WITH ONION, BACON, AND CRÈME FRAÎCHE
SERVES 6

WHAT MAKES THIS A BEST RECIPE: While everyone's familiar with Italian pizza, there are other styles of topped flatbreads and rustic tarts throughout Europe. One of our favorites from Germany is *Flammeküeche*, with its layers of onion, bacon, and crème fraîche on a cracker-thin crust. We like this recipe because it produces an authentically crisp crust and deeply flavored topping without any heroic effort or hard-to-find ingredients. Using our existing thin-crust pizza dough recipe as a starting point, we explored how to get the dough as thin and crisp as possible by experimenting with the recipe's ratio of flour to water, the type of flour (low-protein all-purpose proved best), and how long the dough was allowed to proof. While we liked the 24-hour dough best, the two-hour dough was close enough in flavor and texture to win the contest. We were unable to hand-stretch the dough as thin as we wanted, so we switched to rolling it out on parchment paper. The tackiness of the dough against the parchment prevents the dough from springing and shrinking back, eliminating the need for excess flouring when rolling out the dough. Wanting the cracker-like simplicity of a rich burnished crust, we knew that we would need every bit of conventional oven heat we could get in the five to seven minutes or so it would take to bake. That meant a 500-degree oven and a pizza stone (an essential piece of equipment) with an hour's headstart to preheat. As for the toppings, thin-sliced bacon was quickly dismissed in favor of crisped pieces of thick-sliced bacon (finding the traditional slab bacon proved too difficult); only partially caramelizing the onions helped them retain a bit of bite to contrast with the bacon's richness. And while some recipes call for *fromage blanc* (a fresh, creamy cheese), others swear by crème fraîche, and some recipes combine the two. Crème fraîche proved the most flavorful, but since it can be hard to find, we tested some alternatives, including sour cream, which we think works quite well. (That said, if you can find crème fraîche, we recommend using it.)

TART DOUGH

- 2 cups (10 ounces) unbleached all-purpose flour, plus extra as needed
- ½ teaspoon rapid-rise or instant yeast
- ½ teaspoon honey
- ½ teaspoon salt
- ¾ cup plus 2 tablespoons warm water (110 degrees)
- ¼ cup vegetable oil

TOPPING

- 1 cup crème fraîche or sour cream
  Salt and pepper
- ½ teaspoon freshly grated nutmeg
- 6 slices thick-cut bacon, cut crosswise into ¼-inch-wide strips
- 4 onions, halved and sliced thin (about 4 cups) (see page 24)

1. FOR THE DOUGH: Combine the flour, yeast, honey, and salt together in a food processor. With the machine running, add the water through the feed tube, followed by the vegetable oil. Continue to process until the dough forms a ball, about 30 seconds.

2. Turn the dough out onto a work surface and knead by hand for 30 seconds, adding extra flour if the dough is sticky. Wrap the dough in plastic wrap and refrigerate for 2 hours.

3. Adjust an oven rack to the lowest position, set a baking stone on the rack, and heat the oven to 500 degrees; let the baking stone heat for 1 hour.

4. FOR THE TOPPING: Meanwhile, mix the crème fraîche, 1 teaspoon salt, ½ teaspoon pepper, and nutmeg together, cover with plastic wrap, and refrigerate until needed.

5. Cook the bacon in a 12-inch nonstick skillet over medium heat until browned and most of the fat has rendered, about 10 minutes. Transfer the bacon to a paper towel–lined plate, leaving the fat in the skillet. Add the onions and ½ teaspoon salt to the fat in the skillet, cover, and cook over medium heat, stirring occasionally, until the onions are softened and have released their juices, about 10 minutes. Uncover and continue to cook, stirring often, until the onions begin to brown, about 6 minutes; set aside off the heat.

6. TO ASSEMBLE AND BAKE: Remove the dough from the refrigerator. Divide it into two equal pieces, forming each piece into a ball. Place one ball on a lightly floured

sheet of parchment paper and cover with one large sheet of plastic wrap (or two small overlapping pieces). Using a rolling pin, roll the dough into a 15 by 9-inch oval. Remove the plastic wrap and slide the parchment paper with the dough onto an inverted baking sheet.

7. Spread half of the topping mixture over the dough, leaving a ½-inch border. Scatter half of the onion mixture and half of the bacon over the top. Slide the parchment with the tart onto the heated baking stone. Bake until the edges of the tart are golden brown and the parchment releases from the tart bottom, 5 to 7 minutes. While the first tart bakes, roll out and assemble the second tart on a sheet of parchment paper using the remaining dough and topping. Cut the baked tarts into about 6 pieces each, and serve immediately.

WHERE THINGS CAN GO WRONG: For the crispest crust, it's important to choose a low-protein all-purpose flour, like Gold Medal or Pillsbury brand, and to use a wickedly hot pizza stone. An hour of preheating at 500 degrees may sound excessive, but we found that the extremely high heat is essential for the best results. Lower temperatures meant the tart required longer cooking, which toughened the crust.

WHAT YOU CAN DO AHEAD OF TIME: The dough may be prepared through step 2 and refrigerated, wrapped tightly in plastic, for up to 2 days.

NOTES FROM THE TEST KITCHEN

SLICING ONIONS THIN

To slice an onion thin, halve it pole to pole, peel it, set it on a cut side, and then slice crosswise.

FRISÉE SALAD
WITH BACON AND POACHED EGG
SERVES 6

WHAT MAKES THIS A BEST RECIPE: When we think of bistro fare, one of the first things that come to mind is a classic salad of mildly bitter, curly frisée, smoky-sweet *lardons* (French bacon), and a silky poached egg. Known in France as *Salade Lyonnaise,* it's a perfect balancing of flavor and texture. This recipe adheres to tradition and artfully reproduces an authentic rendition. Frisée on its own can be a little aggressive, so we followed the lead of some of the recipes we found and tempered it with other lettuces like dandelion greens, mâche, or the more widely available mesclun mix. Fresh-baked, crispy croutons added contrasting texture to the otherwise soft and chewy greens. Traditionally the bacon is cut into lardons (thin strips) from a slab, then fried to render out the fat (later used for the vinaigrette). We found it difficult to find slab bacon in our supermarket and decided to use thick-cut bacon, which we diced into pieces and fried to the point where they were just getting crispy, yet still had a slight chew and enough presence that they didn't get lost in the other flavors. The rendered fat from the bacon is the starting point for the vinaigrette. To it, we added a shallot—briefly sweated in the hot fat—red wine vinegar (although sherry vinegar was also quite good in this salad), whole-grain Dijon mustard, and olive oil; bacon fat alone made the vinaigrette too heavy on the palate. Lastly, there were the eggs to poach. We knew from past test kitchen findings that adding a bit of white distilled vinegar to the poaching water prevents the eggs from feathering out and becoming ragged-looking. Why? The vinegar lowers the pH of the water, which results in lowering the temperature of the water. Another key finding was to poach them in still, not simmering, water. The water is brought to a simmer and taken off the heat before the eggs are added. After the eggs are slipped into the hot water, the pan is covered and enough heat remains to cook the eggs perfectly in 5 minutes. From there, we gently slid an egg onto each dressed salad—the crowning touch to an enduring French favorite.

SALAD

- 4 slices high-quality white sandwich bread, cut into ½-inch cubes
- ⅓ cup olive oil plus 1 tablespoon
  Salt and pepper
- 2 medium heads frisée (about 6 ounces), torn into bite-sized pieces
- 3 ounces dandelion greens
- 3 ounces mâche
- 4 slices thick-cut bacon, cut into ½-inch pieces
- 1 shallot, minced (about 3 tablespoons)
- ⅓ cup red wine vinegar
- 1 tablespoon Dijon mustard or whole-grain mustard

EGGS

- 2 tablespoons distilled white vinegar
- 6 large eggs

1. FOR THE SALAD: Adjust an oven rack to the upper-middle position and heat the oven to 400 degrees. Toss the bread cubes with the 1 tablespoon oil, ½ teaspoon salt, and ⅛ teaspoon pepper and spread out over a rimmed baking sheet. Bake until the croutons are golden brown and crisp, 8 to 10 minutes; set aside. Toss the frisée, dandelion greens, and mâche together in a large bowl; set aside.

2. Cook the bacon in an 8-inch skillet over medium-high heat until golden brown and crisp, but still chewy, 4 to 6 minutes. Transfer the bacon to a paper towel–lined plate, leaving the rendered fat in the skillet. Add the shallot to the skillet and cook over medium heat until softened, 2 to 4 minutes. Stir in the vinegar and mustard, scraping up any browned bits, and cook until slightly thickened, about 2 minutes. Off the heat, stir in the remaining ⅓ cup oil; set aside.

3. FOR THE EGGS: Fill a 12-inch nonstick skillet nearly to the rim with water. Add 1 teaspoon salt and the vinegar and bring to a boil over high heat. Meanwhile, following the photo, crack 2 eggs each into three small, handled teacups. When the water boils, turn off the heat, immediately lower the lips of the three cups into the water at once, and tip the eggs into the water. Cover, remove the pan from the heat, and poach the eggs until the whites are cooked but the yolks are still runny in the center, about 5 minutes.

4. TO ASSEMBLE THE SALAD: While the eggs poach, drizzle the vinaigrette over the greens and toss thoroughly to coat. Divide the greens among 6 individual serving plates and sprinkle the bacon and croutons evenly over the top. Using a slotted spoon, quickly and carefully transfer the eggs, one at a time, to a large, clean plate, pausing briefly to let the water drain back into the skillet. Once all of the eggs have been transferred, use your fingers to gently slide one egg onto the top of each salad. Serve immediately.

WHERE THINGS CAN GO WRONG: The vinaigrette will taste far sharper than a conventional vinaigrette, but resist the urge to adjust it. The dressing needs to be acidic to counter the richness of the bacon and egg. Timing is key here; the salad should be dressed while the eggs poach. If the salad is dressed too early the greens will wilt, and if the poached eggs sit for too long the yolks will no longer be runny.

THINGS YOU CAN DO AHEAD OF TIME: The croutons can be prepared up to 2 days ahead of time and stored in a zipper-lock bag at room temperature.

NOTES FROM THE TEST KITCHEN

POACHING EGGS

Regardless of how many eggs you are poaching, the key is to crack them into small, handled cups (2 eggs each). Lower the lips of all the cups just into the water at the same time and tip the eggs simultaneously into the pan.

GREENS SUBSTITUTION

If dandelion greens and mâche are not available at your supermarket, you can use mesclun mix instead (a combination of young greens, which typically includes dandelion greens, mâche, radicchio, and frisée).

SPICY ASIAN CUCUMBER SALAD

SERVES 4

WHAT MAKES THIS A BEST RECIPE: A cool salad made with crisp cucumbers is a refreshing companion to any grilled dish. The cucumbers' high water content is part of what makes them so refreshing, but once sliced they shed some of this water, which dilutes any dressing. The usual solution is to salt and press the sliced cucumbers, but this is time consuming, requiring an hour or more. For quick summer meals or weeknight dinners, this seems excessive. This recipe for cucumber salad provides a quick—and easy—means to an end: The vinaigrette is made "double strength," or strong enough that it retains its potency despite the liquid shed by the fresh-sliced cucumber. Briefly boiled and concentrated rice wine vinegar flavored with sugar is the vinaigrette's base, to which bright lime juice, biting fresh ginger, and spicy red chile are added. Fresh basil balances the sweet, sour, and hot flavors and keeps things refreshing. Instead of fighting the succulent nature of the cucumber as most recipes do, this recipe uses it to great effect.

½   cup rice vinegar
2   tablespoons sugar
2   tablespoons fresh lime juice
2   tablespoons minced fresh ginger
1½ tablespoons minced hot red chile, such as Thai bird
     or red jalapeño
1   tablespoon toasted sesame oil
3   cucumbers, peeled, seeded, and cut crosswise into
     ¼-inch slices
4   scallions, white and light green parts, sliced thin
¼   cup loosely packed fresh basil, chopped
     Salt and pepper

1. Bring the vinegar and sugar to a boil in a saucepan over medium-high heat. Reduce the heat to medium-low and simmer until the mixture reduces by half, 5 to 6 minutes. Transfer to a medium bowl and cool to room temperature.

2. Whisk in the lime juice, ginger, chile, and sesame oil. Toss in the cucumbers, scallions, and basil; season with salt and pepper to taste, and let sit for 10 minutes or up to 1 hour. Serve.

WHERE THINGS CAN GO WRONG: If allowed to sit too long, the salad will turn watery from water leaching from the cucumbers. The salad is best served within 1 hour of being prepared.

WHAT YOU CAN DO AHEAD OF TIME: The vinaigrette can be prepared up to 1 day ahead of time and stored in an airtight container in the refrigerator.

NOTES FROM THE TEST KITCHEN

CUCUMBERS

In addition to the common Kirby cucumber, many supermarkets sell English (or hothouse) cucumbers. English cukes are longer and more slender than their American cousins, and in the test kitchen we prefer them because their skin is perfectly edible, their flesh is slightly firmer, and they have fewer (and smaller) seeds than Kirby cucumbers. Because of their spotty availability, however, we develop our recipes with Kirby cucumbers, which must be peeled and seeded.

HOW TO SEED A CUCUMBER

Peel and halve the cucumber lengthwise. With a spoon, use just enough pressure to scoop away the seeds and the surrounding liquid.

SOUTHWESTERN CAESAR SALAD

SERVES 6 TO 8

WHAT MAKES THIS A BEST RECIPE: Everyone knows Caesar salad—the classic combination of romaine lettuce drizzled with a creamy dressing flavored with garlic, anchovy, Worcestershire, lemon, and Parmesan cheese and topped with seasoned croutons. What most people don't know is that, despite its name and ingredients, Caesar salad was invented in Mexico. This recipe for Southwestern Caesar salad takes liberties with the original that, ironically, brings the salad closer to its Mexican roots than the original. The main alteration is the use of smoky chipotle chiles as the predominant flavoring in the dressing instead of anchovies, which are omitted. And sticking with the Southwestern theme, lime juice replaces the lemon juice and sour cream stands in for the raw egg usually added as a thickener. We kept the Worcestershire sauce for the complexity it contributes and the Parmesan, which everyone agreed was still the best choice for cheese. A Caesar salad wouldn't be right without croutons, and in this case, we found we could use some of the adobo sauce in which the chiles come packed to add a burst of flavor. Toasted in the oven until golden brown and crunchy, these smoky, garlicky croutons paired perfectly with the bright flavors in the salad dressing and the crisp greens.

1   cup olive oil
1   large chipotle chile, minced, plus 1 tablespoon
     adobo sauce
4   garlic cloves, minced
6   slices high-quality white sandwich bread, cut into
     ½-inch cubes
     Salt and pepper
2   ounces Parmesan cheese, grated (about 1 cup)
½   cup sour cream
3   tablespoons fresh lime juice
2   teaspoons Worcestershire sauce
2   teaspoons Dijon mustard
3   romaine hearts, torn into bite-sized pieces
     (about 12 cups)

1. Adjust an oven rack to the middle position and heat the oven to 350 degrees. Whisk ¼ cup of the oil, the adobo sauce, and half of the garlic in a large bowl. Toss in the bread cubes and season with salt and pepper. Spread the bread cubes on a rimmed baking sheet and bake, shaking the pan occasionally, until golden brown, 20 to 25 minutes. Cool completely.
2. Whisk ¼ cup of the Parmesan, sour cream, lime juice, Worcestershire, mustard, chile, and remaining garlic in a bowl until smooth. Whisk in the remaining ¾ cup oil in a steady stream and season with salt and pepper to taste.
3. Toss the romaine, remaining ¾ cup Parmesan, and dressing in a large bowl. Add the croutons and serve.

WHERE THINGS CAN GO WRONG: In stark contrast to a classic Caesar dressing, it's best to use plain olive oil, not stronger extra-virgin olive oil, which can clash with the other ingredients.

WHAT YOU CAN DO AHEAD OF TIME: The croutons and dressing can be made up to 2 days in advance. Store the croutons in a zipper-lock bag at room temperature; the dressing must be stored in an airtight container in the refrigerator.

NOTES FROM THE TEST KITCHEN

CHIPOTLE CHILES

While, strictly speaking, the word chipotle can refer to any smoked chile pepper, it is now used almost exclusively to refer to smoke-dried red-ripe jalapeño chiles. Their smoky flavor—dependent upon the type of hardwood or fruitwood over which they are smoked—is accompanied by undertones of sweetness and even hints of chocolate. But be wary, chipotles are also quite hot—far hotter than fresh jalapeños. While chipotle chiles can be purchased in dry form, they are most commonly sold rehydrated in adobo, a tangy, oily, tomato-and-herb-based sauce that can also be used as a flavoring agent. Cans of chipotles en adobo are available in the Mexican food section of most supermarkets.

FREEZING CHIPOTLE CHILES

It can be difficult to use up a whole can of chipotle chiles—a little goes a long way. To freeze the leftovers, spoon out the chiles, each with a couple of teaspoons of the adobo sauce, onto different areas of a parchment-lined baking sheet. Freeze the chiles, then transfer them to a zipper-lock freezer bag.

ARUGULA SALAD
WITH GRAPES, FENNEL, GORGONZOLA, AND PECANS
SERVES 6

WHAT MAKES THIS A BEST RECIPE: Unlike everyday (read: bland) iceberg, romaine, or butter lettuce, spicy arugula is more than just a leafy backdrop for salad garnishes. Yet that complex, peppery flavor also makes arugula something of a challenge to pair with other ingredients. We wanted to develop a vinaigrette and garnishes that would ideally complement the green's unique bite for the perfect arugula salad. After preparing and tasting countless arugula-based salads, we found we most preferred those that matched the arugula with sweet and salty components; sour or peppery flavorings only served to magnify the green's bite. Fresh fruit, nuts, and cheeses all won favor with tasters. Most salad vinaigrettes are emulsified with the aid of mustard, but we knew that its strong, sharp flavor would be too much in this case. We experimented with a variety of other emulsifiers and landed on a surprising ingredient, apricot jam, as the best choice. Its deep, resonant flavor paired particularly well with white wine vinegar, extra-virgin olive oil, and shallot. Fruity and sweet without being cloying, the vinaigrette brought the assertive greens right into line. So what garnishes best matched the fruity vinaigrette and peppery greens? Out of everything we tried—and there were more than we care to remember—we most preferred a mix of crunchy fennel, sweet grapes, musty Gorgonzola, and bittersweet pecans. Each ingredient contributed a contrasting flavor that brought out the best in the greens.

4 teaspoons apricot jam

3 tablespoons white wine vinegar

3 tablespoons extra-virgin olive oil

1 shallot, minced (about 3 tablespoons)
Salt and pepper

½ small fennel bulb, cored, trimmed of stalks, and sliced thin; fronds chopped coarse

5 ounces lightly packed baby arugula (8 cups)

6 ounces red seedless grapes, halved lengthwise (about 1 cup)

3 ounces Gorgonzola cheese, crumbled (about ¾ cup)

½ cup chopped pecans, toasted

1. Whisk the jam, vinegar, oil, shallot, ¼ teaspoon salt, and ¼ teaspoon pepper in a large bowl. Toss the fennel with the vinaigrette; let stand for 5 minutes.

2. Add the arugula, fennel fronds, and grapes and toss to combine. Season with salt and pepper to taste. Divide the salad among individual plates; top each with a portion of the Gorgonzola and pecans. Serve immediately.

WHERE THINGS CAN GO WRONG: Tender baby arugula is the best choice for salads; bunched, mature arugula can be unpalatably strong and too bitter to enjoy raw.

WHAT YOU CAN DO AHEAD OF TIME: The vinaigrette can be refrigerated in an airtight container for up to 1 day.

NOTES FROM THE TEST KITCHEN
MEASURING GREENS

When we tried to convert our usual formula of 2 ounces (or 2 cups) of lightly packed greens per serving to our arugula salad, we ended up with more greens than we could eat. That's because our calculation is based on head lettuce, which is heavier than baby greens (such as arugula, baby spinach, and mesclun) due to its higher water content. We found that 1 ounce of lightly packed baby greens will yield roughly 1½ cups, just enough for one serving.

FRESH BASIL VINAIGRETTE

MAKES 1½ CUPS

WHAT MAKES THIS A BEST RECIPE: Homemade vinaigrettes are simple to make, good to have on hand for salads or to serve as quick sauces, and, without a doubt, far better than bottled salad dressings. This recipe for emerald-green basil vinaigrette wins our nod for the way it highlights the basil's flavor and the unique approach it takes to capturing that flavor. After experimenting with a handful of different methods for assembling the dressing and maximizing its herbiness—from shaking and whisking to mechanical means like the food processor or blender—we learned that the best way to develop a deep, herbal flavor was to make a quick herb oil. Gently heating olive oil with the basil for just two to three minutes—and allowing a five-minute steep off heat—created an infused oil loaded with a deep basil flavor. We assumed that extra-virgin olive oil would be necessary for the best results, but this proved not to be the case as it muddied matters; plain olive oil was a better choice. To round out the vinaigrette's flavor, we added shallot and garlic. As for vinegar, red wine vinegar tasted best, especially when paired with tangy Dijon mustard, which also helped to blend the vinaigrette into a smooth, stable mixture. Tossed with greens or spooned over roasted chicken or seafood, this vinaigrette tastes like summer distilled.

> ¾ cup olive oil
>
> 2 cups chopped fresh basil
>
> 1 shallot, peeled
>
> 1 garlic clove, peeled
>
> ¼ cup red wine vinegar
>
> ¼ cup water
>
> ½ teaspoon salt
>
> ¼ teaspoon pepper
>
> 2 teaspoons Dijon mustard

1. Heat ¼ cup of the oil with 1 cup of the basil in a medium saucepan over medium heat until the basil turns bright green and small bubbles appear, 2 to 3 minutes. Turn off the heat and let steep 5 minutes.

2. Process the shallot, garlic, vinegar, water, salt, pepper, and mustard in a blender until the garlic and shallot are finely chopped, about 15 seconds. With the blender running, slowly add the remaining ½ cup oil and steeped basil oil and continue to process until the dressing is smooth and emulsified, about 15 seconds. Pack the remaining 1 cup basil into the blender and process until the vinaigrette is smooth, about 15 seconds.

WHAT YOU CAN DO AHEAD OF TIME: The vinaigrette can be refrigerated in an airtight container for up to 3 days.

NOTES FROM THE TEST KITCHEN

THE SECRETS TO BIG HERB FLAVOR

1. Heating fresh herbs in olive oil creates an herb-infused oil that offers a good foundation for our dressing.

2. Making the dressing in a blender (and adding more fresh herbs) extracts every bit of flavor from the herbs.

THE BEST DIJON MUSTARDS

Today Dijon mustard can be made anywhere in the world and still be considered authentic as long as it follows the original recipe established in Dijon—it must be prepared from brown or black ground mustard seeds, the seed coats must be filtered out, and no coloring agents, stabilizing agents, or fillers may be used. The one major difference in modern Dijon mustards is that they are usually made with vinegar (less harsh than originally used) or wine rather than verjus. Out of the supermarket brands we tasted, we quite liked three. **Roland Extra Strong Dijon Mustard** is an American brand manufactured in France that was widely praised for its excellent flavor balance. Everyone knows the second favorite, **Grey Poupon**, which won favor for its "well-rounded flavor," "nice balance," and "smooth," "creamy" texture. And third, **Delouis Fils Moutarde de Dijon** exhibited a multidimensional, deep, well-balanced flavor. Tasters detected sufficient heat, with salt and acidity at levels that pleased them, and used phrases such as "straightforward," "pungent," and "tangy" to describe it.

A GUIDE TO ESSENTIAL KITCHEN TOOLS

Countless gadgets promise convenience but deliver disappointment and lost drawer space. Here are 16 tools that really work.

VEGETABLE PEELER

WHY YOU NEED IT: Most people have a peeler that works on carrots and potatoes. But for other peeling jobs—say, the thick peel of a winter squash or the delicate skin of a pear—we rely on peelers that have maneuverable blades.
WHY WE LIKE IT: Its rubberized handle is easy to grip, and we find its hefty weight adds force to the sharpness of the blade, which can easily follow rounded contours.

TEST KITCHEN FAVORITE
★ OXO I-Series Swivel Peeler ($9.95)

GRATERS

WHY YOU NEED THEM: A sharp box grater is indispensable for many tasks, from uniformly grating blocks of cheddar cheese to shredding potatoes. A finely textured rasp grater is portable, allowing you to grate or zest at the stove or table.
WHY WE LIKE THEM: This razor-sharp box grater requires little effort or pressure to get results. It also comes with a handy container marked with cup measurements that snaps onto the bottom. The handheld grater has razor-sharp teeth that can finely grate Parmesan in a flash, and it can handle shallots, garlic, ginger, nutmeg, chocolate, and citrus zest.

TEST KITCHEN FAVORITES
★ OXO Good Grips Box Grater ($14.99)
★ MICROPLANE Grater/Zester ($12.95)

WHISK

WHY YOU NEED IT: Useful for not only whipping cream and egg whites, a whisk can also mix batters and make pan sauces and gravies.
WHY WE LIKE IT: This long whisk does it all, boasting a tight radius that can easily reach into all areas of a saucepan or bowl. Though agile, its tines do not bend and twist with prolonged use.

TEST KITCHEN FAVORITE
★ BEST MANUFACTURERS 12-inch Standard French Whip ($9.95)

FINE-MESH STRAINER

WHY YOU NEED IT: Essential for such tasks as dusting a tart with sugar, removing bits of curdled egg from a pudding, or turning cooked raspberries into a seedless sauce. It also makes an excellent stand-in for a sifter.
WHY WE LIKE IT: The OXO keeps its shape. The ergonomic handle and deep bowl are nice, too.

TEST KITCHEN FAVORITE
★ OXO Steel Strainer ($24.95)

GARLIC PRESS

WHY YOU NEED IT: A garlic press does a better job of mincing than one can do by hand—producing a fuller, less acrid flavor that is more evenly distributed throughout a dish.
WHY WE LIKE IT: Made of solidly constructed stainless steel, it has comfortable curved handles and a hopper that lifts out automatically for cleaning as you open the handles. It produces fine, uniform garlic with minimum effort.

TEST KITCHEN FAVORITE
★ KUHN RIKON 2315 Epicurean Garlic Press ($34.95)

TONGS

WHY YOU NEED THEM: Acting like an extension of the hand, tongs can lift, flip, turn, and rotate most any type of food.
WHY WE LIKE THEM: These stainless steel tongs have rubber grips that secure them in your hand. They open wide to pick up large items, but have springs that enable them to pick up the smallest of vegetables. Available with nonstick heads.

TEST KITCHEN FAVORITES
★ OXO GOOD GRIPS 12-inch Locking Tongs ($9.95) and OXO GOOD GRIPS Tongs with Nylon Heads ($9.95)

KITCHEN SHEARS

WHY YOU NEED THEM: Our favorite tool for cutting up and trimming chickens, trimming pie dough, snipping herbs, and cutting through twine.
WHY WE LIKE THEM: Precise, super-sharp, and agile. We like their slip-resistant handles and the fact that they can be taken apart and cleaned thoroughly.

TEST KITCHEN FAVORITE
★ MESSERMEISTER Take-Apart Shears ($23.99)

INSTANT-READ THERMOMETER

WHY YOU NEED IT: You'll never overcook meat again. We also use them for sauces, breads, and cheesecakes.
WHY WE LIKE IT: Provides an accurate read each time, and has a quick response, thin probe, and large display. It can register temperatures from –58 to 572 degrees.

TEST KITCHEN FAVORITE
★ THERMOWORKS Super-Fast Thermapen ($85)

COLANDER

WHY YOU NEED IT: How else are you going to drain pasta and vegetables?
WHY WE LIKE IT: It has a large capacity and mesh-like perforations that drain in seconds. A wide base means it can sit in the sink without tipping.

TEST KITCHEN FAVORITE
★ ENDURANCE Pierced Colander/Strainer, 3-quart ($20.95) and 5-quart ($27.95)

OVEN THERMOMETER

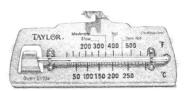

WHY YOU NEED IT: A survey of our ovens at home found that temperatures varied as much as 90 degrees from oven to oven. Knowing that, we always recommend checking an oven's temperature with a reliable thermometer.

WHY WE LIKE IT: It's accurate and easy to read.

TEST KITCHEN FAVORITE
★ TAYLOR Classic Oven Guide Thermometer ($14.99)

SALAD SPINNER

WHY YOU NEED IT: Wet greens can't be dressed properly and result in a soggy salad. We also use a salad spinner to wash and dry herbs.
WHY WE LIKE IT: It has a sturdy, leakproof bowl and its top-mounted pump knob requires little effort to use. The top locks into place for storage, and a nonskid bottom holds the spinner in place.

TEST KITCHEN FAVORITE
★ OXO GOOD GRIPS Salad Spinner ($24.95)

HEATPROOF RUBBER SPATULA

WHY YOU NEED IT: Nothing is better suited to a multitude of tasks, be it cleaning out the corners of bowls and pots, stirring batters, icing cakes, or folding egg whites.
WHY WE LIKE IT: The wide, firm blade is rigid enough to mix the stiffest batter yet flexible enough to reach into the tightest of spaces. It doesn't stain or carry odors—even when used to stir chili. And Rubbermaid's high-heat material is truly heatproof.

TEST KITCHEN FAVORITE
★ RUBBERMAID 13.5-inch High Heat Scraper ($10.48)

MEASURING CUPS AND SPOONS

WHY YOU NEED THEM: Inaccurate measuring of ingredients is one of the most common reasons recipes fail.

WHY WE LIKE THEM: The tops are level with the handles, which makes for accurate measurement of dry ingredients. Set comes in measurements such as ¾ and ⅔ cups, too.

TEST KITCHEN FAVORITE
★ AMCO Stainless Steel Dry Measuring Cups ($14.95)

WHY WE LIKE THEM: These roomy cups are lightweight, able to pour without spilling a drop, and made of unbreakable plastic. Buy the 2-cup and 4-cup sizes.

TEST KITCHEN FAVORITE
★ RUBBERMAID Liquid Measuring Cups ($4.49 for 2-cup; $5.99 for 4-cup)

WHY WE LIKE THEM: The handles and bowl are flush, which facilitates the leveling of dry ingredients. Deep bowls make measuring liquids easier. And they fit in spice jars.

TEST KITCHEN FAVORITE
★ CUISIPRO Stainless Steel Oval Measuring Spoons ($11.95)

SLOW-COOKER GUINNESS BEEF STEW

SOUPS & STEWS

SHRIMP BISQUE **36**

THAI-STYLE CHICKEN SOUP **38**

COLCANNON SOUP **41**

POTATO GARLIC SOUP **42**

SKILLET CREOLE CHICKEN FRICASSEE **45**

BRAZILIAN BLACK BEANS WITH RIBS, PORK TENDERLOIN, AND SAUSAGE **46**

CINCINNATI CHILI **49**

SPANISH SHELLFISH STEW **50**

SLOW-COOKER LENTIL AND SWISS CHARD STEW **53**

SLOW-COOKER GUINNESS BEEF STEW **54**

SHRIMP BISQUE
SERVES 4

WHAT MAKES THIS A BEST RECIPE: Shrimp bisque, or creamy shrimp soup flavored with cognac, is a classic French soup that doesn't see the light of day too much these days. Why? A fussy, time-consuming cooking method. Our updated version achieves deep, rich shrimp flavor with a minimum of effort by combining and/or omitting many of the classic steps. Most of the shrimp are sautéed over high heat to brown them, after which they are flambéed and chopped fine. Flambéing is a classic trick to heighten flavors, especially shellfish, and it works wonders here. Finishing the soup involves cooking the ground shrimp with aromatics—onion, celery, carrot, and garlic—and simmering the shrimp and vegetable mixture with diced tomato, bottled clam juice, and white wine. After the flavors have blended, the soup base is strained smooth through a fine-holed chinois and finished with cream, tarragon, and a stiff shot of sherry. A few chopped shrimp added as a garnish emphasize the soup's flavor and provide textural contrast. All said, our modernized bisque recipe requires only an hour or two of effort—only half that active—and just two pans. Classically flavored to a fault without the usual rigmarole required, this truly is a best recipe.

2	pounds extra-large shell-on shrimp (21 to 25 per pound)
3	tablespoons olive oil
⅓	cup brandy or cognac, warmed
2	tablespoons unsalted butter
1	carrot, peeled and chopped fine
1	celery rib, minced
1	small onion, minced
1	garlic clove, minced
½	cup unbleached all-purpose flour
1½	cups dry white wine
4	(8-ounce) bottles clam juice
1	(14.5-ounce) can diced tomatoes, well drained
1	small sprig fresh tarragon
1	cup heavy cream
1	tablespoon fresh lemon juice
	Pinch cayenne pepper
2	tablespoons dry sherry or Madeira
	Salt and pepper

1. Peel ½ pound of the shrimp, reserving the shells, and cut each peeled shrimp into thirds. With paper towels, thoroughly pat dry the remaining shrimp and reserved shells.

2. Heat 1½ tablespoons of the oil in a 12-inch heavy-bottomed skillet over high heat until just smoking. Add half of the shell-on shrimp and half of the reserved shells, spread into an even layer, and cook, stirring infrequently, until the shrimp are deep pink and the shells are lightly browned, about 2 minutes. Transfer the shrimp to a bowl and repeat the process with the remaining 1½ tablespoons oil, remaining shell-on shrimp, and the remaining shells. Return the first browned batch to the pan, remove the pan from the heat, and pour the warmed brandy over the shrimp; wave a lit match over the pan until the brandy ignites, shaking the pan. When the flames subside, transfer the shrimp and shells to a food processor and process until the mixture resembles fine meal, about 10 seconds.

3. Heat the butter in a heavy-bottomed Dutch oven over medium heat until foaming subsides. Add the carrot, celery, onion, garlic, and ground shrimp; cover and cook, stirring frequently, until the vegetables are slightly softened and the mixture is fragrant, about 5 minutes. Add the flour and cook, stirring constantly, until well blended, about 1 minute. Stir in the wine, clam juice, and tomatoes, scraping the pan bottom with a wooden spoon to loosen the browned bits, if any exist. Cover, increase the heat to medium-high, and bring to a boil; then reduce the heat to low and simmer, stirring frequently, until thickened and the flavors meld, about 20 minutes.

4. Strain the bisque through a chinois into a large bowl, pressing on the solids with the back of a ladle to extract all the liquid. Wash and dry the now-empty Dutch oven; return the strained bisque to the pot and stir in the tarragon, cream, lemon juice, and cayenne. Bring to a simmer over medium-high heat; add the reserved peeled-and-cut shrimp and simmer until the shrimp are firm but tender, about 1½ minutes. Discard the tarragon sprig; stir in the sherry, season with salt and pepper to taste, and serve hot.

SHRIMP BISQUE

WHAT YOU CAN DO AHEAD OF TIME: For the freshest flavor, the bisque should be prepared the same day it is to be served. That said, the soup base (the strained broth) can be prepared up to 8 hours ahead of time and refrigerated in an airtight container. The cream and flavorings should be added just before serving.

NOTES FROM THE TEST KITCHEN

STRAINING THE BISQUE
For the silkiest texture, strain the bisque through a chinois, or a deep, conical strainer made from supple, fine, mesh. The liquid must be forced through with the back of a ladle or wooden spoon.

If you don't own a chinois, it is possible to achieve a similarly smooth texture with a basic fine-mesh strainer lined with cheesecloth. (Try to buy it at a fabric store from large, wide bolts—and buy it in ample amounts, so that you're not out every time you need it.)

FEARLESS FLAMBÉ
Igniting alcohol helps develop a deeper, more complex flavor in sauces, thanks to flavor-boosting chemical reactions that occur only at the high temperatures reached in flambéing. Here are some tips for successful—and safe—flambéing at home.

BE PREPARED: Turn off the exhaust fan, tie back long hair, and have a lid ready to smother dangerous flare-ups.

USE THE PROPER EQUIPMENT: A pan with flared—not straight—sides (such as a skillet) allows more oxygen to mingle with the alcohol vapors, increasing the chance that you'll spark the desired flame. Use long, wooden chimney matches, and light the alcohol with your arm extended to full length.

IGNITE WARM ALCOHOL: If the alcohol becomes too hot, the vapors can rise to dangerous heights, causing large flare-ups once lit. Inversely, if the alcohol is too cold, there won't be enough vapors to light at all. We found that heating alcohol to 100 degrees Fahrenheit (best achieved by adding alcohol to a pan off the heat, then letting it heat for 5 to 10 seconds) produced the most moderate, yet long-burning flames.

LIGHT THE ALCOHOL OFF THE HEAT: If using a gas burner, be sure to turn off the flame to eliminate accidental ignitions near the side of the pan.

IF A DANGEROUS FLARE-UP SHOULD OCCUR: Simply slide the lid over the top of the skillet (coming in from the side of, rather than over, the flames) to put out the fire quickly. Let the alcohol cool down and start again.

THAI-STYLE CHICKEN SOUP
SERVES 4

WHAT MAKES THIS A BEST RECIPE: While Thai-style chicken soup may not look like much—a creamy, pale broth laced with chicken slices, mushrooms, and cilantro—what it lacks in looks it makes up for in flavor. Sweet-and-sour components balance the richness of lemongrass-and-lime-infused coconut milk, which, in turn, tempers a slow-building chile burn. It makes most styles of chicken soup seem as enticing as hospital food. However, most recipes for Thai chicken soup require a shopping list's worth of exotica available only at Asian markets. This recipe, however, takes the trouble out of the soup and makes it doable for any home cook. And it's quick too, requiring minimal effort and little time. While most traditional recipes stew a whole chicken in water with aromatic ingredients to lay the soup's foundation, we found that we could achieve the same flavor faster by simply simmering prepared chicken broth and a portion of the soup's coconut milk (the fat in the milk "clung" to the aromatics' flavors better than broth alone)—and a little potent fish sauce—with the aromatics. Within 10 minutes, the broth was ready to be strained and enriched with the remaining coconut milk, sugar for balance, mushrooms, and paper-thin slices of chicken breast. As for those exotic Asian aromatics and flavorings, we could locate lemongrass and fish sauce at most supermarkets, though no such luck with galangal, Kaffir lime leaves, or bird's eye chiles. Those flavors, however, make up Thai red curry paste, a bottled paste that is available at most supermarkets. Stirring a spoonful into the soup—dissolved into a slurry with fish sauce and lime juice—just before serving gave our soup the heady aroma and resonant flavor of the authentic versions we sought to replicate.

1   teaspoon vegetable oil

3   lemongrass stalks, tough outer leaves removed, bottom
    5 inches halved lengthwise and sliced thin crosswise

3   shallots, chopped (about ½ cup)

8   sprigs fresh cilantro, chopped

3   tablespoons fish sauce

4   cups low-sodium chicken broth

2   (14-ounce) cans coconut milk, well shaken

1   tablespoon sugar

½   pound white mushrooms, cut into ¼-inch slices

3   boneless, skinless chicken breasts (5–6 ounces each),
    halved lengthwise and sliced on the bias into
    ⅛-inch-thick pieces

3   tablespoons fresh lime juice from 2 to 3 limes

2   teaspoons Thai red curry paste

GARNISH

½   cup fresh cilantro leaves

2   serrano chiles, sliced thin

2   scallions, sliced thin on the bias

1   lime, cut into wedges

1. Heat the oil in a large saucepan over medium heat until just shimmering. Add the lemongrass, shallots, cilantro, and 1 tablespoon of the fish sauce; cook, stirring frequently, until just softened, 2 to 5 minutes (the vegetables should not brown). Stir in the broth and 1 can coconut milk; bring to a simmer over high heat. Cover, reduce the heat to low, and simmer until the flavors have blended, 10 minutes. Pour the broth through a fine-mesh strainer and discard the solids in the strainer. Rinse the saucepan and return the broth mixture to the pan.

2. Return the pan to medium-high heat. Stir the remaining can of coconut milk and sugar into the broth mixture and bring to a simmer. Reduce the heat to medium, add the mushrooms, and cook until just tender, 2 to 3 minutes. Add the chicken and cook, stirring constantly, until no longer pink, 1 to 3 minutes. Remove the soup from the heat.

3. Combine the lime juice, curry paste, and remaining 2 tablespoons fish sauce in a small bowl; stir into the soup. Ladle the soup into bowls and garnish with the cilantro, chiles, and scallions. Serve immediately with lime wedges.

WHERE THINGS CAN GO WRONG: Fresh lemongrass can be omitted, but don't be tempted to use jarred or dried lemongrass—their flavor is characterless.

WHAT YOU CAN DO AHEAD OF TIME: The soup can be prepared through step 1 up to 1 day ahead of time and refrigerated in an airtight container. Finish the soup just before serving, as the chicken and mushrooms can easily overcook.

NOTES FROM THE TEST KITCHEN

COCONUT MILK

Coconut milk is made by steeping equal parts shredded coconut meat in either warm milk or water. The meat is pressed or mashed to release as much liquid as possible, the mixture is strained, and the result is coconut milk. We tasted seven nationally available brands (five regular and two light) in coconut pudding, coconut rice, Thai-Style Chicken Soup, and green chicken curry. In the soup and curry, tasters preferred **Chaokoh** because of its exceptionally low sugar content (less than 1 gram per ⅓ cup). By comparison, brands with more than twice as much sugar (Ka-Me, Goya, Thai Kitchen) tasted "saccharine." In the sweet recipes, tasters gave velvety Ka-Me top votes for its "fruity" and "complex" flavor. In these recipes, the extra sugar was an advantage. If you're counting your fat grams, we can recommend **A Taste of Thai** as a light alternative (though we wouldn't recommend using it in desserts).

CREAM OF THE CROP   **THE LEAN CHOICE**

FISH SAUCE

Fish sauce is a salty, amber-colored liquid made from fermented fish. It is used as an ingredient and condiment in certain Asian cuisines, most commonly in the foods of Southeast Asia. In very small amounts, it adds a salty complexity to sauces, soups, and marinades that is nearly impossible to replicate.

SLICING CHICKEN BREASTS

Our Thai-Style Chicken Soup calls for thin slices of boneless, skinless chicken breast that will cook in just a minute or two. To make slicing easier, place the chicken in the freezer for 30 minutes, then cut the breasts in half lengthwise. Firmer, narrower strips of chicken will be easier to slice on the bias into ⅛-inch-thick pieces.

COLCANNON SOUP

SERVES 4

WHAT MAKES THIS A BEST RECIPE: Colcannon is an age-old dish of Ireland and Western Scotland in which mashed potatoes are enriched with cabbage, leeks, onions, and scallions or chives. In recent years, colcannon has interestingly morphed into a thick potage that is just the kind of soup to warm you up on the coldest winter night. We recently tackled colcannon soup for *The Best International Recipe* and find our version without equal. The soup's deep flavor is developed in part by blending three alliums—leeks, onion, and garlic—and cooking them in rendered bacon fat (the crisped bacon is reserved for the garnish) prior to adding chicken broth. As for the potatoes, we preferred Red Bliss for their characteristic flavor and firm texture. Most recipes thicken the soup by simply mashing a portion of the potatoes, but we were disappointed in the grainy texture this lent the soup. Instead, we added a little flour, which made the broth silky-smooth. As for the cabbage, we tried Savoy and Napa, but tasters liked straightforward green cabbage for its substantial texture—it remained distinct, even after simmering. With a splash of white wine for brightness and heavy cream for body, we had a flavorful bowl of soup sporting the rich and layered flavors of a favorite Irish potato dish.

- 3 slices bacon, cut into ½-inch pieces
- 1 onion, minced (about 1 cup)
- 1 pound leeks, white and light green parts only, halved lengthwise, sliced thin, and rinsed thoroughly
- ½ head green cabbage (about 8 ounces), cored and chopped medium (about 4 cups)
- 2 garlic cloves, minced
- 2 tablespoons unbleached all-purpose flour
- ½ cup white wine
- 4 cups low-sodium chicken broth
- 12 ounces red potatoes (about 3 medium), cut into ¾-inch chunks
- ½ cup heavy cream

Salt and pepper
- 2 tablespoons minced fresh chives, dill, or parsley, for serving

1. Cook the bacon in a large Dutch oven over medium-low heat until the fat is rendered and the bacon is crisp, 5 to 7 minutes. Transfer the bacon to a paper towel–lined plate, leaving the rendered fat in the pot.

2. Add the onion, leeks, and cabbage to the fat in the Dutch oven and stir to coat. Cover and cook over medium heat until the vegetables are tender, about 10 minutes. Stir in the garlic and cook until fragrant, about 30 seconds. Stir in the flour and cook for about 1 minute.

3. Stir in the wine, scraping up any browned bits, and simmer until thickened slightly, about 2 minutes. Stir in the broth and potatoes and bring to a boil. Reduce the heat to a simmer and cook until the potatoes are tender, about 15 minutes.

4. Off the heat, stir in the cream and season with salt and pepper to taste. Portion the soup into individual serving bowls and sprinkle with the reserved crumbled bacon and chives before serving.

NOTES FROM THE TEST KITCHEN

PREPARING LEEKS

1. Trim and discard the roots and the dark green leaves.

2. Slice the trimmed leek in half lengthwise, then slice thin.

3. Rinse the cut leeks thoroughly to remove dirt and sand.

POTATO GARLIC SOUP

SERVES 6

WHAT MAKES THIS A BEST RECIPE: This thick potato soup flavored with garlic *(Potage Parmentier)* was invented as a stopgap measure to prevent famine during a disastrous wheat crop in 18th century France. It may be a classic now, but its canonical stature is in no way a guarantee that it's all that good. We tasted dozens of recipes that proved unsatisfying because they were too simple, too complicated, or had a displeasing texture. How could such a simple soup go so wrong? Our recipe succeeds where the others fail. First of all, for the potatoes, we liked the contrasting flavors and textures of a soup made with both russet and Red Bliss potatoes. The duo invests the soup with a well-rounded flavor and a creamy texture punctuated by toothsome chunks. As for the garlic, we much preferred the mellow, sweet flavor lent by whole heads of poached garlic combined with the potency of sautéed garlic. It couldn't have been easier to poach the garlic heads in the soup, squeeze them from their papery skins, mash them smooth, and return the paste to the soup. Chicken broth enriched with cream proved the best liquid component and leeks alone, rather than a full mirepoix, contributed a full flavor without distracting from the potatoes or garlic. And finally, garnishing the soup with crisp-fried garlic chips added a pleasantly bittersweet flavor, not to mention a crispy crunch to accent the soup's creaminess.

GARLIC CHIPS

3 **tablespoons olive oil**

6 **garlic cloves, sliced thin lengthwise**
  Salt

SOUP

3 **tablespoons unsalted butter**

1 **medium leek, white and light green parts only, halved lengthwise, washed, and chopped small**

3 **garlic cloves, minced, plus 2 whole garlic heads, rinsed, top third cut off and discarded, and loose outer skins removed**

6 **cups low-sodium chicken broth, plus extra to thin soup, as needed**

2 **bay leaves**
  Salt

1½ **pounds russet potatoes (about 3 medium), peeled and cut into ½-inch cubes**

1 **pound red potatoes (about 6 small), unpeeled and cut into ½-inch cubes**

½ **cup heavy cream**

1½ **teaspoons minced fresh thyme**
  Pepper

¼ **cup minced fresh chives**

1. FOR THE GARLIC CHIPS: Heat the oil and sliced garlic in a 10-inch skillet over medium-high heat. Cook, turning frequently, until light golden brown, about 3 minutes. Transfer the garlic to a paper towel–lined plate and sprinkle lightly with salt; set aside until ready to serve. Discard the oil.

2. FOR THE SOUP: Melt the butter in a large Dutch oven over medium heat. When the foaming subsides, add the leek and cook until softened but not browned, 5 to 8 minutes. Stir in the minced garlic and cook until fragrant, about 30 seconds. Add the garlic heads, broth, bay leaves, and ¾ teaspoon salt; partially cover the pot and bring to a simmer over medium-high heat. Reduce the heat to medium-low and simmer until the garlic is very tender when pierced with the tip of a knife, 30 to 40 minutes. Add the potatoes and continue to simmer, partially covered, until the potatoes are tender, 15 to 20 minutes.

3. Remove and discard the bay leaves. Remove the garlic heads; using tongs or paper towels, squeeze the garlic heads at the root end until the cloves slip out of their skins into a bowl. Mash the garlic to a smooth paste with a fork.

4. Stir the cream, thyme, and half of the mashed garlic into the soup; heat the soup until hot, about 2 minutes. Taste the soup and add the remaining garlic paste if desired. Using an immersion blender, process the soup until creamy, with some potato chunks remaining.

(Alternatively, transfer 1½ cups of the potatoes and 1 cup of the broth to a blender or food processor and process until smooth. Process more of the potatoes for a thicker consistency, if desired.) Return the puree to the pot and stir to combine, adjusting the consistency with more broth, if necessary. Season with salt and pepper to taste. Ladle into bowls and garnish each serving with a sprinkling of chives and the reserved garlic chips.

GREAT DISCOVERIES

THREE WAYS TO GREAT GARLIC FLAVOR

Working my way through dozens of heads of garlic while developing this recipe, I clarified some of the mysteries surrounding the bulbous plant. First, the extent to which a garlic clove is cut determines the amount of flavor it will exude. When the cells of a garlic clove are ruptured, an odorless chemical called *allyl sulfenic acid* is released and comes into contact with an enzyme called *alliinase*. The reaction of the two produces a new compound called *allicin*, which is responsible for the characteristic fiery flavor and scent of garlic. The more a garlic clove is broken down, the more enzymes are released and the more allicin—and therefore flavor—is produced. Second, cooking affects the flavor intensity of garlic. Garlic is at its sharpest when raw. When heated beyond 150 degrees, the enzymes in garlic are destroyed and no new flavor is produced; only flavor produced up to the inactivation temperature remains. One caveat: When garlic is browned at very high temperatures (300 to 350 degrees, as when making our garlic chips), some of the flavor compounds are converted into slightly bitter molecules. What does this mean for the garlic in our recipe? To extract the maximum garlic flavor from our soup, we used garlic in three ways: whole heads of garlic simmered in the soup added sweet, mild notes; sautéed minced garlic contributed potent flavor; and finally, a garnish of toasted garlic chips added bold flavor and pleasantly bitter notes.

REBECCA HAYS | MANAGING EDITOR, *COOK'S ILLUSTRATED*

NOTES FROM THE TEST KITCHEN

TWO SPUDS ARE BETTER THAN ONE

Our potato garlic soup uses both russet and Red Bliss potatoes for ultimate potato flavor and texture. Peeled starchy russet potatoes break down during cooking to thicken the soup, while unpeeled Red Bliss potatoes give the soup both a rustic, chunky texture and rich potato flavor.

RED BLISS UNCOOKED

RED BLISS COOKED

RUSSET UNCOOKED

RUSSET COOKED

THE ANATOMY OF A PERFECT LADLE

You might think one ladle is pretty much the same as the next. But after dunking eight stainless steel models (plastic stains and can melt on the stovetop) into pots of chicken noodle soup and hearty beef stew, scattered puddles on the test kitchen countertop made it clear that not all ladles are ergonomically equal. Ladles with handles shorter than 9 inches simply sank in deeper pots, while more than 10 inches of grip proved cumbersome to maneuver. Ladles with small bowls are better suited to sauces than soups, and an offset handle is a must—without some slight bend in the handle, cleanly transferring the ladle's contents into a bowl is nearly impossible. A handle that bends too dramatically, however, makes it difficult to dip the ladle into a tall, narrow stockpot. The **Rösle Ladle with Pouring Rim & Hook Handle** ($23.95) had everything we were looking for—including a hook handle and a drip-prevention pouring rim, which kept even wiggly noodles intact all the way to the bowl.

SKILLET CREOLE CHICKEN FRICASSEE

SERVES 4

WHAT MAKES THIS A BEST RECIPE: Classically defined, a fricassee involves simmering browned meat—usually chicken—and vegetables in a flour-thickened sauce until tender and flavorful. It's a great way to produce a one-pot meal, though it's a slow and time-consuming process. Our Skillet Creole Chicken Fricassee, however, takes liberties with the classic method and produces a finished, Cajun-inspired meal in just thirty minutes. How is it done? The biggest change we made was to switch from whole chicken pieces to boneless, skinless chicken breasts, which took a fraction of the time to cook. To compensate for the milder flavor of the boneless breasts, we browned the chicken in fat rendered from spicy *andouille* sausage. Cajun dishes just don't taste quite right unless flavored with the trinity of onion, celery, and bell pepper, so we added the three vegetables and sautéed them briefly. Garlic, too, helps define Cajun cooking, so we added a hefty four cloves. Browning the flour before adding the liquid intensified its flavor and the color of the finished dish, making it reminiscent of gumbo (with a fraction of the effort). And for a Cajun flourish, we relied on prepared Cajun seasoning, which is available at most supermarkets. Within a half hour, 10 minutes of which was hands-off simmering, our "quick" version of fricassee was on the table.

4 boneless, skinless, chicken breasts (5–6 ounces each), halved lengthwise

3 teaspoons Creole seasoning

8 ounces andouille or chorizo sausage, cut into ½-inch rounds

3 tablespoons vegetable oil

1 onion, chopped (about 1 cup)

3 celery ribs, sliced thin

1 red bell pepper, stemmed, seeded, and chopped

4 garlic cloves, minced

¼ cup unbleached all-purpose flour

2 cups low-sodium chicken broth

1. Pat the chicken dry with paper towels and sprinkle with 2 teaspoons of the Creole seasoning. Cook the sausage in a 12-inch nonstick skillet over medium-high heat until browned, about 5 minutes. Transfer the sausage to a paper towel–lined plate, leaving the fat in the skillet. Cook the chicken in the sausage fat until browned, about 2 minutes per side. Transfer to the plate with the sausage.

2. Add the oil, onion, celery, and pepper to the now-empty skillet and cook until lightly browned, about 5 minutes. Add the garlic and cook until fragrant, about 30 seconds. Stir in the flour and the remaining 1 teaspoon Creole seasoning and cook until the flour begins to brown, about 1 minute.

3. Slowly stir in the broth until smooth. Return the chicken and sausage to the skillet. Cover and simmer until the chicken registers 160 degrees on an instant-read thermometer, about 10 minutes. Serve.

NOTES FROM THE TEST KITCHEN

CREOLE SEASONING
Creole seasoning is a spicy blend of salt, paprika, cayenne pepper, thyme, garlic, and other herbs and spices. We've had good results with **Chachere's Brand.**

PREPARING BELL PEPPERS

1. Slice ¼ inch from the top and bottom of each pepper and then gently remove the stem from the top lobe.

2. Pull the core out of the pepper. Make a slit down one side of the pepper and lay it flat, skin-side down, in one long strip.

3. Slide a sharp knife along the inside of the pepper to remove all the ribs and seeds. Cut into strips and chop.

BRAZILIAN BLACK BEANS
WITH RIBS, PORK TENDERLOIN, AND SAUSAGE
SERVES 8 TO 10

WHAT MAKES THIS A BEST RECIPE: Considered one of Brazil's national dishes, this hearty black bean stew (*Feijoada*) is typically loaded with all manner of pork (and pig parts, like feet, ears, tail, and snout) and flavored with two traditional accompaniments: *molho appimentado,* a fresh salsa-like hot sauce, and *farofa,* a toasted manioc flour that is sprinkled over the top. Feijoada is as much an event as it is a meal. For *The Best International Recipe,* we whittled the dish down to a more approachable—though still authentic-tasting—recipe, one easily prepared from supermarket staples. We limited the selection of meats to just four: baby back ribs, linguiça (a Portuguese sausage), pork tenderloin, and bacon—no parts. The biggest challenge we faced was the cooking method. Traditional recipes stew the beans and unbrowned meats together for hours over low heat, resulting in overcooked meat, mushy beans, and too much liquid. We solved this problem by adding the meat to the simmering beans in stages, according to how long it would take for the meat to cook to its ideal doneness (after browning the meat first to intensify its flavor and enrich the broth). The ribs and sausage went in early and we arranged the delicate tenderloins on top of the beans—above the liquid—so that they effectively steamed and remained tender and moist. As for the beans, we discovered that they could be successfully simmered and cooked to a creamy texture without being soaked first, which saved us a significant amount of time. A pinch of baking soda helps the beans retain their deep color. Flavorings, outside of the hot sauce and manioc flour, are traditionally kept simple: garlic, onion, and bay leaf sufficed. We sautéed the aromatics, with bacon, prior to adding the beans so that they would be infused with the flavorings as they hydrated. If you like, serve this stew with its classic condiments—orange segments, sautéed kale, and rice—for a carnival-worthy experience.

HOT SAUCE

- 2 medium firm, ripe tomatoes, cored, seeded, and chopped fine
- 1 onion, minced (about 1 cup)
- 1 green bell pepper, stemmed, seeded, and chopped fine
- 1 jalapeño chile, seeds and ribs removed, then minced
- ⅓ cup white wine vinegar
- 3 tablespoons extra-virgin olive oil
- 1 tablespoon minced fresh cilantro
- ½ teaspoon salt

TOASTED MANIOC FLOUR

- 2 tablespoons unsalted butter
- 1 cup manioc flour

STEW

- 4 slices bacon, minced
- 1 onion, minced (about 1 cup)
- 4 garlic cloves, minced
- 10½ cups water
- 2 pounds (about 4½ cups) dried black beans, rinsed and picked over
- 2 bay leaves
- ⅛ teaspoon baking soda
  Salt
- 2 (1-pound) pork tenderloins, trimmed and cut in half crosswise
- 2 racks baby back ribs (2½ to 3 pounds each), trimmed and each rack cut into 3 pieces
  Pepper
- ¼ cup vegetable oil
- 1 pound linguiça, cut into 6-inch lengths

1. FOR THE HOT SAUCE: Combine all the ingredients in a bowl and let stand at room temperature until the flavors meld, about 30 minutes; cover and refrigerate until needed.

2. FOR THE TOASTED MANIOC FLOUR: Melt the butter in a 10-inch skillet over medium heat. Add the manioc flour and cook, stirring frequently, until golden brown, 5 to 7 minutes. Transfer to a bowl and let cool, about 5 minutes; set aside.

3. FOR THE STEW: Cook the bacon in a 12-quart heavy-bottomed stockpot over medium heat until partly rendered and lightly browned, about 5 minutes. Stir in the onion and cook until the onion is softened, 5 to 7 minutes. Stir in the garlic and cook until fragrant, about

30 seconds. Stir in 10 cups of the water, beans, bay leaves, baking soda, and 1 teaspoon salt, and bring to a boil over high heat, skimming any impurities that rise to the surface. Reduce the heat to low, cover, and cook, stirring occasionally, until the beans begin to soften, about 1 hour.

4. Meanwhile, pat the pork tenderloins and ribs dry with paper towels and season with salt and pepper. Heat 1 tablespoon of the oil in a 12-inch skillet over medium-high heat until just smoking. Brown the tenderloins on all sides, 8 to 10 minutes, reducing the heat if the pan begins to scorch. Transfer the tenderloins to a plate and set aside. Add ¼ cup of the remaining water to the skillet, return to low heat, and scrape up the browned bits; add the water and bits to the simmering beans.

5. Wipe the skillet dry, add 1 tablespoon more oil, and return to medium-high heat until just smoking. Brown 2 of the rib pieces, on the meat side only, about 5 minutes, reducing the heat if the pan begins to scorch. Transfer the browned ribs to a plate, and repeat twice more with the remaining 2 tablespoons oil and 4 rib pieces. After all of the ribs are browned, add the remaining ¼ cup water to the skillet, return to low heat, and scrape up the browned bits; add the water and bits to the simmering beans.

6. After the beans have cooked for 1 hour, nestle the linguiça and browned ribs into the beans, submerging them as much as possible. Continue to cook the beans over low heat, covered, until the beans are soft, about 40 minutes, stirring thoroughly about halfway through the cooking time.

7. Gently lay the browned pork tenderloins on top of the beans (it's OK if they sink in a little), and continue to cook, covered, until the beans are tender and the center of the tenderloins register 145 degrees on an instant-read thermometer, 20 to 30 minutes longer.

8. Using tongs, transfer the tenderloins, ribs, and linguiça to a large carving board and tent with aluminum foil. Remove and discard the bay leaves. Remove 1 cup of the bean cooking liquid and reserve. Transfer 2 cups of the beans and ½ cup more of the bean liquid to a bowl and mash smooth with a potato masher or fork, then return to the pot. Add the reserved cooking liquid back to the beans as needed to keep the consistency loose but not soupy.

9. Slice the pork tenderloin into ½-inch-thick slices. Slice the linguiça into ¾-inch-thick slices. Slice the ribs between each bone into single rib portions. Arrange the meats on a large, warmed serving platter. Season the beans with salt and pepper to taste, then serve with the meats, passing the hot sauce and toasted manioc flour separately.

WHERE THINGS CAN GO WRONG: Make sure to rinse and sort the beans carefully to remove any errant bits of dirt or pebbles.

WHAT YOU CAN DO AHEAD OF TIME: The stew can be refrigerated in an airtight container for up to 2 days. Hold on to the 1 cup reserved bean liquid and add it as needed to prevent the stew's texture from being too thick. The stew should be reheated over gentle heat. The hot sauce can be refrigerated in an airtight container for up to 2 days. The farofa (toasted flour) can be refrigerated in an airtight container for up to 5 days.

NOTES FROM THE TEST KITCHEN

BRAZILIAN ACCOMPANIMENTS

While researching recipes for *feijoada*, we found a continuing reference to two traditional accompaniments: a toasted meal that is sprinkled over the beans called *farofa*, and a salsa-like sauce called *molho appimentado*. Giving both of these accompaniments a whirl, we quickly fell in love with the exotic texture of the farofa, and spicy, fresh flavor of the molho appimentado. Manioc flour/meal can be found in most Latin American specialty stores in a variety of textures ranging from fine to coarse (much like cornmeal); finely ground is most common but any will work. The hot sauce is typically enlivened with Malagueta chiles, small hot Brazilian chiles, which may be tricky to find; a jalapeño chile is a suitable alternative.

OUR FAVORITE STOCKPOT

We think a 12-quart stockpot is the most useful size—it's the "smallest" big pot, meaning it can handle most big jobs yet is small enough to store with your other pots and pans. So how much do you have to spend to get a good one? With its heft, greater width, easy to grip handles, and ability to heat evenly, the **All-Clad Stainless 12-Quart Stockpot** (left), $325, can't be beat. Don't want to spend $325 on a pot? The **Cuisinart Chef's Classic Stainless 12-Quart Stockpot** (right) performed almost as well and costs a reasonable $65.

CINCINNATI CHILI

SERVES 6 TO 8

WHAT MAKES THIS A BEST RECIPE: Invented by Greek immigrants early in the century, Cincinnati chili tastes more of the Mediterranean than of Texas. Warm spices—though not spicy "hot"—lend complexity to a sweet, tender mixture of ground beef, tomatoes, and onion. The chili is never served solo; instead it's ladled over spaghetti and topped with the classic condiments: beans (kidney), chopped onions, cheese, and oyster crackers. (Each topping is a called a "way"; if you opt for spaghetti and all the toppings, it's called a "five way.") We like this recipe because it makes this regional version of chili accessible to everyone, whether you live in Ohio, Oregon, or daresay it, Texas. Many recipes called for a spice cabinet's worth of seasoning, but through several tests, we cut the ingredients down to a manageable list. Cinnamon, allspice, chili powder, and oregano made the cut. Chocolate, cocoa or bar (despite whisperings that it's a secret ingredient in some of the city's chili parlors), didn't. With a bit of tomato paste for color and richness, dark brown sugar to add a molasses tang, and onions and a hint of garlic for body, we achieved rich flavor without a grocery list of items. But Cincinnati chili isn't defined by flavor alone—another hallmark is the saucy, ultra-tender texture of the ground beef. We knew that most chili parlors boil the raw meat in water, drain it, and then add it to the spiced liquid. Boiling helps keep the beef extremely tender during the cooking process, which takes just minutes, not hours like most chili recipes. To save on both time and dishes, we found we could achieve the same soft texture by simmering the uncooked beef with the flavorings in the chili's liquid components. Within 20 minutes, we had chili every bit as good—and authentic—as that slung at parlors throughout Cincinnati. Make ours a "five way."

1 tablespoon vegetable oil
2 onions, minced (2 cups)
1 garlic clove, minced
2 tablespoons tomato paste
2 tablespoons chili powder

1 tablespoon dried oregano
1½ teaspoons ground cinnamon
Salt
¾ teaspoon pepper
¼ teaspoon ground allspice
2 cups low-sodium chicken broth
2 cups canned tomato sauce
2 tablespoons cider vinegar
2 teaspoons dark brown sugar
1½ pounds 85 percent lean ground beef

CONDIMENTS

1 onion, chopped (about 1 cup)
4 ounces cheddar cheese, shredded (about 1 cup)
1 (15-ounce) can kidney beans, rinsed and drained

1. Heat the oil in a Dutch oven over medium-high heat until shimmering. Cook the onions until softened, about 8 minutes. Add the garlic, tomato paste, chili powder, oregano, cinnamon, 1 teaspoon salt, pepper, and allspice and cook until fragrant, about 30 seconds. Stir in the broth, tomato sauce, vinegar, and sugar.

2. Add the beef and stir to break up the meat. Bring to a boil, reduce the heat to medium-low, and simmer until the chili is deep brown and slightly thickened, 15 to 20 minutes. Season with salt to taste and serve with condiments if desired.

WHAT YOU CAN DO AHEAD OF TIME: The chili can be refrigerated in an airtight container for up to 3 days or frozen for up to 2 months.

NOTES FROM THE TEST KITCHEN

OUR FAVORITE MODERATELY-PRICED DUTCH OVEN
After testing seven inexpensive Dutch ovens alongside previous test kitchen winners made by All-Clad and Le Creuset, we have found that they are still the two to beat. but for those looking to spend less on this piece of equipment, we have found a solid alternative. **The Mario Batali Italian Essentials** Dutch oven is on the heavy side and could use bigger handles, but it is comparable in size to the All-Clad and Le Creuset ovens and performs nearly as well. Better yet, at $99.99 it costs less than half the price of either.

SPANISH SHELLFISH STEW

SERVES 4

WHAT MAKES THIS A BEST RECIPE: Less well known than France's *bouillabaisse* and Italy's *cioppino*, but equally flavorful is Spain's shellfish stew known as *zarzuela*, a stew infused with the flavors of saffron, paprika, and tomato. A *picada*, or a flavorful mixture of ground almonds, bread crumbs, and olive oil, is added at the last minute as a thickener and flavor enhancer. Unlike most seafood stews, zarzuela contains no fish stock—instead the shellfish release their rich liquors into the pot as they cook. It's a unique combination that's utterly delicious. Zarzuela starts with a slow-cooked *sofrito* of onion, garlic, and red bell pepper. Paprika, saffron, red pepper flakes, and bay leaves join the sofrito to form a distinctly Spanish flavor base to which tomatoes, dry white wine, and brandy are added. Typically, the dish includes lobster, shrimp, scallops, mussels, and clams. We decided to omit lobster for convenience's sake, compensating for its rich flavor by steeping sautéed shrimp shells in the wine before straining it and adding it to the broth. To insure that the different types of seafood cooked evenly, we added it to the broth in stages, the tender shelled shrimp going in last. As for the picada, we found that fried bread (which required a significant amount of oil) turned the stew greasy. Instead we toasted fresh bread crumbs with a little olive oil. We also tossed the almonds in with the crumbs, so they too toasted, intensifying their flavor. Stirring the picada into the stew once the shellfish were cooked thickened the broth perfectly and its rich mellow flavor rounded out the bold stew. A handful of chopped fresh parsley and a squeeze of lemon are the perfect finishing touches to this Spanish favorite.

PICADA

- ¼ cup slivered almonds
- 2 slices high-quality white sandwich bread, torn into quarters
- 2 tablespoons extra-virgin olive oil
- ⅛ teaspoon salt
  Pepper

STEW

- ¼ cup olive oil
- 16 extra-large shrimp (21 to 25 per pound), peeled, deveined, and shells reserved
- 1½ cups dry white wine
- 1 onion, minced (about 1 cup)
- 1 red bell pepper, stemmed, seeded, and chopped fine
  Salt
- 3 garlic cloves, minced
- 1 teaspoon sweet paprika
- ¼ teaspoon saffron threads, crumbled
- ⅛ teaspoon red pepper flakes
- 2 bay leaves
- 2 tablespoons brandy
- 1 (28-ounce) can whole tomatoes in juice, tomatoes chopped medium and juice reserved
- 16 littleneck clams (about 1½ pounds), scrubbed
- 16 mussels (about 8 ounces), scrubbed and debearded if necessary (see page 52)
- 8 large sea scallops (about 8 ounces), tendons removed (see page 52)
- 1 tablespoon minced fresh parsley
  Pepper
- 1 teaspoon lemon juice

1. FOR THE PICADA: Adjust an oven rack to the middle position and heat the oven to 375 degrees. Pulse the nuts in the food processor to fine crumbs, about 15 pulses. Add the bread, olive oil, salt, and pepper to taste and continue to pulse the bread to coarse crumbs, about 10 pulses. Spread the mixture out evenly over a rimmed baking sheet and toast, stirring often, until golden brown, about 10 minutes; set aside to cool.

2. FOR THE STEW: Heat 1 tablespoon of the oil in a medium saucepan over medium heat until shimmering. Add the reserved shrimp shells and cook until pink, about 5 minutes. Off the heat, stir in the wine, cover, and let steep until ready to use.

3. Meanwhile, heat the remaining 3 tablespoons oil in a large Dutch oven over medium heat until shimmering. Add the onion, bell pepper, and ¼ teaspoon salt and cook until the onion is softened and lightly browned, 7 to 10 minutes. Stir in the garlic, paprika, saffron, pepper flakes, and bay leaves and cook until fragrant, about 30 seconds. Stir in the brandy and simmer for 30 seconds. Stir in the tomatoes with their juice and

cook until slightly thickened, 5 to 7 minutes.

4. Strain the wine mixture into the Dutch oven through a fine-mesh strainer, pressing on the shrimp shells to extract as much liquid as possible; discard the shells. Continue to simmer until the flavors have melded, 3 to 5 minutes.

5. Increase the heat to medium-high, add the clams, cover, and cook, stirring occasionally, until the first few clams begin to open, about 5 minutes. Add the mussels and scallops, cover, and continue to cook until most of the clams have opened, about 3 minutes longer. Add the shrimp, cover, and continue to cook until the shrimp are pink and cooked through and the clams and mussels have opened, about 2 minutes longer.

6. Remove and discard the bay leaves and any mussels or clams that have not opened. Fold in the reserved picada and parsley, and season with salt, pepper, and lemon juice to taste. Serve immediately.

WHERE THINGS CAN GO WRONG: Properly prepping the seafood is important to the dish's success. The mussels and clams should be well rinsed and scrubbed to remove any grit; the mussels should also have their "beard" pulled free. As for the scallops, the small, rough-textured, crescent-shaped muscle that attaches the scallop to the shell will toughen when cooked. Use your fingers to peel the tendon away from the side of each scallop before cooking. The cooking time of the sea scallops will depend on their size; we used extra-large scallops (about 2 inches in diameter and 1 inch thick), but if your scallops are smaller (about 1 inch in diameter and ½ inch thick), they will cook more quickly and should be added to the pot with the shrimp. Be sure to choose an appropriately dry white wine like Spain's Rueda or Sauvignon Blanc. A Chardonnay will also work, but avoid any that have been aged in oak.

WHAT YOU CAN DO AHEAD OF TIME: The broth can be prepared through step 4, cooled, and refrigerated in an airtight container for up to 1 day. Bring the broth to a simmer in a large Dutch oven, covered, over medium heat before continuing. The picada can be stored in an airtight container at room temperature for up to 3 days.

NOTES FROM THE TEST KITCHEN

DEBEARDING MUSSELS

Occasionally, mussels will have a harmless weedy piece (known as the beard) protruding from between the shells. Before cooking, a quick tug between your thumb and a butter knife or the flat side of a paring knife is all it takes to remove it.

PREPARING SCALLOPS

The small, crescent-shaped muscle that is sometimes attached to the scallop will be incredibly tough when cooked. Use your fingers to peel this muscle away from the side of each scallop before cooking.

CANNED WHOLE TOMATOES

After tasting ten brands of whole canned tomatoes straight and prepared in two different sauces, we were most impressed with the firm texture, bright acidity, and fresh, lively flavor of **Progresso "Italian-Style" Whole Peeled Tomatoes with Basil** (the basil adds nominal flavor at best and can easily be removed for recipes where it might taste out of place). That said, buy carefully: Progresso also sells whole peeled tomatoes packed in tomato puree and basil, which tastes decidedly blander—the puree mutes the tomato's brightness. The two cans look remarkably similar, so read the labels carefully and make sure to choose the tomatoes packed in juice.

SLOW-COOKER LENTIL AND SWISS CHARD STEW

SERVES 6 TO 8

WHAT MAKES THIS A BEST RECIPE: While the slow cooker works wonders with hearty meat-based stews and thick roasts, we've been ambivalent about most slow-cooker-made vegetarian recipes, which typically turn bland and one-dimensional during the long simmer. That is until now. This lentil and Swiss chard stew from *The Best Make-Ahead Recipe* is complexly flavored and deeply satisfying—all without a hint of meat. How did we do it? By layering flavors and textures. Initial recipe testing proved that, first, garlic, herbs, onions, and tomatoes were a must for both flavor and color. And secondly, texture is a big issue; nobody liked the soup that was brothy or, at the other extreme, thick as porridge. We quickly decided on vegetable broth as more flavorful than water for the base; choosing the right type of lentils proved a little trickier. After testing all shapes, sizes, and textures, we found it crucial to use large-sized green or brown lentils. Despite the extensive amount of time they spent in the slow cooker, they retained a desirable texture. While we pureed a portion of the cooked soup to lend it a creamy consistency, tasters wanted that creaminess punctuated with chunky vegetables, so we turned to meaty portobello mushrooms. To enhance the now-earthy flavor of the soup, we found that adding ½ ounce of dried porcini mushrooms was key. Bay leaves and thyme rounded out the other flavors, but the soup was a rather muddy color. To remedy the problem, and add yet more flavor (not to mention color), we stirred in chopped Swiss chard leaves after the soup was basically done. The contrast of the bright chard with the earthy tones of the soup was perfect, except there remained one last issue: The chard stems were tough and stringy. We decided to sauté the stems along with the onions at the onset of cooking, which solved the problem. A splash of balsamic vinegar stirred into the pot at completion, and tasters gave this soup a perfect 10.

2 tablespoons vegetable oil

3 onions, minced (about 3 cups)

1 pound Swiss chard, stems and leaves separated; stems cut into ¼-inch pieces and leaves chopped coarse

6 garlic cloves, minced

Salt

6 cups vegetable broth

1 pound carrots, peeled and cut into 1-inch chunks

1 (15-ounce) can tomato sauce

12 ounces portobello mushroom caps, gills removed (see page 54) and cut into ½-inch chunks

1 cup brown or green lentils, rinsed and picked over

2 bay leaves

1 tablespoon minced fresh thyme or 1 teaspoon dried

½ ounce dried porcini mushrooms, rinsed and minced

1 tablespoon balsamic vinegar

Pepper

Grated Parmesan cheese, for serving (optional)

Extra-virgin olive oil, for serving (optional)

1. Heat the oil in a 12-inch nonstick skillet over medium heat until shimmering. Add the onions, chard stems, garlic, and ¼ teaspoon salt and cook until the vegetables are softened and lightly browned, 10 to 12 minutes.

2. Transfer the onion mixture to the slow cooker insert and stir in the broth, carrots, tomato sauce, portobello mushroom caps, lentils, bay leaves, thyme, and dried porcini mushrooms until evenly combined. Cover and cook on low until the stew is thickened and the lentils are tender, 8 to 10 hours. (Alternatively, cover and cook on high for 5 to 7 hours.)

3. Remove and discard the bay leaves. Puree 2 cups of the soup in a blender until smooth, then stir back into the slow cooker insert. Stir in the chard leaves, cover, and continue to cook until the leaves are wilted and tender, 10 to 15 minutes longer. Stir in the vinegar, season with salt and pepper to taste, and serve, passing grated Parmesan cheese and extra-virgin olive oil, if desired.

WHERE THINGS CAN GO WRONG: Be sure to choose large green or brown lentils and avoid red lentils, which will overcook. Rinse the lentils, then carefully sort through them to remove small stones and pebbles.

WHAT YOU CAN DO AHEAD OF TIME: The onion-chard stem mixture may be prepared through step 1 and refrigerated in an airtight container up to 1 day in advance. The remaining vegetables may also be prepared and refrigerated up to 1 day ahead.

NOTES FROM THE TEST KITCHEN

REMOVING GILLS FROM PORTOBELLO MUSHROOMS
We found that it was necessary to remove the black gills from the portobello mushrooms because they made the stew muddy in appearance. Using a soup spoon, scrape and discard the dark-colored gills from the underside of each mushroom.

TAKING STOCK OF VEGETABLE BROTH
After tasting nine popular brands of vegetable broth straight and prepared in two separate dishes, we were somewhat surprised to find the differences subtle, the biggest difference being the amount of sodium each contained. Tasted straight, the clear winner was Swanson, which also happened to have the highest sodium levels out of all the samples. Prepared in a stew, however, the differences between Swanson and the broth containing the least amount of sodium, Kitchen Basics, were less pronounced than we expected. Which vegetable broth should you buy? **Swanson's Vegetable Broth** was the winner of our tasting, but the differences among brands when used in cooking (rather than tasting them straight) are not terribly significant.

SLOW-COOKER GUINNESS BEEF STEW
SERVES 6 TO 8

WHAT MAKES THIS A BEST RECIPE: While slow cookers and beef stews are usually a match made in heaven—their shared mantra of "slow and low" produces succulent meat, fork-tender vegetables, and a rich, beefy broth—we've had poor luck with slow-cooker versions of Ireland's Guinness Beef Stew. Instead of a rich stew infused with the stout's characteristic maltiness, the beer's bitterness runs amok and makes the stew harsh. This recipe, however, succeeds where others have failed. The recipe initially reads like other Guinness stews, relying on well-marbled chuck roast for a deep beefiness (seared prior to simmering to maximize that beefiness) and carrots, parsnips, and potatoes for rustic charm and a satisfying texture, but then the recipe takes some interesting approaches to both tempering the beer's bitterness and maximizing its flavor. Where many recipes add a six pack's worth of beer, we found a little—just 1½ cups—added plenty of flavor if added twice: the bulk at the beginning and a tipple to finish. But that was only half the solution. Since stout drinkers often extol the beer's complex coffee-chocolate aroma, we wondered if enhancing these flavors might bolster the perceived stout character of the stew without adding any harshness. We first tested coffee (both instant and fresh-brewed) in the stew, but tasters instantly rejected its distinctive taste. Cocoa, however, drew rave reviews as it heightened the stout flavor and mellowed out the stew overall. The only downside to the cocoa was its slightly acidic nature, but a quick switch to bittersweet chocolate left us with a beefy stew that was long on flavor and short on bitterness. Chocolate in beef stew—who would have guessed? This is a beef stew any Irish pub would be proud to serve.

4 pounds boneless beef chuck roast, trimmed and cut into 1½-inch chunks

Salt and pepper

2 tablespoons vegetable oil

2 onions, chopped (about 2 cups)

4 cups low-sodium chicken broth

1½ cups Guinness Draught

1 tablespoon light brown sugar

1 teaspoon dried thyme

1 ounce bittersweet chocolate, chopped

2 bay leaves

5 carrots, peeled and cut into 1-inch chunks

1 pound parsnips, peeled and cut into 1-inch chunks

1½ pounds baby red potatoes (about 24), scrubbed

¼ cup unbleached all-purpose flour

2 tablespoons minced fresh parsley

1. Pat the beef dry with paper towels and season with salt and pepper. Heat 2 teaspoons of the oil in a large skillet over medium-high heat until just smoking. Cook half of the beef until browned on all sides, about 8 minutes. Transfer to the slow cooker insert and repeat with an additional 2 teaspoons oil and the remaining beef.

2. Add the remaining 2 teaspoons oil, onions, and ¼ teaspoon salt to the skillet and cook until the onions are lightly browned, about 5 minutes. Add the broth, 1¼ cups of the beer, sugar, thyme, chocolate, and bay leaves and bring to a boil, using a wooden spoon to scrape up any browned bits. Transfer to the slow cooker insert.

3. Add the carrots, parsnips, and potatoes to the slow cooker insert. Cover and cook on low until the meat is tender, 9 to 10 hours (or cook on high for 6 to 7 hours). Set the slow cooker to high. Whisk the flour and remaining ¼ cup beer until smooth, then stir the mixture into the slow cooker. Cook, covered, until the sauce thickens, about 15 minutes. Remove and discard the bay leaves, stir in the parsley, and season with salt and pepper to taste. Serve.

WHERE THINGS CAN GO WRONG: Be gentle when adding the flour slurry in step 3—the fork-tender beef will fall apart if stirred too aggressively.

WHAT YOU CAN DO AHEAD OF TIME: You can prepare the recipe through step 2 the night before the ingredients go into the slow cooker. Refrigerate the browned beef and the onion mixture in separate containers. In the morning, transfer the beef and the onion mixture to the slow cooker and proceed with step 3. The cooking time will run to the high end of the ranges given in the recipe.

NOTES FROM THE TEST KITCHEN

CHOOSING THE RIGHT BEER

While shopping for our Guinness Beef Stew recipe, we were surprised to find two options in the beer aisle: Guinness Extra Stout and Guinness Draught. Straight from the bottle, both beers have their merits. But after nine hours in the slow cooker, **Guinness Draught** was the clear winner. Tasters noticed the "clean, toasted taste" of the stew made with Guinness Draught, while the stew made with Guinness Extra Stout, although still acceptable, was noted for having a slightly "tannic, bitter" aftertaste.

THE RIGHT CUT

Our favorite cut of beef for stewing and braising is chuck roast, which is located in the animal's shoulder. Shoulder cuts are "working muscles," and are, therefore, well marbled with fat and connective tissue, which melts to gelatin during a long, slow simmer. We recommend that you cut the meat yourself as prepackaged stew meat is often made up of irregularly shaped end pieces from different cuts and thus may cook differently and have varying textures and flavors.

CHOCOLATE TO THE RESCUE

We found that chocolate emphasized the rich flavor in Guinness without adding any bitterness. But not all chocolate worked in our recipe. Unsweetened chocolate was much too astringent and imparted chalkiness to the stew. Semisweet chocolate was too sweet, making the stew taste like a "meaty candy bar." Bittersweet chocolate was the perfect compromise. It enhanced the flavor of the beer without adding any harsh notes.

VEGETABLES & SIDE DISHES

GARDEN FRESH CORN **58**

ZUCCHINI AND TOMATO TIAN **59**

STIR-FRIED SICHUAN GREEN BEANS **60**

ROASTED GLAZED TURNIPS
WITH BACON AND BALSAMIC VINEGAR **63**

ROASTED CAULIFLOWER WITH CURRY-YOGURT SAUCE **65**

FROM-THE-FREEZER STUFFED PEPPERS **66**

STUFFED PLUM TOMATOES **68**

GREEN BEAN CASSEROLE **71**

CREAMY CAULIFLOWER CASSEROLE
WITH BACON AND CHEDDAR **73**

POTATO ROESTI **74**

SMOKY SCALLOPED POTATOES **77**

CRUNCHY POTATO WEDGES **78**

GARLICKY STUFFED BAKED POTATOES **80**

GARLIC MASHED POTATOES WITH CHEESE **82**

MASHED POTATO CASSEROLE **83**

ORANGE-CRANBERRY RICE PILAF **84**

OVEN-BAKED HOLIDAY STUFFING **86**

INDIAN-STYLE CURRY WITH POTATOES,
CAULIFLOWER, PEAS, AND CHICKPEAS **87**

GARDEN FRESH CORN

SERVES 4

WHAT MAKES THIS A BEST RECIPE: While we love simply steamed fresh corn on the cob, it can grow old by mid-summer. Looking for alternative dishes in which to serve it, we realized that cooked corn dishes present a two-fold problem: successfully removing the corn from the cob and finding a cooking method that best preserves its sweet, delicate flavor. Removing corn from the cob isn't a difficult job, but we've found most home cooks do a pretty poor job of it. While a perfect "decobbing" would cleanly cleave every kernel from the cob, in the real world the knife usually cuts open the kernels, releasing (and wasting) the sweet "milk" inside and leaving part of the kernel behind. To capture every bit of sweetness from the cobs, we "milked" them after removing the kernels by scraping the back of the knife up and down each side of the cob. We then added the resulting milk to the kernels (getting anywhere from 1 to 2 tablespoons per cob). So what's the best way to cook the corn kernels? We didn't want to cook the corn too much—and risk losing the fresh flavor—so we tried two quick-cooking options: blanching and sautéing. Tasters much preferred the flavor of the sautéed corn, and the method allowed us to incorporate other flavors easily. Ingredients that found favor included fresh herbs, like basil, chives, and parsley, and the bite of fresh garlic. To contrast the chewy, succulent texture of the corn, we opted to add diced zucchini (another star of the summer garden). With a splash of fresh lemon juice, this dish was ready to go—a snapshot of summer flavors.

1	tablespoon vegetable oil
2	small zucchini, ends trimmed and diced
5	medium ears corn, prepared according to the photos
3	garlic cloves, minced
2	tablespoons minced fresh basil
1	tablespoon minced fresh chives
1	tablespoon minced fresh parsley
1½	teaspoons fresh lemon juice
	Salt and pepper

Light cooking keeps summer corn super-sweet and fresh.

Heat the oil in a large skillet over medium-high heat until shimmering. Add the zucchini and cook until softened and browned at the edges, about 3 minutes. Add the corn and cook until deep yellow and softened, about 2 minutes. Add the garlic and cook until fragrant, about 30 seconds. Off the heat, stir in the herbs and lemon juice, and season with salt and pepper to taste. Serve.

NOTES FROM THE TEST KITCHEN

CUTTING CORN OFF THE COB
To get every bit of sweet summer goodness from fresh corn, we cut the kernels from the cobs, then use the back of a knife to scrape all the "milk" from the cobs.

1. Cut the kernels from the ears.

2. Run the back of the knife down each corn cob to scrape away the milk.

ZUCCHINI AND TOMATO TIAN

SERVES 6

WHAT MAKES THIS A BEST RECIPE: This Provençal-inspired recipe is a classic side dish in which two of summer's best vegetables are dressed with olive oil and thyme, topped with Gruyère cheese, and baked until the flavors have blended into something far greater than the sum of its parts. That's when it's good; too often, however, it's a muddy-flavored, mushy-textured casserole. We spent the better part of a summer ruining countless pounds of tomatoes and zucchini to discover the secret to a perfect tian. First of all, size, on a number of fronts, mattered. We chose plum tomatoes over globe tomatoes because their size better paralleled that of the squash. We also sought out squash that were all about the same size so that the shingled rows would look uniform and cook evenly. Slicing the vegetables thin (¼ inch) and evenly enough challenged our knife skills, so we turned to mechanical means: a mandoline (a compact, hand-operated machine that ensures evenly thin, or thick, slices). With this handy gadget, we were able to slice the vegetables perfectly in seconds. (You can also use a food processor fitted with a ¼-inch-thick slicing blade, although because of the quickness of the machine, there is less control.) Now it was a matter of assembling the sliced vegetables. Alternating the slices and keeping them fairly tightly shingled was easy—once we added a layer of garlic-scented caramelized onions to the bottom of the baking dish for a bit of "traction." We sprinkled fresh thyme and drizzled olive oil over the vegetables and from there it went into the oven. Baking a tian is usually a two-step process: The vegetables are baked, after which the cheese is added and the casserole goes back into the oven until browned and bubbly. Baked uncovered, the vegetables took a long time to cook, dried out, and lost flavor and color by the time the cheese had melted. Covering the casserole with foil for the first go-around, however, trapped escaping steam, which cooked the vegetables faster and kept them moist for the 25 minutes it took the cheese to melt. No one would ever know this tian didn't arrive express from Provence.

¼ cup extra-virgin olive oil
3 onions, halved and sliced ¼ inch thick (about 3 cups) (see page 24)
    Salt
2 garlic cloves, minced
1 pound zucchini, ends trimmed and sliced ¼ inch thick
1 pound yellow squash, ends trimmed and sliced ¼ inch thick
1 pound plum tomatoes, cored and sliced ¼ inch thick
1 teaspoon minced fresh thyme
    Pepper
2 ounces Gruyère cheese, shredded (about ½ cup)

1. Adjust an oven rack to the middle position and heat the oven to 375 degrees. Brush a 13 by 9-inch baking dish with 1 tablespoon of the oil; set aside.

2. Heat 2 tablespoons more oil in a 12-inch nonstick skillet over medium heat until shimmering. Add the onions and ½ teaspoon salt, and cook until softened and lightly browned, 12 to 15 minutes. Stir in the garlic and cook until fragrant, about 30 seconds. Spread the onion mixture into the bottom of the prepared baking dish.

3. Following the photo on page 60, alternately shingle the sliced zucchini, yellow squash, and tomato into a single layer of four tightly fit rows on top of the onions. Sprinkle with the remaining 1 tablespoon oil and thyme and season with salt and pepper to taste. Cover the dish with foil and bake until the vegetables are tender, about 30 minutes.

4. Remove the foil, sprinkle the cheese over the top, and continue to bake until bubbling around the edges and lightly browned on top, 20 to 30 minutes. Let rest for 10 minutes before serving.

WHERE THINGS CAN GO WRONG: Slicing the vegetables ¼ inch thick is crucial for the success of this dish; use a mandoline, a V-slicer, or a food processor fitted with a ¼-inch-thick slicing blade. You can also slice them carefully by hand using a very sharp knife. An oven-safe, Provençal-style gratin dish can be substituted for the 13 by 9-inch baking dish, as long as it's of similar size.

WHAT YOU CAN DO AHEAD OF TIME: The onion mixture can be cooked and refrigerated in an airtight container for up to 2 days.

NOTES FROM THE TEST KITCHEN

MAKING A VEGETABLE TIAN
Alternately shingle the vegetables—zucchini, yellow squash, and tomatoes—on top of the onions in tidy, tight rows.

THE BEST INEXPENSIVE MANDOLINE
What's cheaper than a food processor and faster (if not also sharper) than a chef's knife? A mandoline. We highly recommend using one to ensure that the vegetables are cut thinly and evenly. And you don't have to spend a fortune on this handy slicer; in fact, after testing five models we found several that fit the bill. The best buy: the **Pyrex Slicer** at just $5.99.

STIR-FRIED SICHUAN GREEN BEANS
SERVES 4

WHAT MAKES THIS A BEST RECIPE: The flavors of this addictive concoction—with its wrinkly, sweet beans, sprinkled with morsels of flavorful pork and coated in a pungent sauce—are hot, aromatic, and tangy all at the same time. We usually pick up an order with our carry-out, but an urge to make them at home led us to develop a recipe that we think bests the best of our local restaurants. First things first, we had to cook the green beans. Traditionally, the beans are deep-fried to a wrinkled appearance, slightly chewy texture, and intense flavor. In an effort to replicate these effects minus the grease and mess, we tried roasting the beans in the oven, but it just wasn't the same. Stir-frying got us closer to that elusive texture and flavor we wanted, especially when we cooked the beans a little longer than we would have under normal conditions. Authentic recipes rely on elusive ingredients such as Sichuan preserved mustard stems to produce the characteristic tang and modest heat. We tried substituting pickled ginger, pickled jalapeños, and even dill pickle, but their individual assertive flavors showed through. Fresh mustard was also too strong, but dry mustard added a nice, subtle tang. Dry sherry plus a little sugar produced the right level of acidity and sweetness once combined with soy, fresh ginger, and garlic. The sauce now had the proper tang but still needed more heat. Adding more mustard didn't work, so we tried fresh chiles and red pepper flakes. The pepper flakes had a straightforward punch, and ground white pepper added aromatic warmth and a complex muskiness. A touch of cornstarch made the sauce cling to each bean, delivering more pungent flavor with each bite. Some chopped scallions and a drizzle of sesame oil were the perfect finishing touches. In restaurants, it is common to find chopped or shredded bits of Chinese barbecued pork mingling with the beans, but we found that simple ground pork worked fine at home. With their crinkled, chewy texture and intriguing spicy flavor, Sichuan green beans were no longer lost in translation. They were easily made at home—and without the mess of deep-frying.

STIR-FRIED SICHUAN GREEN BEANS

2 tablespoons soy sauce

2 tablespoons water

1 tablespoon dry sherry

1 teaspoon sugar

½ teaspoon cornstarch

¼ teaspoon ground white pepper

¼ teaspoon red pepper flakes

¼ teaspoon dry mustard

2 tablespoons vegetable oil

1 pound green beans, stem ends snapped off and cut into 2-inch pieces

¼ pound ground pork

3 garlic cloves, minced

1 tablespoon minced fresh ginger

3 scallions, sliced thin

1 teaspoon toasted sesame oil

1. In a small bowl, stir together the soy sauce, water, sherry, sugar, cornstarch, white pepper, pepper flakes, and mustard until the sugar dissolves; set aside.

2. Heat the vegetable oil in a 12-inch nonstick skillet over high heat until just smoking. Add the beans and cook, stirring frequently, until crisp-tender and the skins are shriveled and blackened in spots, 5 to 8 minutes (reduce heat to medium-high if beans darken too quickly). Transfer the beans to a large plate.

3. Reduce the heat to medium-high and add the pork to the now empty skillet. Cook, breaking the pork into small pieces, until no pink remains, about 2 minutes. Add the garlic and ginger; cook, stirring constantly, until fragrant, about 30 seconds. Stir the sauce to recombine and return the beans to the pan with the sauce. Toss and cook until the sauce is thickened, 5 to 10 seconds. Remove the pan from the heat and stir in the scallions and sesame oil. Serve immediately.

WHAT YOU CAN DO AHEAD OF TIME: The sauce can be prepared up to 1 day ahead of time and stored at room temperature. Stir thoroughly to recombine before adding to the beans in step 3.

NOTES FROM THE TEST KITCHEN

A VEGETARIAN OPTION

To make this dish vegetarian, substitute 4 ounces of shiitake mushrooms, stemmed and minced, for the pork. You will need to add 1 teaspoon vegetable oil to the pan in step 3 before adding the minced mushrooms.

PEELING GINGER

Because of its shape, ginger can be difficult to peel, especially if using a knife. Try this method to reduce waste.

Use the bowl of a teaspoon to scrape off the knotty skin from a knob of ginger. The spoon moves easily around the knots in the ginger, so you remove just the skin.

WHITE PEPPER

The berries used to make white pepper are the same as those used to make black pepper, but they are harvested at a riper stage. The hulls are then removed and with them goes some of the heat characteristic of black pepper. White peppercorns are often used when the appearance of a dish would be marred by flecks of black. Many Asian recipes rely on the fragrant, citrusy flavor of white pepper. We use white pepper so infrequently that we can't justify purchasing a pepper mill for the sole purpose of grinding it, nor can we be bothered emptying and then refilling the black-pepper mill. Instead, we buy ground white pepper and replenish our stock when the pepper loses its fragrance.

ROASTED GLAZED TURNIPS
WITH BACON AND BALSAMIC VINEGAR
SERVES 6

Our oven-glazing technique makes root vegetables (in this case, turnips) look good—and taste even better.

WHAT MAKES THIS A BEST RECIPE: This oft-maligned, starchy root vegetable can be delicious—if prepared in just the right fashion. Many recipes roast them, but we found this made them leathery and dry. Instead, we found that cooking them with some liquid was key. We added a small amount of liquid to the baking dish with the vegetables and then covered the dish with foil. About halfway through the cooking time, we removed the foil, allowing the liquid to evaporate and the flavors to concentrate. The vegetables even caramelized in spots. Water (rather than overpowering chicken broth) mixed with balsamic vinegar and maple syrup lent the turnips an appealing sweet-and-sour flavor and rich coloring. For complexity, we added thin-sliced shallot, which caramelized nicely, and rosemary, which accented the turnips' earthy flavor. The only thing missing was something crunchy, and for that, we turned to crisp-fried bacon bits, the smoky flavor of which also served to cut the turnips' sweetness. A knob of butter tossed in with the turnips just before serving lent them a glossy, glazed appearance that nobody in the test kitchen could resist. The lowly turnip taking a turn as a superstar? We think it's time.

- 2 **pounds purple-top turnips, peeled and cut into ¾-inch cubes**
- 4 **shallots, peeled and sliced thin (about ¾ cup)**
- 2 **tablespoons maple syrup**
- 2 **tablespoons balsamic vinegar**
- 1 **tablespoon chopped fresh rosemary**
  Salt and pepper
- 3 **tablespoons unsalted butter (1 tablespoon melted and 2 tablespoons cubed)**
- ½ **cup water**
- 6 **slices bacon, cut into ¼-inch strips and cooked until crisp**

1. Adjust an oven rack to the middle position and heat the oven to 450 degrees. Toss the turnips, shallots, syrup, vinegar, rosemary, ½ teaspoon salt, ⅛ teaspoon pepper, and melted butter in a 13 by 9-inch baking dish. Pour the water over the vegetables, cover with foil, and roast until the turnips begin to soften, about 25 minutes.

2. Remove the foil and continue to roast, tossing occasionally, until the turnips are tender and spotty brown and the liquid is reduced to a thick glaze, 25 to 30 minutes. Add the bacon and cubed butter and toss. Season with salt and pepper to taste. Serve.

WHERE THINGS CAN GO WRONG: Use only purple-top turnips for this recipe; yellow turnips, otherwise known as rutabagas, take longer to cook.

NOTES FROM THE TEST KITCHEN

THE BEST BALSAMIC VINEGAR
Traditional balsamic vinegar takes a minimum of 12 years to make and costs an astonishing $60 per ounce. We were happy to discover that for use in salad dressings or for cooking, you don't need to spend a fortune for this ingredient—a supermarket balsamic works just fine. Tasters thought **Lucini Gran Riserva Balsamico** most closely resembled a traditional balsamic vinegar with its balance of sweet and tart and its viscosity. And at $2 an ounce, it won't break the bank.

ROASTED CAULIFLOWER
WITH CURRY-YOGURT SAUCE
SERVES 4 TO 6

WHAT MAKES THIS A BEST RECIPE: While roasting is a common trick for coaxing big flavor from vegetables, it is not a method commonly applied to cauliflower. Until now, that is. We found that it is one of the best methods going for intensifying cauliflower's usually bland flavor and lending character to its often lifeless, waterlogged texture. The few recipes we did find for roasted cauliflower typically blanched the cauliflower prior to roasting to ensure even cooking. We agreed that roasting alone wasn't sufficient for even cooking—it produced dry, withered, and gritty cauliflower—but found blanched cauliflower soggy even after roasting. Instead, we developed a method in which we covered the baking sheet with foil for the first 10 minutes of cooking so that it effectively steamed the cauliflower in its own juices. Then, once softened, we removed the foil and roasted it for 20 minutes until caramelized and tender. With cauliflower this good, there's no need to bury it beneath a cheesy sauce. Instead, we flavored it simply before roasting with a liberal amount of extra-virgin olive oil, salt, and pepper, and paired it with an Indian-inspired yogurt sauce.

SAUCE
- 1 tablespoon vegetable oil
- 1 shallot, minced (about 3 tablespoons)
- 2 teaspoons curry powder
- ¼ teaspoon red pepper flakes
- ⅓ cup water
- ¼ cup plain yogurt
- 1 teaspoon fresh lime juice
- 2 tablespoons minced fresh cilantro
- Salt and pepper

CAULIFLOWER
- 1 medium head cauliflower (about 2 pounds)
- ¼ cup extra-virgin olive oil, plus extra for drizzling
- Kosher salt and pepper

1. FOR THE SAUCE: Heat the oil in a small skillet over medium-high heat until shimmering. Add the shallot and cook until softened, about 2 minutes. Stir in the curry powder and pepper flakes; cook until fragrant, about 1 minute. Remove from the heat and whisk in the water, yogurt, lime juice, cilantro, and salt and pepper to taste, and set aside.

2. FOR THE CAULIFLOWER: Adjust an oven rack to the lowest position and heat the oven to 475 degrees. Trim the outer leaves of the cauliflower and cut the stem flush with the bottom. Cut the head into 8 equal wedges so that the core and florets remain intact. Place the wedges cut side down on a foil- or parchment-lined rimmed baking sheet. Drizzle with 2 tablespoons of the oil and sprinkle with kosher salt and pepper; gently rub to distribute the oil and seasonings evenly. Gently flip the cauliflower and season the other cut side with the remaining 2 tablespoons oil and kosher salt and pepper.

3. Cover the baking sheet tightly with foil and cook for 10 minutes. Remove the foil and continue to roast until the bottoms of the cauliflower pieces are golden, 8 to 12 minutes. Remove the baking sheet from the oven, and, using a spatula, carefully flip the wedges. Return the sheet to the oven and continue to roast until the cauliflower is golden all over, 8 to 12 minutes longer. Season with salt and pepper to taste, drizzle with the sauce, and serve immediately.

WHERE THINGS CAN GO WRONG: Pay close attention to timing as cauliflower can easily overcook and turn mushy.

WHAT YOU CAN DO AHEAD OF TIME: The yogurt sauce can be prepared up to 1 day ahead of time and refrigerated in an airtight container.

NOTES FROM THE TEST KITCHEN

CUTTING THE CAULIFLOWER
Cutting the cauliflower head from pole to pole into large wedges (about the length of a pencil) exposes more surface area to the hot baking sheet. And leaving the core intact makes it easy to flip the pieces halfway through the caramelization stage so that both sides gain a golden exterior.

FROM-THE-FREEZER STUFFED PEPPERS

SERVES 4 TO 6

WHAT MAKES THIS A BEST RECIPE: This recipe for meat-stuffed peppers is wholly unique in that it is designed to be made well ahead of time, not frozen as a leftover or afterthought. The prepared peppers can be pulled from the freezer, plunked right in the oven, and on the table without a thought. Here's how it works. Peppers to be stuffed are typically blanched before stuffing to soften their skins and crunchy texture. Blanched peppers, however, turn to mush if frozen. We found that we could skip the blanching step altogether and rely on freezing alone to soften the pepper. That was only a small part of the solution. We found that baking the peppers directly from the freezer best maintained their flavors, but the filling was taking two hours to reach a safe temperature, by which time the peppers were swimming in a sea of their own juices. Splitting the peppers through the stem (instead of lopping off the top) halved the cooking time and flipping them upside down, wrapping them in foil lanced with holes for drainage, and baking them on a broiler tray dealt with the moisture issue (and we finished them right side up to crisp). The pepper's skin baked up tough, but brushing it with oil before baking and increasing the baking temperature to 450 degrees took care of that issue. The skin softened and browned—not unlike that of a roasted pepper. With a technique in hand, we could finally work on the flavors of the filling. We knew freezing muted flavors, so we found it imperative to season the filling assertively. We favored a blend of ground beef and sausage for the main thrust of flavor, garlic and tomatoes for punch, and a mixture of Parmesan and mozzarella cheeses to tie things together. Rice bested bread crumbs or pasta for a filling binder.

PEPPERS AND STUFFING

- 1 tablespoon olive oil
- 1 onion, minced (about 1 cup)
- 8 ounces 85 percent lean ground beef or ground turkey
- 4 ounces hot or sweet Italian sausage, casings removed

   Salt and pepper
- 4 garlic cloves, minced
- 2 cups cooked rice
- 1 (14.5-ounce) can diced tomatoes, drained
- 4 ounces mozzarella cheese, shredded (about 1 cup)
- 1 ounce Parmesan cheese, grated (about ½ cup)
- 3 tablespoons chopped fresh parsley
- 4 red bell peppers, cut in half through the stem end (stem left intact), cored, and seeded (see page 68)

FOR SERVING

- 2 tablespoons olive oil
   Salt and pepper
- 4 ounces mozzarella cheese, shredded (about 1 cup)

1. FOR THE PEPPERS AND STUFFING: Heat the oil in a large skillet over medium heat until shimmering. Cook the onion until softened and beginning to brown, about 5 minutes. Increase the heat to medium-high and add the beef, sausage, ½ teaspoon salt, and ¼ teaspoon pepper; cook, breaking the meat into small pieces with a wooden spoon, until the meat begins to brown, 6 to 8 minutes. Add the garlic and cook until fragrant, about 30 seconds. Drain the mixture in a colander for 1 minute.

2. Transfer the meat mixture to a large bowl and mix with the rice, tomatoes, mozzarella, Parmesan, parsley, ½ teaspoon salt, and ¼ teaspoon pepper. Refrigerate until well chilled, at least 20 minutes.

3. Spoon the filling evenly into the bell peppers. Wrap each pepper in 2 layers of plastic wrap and 1 layer of foil. Place in a baking dish and freeze until firm. Transfer to a zipper-lock plastic bag and freeze up to 2 months.

4. WHEN READY TO SERVE: Adjust an oven rack to the middle position and heat the oven to 450 degrees. Cut 8 pieces of foil large enough to just cover the stuffing and the peppers, and spray with cooking spray. Unwrap the peppers and cover the filling sides with the new foil squares. Using a skewer, poke several holes through the foil. Place the peppers, foil side down, over the vents of a slotted broiler-pan top set over a broiler-pan bottom.

5. Brush the peppers with the oil and season with salt and pepper to taste. Bake until the peppers are spotty brown, 30 to 35 minutes. Flip the peppers filling side up, remove the foil, and sprinkle with the mozzarella. Bake until the cheese is melted, about 5 minutes. Let rest 5 minutes before serving.

FROM-THE-FREEZER STUFFED PEPPERS

NOTES FROM THE TEST KITCHEN

A BETTER WAY TO STUFF PEPPERS

1. Cut each pepper in half through the stem end to create two shallow boats. Discard the core and seeds.

2. When ready to bake, unwrap the stuffed pepper halves, cover the filling with foil, and poke several holes to allow excess liquid to drain off.

3. Place the pepper halves foil side down over the vents on the slotted top of a broiler pan.

GREAT DISCOVERIES

SOLVING THE SOGGY PEPPER PROBLEM

I knew that creating stuffed peppers that could go from freezer to oven would be challenging. Freezing dulls the flavor of the filling and makes the peppers mushy (the water in the peppers expands as it freezes, causing the cell walls, which give the pepper structure, to rupture). To solve the flavor problem, I packed the peppers with potent ingredients like sausage, Parmesan, and fresh herbs. To avoid mushy peppers, I thought I might be able to make the freezer's softening power work for me and eliminate the usual step of blanching the peppers before stuffing them. After many tests, it was clear that you can either blanch the peppers or you can freeze them, but you can't do both. So for our freezer stuffed peppers, we skipped the blanching. To cook the filling and peppers perfectly from the freezer, we put them in a really hot oven, filling side down (covering the filling side with perforated foil so the fat could drip out), and brushing the exterior of the peppers with oil. These peppers were perfectly cooked after just 30 minutes—no thawing required.

CALI RICH | TEST COOK, *COOK'S COUNTRY*

STUFFED PLUM TOMATOES
SERVES 8

WHAT MAKES THIS A BEST RECIPE: With their bright red tomato bases filled with golden, garlicky bread crumbs, chopped basil, and grated Parmesan cheese, stuffed tomatoes can be real lookers. Sadly, their appeal usually fades after the first bite reveals the dull, soggy, and flavorless truth. All the moisture that makes tomatoes so inviting wreaks havoc on the stuffing. This recipe, however, keeps the flavors high and eradicates excess moisture. First of all, we skipped over the globe tomato typically used for the base in favor of meatier plum tomatoes. We tried roasting the tomatoes to intensify their flavor and wick away moisture, but they shriveled up too much to stuff with more than a teaspoon or two of filling. Instead, we found salting the halved and seeded tomatoes and allowing them to drain upside down drew off a significant amount of liquid. In addition, the salt brightened and enhanced the tomatoes' flavor. We found that kosher salt worked best here because the larger crystals are easier to sprinkle and disperse more evenly over the tomatoes than regular table salt. For the filling, homemade bread crumbs easily bested store-bought crumbs. In terms of flavor, we found olive oil, garlic, Parmesan cheese, and fresh basil to be crucial additions to the toasted crumbs. Experimenting with different cheeses, we landed on a surprising and winning idea. In the hollow of the tomato, underneath the cover of garlicky bread crumbs, we spread some goat cheese lightly flavored with olive oil and basil. Nearly hidden from view inside the tomato, the creamy goat cheese centers both surprised and impressed the tasters. And as an added bonus, the goat cheese helped prevent the crumbs from absorbing any juice released by the tomatoes and this helped the stuffing remain super-crisp, even when the tomatoes were made a day or two ahead of time. As for baking these beauties straight from the refrigerator, we found that a 325-degree oven worked best. This moderate temperature gave the tomatoes time to soften (but not overcook) while the goat cheese heated through and the crumbs crisped up perfectly.

2 slices high-quality white sandwich bread, quartered

3 garlic cloves, minced

3 tablespoons extra-virgin olive oil

1 ounce Parmesan cheese, grated (about ½ cup)

¼ cup chopped fresh basil

Kosher salt and pepper

8 medium, firm, ripe plum tomatoes (3 to 4 ounces each)

6 ounces goat cheese, softened

1. Adjust an oven rack to the middle position and heat the oven to 300 degrees. Pulse the bread in a food processor to coarse crumbs, about 6 pulses. Toss the crumbs, garlic, and 2 tablespoons of the oil together. Spread the crumbs on a rimmed baking sheet and bake, stirring occasionally, until lightly browned and dry, about 20 minutes; set aside to cool. When cool, toss the crumbs with the Parmesan, 2 tablespoons of the basil, and season with salt and pepper to taste; set aside.

2. Meanwhile, slice the tomatoes in half lengthwise and, following the photos, scoop out the inner ribs and seeds. Sprinkle the insides of the tomatoes with 1½ teaspoons kosher salt, then lay them, cut sides down, on several layers of paper towels. Let stand at room temperature to drain, 30 to 60 minutes. Increase the oven temperature to 325 degrees.

3. Mix the goat cheese with the remaining 1 tablespoon oil and remaining 2 tablespoons basil. Season with salt and pepper to taste, then transfer to a small zipper-lock bag; snip a small piece from one bottom corner of the bag.

4. Pat the insides of the tomatoes dry with paper towels. Following the photos, pipe about 1 teaspoon of the goat cheese mixture into the bottom of each tomato. Spoon the bread-crumb mixture into the tomatoes, pressing on it to adhere to the cheese. Arrange the tomatoes in a 13 by 9-inch baking dish. Bake the tomatoes until the cheese is heated through and the crumbs are crisp, 15 to 20 minutes.

WHERE THINGS CAN GO WRONG: Do not overprocess the bread into fine, even crumbs; the rustic texture of coarse, slightly uneven bread crumbs is preferable here.

WHAT YOU CAN DO AHEAD OF TIME: The tomatoes can be filled, wrapped tightly with plastic wrap, and refrigerated for up to 2 days before baking as directed in step 4.

A hidden bottom layer of creamy goat cheese adds rich flavor to these stuffed tomatoes and shields the crumbs from the tomatoes' moisture.

NOTES FROM THE TEST KITCHEN

MAKING STUFFED TOMATOES

1. Cut the tomato in half lengthwise and, using a sharp-edged spoon, scoop out the seeds and inner flesh. Salt the tomatoes for at least 30 minutes.

2. Pat the inside of the tomatoes dry and pipe about 1 teaspoon of the goat cheese into the bottom of each tomato.

3. Spoon the bread-crumb mixture into the tomatoes, pressing on it to adhere the crumbs to the cheese.

GREEN BEAN CASSEROLE

GREEN BEAN CASSEROLE

SERVES 10 TO 12

WHAT MAKES THIS A BEST RECIPE: Green bean casserole was originally created in the kitchens of the Campbell Soup Company in 1955, solely to feature one of its star products, condensed cream of mushroom soup. In fact, it's estimated that as many as 20 million portions of green bean casserole are served every year—a dozen of which are consumed by test kitchen staffers on Thanksgiving. Fond memories of this dish notwithstanding, the original recipe is disappointingly stodgy and bland; all the canned and prepared foodstuffs didn't make the cut to us. This recipe is our reinterpretation of the original and one we deem a classic in its own right. Starting with fresh green beans, we tried all the usual methods to cook them, finally settling on blanching—or dropping the raw beans into boiling, salted water and cooking them until tender (about 6 minutes), then "shocking" them (to stop the cooking) in an ice water bath. Foolproof and straightforward, this method worked; the beans were perfectly cooked, consistent in texture, and colored a beautiful bright green. They were also nicely seasoned. Creating a suitable replacement for the canned mushroom soup involved sautéing fresh mushrooms and binding them in a roux-thickened blend of equal parts chicken broth and heavy cream—a classic French *velouté*-style sauce. A bit of minced garlic sautéed with the mushrooms contributed some much-needed depth. Trouble came with the fried onion topping. Nothing, outside of deep-frying our own onions, could come close to touching the flavor of the canned fried onions. Not willing to go through the hassle of deep-frying, we gave in and tried canned onions. But tasters balked; the canned onions tasted shockingly "commercial" against the fresh beans and sauce. We switched to buttered bread crumbs, and while the crisp texture and fresh flavor was appreciated, the onion flavor was missing. The solution proved simple: blend bread crumbs with the canned onions. Both the flavor and texture was deemed right-on, and our green bean makeover was complete.

TOPPING

- 4 slices high-quality white sandwich bread, each slice torn into quarters
- 2 tablespoons unsalted butter, softened
- ¼ teaspoon salt
- ⅛ teaspoon pepper
- 3 cups canned fried onions (about 6 ounces)

BEANS AND SAUCE

- Salt
- 2 pounds green beans, trimmed and halved (see page 72)
- 3 tablespoons unsalted butter
- 1 pound white mushrooms, stemmed and quartered (see page 72)
- 3 garlic cloves, minced
- Pepper
- 3 tablespoons unbleached all-purpose flour
- 1½ cups low-sodium chicken broth
- 1½ cups heavy cream

1. FOR THE TOPPING: Pulse the bread, butter, salt, and pepper in a food processor until the mixture resembles coarse crumbs, about ten 1-second pulses. Transfer to a large bowl and toss with the onions; set aside.

2. FOR THE BEANS AND SAUCE: Adjust an oven rack to the middle position and heat the oven to 425 degrees. Fill a large bowl with ice water. Bring 4 quarts of water to a boil in a large Dutch oven. Add 2 tablespoons salt and the beans. Cook until bright green and crisp-tender, about 6 minutes. Drain the beans in a colander and plunge immediately into the ice water to stop the cooking. Spread the beans on a paper towel–lined baking sheet to drain.

3. Add the butter to the now-empty Dutch oven and melt over medium-high heat until the foaming subsides. Add the mushrooms, garlic, ¾ teaspoon salt, and ⅛ teaspoon pepper; cook until the mushrooms release their moisture and the liquid evaporates, about 6 minutes. Add the flour and cook for 1 minute, stirring constantly. Stir in the broth and bring to a simmer, stirring constantly. Add the cream, reduce the heat to medium, and simmer until the sauce is thickened and reduced to 3½ cups, about 12 minutes. Season with salt and pepper to taste.

4. Add the beans to the sauce and stir until evenly

coated. Arrange in an even layer in a 3-quart (or 13 by 9-inch) baking dish. Sprinkle with the topping and bake until the top is golden brown and the sauce is bubbling around the edges, about 15 minutes. Serve immediately.

WHERE THINGS CAN GO WRONG: Do not overcook the green beans; otherwise the casserole's flavor and color will be wan. Plunging the just-cooked beans in ice water stops their cooking instantaneously.

WHAT YOU CAN DO AHEAD OF TIME: The components of the casserole can easily be prepared ahead of time. Store the bread-crumb topping in an airtight container in the refrigerator for up to 3 days in advance and combine with the onions just before cooking. Combine the beans and cooled sauce in a baking dish, cover tightly with plastic wrap, and refrigerate for up to 24 hours. To serve, remove the plastic wrap and heat the casserole in a 425-degree oven for 10 minutes, then add the topping and bake as directed.

NOTES FROM THE TEST KITCHEN

PREPARING THE MUSHROOMS
While you can certainly quarter each mushroom using a paring knife, here's a quick method (sans knife) to break the mushrooms into four pieces each.

1. Using your thumb, pop the caps off their stems.

2. Squeeze both the stem and the cap between your thumb and forefinger to break each into pieces.

TRIMMING GREEN BEANS QUICKLY
Line up about 8 beans in a row on a cutting board. Trim about ½ inch from each end, then cut the beans in half.

CAN "CONVENIENCE" GREEN BEANS RIVAL FRESH?
For those of us without a willing partner (or sous chef) to trim and cut 2 pounds of fresh green beans for our green bean casserole, a package of trimmed and cut beans can look pretty enticing. But how do they taste? We went out and bought eight types of convenience green beans: three canned, four frozen, and one brand of packaged already trimmed fresh green beans. When used in our green bean casserole, the canned beans were pale, bland, and "beyond mushy." Slightly better were the frozen green beans, though they were somewhat "waterlogged" and "spongy," with a diluted flavor. The trimmed fresh beans sounded promising, but the cut ends of the beans in the five different bags we bought had dried out and needed a re-trim once we got them home—not much of a time-saver. In the end, none of these products warranted an enthusiastic nod. Our recommendation? Spend a few minutes to trim—and blanch—fresh green beans and take a shortcut somewhere else in the menu.

TO MAKE A SMALLER BATCH
If you prefer, the recipe can be halved and baked in a 2-quart (or 8-inch square) baking dish. If making a half batch, reduce the cooking time of the sauce in step 3 to about 6 minutes (with a yield of 1¾ cups) and the baking time in step 4 to 10 minutes.

CREAMY CAULIFLOWER CASSEROLE
WITH BACON AND CHEDDAR
SERVES 6 TO 8

WHAT MAKES THIS A BEST RECIPE: The winner of our holiday side dish recipe contest, this recipe (submitted by *Cook's Country* reader Lisa Ashton), takes cauliflower mainstream. Covering cauliflower with a cheese-flavored sauce is a classic approach to making this strong-flavored vegetable likeable. And it works, though most recipes are compromised by overcooked, bland cauliflower—which is exceptionally mushy—or a weak-flavored or poor-textured sauce that doesn't really mate well with the cauliflower. This dish solves these problems. First of all, the cauliflower is blanched until just tender in well-salted water (insuring the cauliflower is properly seasoned). Then, in an interesting method, a portion of the cauliflower is coarsely chopped and the remainder is left whole. The chopped portion acts as a casserole "filler," much like rice or pasta, so that the sauce doesn't pool in the bottom of the baking dish. Speaking of the sauce, it's an easy-to-prepare blend of cream cheese, heavy cream, sour cream, and cheddar cheese. The cream cheese helps to keep the sauce thick and creamy, without requiring flour or cornstarch. Crisp, smoky-tasting bacon, combined with a little cheese and parsley, is the crowning touch. With a quick bake, the flavors of the sauce and vegetable are married and the cheese on top browns a bit for additional flavor. This is cauliflower *anybody* will love.

8 slices bacon, chopped, cooked until crisp, and cooled

12 ounces cheddar cheese, shredded (about 3 cups)

1 tablespoon chopped fresh parsley
  Salt

2 large heads cauliflower, trimmed and cut into 1-inch florets (about 8 cups)

4 ounces cream cheese

¼ cup heavy cream

¼ cup sour cream

½ teaspoon pepper

1. Mix the bacon, ½ cup of the cheese, and parsley in a small bowl. Set aside for the topping.

2. Adjust an oven rack to the middle position and heat the oven to 350 degrees. Bring 4 quarts of water to a boil in a large pot. Add 1 tablespoon salt and the cauliflower and cook until tender, about 7 minutes. Drain and rinse the cauliflower with cold water. Transfer half of the cauliflower to a cutting board and chop roughly.

3. Melt the cream cheese in the now empty pot over low heat. Stir in the heavy cream and remaining 2½ cups cheese and cook until the cheese starts to melt, about 3 minutes. Off the heat, stir in the sour cream, cauliflower, ½ teaspoon salt, and pepper. Transfer the mixture to a 2-quart baking dish, sprinkle with the topping, and bake until browned and bubbly, about 15 minutes. Serve.

WHERE THINGS CAN GO WRONG: Pay close attention when blanching the cauliflower to prevent overcooking; cauliflower goes from crisp to mushy in seconds.

WHAT YOU CAN DO AHEAD OF TIME: The topping can be prepared and the cauliflower can be cooked up to 1 day ahead of time and refrigerated in separate airtight containers.

NOTES FROM THE TEST KITCHEN
CUTTING CAULIFLOWER

1. Pull off any leaves, then cut out the core of the cauliflower using a paring knife.

2. Separate the florets from the inner stem using the tip of a paring knife.

3. Cut the larger florets into smaller pieces by slicing them through the stem.

POTATO ROESTI
SERVES 4

1½ pounds Yukon Gold potatoes (3 to 4 medium), peeled and shredded (see page 76)
½ teaspoon salt
1 teaspoon cornstarch
Pepper
4 tablespoons (½ stick) unsalted butter

WHAT MAKES THIS A BEST RECIPE: Switzerland's national dish is *roesti* (aka *roschti* or *rosti*). Grated potato, seasoned plainly with salt and pepper, is packed into a pan and fried in loads of butter into a broad, golden-brown cake. The crunchy, crisp exterior encases a tender, creamy interior tasting of little but earthy potato and, of course, rich butter. It's somewhat like a large hash brown, just thicker and heartier. But as any cook knows, simple does not mean easy, and roesti can be as hard to master as any "simple" pie crust or omelet. We know: We peeled our way through one hundred some pounds of potatoes to find a foolproof method. While roesti can be prepared from either cooked or raw potatoes, we favored the ease and convenience of the latter. After testing a dozen recipes, we knew that moisture in the potatoes was the number-one problem to resolve. To eliminate as much moisture as possible, we squeezed the grated potatoes in a twisted towel. (You will need plenty of upper-body strength for this.) Then there was the potato's starch to contend with, which if left unchecked, made for a roesti with a gummy, unappetizing interior. Soaking the potatoes briefly in water (prior to squeezing, of course) effectively washed the starch away. Too effectively in fact, so we returned some starch in the form of cornstarch. A nonstick skillet and a large nugget of butter prevented the cake from sticking, and moderate heat evenly browned each side of the cake after a midpoint flip (requiring only a modicum of kitchen bravado). While almost perfect, the cake's texture was still on the dense side. After a complete reevaluation of our recipe, we realized our misstep: We were overpacking the grated potato into the pan. Pressing the grated potato gently into the skillet yielded an airy-light, crisp-crusted cake without a hint of gumminess. We couldn't have asked for better results.

1. Place the potatoes in a large bowl and fill with cold water. Using your hands, swirl to remove the starch; then drain in a strainer.

2. Wipe the bowl dry. Place half of the potatoes in the center of a kitchen towel. Gather the ends together and twist as tightly as possible to expel the maximum amount of moisture. Transfer the potatoes to the bowl and repeat with the remaining potatoes.

3. Sprinkle the salt, cornstarch, and pepper to taste over the potatoes. Using your hands or a fork, toss the ingredients together until well blended.

4. Melt 2 tablespoons of the butter in a 10-inch nonstick skillet over medium heat. When the foaming subsides, add the potato mixture and spread into an even layer. Cover and cook 6 minutes. Remove the cover and, using a spatula, gently press the potatoes down to form a round cake. Cook, occasionally pressing on the potatoes to shape into a uniform round cake, until the bottom is deep golden brown, 4 to 6 minutes longer.

5. Shake the skillet to loosen the roesti and slide it onto a large plate. Add the remaining 2 tablespoons butter to the skillet and swirl to coat the pan. Invert the roesti onto a second plate and slide it, browned side up, back into the skillet. Cook, occasionally pressing down on the cake, until the bottom is well browned, 7 to 9 minutes. Remove the pan from the heat and allow the cake to cool in the pan for 5 minutes. Transfer the roesti to a cutting board, cut into 4 pieces, and serve immediately.

WHERE THINGS CAN GO WRONG: It is imperative to squeeze the grated potatoes as firmly as possible to eliminate as much moisture as possible. It is also important to use a nonstick skillet or a well-seasoned cast-iron skillet to prevent the cake from sticking to the pan.

NOTES FROM THE TEST KITCHEN

SAFER FLIPPING

While certain expert chefs (or particularly buff individuals) may think nothing of flipping a piping hot skillet to turn a roesti out onto a plate, it can be a scary endeavor for mere mortals. A weak wrist can send dinner crashing to the floor. Fortunately, there is a safer and less intimidating way to turn something over in a large skillet. Working with two plates, slide whatever you wish to flip onto one plate and top it with the other. Then, holding the two plates together, flip them over; slide the inverted food back into the pan to finish cooking.

GRATING THE POTATOES

We prefer a roesti prepared with potatoes that have been cut through the large shredding disk of a food processor. You can use a box grater, but be sure to cut the potatoes lengthwise, so you are left with long shreds.

PROBLEMS TO AVOID

Here are three common problems we encountered when testing roesti recipes:

BURNT SPOTS. Too much butter in the pan or too much heat will cause the roesti to burn in spots. The solution: 2 tablespoons butter per side and medium heat are all you need to brown the cake beautifully.

GUMMINESS. Excess moisture will turn your roesti into a gray, sticky mess. The solution: Squeeze out moisture in a kitchen towel.

CRUMBLING. Rinsing the potatoes eliminates excess starch but causes another problem—no structure. The solution: Toss the potatoes with a little cornstarch.

THE BEST PLASTIC NONSTICK SPATULA

Unless you like to eat flaked-off nonstick coating, you need to use a plastic spatula with your nonstick cookware. But with most stores stocking at least five models, how do you know which one is best? A slotted spatula, with slots that allow grease and liquid to drain but that still provide the support of a solid spatula, is the most versatile. The best spatulas have large blades with ample surface area but are thin enough to easily slide under food. At just $4.99, our favorite, the **Calphalon N04 Tools Large Nylon Slotted Spatula**, also happens to be one of the least expensive.

GREAT DISCOVERIES

THE STARCHY TRUTH

After shredding more pounds of potatoes than I care to admit, and making countless batches of roesti, I was within striking distance of the perfect roesti. Turning to the Internet for clues on what I might be missing, I found a professional chef's site where there were pages of commentary from readers on roesti, including one from a chef who had cited recipes from both Madeleine Kamman and Craig Claiborne. In each of their recipes, both authors rinsed the potatoes in cold water before squeezing them out and proceeding. I was skeptical about the rinsing, thinking that the potatoes would absorb the water and become even wetter. I was wrong. Dried, rinsed potatoes yielded the best cakes yet: lighter, drier, and without a hint of gumminess. But some of that starch was needed to keep the cake bound together. Kamman's roesti may have had the best interior, but it fell apart once sliced. Claiborne solved the problem by collecting the starch from the bottom of the expelled potato liquid—a fussy step we weren't willing to take. The solution? I tossed the dried shredded potatoes with a little cornstarch. The result: a caramel-gold crust, creamy, just-cooked-through interior, and airy, light texture that was perfectly sliceable.

MATT CARD | CONTRIBUTING EDITOR, *COOK'S ILLUSTRATED*

SMOKY SCALLOPED POTATOES

SERVES 10 TO 12

WHAT MAKES THIS A BEST RECIPE: Scalloped potatoes are typically a pretty pedestrian affair of sliced potatoes swimming in a cream-thickened sauce. This version, however, is a world apart: The tender potato slices are dressed in a silky-smooth, complexly flavored sauce suffused with a subtle tang and smokiness. And it couldn't be easier to prepare. The sauce is prepared in one pot, the potatoes are then simmered in the sauce until tender, and then the mixture is transferred to a baking dish and baked with cheese on top until bubbling and browned. Sautéed onions and garlic lay the groundwork for the sauce's flavor, and dry mustard and thyme round out the edges. Spicy cayenne pepper adds a boost to the mustard's heat. The real twist, though, is the inclusion of buttermilk along with the heavy cream, the tartness of which cuts the richness of the cream and brings out the best in the flavor of the potatoes and the sauce. The smoky flavor comes via the smoked gouda that is stirred in as a last step prior to baking.

4	tablespoons (½ stick) unsalted butter
1	onion, minced (about 1 cup)
4	garlic cloves, minced
4	teaspoons dry mustard
1	tablespoon minced fresh thyme
2½	teaspoons salt
½	teaspoon cayenne pepper
5	pounds russet potatoes (about 8 large), peeled and sliced thin
1½	cups heavy cream
1½	cups buttermilk
¼	teaspoon baking soda
8	ounces smoked Gouda cheese, shredded (about 2 cups)

1. Adjust an oven rack to the middle position and heat the oven to 425 degrees. Melt the butter in a Dutch oven over medium-high heat. Add the onion and cook until softened, about 5 minutes. Add the garlic, mustard,

Our scalloped potatoes pack a spicy, smoky punch.

thyme, salt, and cayenne and cook until fragrant, about 30 seconds. Stir in the potatoes, cream, buttermilk, and baking soda and bring to a simmer. Reduce the heat to medium-low, cover, and cook until the potatoes are almost tender, about 15 minutes. Stir in the cheese and transfer the mixture to a 13 by 9-inch baking dish.

2. Bake until the cream is bubbling around the edges and the top is golden brown, about 15 minutes. Cool 10 minutes before serving.

WHERE THINGS CAN GO WRONG: Pay close attention when cooking the potatoes in step 1 to avoid overcooking them.

WHAT YOU CAN DO AHEAD OF TIME: The casserole can be prepared through step 1, covered with foil, and refrigerated for up to 24 hours. Bake, still covered with foil, in a 400-degree oven until hot and bubbly, about 40 minutes. Remove the foil and continue cooking until the top is golden brown, about 30 minutes.

NOTES FROM THE TEST KITCHEN

THE ROLE OF BAKING SODA
While baking soda seems like an odd addition to scalloped potatoes, it is added as a tenderizer to ensure that the potato slices are soft. Baking soda used to be frequently added to vegetable and legume dishes for just this reason, though it is less common these days.

CRUNCHY POTATO WEDGES

SERVES 6

WHAT MAKES THIS A BEST RECIPE: We admit that sometimes, on the rarest of occasions, we eat fast food. And one of our favorite treats here in the test kitchen is the spicy, crunchy-coated potato wedges prepared by one of the fried-chicken chains. The wedges taste so similar to the chicken that the two must share the same coating. Driven to replicate those wedges at home, we developed this recipe, which has all the flavor of the original, with none of the fast-food guilt. To obtain a perfectly cooked interior and a nicely crisped exterior, we knew we'd have to precook the potato wedges before they were fried. Taking a cue from a previously developed recipe for steak fries, we tossed the wedges with a little oil, covered them with plastic, and microwaved them until they were just shy of being done. Since the potatoes were tightly covered, they didn't lose any moisture, which made them fry up especially fluffy inside. Some coatings were definitely more successful than others. Our favorite was simple, but effective: A little baking soda was mixed into the buttermilk in which the wedges were dipped before being dredged in flour. You could see the soda reacting with the buttermilk, making it foam and bubble. Potatoes coated with this mixture were especially crunchy and deep golden brown and even lighter textured when we replaced a portion of the flour with cornstarch. Even better, the cornstarch helped keep the fries from turning soggy even after they'd sat around for a few minutes. And finally, there were those spices. After trying countless combinations of herbs and spices, we settled on just six: salt, pepper, onion powder, garlic powder, cayenne, and oregano. Together these seasonings approximated the chicken chain's secret blend. Adding a pinch to the potatoes as they parcooked in the microwave, in addition to the flour mixture, guaranteed each wedge was shot through with flavor.

4	teaspoons kosher salt
½	teaspoon pepper
2	teaspoons onion powder
1	teaspoon garlic powder
¾	teaspoon cayenne pepper
1	teaspoon dried oregano
1¾	pounds russet potatoes (about 3 large), cut into ¼-inch wedges
¼	cup vegetable or peanut oil, plus 3 quarts for frying
1½	cups unbleached all-purpose flour
½	cup cornstarch
1	cup buttermilk
½	teaspoon baking soda

1. Combine the salt, pepper, onion and garlic powders, cayenne, and oregano in a small bowl.

2. Toss the potato wedges with 4 teaspoons of the spice mixture and ¼ cup oil in a large microwave-safe bowl; cover tightly with plastic wrap. Microwave on high until the potatoes are tender but not falling apart, 7 to 9 minutes, shaking the bowl (without removing the plastic) to redistribute the potatoes halfway through cooking. Slowly remove the plastic wrap from the bowl (be careful of the steam) and drain the potatoes. Arrange the potatoes on a rimmed baking sheet and cool until they firm up, about 10 minutes. (The potatoes can be held at room temperature for up to 2 hours.)

3. Heat the remaining 3 quarts oil in a large Dutch oven over high heat to 340 degrees. Meanwhile, combine the flour and cornstarch in a medium bowl and whisk the buttermilk and baking soda in a large bowl. Working in 2 batches, dredge the potato wedges in the flour mixture, shaking off the excess. Dip in the buttermilk mixture, allowing the excess to drip back into the bowl, then coat again in the flour mixture. Shake off the excess and place on a wire rack. (The potatoes can be coated up to 30 minutes in advance.)

4. When the oil is ready, add half the coated wedges and fry until deep golden brown, 4 to 6 minutes. Transfer the wedges to a large bowl and toss with 1 teaspoon of the spice mixture. Drain the wedges on a baking sheet lined with paper towels. Return the oil to 340 degrees and repeat with the second batch of wedges. Serve with extra seasoning on the side.

WHERE THINGS CAN GO WRONG: For the crispest texture, be sure to keep the cooking oil at the right temperature. Use an instant-read thermometer to monitor the temperature and be patient enough to bring it back to a full 340 degrees before adding the second batch of potato wedges.

WHAT YOU CAN DO AHEAD OF TIME: The potato wedges can be prepared and coated up to 30 minutes in advance; place them on a wire rack set over a baking sheet and store at room temperature. They also freeze very well. Follow steps 1 through 4, frying each batch of wedges until light golden brown, 2 to 3 minutes. Do not toss with seasoning, and drain and cool the potatoes completely on a baking sheet lined with paper towels. Freeze the wedges on a baking sheet until completely frozen, about 2 hours, then transfer the potatoes to a zipper-lock storage bag for up to 2 months. To fry, heat 3 quarts oil to 340 degrees and cook in two batches until deep golden brown, about 3 minutes. Toss with the spice mixture, drain, and serve.

NOTES FROM THE TEST KITCHEN

THE SECRET TO CRUNCHY POTATO WEDGES

1. Precook the wedges in the microwave with the spice mixture for a fluffy, well-seasoned interior when fried.

2. A triple coating of flour/cornstarch, buttermilk, and flour/cornstarch gives these wedges a super-crunchy exterior.

3. After frying, a final toss with seasoning provides an extra flavor boost.

GARLICKY STUFFED BAKED POTATOES
SERVES 6

WHAT MAKES THIS A BEST RECIPE: Inspired by a steakhouse specialty, this recipe stuffs crisp-skinned baked potatoes with a creamy filling flavored with pungent garlic and creamy cheese. While we were most concerned with maximizing the filling's flavor, we also wanted to trim some prep time. Most stuffed (or "twice-baked") potatoes take hours to prepare because the potatoes require full baking before the filling can be made, the potatoes stuffed, and baked again. We found that the potatoes could be started in the microwave and finished in the oven. The texture wasn't quite as fluffy as that of potatoes that were fully baked, but the microwave shaved an hour off the cooking time and the differences in texture between the two styles disappeared once we prepared the filling. Baking the hollowed-out shells— while whipping up the filling—guaranteed an extra-crisp and fully flavored potato skin. We tried fillings based on cream cheese, sour cream, heavy cream, and evaporated milk, but tasters unanimously preferred Boursin cheese, which gave the filling a rich garlic and herb flavor and a smooth texture. We boosted the flavor even more by cooking minced garlic in butter and adding that to the cheese mixture. After hollowing out the potatoes, there was enough filling for each, but not enough to mound on top for an attractive "overstuffed" appearance. More cheese just weighed down the potato, so we opted to cook an extra potato for its "guts," which we added to bulk up the filling (we discarded the skin from this potato). With a bit more cheese sprinkled over the top for a final burst of flavor, these steakhouse-style stuffed potatoes were ready to go.

These stuffed baked potatoes are generously sized and made super creamy with a mixture of Boursin and half-and-half.

7   large russet potatoes (about 12 ounces each), scrubbed

6   tablespoons unsalted butter, 3 tablespoons melted

¾   teaspoon salt

1   (5.2-ounce) package Boursin cheese, crumbled

½   cup half-and-half

2   garlic cloves, minced

¼   cup chopped fresh chives

1   teaspoon pepper

1. Adjust an oven rack to the middle position and heat the oven to 475 degrees. Set a wire rack inside a rimmed baking sheet. Prick the potatoes all over with a fork, place on a paper towel, and microwave on high until tender, 20 to 25 minutes, turning the potatoes over after 10 minutes.

2. Following the photos, slice and remove the top quarter of each potato, let cool 5 minutes, then scoop out the flesh, leaving a ¼-inch layer of the potato on the inside. Discard 1 potato shell. Brush the remaining shells inside and out with the melted butter and sprinkle the interiors with ¼ teaspoon salt. Transfer the potatoes, scooped side up, to a baking sheet fitted with a wire rack and bake until the skins begin to crisp, about 15 minutes.

3. Meanwhile, mix half of the Boursin and the half-and-half until blended in a bowl. Cook the remaining 3 tablespoons butter with the garlic in a saucepan over medium-low heat until the garlic is straw-colored, 3 to 5 minutes. Stir in the Boursin mixture until combined.

4. Set a ricer or food mill over a medium bowl and press or mill the potato flesh into the bowl. Gently fold in the warm Boursin mixture, 3 tablespoons of the chives, remaining ½ teaspoon salt, and pepper until well incorporated. Remove the potato shells from the oven and fill with the potato-cheese mixture. Top with the remaining Boursin and bake until the tops of the potatoes are golden brown, about 15 minutes. Sprinkle with the remaining 1 tablespoon chives. Serve.

WHAT YOU CAN DO AHEAD OF TIME: After filling the potato shells in step 4, they can be covered tightly with plastic wrap and refrigerated for up to 2 days or frozen for up to 1 month. Bake as directed in step 4, extending the baking time by 15 to 20 minutes and adding the additional Boursin after 15 minutes of baking.

NOTES FROM THE TEST KITCHEN

BIGGER, BETTER STUFFED POTATOES
While most recipes called for the potatoes to be cut in half before being filled, we found that these skimpy spuds were far from the super-stuffed potatoes we were after. Cut off only the top quarter of the potato and you'll have a much more substantial spud to stuff.

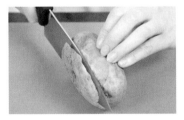

1. Slice the top quarter off the potato before scooping out its interior.

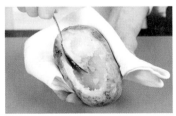

2. Use a spoon to scoop out the interior of the potato, being careful to leave a ¼-inch layer of potato in the shell.

GARLIC MASHED POTATOES WITH CHEESE
SERVES 4 TO 6

2 pounds russet potatoes (about 4 medium), peeled and sliced into ¾ inch thick
Salt
6 ounces cheddar cheese, shredded (about 1½ cups)
4 ounces mozzarella cheese, shredded (about 1 cup)
4 ounces Gruyère cheese, shredded (about 1 cup)
8 tablespoons (1 stick) unsalted butter, cut into ½-inch pieces
3 garlic cloves, minced
1 cup sour cream or crème fraîche
Pepper

WHAT MAKES THIS A BEST RECIPE: Originating in Southwest France, these special potatoes, called *aligot*, are an inspired coupling of mashed potatoes and a local fresh cow's milk cheese, called *tome fraîche de Cantal*. The cheese adds rich flavor, of course, but it also makes the dish particularly intriguing because when the cheese melts, aligot can be stretched into long, tantalizing strands. Early testing proved that starchy russet potatoes were a must. As for the dairy components—and there are a few—traditional aligot includes great lashings of both crème fraîche and butter, and we could find little to disagree with, outside of securing crème fraîche in our local supermarkets (sour cream made a fine substitute). The addition of a bit of minced garlic served as a welcome relief to the sudden stunning richness. Our usual method for mashing potatoes (by hand) wouldn't produce the creamy texture aligot demands, but a food processor did, although not without a *frisson* of concern as the potatoes can go from smooth to gummy in seconds. We found that it was essential to have all the ingredients at the ready when it came time to process the boiled potatoes and just as important to keep the processing to a few seconds. We left the trickiest ingredient for last: the cheese. Since Cantal, a young cow's milk cheese, is rare in this country outside of specialty shops, we determined that the flavor was most like a sharp cheddar, but with a hint of an assertive, nutty Swiss, like Gruyère. So we added a combination of sharp cheddar and Gruyère to our pureed potato blend, then tasted our handiwork. The flavors were there, but the much sought-after singular stringiness was not. So we added mozzarella to the mix. With this, we had achieved the aligot of our dreams.

1. Cover the potatoes by 1 inch of water in a large saucepan and add 1 tablespoon salt. Bring to a boil, then reduce to a simmer and cook until the potatoes are tender and a fork can be slipped easily into the center, 10 to 12 minutes. Reserve ¼ cup of the cooking water, then drain the potatoes in a colander. Wipe the saucepan dry and set aside. While the potatoes cook, toss the cheeses together in a medium bowl until evenly combined; set aside.

2. Pulse the cooked potatoes, ¼ cup reserved water, butter, garlic, and 1½ teaspoons salt in a food processor until the butter is melted and incorporated, about 5 pulses. Add the sour cream and continue to process until the potatoes are smooth and creamy, about 20 seconds.

3. Transfer the potato mixture back to the saucepan and cook over medium heat, slowly stirring in the cheese, one handful at a time, until all the cheese is incorporated. Continue to cook the cheese and potatoes, beating vigorously and constantly with a wooden spoon, until all the cheese is melted and the mixture is smooth and elastic, 4 to 6 minutes. Season with salt and pepper to taste and serve immediately.

WHERE THINGS CAN GO WRONG: Overprocessing the potatoes in the food processor in step 2 will turn them gummy, so have the ingredients ready and work quickly. And be careful to not overcook the potatoes in step 3, otherwise the cheese will become rubbery. Serve this dish immediately.

MASHED POTATO CASSEROLE

SERVES 8 TO 10

WHAT MAKES THIS A BEST RECIPE: Mashed potato casseroles transform the humble potato into a side dish that is more than the sum of its parts. Smooth, cheesy, and topped off with a crunchy topping, this casserole shouts comfort food. While we typically boil potatoes whole in their jackets (a slow process), we wanted to save time and assumed that the slight difference in texture between cooked whole and peeled, sliced potatoes wouldn't be noticeable here with everything else going on. And we were right. Based on our initial testing of mashed potato casseroles, we already knew that the secret to keeping the potatoes creamy and smooth was to mix them with a variety of dairy products. Butter and milk were obvious shoo-ins because they added good flavor and helped loosen the mashed potatoes to a softened consistency. But using butter and milk alone didn't work; the potatoes tasted dry and grainy. Tangy sour cream made the casserole smooth and creamy, though when we added too much its flavor became overpowering—there can be too much of a good thing. Looking for ways to increase the overall flavor of the casserole, we tried adding powdered mustard, but found that Dijon tasted better, especially when paired with cheddar cheese and a pinch of cayenne. Although we didn't have luck stirring the cheddar into the potatoes, we found that sprinkling it over the top of the casserole worked perfectly. Lastly, to complete the dish, we sprinkled a breadcrumb topping over the cheese. This casserole not only holds well for days in the refrigerator before baking, but the potatoes reheat to a smooth, creamy consistency and retain all of their flavor.

TOPPING

- 4 slices high-quality white sandwich bread, quartered
- 2 tablespoons unsalted butter, melted
- ¼ cup minced fresh parsley
- Salt and pepper

CASSEROLE

- 5 pounds russet potatoes (about 8 large), peeled, sliced into ¾-inch-thick rounds, and rinsed thoroughly
- 2½ cups whole milk, warmed
- 1 cup sour cream
- 8 tablespoons (1 stick) unsalted butter, melted
- 2½ teaspoons Dijon mustard
- 1 garlic clove, minced
- ⅛ teaspoon cayenne pepper
- Salt and pepper
- 8 ounces extra-sharp cheddar cheese, shredded (about 2 cups)

1. FOR THE TOPPING: Adjust an oven rack to the middle position and heat the oven to 350 degrees. Pulse the bread in a food processor to coarse crumbs, about 6 pulses. Toss the crumbs with the butter, and spread them out over a rimmed baking sheet. Bake, stirring occasionally, until golden and dry, about 20 minutes. Let the crumbs cool, then toss with the parsley and season with salt and pepper to taste; set aside.

2. FOR THE CASSEROLE: Meanwhile, place the potatoes in a large Dutch oven and cover by 1 inch of water. Bring to a boil over high heat, then reduce to a simmer and cook until the potatoes are tender (a paring knife can be slipped into and out of the center of the potatoes with very little resistance), about 15 minutes.

3. Drain the potatoes in a colander. Set a food mill (or ricer) over the now-empty, but still warm, saucepan. Working in batches, drop the potatoes into the hopper of the food mill and process the potatoes into the saucepan. Stir in the milk, sour cream, butter, Dijon, garlic, and cayenne until uniform. Season with salt and pepper to taste.

4. Spread the potato mixture into a 13 by 9-inch baking dish. Sprinkle the cheddar cheese evenly over the top, followed by the bread crumbs. Bake until hot throughout, 25 to 30 minutes.

WHAT YOU CAN DO AHEAD OF TIME: The casserole may be prepared through step 4 (but not baked), covered tightly with plastic wrap, and refrigerated for up to 2 days. To reheat, remove the plastic wrap, cover the casserole with foil, and bake in a 350-degree oven for 20 minutes. Remove the foil and continue to bake until the casserole is heated through and the crumbs are crisp, 20 to 30 minutes longer.

ORANGE-CRANBERRY RICE PILAF

SERVES 4 TO 6

WHAT MAKES THIS A BEST RECIPE: At its most basic, rice pilaf is long-grain rice first toasted in butter or oil until the grains are fragrant and nutty, and then simmered in water. Onions, dried fruits, herbs, and spices are often added for depth of flavor and texture. We wanted a simple autumnal-flavored pilaf that would complement the deep, rich flavors of roasted meats. The tartness of cranberries made a good deal of sense and nothing pairs with cranberries quite like a bracing shot of orange. How to add those cranberries and a deep orange flavor was the crux of our testing. We started off with the test kitchen's recipe for basic rice pilaf and tried replacing half of the water in which the rice is simmered with fresh squeezed orange juice. Our instincts were right on, but the proportion was way off. A scant ½ cup of juice proved potent enough to flavor the rice. Swapping the remaining water for chicken broth gave our pilaf richness and tempered the sweetness of the juice. A few strips of zest added more orange flavor without adding sweetness, and a single bay leaf suffused the rice with its characteristic warmth. As for the cranberries, we used dried and found they were best sprinkled on top of the rice while it rested off the heat for 10 minutes before serving. (If added earlier, the fruit became bloated and discolored the rice.) Whole dried cranberries proved too leathery; chopping them was the easy solution.

> 3 tablespoons unsalted butter
> 1 onion, minced (about 1 cup)
> Salt
> 1½ cups long-grain rice
> 1¾ cups low-sodium chicken broth
> 3 strips zest, plus ½ cup fresh orange juice, from 1 to 2 oranges
> 1 bay leaf
> ½ cup dried cranberries, chopped fine
> 6 scallions, chopped fine
> Pepper

1. Melt the butter in a large saucepan over medium heat. Add the onion and ½ teaspoon salt and cook until softened, about 3 minutes. Stir in the rice and cook, stirring occasionally, until fragrant and the edges begin to turn translucent, about 3 minutes.

2. Stir in the broth, orange zest and juice, and bay leaf and bring to a boil over medium-high heat. Cover, reduce the heat to low, and cook until the liquid is absorbed and the rice is tender, about 20 minutes. Quickly sprinkle the cranberries and scallions over the rice (do not stir), replace the lid, and let the rice stand off the heat 10 minutes. Discard the bay leaf and zest and fluff the rice with a fork. Season with salt and pepper to taste. Serve.

WHERE THINGS CAN GO WRONG: This recipe was developed for long-grain rice, so resist the urge to use any other variety, as it will not hydrate properly. Be sure to remove as much pith—the white part of the peel—as possible; otherwise it can impart a bitterness to the pilaf. Using a sharp vegetable peeler helps in removing only the flavorful zest in a wide strip.

NOTES FROM THE TEST KITCHEN

CHOOSING RICE

Varieties of rice are loosely categorized according to their grain length as short-, medium-, or long-grain rice. Length is indicative of the cooked texture of the rice. Short-grain rice is starchy and will cook up with a creamy, sticky texture—think sushi rice or risotto. Medium-grain rice is a little less sticky—ideal for paella. Long-grain rice is the least sticky and thus the best choice for dishes in which discrete grains are desired, like pilaf.

ZESTING CITRUS FRUIT WITH A VEGETABLE PEELER

A vegetable peeler is a great tool for removing the zest from citrus fruit. Gently peel away a 1-inch-wide piece of zest, trying to avoid any of the bitter white pith beneath it.

ORANGE-CRANBERRY RICE PILAF

OVEN-BAKED HOLIDAY STUFFING

SERVES 10 TO 12

WHAT MAKES THIS A BEST RECIPE: For the sake of moist meat and food safety, we highly recommend cooking the stuffing outside of the holiday turkey (stuffed turkeys must be cooked longer than unstuffed turkeys to raise the internal temperature high enough to prevent bacteria from forming). That said, we recognize that the turkey drippings add a good deal of rich flavor and moisture to the stuffing. This recipe, however, produces oven-baked stuffing every bit as good as that baked inside the turkey by compensating for the turkey juices in a variety of ways. First of all, we found that French bread was the best bread for the job as it held up well to added moisture and provided a neutral base for flavorings. Challah and potato bread were also attractive possibilities, adding a hint of sweetness and richness to the finished product. Stuffing cooked outside a bird requires not only a higher proportion of liquid to bread (we chose unembellished chicken broth for a clean, birdy flavor), but also some way of adding the richness and flavor that the drippings would have provided. A combination of eggs and butter proved a quick fix and, as an added bonus, lent the stuffing structure and improved the browning. Sautéed onion and celery added their requisite charm, and herbs—the classic stuffing flavorings sage, thyme, and marjoram—were a must. Fresh herbs made a filling that tasted slightly brighter, but dried herbs worked fine too. Ingredients were half the battle; cooking method the rest. Baking the stuffing uncovered for the entire time developed a crunchy crust, but it also dried out the bread, unless it was swimming in broth, which foiled crust development. Cooking it covered the entire time kept the bread moist, but produced no crust. A compromise was in order: We started the stuffing covered, so that it would steam and fully moisten the bread, then finished it uncovered to brown and develop a toasty flavor.

8 tablespoons (1 stick) unsalted butter, plus extra for the baking dish

1 onion, chopped (about 1 cup)

4 celery ribs, diced

1½ teaspoon each minced fresh sage, thyme, and marjoram or ½ teaspoon each dried

½ cup minced fresh parsley

½ teaspoon pepper

12 cups dried ½-inch cubes from one 1-pound bag French, potato, or challah bread

2 cups low-sodium chicken broth

3 large eggs, beaten lightly

1¼ teaspoons salt

1. Adjust an oven rack to the middle position and heat the oven to 400 degrees (350 degrees if using challah). Butter a 13 by 9-inch baking dish. Heat the butter in a large skillet over medium-high heat until melted; pour off 2 tablespoons of the butter and reserve. Return the skillet to the heat; add the onion and celery and cook, stirring occasionally, until translucent, about 8 minutes. Stir in the sage, thyme, marjoram, parsley, and black pepper and cook until just fragrant, about 1 minute longer. Turn the onion mixture into a large mixing bowl. Add the bread cubes, broth, eggs, and salt and toss gently to distribute the dry and wet ingredients evenly.

2. Turn the mixture into the prepared baking dish, and drizzle with the reserved melted butter. Cover tightly with foil, and bake until fragrant, about 25 minutes (30 minutes for challah). Remove the foil and bake until a golden brown crust forms on top, 15 to 20 minutes longer. Serve warm.

WHERE THINGS CAN GO WRONG: The bread must be thoroughly "staled" so that it will absorb the flavors and liquid added to it. If your bread is not stale, cut it into ½-inch slices and lay them in a single layer on baking sheets. Dry them in a 225-degree oven until brittle but not brown, 30 to 40 minutes. Then cut them into cubes and proceed.

WHAT YOU CAN DO AHEAD OF TIME: The onion mixture can be cooked and refrigerated in an airtight container for up to 2 days ahead of time.

INDIAN-STYLE CURRY
WITH POTATOES, CAULIFLOWER, PEAS, AND CHICKPEAS
SERVES 4 TO 6

WHAT MAKES THIS A BEST RECIPE: While Indian cooks spend hours making vegetable curries, not all of us have the time to do a traditional recipe justice. This recipe captures the classic flavors of a vegetarian curry with an hour's labor and without any special ingredients. Testing boiled down to three main issues: the spices with which to flavor the curry, the vegetables, and the cooking technique. With a homemade spice blend taking too much time to grind and mix, we decided early on to go with prepared curry powder. We found that as long as we used enough and toasted it first in a dry skillet to maximize its flavor, store-bought curry powder was serviceable. Spices are just the start of the dish's flavor. Many classic recipes begin with a generous amount of sautéed onion as well as equal amounts of garlic and ginger, and we found no reason to stray from this well-balanced tradition. Fresh chile added some heat and, while inauthentic, we really like the addition of a tablespoon of tomato paste for sweetness. As the onions caramelized with the other ingredients, *fond* (flavorful dark bits) developed, to which we stirred in the toasted curry powder and let it dissolve. Creating a supercharged base took about 20 minutes, then we added our chosen vegetables to the pot: chickpeas and potatoes for heartiness, along with cauliflower and peas. A bit bland. We evaluated our basic cooking method and decided on a few changes. We browned the potatoes along with the onions and also picked up an Indian cooking technique called *bhuna*, which involves sautéing the spices and main ingredients together to develop and meld flavors. We determined that a combination of water and pureed canned tomatoes along with a splash of cream or coconut milk allowed the delicate vegetables and fragrant spices to shine. The coup de grace turned out to be the addition of a second spice blend: garam masala, a mixture of black pepper, cinnamon, coriander, and cardamom. A few pinches toasted along with the curry powder added a second wave of flavor. Serve over basmati rice.

2 tablespoons sweet or mild curry powder

1½ teaspoons garam masala

¼ cup vegetable oil

2 onions, minced (about 2 cups)

12 ounces Red Bliss potatoes (about 2 medium), cut into ½-inch pieces

3 garlic cloves, minced

1 tablespoon grated fresh ginger

1 serrano chile, ribs, seeds, and flesh minced

1 tablespoon tomato paste

½ medium head cauliflower, trimmed, cored, and cut into 1-inch florets (about 4 cups)

1 (14.5-ounce) can diced tomatoes, pulsed in a food processor until nearly smooth with ¼-inch pieces visible

1¼ cups water

1 (15-ounce) can chickpeas, drained and rinsed
   Salt

1½ cups frozen peas (8 ounces)

¼ cup heavy cream or coconut milk

CONDIMENTS
   Plain whole-milk yogurt
   Mango chutney

1. Toast the curry powder and garam masala in a small skillet over medium-high heat, stirring constantly, until the spices darken slightly and become fragrant, about 1 minute. Remove the spices from the pan and set aside.

2. Heat 3 tablespoons of the oil in a large Dutch oven over medium-high heat until shimmering. Add the onions and potatoes and cook, stirring occasionally, until the onions are caramelized and the potatoes are golden brown on the edges, about 10 minutes. (Reduce the heat to medium if the onions darken too quickly.)

3. Reduce the heat to medium. Clear the center of the pan and add the remaining 1 tablespoon oil and the garlic, ginger, chile, and tomato paste; cook, stirring constantly, until fragrant, about 30 seconds. Add the toasted spices and cook, stirring constantly, about 1 minute longer. Add the cauliflower and cook, stirring constantly, until the spices coat the florets, about 2 minutes longer.

4. Add the tomatoes, water, chickpeas, and 1 teaspoon salt; increase the heat to medium-high and bring the mixture to a boil, scraping the bottom of the pan with a wooden spoon to loosen the browned bits. Cover and reduce the heat to medium. Simmer briskly, stirring

INDIAN-STYLE VEGETABLE CURRY

occasionally, until the vegetables are tender, 10 to 15 minutes. Stir in the peas and the cream; continue to cook until heated through, about 2 minutes longer. Adjust the seasoning with salt and serve immediately, passing the condiments separately.

NOTES FROM THE TEST KITCHEN

THE BEST CURRY POWDER

Though blends can vary dramatically, curry powders come in two basic styles—mild or sweet and a hotter version called Madras. The former combines as many as 20 different ground spices, herbs, and seeds. We tasted six curry powders—mixed into rice pilaf and in our vegetable curry. And the result? Our favorite is **Penzeys Sweet Curry Powder** ($4.39 for 2.2 ounces) though Durkee Curry Powder came in a close second.

THE BEST MANGO CHUTNEY

Mango chutney (sometimes called Major Grey's chutney) is a welcome accompaniment to many curries. Classic preparations cook unripe green mangoes with sugar, vinegar, and aromatic spices. We sampled four supermarket brands to see which we liked best. High levels of fructose corn syrup and caramel color in the Crosse and Blackwell Major Grey's Chutney overshadowed any natural mango flavors, making for what testers found "sickly sweetness" and "insipid, weak" flavor. A substantial dollop of ginger oil spiced Patak's Sweet Mango Chutney so heavily that tasters were torn; some appreciated the "pungent," "perfumey" zing, while others complained about the "ginger overload." Our tasters liked the balanced sweetness and acidity in both Sharwood's Major Grey Mango Chutney and **The Silver Palate Mango Chutney**. But the addition of lemon juice and peel gave The Silver Palate chutney a tangy boost that made it our favorite.

BUILDING FLAVOR QUICKLY

Indian curries are defined by hours of cooking that result in complex layers of flavor. Here are the key steps we took to create big flavors in less time.

1. Toast the curry powder and garam masala in a dry skillet.

2. Rather than simmering potatoes in the curry, brown them with the onions.

3. Add tomato paste to the traditional garlic and ginger for a hint of sweetness and depth.

4. Add the toasted spices to the flavor base to infuse the dish with flavor.

5. Sauté the vegetables in the spices, following a simple Indian technique called *bhuna*.

POTATOES 101

Until recently, most markets sold potatoes under generic names, such as "baking potato" or "boiling potato," which helped shoppers choose the right potato for each recipe. But now many markets sell potatoes by varietal name, such as Yukon Gold and Red Creamer. So how do you use these potatoes? We find that potato varieties can be divided into three major categories based on texture. What causes different potatoes to have different textures? In a word, starch.

NEW VERSUS OLD POTATOES

Potatoes can be categorized as "new" or "early" potatoes and "old" or "main crop" potatoes. Both new and old potatoes can come from any variety of potato. New potatoes are thin-skinned, less mature potatoes harvested in the late spring and summer. They are less starchy than "old" potatoes, because they haven't had time to convert their sugar into starch. These potatoes should be used as firm, waxy potatoes, regardless of variety. Old potatoes are fully mature and are harvested in the fall. They are usually starchier and have thick skins. These potatoes are often held in cold storage, or cured, in order for their skins to toughen, which helps protect their flesh for better storage. Most potatoes sold in supermarkets have been cured and can be considered "old" potatoes.

GREEN POTATOES

The green patches found on some potatoes are caused by prolonged exposure to light or improper storage. This discoloration is produced by chlorophyll and is usually an indication of increased levels of a naturally occurring toxic alkaloid called solanine. Ingesting solanine can lead to illness, so if you discover green patches when peeling your potatoes, simply cut off the affected areas.

POTATO VARIETIES

DRY, FLOURY POTATOES

WHAT YOU NEED TO KNOW: This group contains more total starch (20 to 22 percent) and amylose than other categories, giving these varieties a dry, mealy texture.
HOW TO USE THEM: Good for baking, frying, and mashing (they drink up butter and cream), as well as for thickening soups and stews.
COMMON VARIETIES: Russet, Burbank, Idaho

"IN-BETWEEN" POTATOES

WHAT YOU NEED TO KNOW: These potatoes contain less total starch (18 to 20 percent) and amylose than dry, floury potatoes but more than firm, waxy potatoes. Their texture is more mealy than firm, putting them closer to dry, floury potatoes.
HOW TO USE THEM: They can be mashed or baked but won't be as fluffy as dry, floury potatoes; they can be used in salads and soups but won't be quite as firm as waxy potatoes.
COMMON VARIETIES: Yukon Gold, Yellow Finn, Purple Peruvian, Kennebec, Katahdin

FIRM, WAXY POTATOES

WHAT YOU NEED TO KNOW: These potatoes contain a relatively low amount of total starch (16 to 18 percent) and very little amylose, which means they have a firm, smooth, waxy texture. Freshly dug "new" potatoes fall into this group.
HOW TO USE THEM: Perfect when you want the potatoes to hold their shape, as with potato salad; also a good choice when roasting or boiling.
COMMON VARIETIES: Red Bliss, French Fingerling, Red Creamer, White Rose

THE STARCH MATTERS

Total starch content in potatoes can range from 16 percent to 22 percent. But just as important as the total amount of starch is the type of starch. There are two kinds of starch molecules—amylose and amylopectin—and they behave quite differently. Amylose molecules, which are shaped like long chains, easily separate when cooked in the presence of water.

This explains why russet potatoes, which have a high amount of amylose, are the best choice for mashing. In contrast, amylopectin molecules have a compact, branched shape that holds together when cooked and helps the potato remain intact. Varieties with more amylopectin, such as Red Bliss, are the best choice for boiling.

RED BLISS POTATO
Remains Firm When Cooked

RUSSET POTATO
Turns Crumbly When Cooked

HOW TO COOK POTATOES

MASHED

Start with dry, floury potatoes and simmer them with their peels on. Yes, this is more work than the usual peel-and-dice method, but keeping water out ensures fluffy mashed potatoes with an earthy flavor. It is also important when mixing the potatoes to add the melted butter before the half-and-half. When butter is added before the half-and-half, the fat coats the starch molecules, inhibiting their interaction with the water in the half-and-half. The result is a silkier, creamier mashed potato.

HOW TO PEEL: The most efficient way to peel a just-boiled potato is to spear it with a fork and then use a paring knife to remove the peel.

ROASTED

Start with waxy potatoes (they have more moisture than other varieties) and cover the pan with foil for the first half of the roasting time so the potatoes steam in their own moisture and become creamy. Remove the foil and continue roasting until the exteriors are crisp.

HOW TO FLIP ROAST POTATOES: Press a metal spatula against the pan as you slide it under the potatoes to protect the crisp crust. Flip the potatoes so the other cut sides come in contact with the hot pan.

BAKED

Start with a dry, floury potato and bake it at a relatively low temperature, which allows some of the starch in the flesh just inside the skin to break down into sugar and gives the potato a rich flavor. To ensure that the flesh does not steam and become dense, open a baked potato as soon as it comes out of the oven.

HOW TO OPEN A BAKED POTATO: Use the tines of a fork to make a dotted X on top of each potato. Press in at the ends of the potato to push the flesh up and out. Besides releasing the steam quickly, this method helps trap and hold on to bits of butter.

BOILED

Start with firm, waxy potatoes and boil them with their skin intact. Toss with butter and serve, or, for salad, cut and toss potatoes with vinegar, salt, and pepper. This technique allows the potatoes to easily absorb the vinegar, creating a fuller-flavored salad.

HOW TO KNOW WHEN IT'S DONE: Poke the potato with a sharp paring knife and then try to lift it out of the water. If the potato clings to the knife even for a second, back into the pot it goes.

POTATO RECIPES

MASHED POTATOES

Place 2 pounds scrubbed (and unpeeled) dry, floury potatoes in a large saucepan with cold water to cover by about 1 inch. Bring to a boil, then simmer over medium-low heat until tender and fully cooked, 20 to 30 minutes. Drain and peel the potatoes. Mill, rice, or mash the potatoes. Stir in 8 tablespoons melted unsalted butter, followed by 1 cup warm half-and-half. Season with 1½ teaspoons table salt and ground black pepper to taste. Serves 4.

BAKED POTATOES

Place 4 medium dry, floury potatoes directly on the middle rack in a 350-degree oven. Bake the potatoes until a skewer glides easily through the flesh, about 1 hour and 15 minutes. Open immediately (see illustration at left), and serve with butter and salt. Serves 4.

ROASTED POTATOES

Toss 2 pounds firm, waxy potatoes, cut into ¾-inch wedges, with 3 tablespoons olive oil, salt, and pepper. Place the potatoes flesh side down on a rimmed baking sheet and cover tightly with foil. Cook the potatoes on a middle rack in a 425-degree oven for 20 minutes. Remove the foil and continue to roast until the sides of the potatoes touching the pan are golden brown, about 15 minutes. Carefully turn the potatoes over and continue to roast until golden brown on the second side, 5 to 10 minutes. Serves 4.

BOILED POTATOES

Place 2 pounds scrubbed firm, waxy potatoes in a large saucepan with cold water to cover by about 1 inch. Bring to a boil, then simmer over medium-low heat until tender, at least 10 minutes for 1-inch potatoes and up to 18 minutes for 2½-inch potatoes. Drain and toss with butter. Serves 4.

FOR SALAD: Cool potatoes slightly, cut with serrated knife into ¾-inch chunks, and place on rimmed baking sheet. Drizzle with ¼ cup red wine vinegar, ½ teaspoon salt, and ¼ teaspoon pepper. Let stand for 20 minutes, then transfer to bowl and dress as desired.

MULTIGRAIN PANCAKES

MAKES ABOUT SIXTEEN 4-INCH PANCAKES

WHAT MAKES THIS A BEST RECIPE: There are a lot of multigrain pancake recipes out there, each more wholesome, heavier, or blander than the last. Sure we like to eat healthy, but first thing in the morning, we want breakfast, not penance. That being said, our dilemma has been solved with this recipe for multigrain pancakes that are nutritious—chocked full of whole grains, nuts, and dried fruit—and flavorful without being the least bit dense. No "mulch pucks here." The solution came after testing and discounting a dozen-odd whole grain blends. (Requiring a long list of different flour and grains for the recipe was quickly ruled out as overly ambitious for breakfast.) Fishing around for inspiration in the cereal aisle of the supermarket, we came up with a rather unorthodox idea: Why not use ground-up breakfast cereal? We bought all of the "healthy" cereals we could find and made dozens of different pancakes in which we substituted cereal for a portion of the flour. While each had its merits—outside of gritty textured Grape Nuts pancakes—we were most smitten with pancakes prepared with muesli. Made from raw whole oats, wheat germ, rye flakes, barley, toasted nuts, and dried fruit, muesli had everything we wanted in one convenient package. And that convenience translated to great flavor; the dried fruit and toasted nuts—usually almonds and/or hazelnuts—provided a huge flavor boost. The cereal alone, however, wasn't quite enough for great-tasting multigrain pancakes. Blending a bit of whole wheat flour with white flour underpinned the "wholesomeness" of the pancakes without detrimentally affecting the texture; they were surprisingly light due to a fine-tuned balance of baking powder and baking soda. A stiff shot of vanilla emphasized the flavor of the grains and nuts, and brown sugar added an earthy note and improved the pancake's

browning. And while we usually prepare pancakes with buttermilk (the acid is required for leavening), we preferred a less sour blend of whole milk acidulated with lemon juice. The last touch was stirring in a handful of unground muesli for texture; a teasing reminder, perhaps, of how far these pancakes had come from their dense beginnings.

    4   teaspoons fresh lemon juice
    2   cups whole milk
 1¼   cups (6 ounces) plus 3 tablespoons no-sugar-added
        muesli (see note)
    ¾   cup (3¾ ounces) unbleached all-purpose flour
    ½   cup (2¾ ounces) whole wheat flour
    2   tablespoons light or dark brown sugar
 2¼   teaspoons baking powder
    ½   teaspoon baking soda
    ½   teaspoon salt
    2   large eggs
    3   tablespoons unsalted butter, melted and cooled
    ¾   teaspoon vanilla extract
        Vegetable oil

1. Whisk the lemon juice and milk together in a medium bowl or 4-cup measuring cup; set aside to thicken while preparing the other ingredients.

2. Process 1¼ cups of the muesli in a food processor until finely ground, 2 to 2½ minutes; transfer to a large bowl. Add the remaining 3 tablespoons unground muesli, flours, brown sugar, baking powder, baking soda, and salt; whisk to combine.

3. Whisk the eggs, melted butter, and vanilla into the milk until combined. Make a well in the center of the dry ingredients in the bowl; pour in the milk mixture and whisk very gently until just combined (a few streaks of flour and lumps should remain). Do not overmix. Allow the batter to sit while the pan heats.

4. Heat a 12-inch nonstick skillet over medium-low heat for 5 minutes. Add 1 teaspoon oil and brush to coat the skillet bottom evenly. Following the instructions on page 99, add 1 tablespoon batter to gauge the temperature of

Muesli is the secret to fluffy pancakes packed with rich multi-grain flavor.

the pan. Pour ¼ cup batter onto 3 spots in the skillet, using the bottom of the ladle to spread the batter smooth if necessary. Cook the pancakes until small bubbles begin to appear evenly over the surface, 2 to 3 minutes. Using a thin, wide spatula, flip the pancakes and cook until golden brown on the second side, 1½ to 2 minutes longer. Serve immediately. Repeat with the remaining batter, brushing the surface of the pan lightly with the oil between batches and adjusting the heat if necessary.

WHERE THINGS CAN GO WRONG: Familia brand, no-sugar-added muesli is the best choice for this recipe. If you can't find Familia, look for Alpen or any no-sugar-added muesli. (If you can't find muesli without sugar, muesli with sugar added will work; reduce the brown sugar in the recipe to 1 tablespoon.) If you want to keep cooked pancakes warm and moist as you cook the rest, place them on a greased wire rack in a 200-degree oven.

WHAT YOU CAN DO AHEAD OF TIME: The muesli may be processed and the dry ingredients may be blended up to 1 week ahead of time and stored at room temperature in a zipper-lock bag.

NOTES FROM THE TEST KITCHEN

PANCAKES 101: IS THE PAN READY?
The best way to determine when the skillet is ready is to make a test pancake the size of a half-dollar (use 1 tablespoon of batter). If after 1 minute the pancake is golden brown, the pan is ready. If the bottom of the pancake remains blond—or is close to burning—adjust the heat accordingly.

LET THAT BATTER REST
To achieve light, fluffy pancakes, it's important to let the batter rest while the pan heats (a full 5 minutes). The flour needs this time to absorb all the liquid, thus ensuring that the batter sets up properly. Skip this step and the pancakes will run together in the pan (left) and cook up flat, not to mention misshapen. Properly rested batter will maintain its shape when poured into the pan and will produce puffed and fluffy pancakes (right).

| UNRESTED | RESTED |

MULTIGRAIN MAKEOVER
Some multigrain pancake recipes load up on unprocessed grains—great for flavor but bad for texture. To avoid gummy, chewy pancakes, we made our own multigrain "flour" by processing store-bought muesli cereal in a food processor. To give our pancakes a subtle hint of that hearty whole grain texture, we added a few tablespoons of unprocessed muesli to the batter.

TOO TOOTHSOME
Pancakes made with unprocessed muesli had great flavor but too much chew.

PERFECT COMBO
Processing some muesli into "flour" and leaving some muesli whole gave us great texture.

POTATO AND SAUSAGE BREAKFAST POPOVER CASSEROLE

POTATO AND SAUSAGE BREAKFAST POPOVER CASSEROLE

SERVES 6

WHAT MAKES THIS A BEST RECIPE: The folks at Betty Crocker brought forth the "impossible pie" back in the 1970s as yet another use for its ubiquitous Bisquick mix. The idea was to pour a thinned-out biscuit batter (made with Bisquick, milk, and eggs) on top of a hearty filling in a pie plate; the batter sinks to the bottom of the dish and "impossibly" forms its own crust when baked. Sorry, Betty Crocker, but what sounds good in theory, doesn't quite work in practice: Those we tried were "impossibly" dense or heavy. That said, we took our own stab at it and came up with a solution that really works. We reenvisioned the pie with a lighter, crisper, popover-inspired batter (no Bisquick required). Popovers also seem to do the "impossible," as the high heat of the oven transforms their humble ingredients—eggs, milk, flour, salt, and butter—into the culinary equivalent of a hot air balloon. They are crisp and golden brown on the outside, tender and moist inside—perfect for a "pie." For the best rise and crispiest texture, we found it necessary to replace the pie plate traditionally used with a springform pan so that it could be preheated in the oven for the best rise and crispest texture. As for filling our "impossible pie," we turned to a blend of sausage and potato. Tasters preferred ground, bulk sausage over diced links, and diced Yukon Golds, precooked in the microwave before being browned in a skillet, were perfect.

- 2 large eggs
- 1 cup whole milk
- Salt
- 1 cup unbleached all-purpose flour
- 1 tablespoon unsalted butter, melted
- 2 scallions, chopped
- ¾ pound Yukon Gold potatoes (about 2), peeled and cut into ¼-inch dice
- 1 (12-ounce) package bulk sausage meat
- 2 tablespoons vegetable oil
- 1 ounce grated Parmesan cheese (½ cup)

1. Adjust an oven rack to the upper-middle position and heat the oven to 425 degrees. Prepare a 9-inch springform pan (see page 102), and set aside on a rimmed baking sheet.

2. Whisk the eggs, milk, and ½ teaspoon salt in a bowl until well combined. Stir in the flour until just incorporated—the mixture will still be a bit lumpy. Whisk in the butter until the batter is smooth. Stir in the scallions and set the batter aside while preparing the filling.

3. Toss the potatoes with 1 tablespoon of water in a large microwave-safe bowl. Cover with plastic wrap, cut vent holes in the plastic, and microwave on high power until the potatoes just begin to soften, 3 to 4 minutes. Meanwhile, cook the sausage in a large nonstick skillet over medium heat, breaking up the clumps, until the meat has lost most of its pink color, about 4 minutes. Using a slotted spoon, spread the sausage evenly over the bottom of the prepared springform pan.

4. Heat the oil in the skillet with the sausage fat over medium-high heat until shimmering. Add the cooked potatoes and ¼ teaspoon salt and cook until the potatoes are golden and crisp, 8 to 10 minutes. Drain the potatoes on paper towels.

5. While the potatoes are cooking, place the springform pan with the sausage in the oven for 10 minutes. Remove the pan from the oven and, working quickly, sprinkle ¼ cup of the cheese over the sausage and pour the batter evenly over the filling. Scatter the potatoes on top and sprinkle with the remaining cheese. Bake until puffed and golden, 25 to 30 minutes. Remove the pan from the oven, run a knife around the edges of the pan, and let cool 5 minutes. Release the outer ring and, using a spatula, transfer the casserole to a serving plate. Serve.

WHERE THINGS CAN GO WRONG: This recipe requires careful timing. Once the batter is prepared and set aside to rest, the potatoes can be microwaved while the sausage is cooking. While the potatoes are pan-fried, the springform pan (with the cooked sausage) should be preheated in the oven.

NOTES FROM THE TEST KITCHEN

DOUBLE UP ON THE NONSTICK

Even when we used a nonstick springform pan, we found that our breakfast casserole stubbornly stuck to the bottom of the pan, making it difficult to slice the casserole into wedges. Lining a springform pan (nonstick or regular) with foil (preferably nonstick) and then coating the foil with nonstick cooking spray ensured that our popover casserole released from the pan every time.

1. Line the bottom of a springform pan with aluminum foil (preferably nonstick), attach the sides of the pan, and tuck the foil underneath the pan bottom.

2. Coat the sides and bottom with cooking spray.

CHEESE SOUFFLÉ
SERVES 4

WHAT MAKES THIS A BEST RECIPE: A perfect cheese soufflé has a dramatic lift above the rim of the dish, a crusty, burnished exterior, and a rich, moist, almost wobbly center shot through with rich flavor. Despite the soufflé's long-standing reputation for fickleness—deflating on a whim and bland flavor—we developed a foolproof cheese soufflé for *The Best International Recipe* that couldn't be easier to whip up. Essentially, a soufflé is a sauce into which stiffly beaten egg whites are incorporated. The lightened sauce is then turned into a prepared mold and baked. Our first hurdle was picking a "base," the mixture that supplies substance and flavor to the soufflé, as opposed to the airiness and "lift" provided by the whipped egg whites. The base can be a *béchamel* (equal amounts of butter and flour, whisked with milk over heat), or a *bouillie* (flour cooked with milk until thickened). After testing a few of each style, we consistently preferred the béchamel base. Three whipped egg whites sufficiently leavened the base (the yolks were used in the béchamel). As for the cheese, Gruyère is the traditional choice. Our testing proved that any more than four ounces of grated cheese prevented a perfect rise. Some recipes we came across in our research coated the soufflé dish with a dusting of cheese (and sprinkled cheese over the soufflé as well). After greasing our soufflé dish with butter, we added Parmesan to coat the dish and after pouring in the soufflé, we dusted more Parmesan on top. The addition was a success—the Parmesan helped to give the soufflé an attractive golden brown color and, by virtue of its salty nature, heightened the flavor of the Gruyère. Most recipes call for baking a soufflé at 350 degrees, and we stuck with the pack as there was plenty of rise, a crisp exterior, and a moist interior with that level of heat. The right-size soufflé dish was a must, as were friends ready and waiting at the table. You want to serve a soufflé while it is towering and hot, not just for the flavor, but also for the drama.

3   tablespoons unsalted butter cut into ½-inch chunks, plus extra for coating the dish

½   ounce Parmesan cheese, grated (¼ cup)

3   tablespoons unbleached all-purpose flour

1   cup whole milk

4   ounces Gruyère cheese, shredded (1 cup)

½   teaspoon salt

¼   teaspoon pepper

Pinch nutmeg

3   large eggs, separated

¼   teaspoon cream of tartar

1. Adjust an oven rack to the middle position and heat the oven to 350 degrees. Thoroughly butter the inside of a 2-quart soufflé dish, then coat evenly with 2 table-spoons of the Parmesan; set aside.

2. Melt the butter in a medium saucepan over medium heat. Stir in the flour and cook until golden, about 1 minute. Slowly whisk in the milk. Bring to a simmer and cook, whisking constantly, until thickened and smooth, about 1 minute. Off the heat, whisk in the Gruyère, salt, pepper, and nutmeg. Transfer the mixture to a large bowl. Whisk in the egg yolks until completely incorporated and set aside.

3. Using an electric mixer, whip the egg whites in a separate bowl on medium-low speed until they are opaque and frothy, about 30 seconds. Add the cream of tartar, increase the speed to medium-high, and continue to whip, watching carefully, until they are thick and form stiff peaks, about 2½ minutes.

4. Working with one-quarter of the whipped egg whites at a time, gently fold them into the yolk mixture until almost no white streaks remain (a few streaks are okay). Gently pour the mixture into the prepared soufflé dish and sprinkle with the remaining 2 tablespoons Parmesan.

5. Bake until the top is nicely browned, the center jiggles slightly, and an instant-read thermometer inserted through the top side registers 170 degrees, 25 to 30 minutes. Serve immediately.

NOTES FROM THE TEST KITCHEN

DISCERNING PROPERLY BEATEN EGG WHITES

OVERBEATEN EGG WHITES will look dry and grainy and will begin to separate. They will not fold in easily with other batter ingredients, will clump up in the batter, and will produce a finished baked good that looks spotted and sunken.

UNDERBEATEN EGG WHITES are foamy and soft. They will turn a batter watery and produce a finished baked good that looks flat.

PROPERLY BEATEN EGG WHITES will look creamy and glossy. They will hold a stiff peak yet fold in easily with other batter ingredients, will give the batter a billowy texture, and will produce a soufflé or finished baked good that has uniformly lofted texture.

WHEN IS IT DONE?

During the course of all this testing, we found a cheese soufflé will give you three indications of when it is done: when you can smell the cheese, when it stops rising, and when only the very center of the top jiggles when gently shaken. Of course, these are all imprecise methods. If you have an instant-read thermometer, slide it through the side of the top—it should measure 170 degrees. If you don't have a thermometer, simply take two large spoons, pull open the top of the soufflé, and peek inside. If the center is still soupy, simply put the dish back in the oven! Much to our surprise, and as heretical as it may sound, this probing in no way harmed the soufflé—it lost no volume and no one noticed the spot punctured by the spoons.

SOUFFLÉ DISHES

We tried baking our soufflé in a variety of baking dishes, but only a soufflé dish with its characteristic straight sides guaranteed that our soufflé rose evenly and stayed in the dish, and did not spill all over the bottom of our oven. Soufflé dishes are relatively inexpensive and can be found in a variety of cookware stores.

BETTER BRAN MUFFINS
MAKES 12 MUFFINS

WHAT MAKES THIS A BEST RECIPE: Whipping up muffins from breakfast cereal is nothing new—one of the first such recipes appeared on the package of Kellogg's Krumbled Bran cereal in 1916—but a pedigree is no guarantee of great flavor. Those we've tasted have largely been dense and gummy. This recipe, however, uses breakfast cereal to great effect and produces a moist, hearty muffin redolent of bran's earthy flavor. Working with a basic recipe, we tested every different cereal we could get our hands on. Bran flakes came out flavorless and looked like springy cupcakes; bran granules were also flavorless, and their texture was dense and pasty. The twigs (Kellogg's All-Bran Original was the best flavored of this style cereal) provided a deep bran flavor, but they wouldn't fully dissolve into the batter and were even sticking out of the tops of the baked muffins. We tried grinding the twigs to a powder in a food processor before adding them to the batter. Much better—the muffins had an even crumb, but they were a bit heavy. A compromise was in order, so we pulverized half of the cereal and kept the other half whole. Fine-tuning the recipe, we discovered that one egg didn't add enough structure, and two eggs made the muffins too springy; a whole egg plus a yolk worked best. And the muffins seemed lean and dry until we switched to whole-milk yogurt for the liquid component. Mixing some whole wheat flour with the all-purpose flour reinforced the flavor of the bran, as did replacing the granulated sugar with brown sugar and increasing the molasses. Now here's a moist, tender muffin with big bran flavor.

1 cup raisins
1 teaspoon water
2¼ cups (5 ounces) All-Bran Original cereal (see page 106)
1¼ cups (6¼ ounces) unbleached all-purpose flour
½ cup (2½ ounces) whole wheat flour
2 teaspoons baking soda

½ teaspoon salt
1 large egg plus 1 large yolk
⅔ cup (4⅔ ounces) packed light brown sugar
3 tablespoons mild or light molasses
1 teaspoon vanilla extract
6 tablespoons (¾ stick) unsalted butter, melted and cooled
1¾ cups plain whole-milk yogurt

1. Adjust an oven rack to the middle position and heat the oven to 400 degrees. Spray a standard muffin tin with nonstick cooking spray. Combine the raisins and water in a small microwave-safe bowl, cover with plastic wrap, cut several steam vents in the plastic with a paring knife, and microwave on high power for 30 seconds. Let stand, covered, until the raisins are softened, about 5 minutes. Transfer the raisins to a paper towel–lined plate to cool.

2. Process half of the bran cereal in a food processor until finely ground, about 1 minute. Whisk together the flours, baking soda, and salt in a large bowl; set aside. Whisk the egg and yolk together in a medium bowl until well combined and light colored, about 20 seconds. Add the sugar, molasses, and vanilla; whisk until the mixture is thick, about 30 seconds. Add the melted butter and whisk to combine; add the yogurt and whisk to combine. Stir in the processed cereal and unprocessed cereal; let the mixture sit until the bran cereal is evenly moistened (there will still be some small lumps), about 5 minutes.

3. Add the wet ingredients to the dry ingredients and gently mix with a rubber spatula until the batter is combined and evenly moistened. Do not overmix. Gently fold the raisins into the batter. Using a ⅓-cup measure or ice cream scoop, divide the batter evenly among the prepared muffin cups, dropping the batter to form mounds. Do not level or flatten the mounds.

4. Bake until the muffins are dark golden and a toothpick inserted into the center of a muffin comes out with a few crumbs attached, 16 to 20 minutes, rotating the pan halfway through baking. Cool the muffins in the tin for 5 minutes, then transfer to a wire rack and cool for 10 more minutes. Serve warm.

WHAT YOU CAN DO AHEAD OF TIME: The muffins can be stored in an airtight container at room temperature for 3 days.

NOTES FROM THE TEST KITCHEN

BRAN CEREAL

Bran is the outer layer of the wheat grain that is removed during milling. A good source of calcium, phosphorous, and fiber, bran cereal comes in various forms. Here's how they stack up in muffins.

TWIGS
We found that All-Bran Original gave our muffins the most robust bran flavor.

FLAKES
Bran flakes are mostly made of wheat and made muffins with very little bran flavor.

GRANULES
Small granules of bran cereal made very dense muffins with almost no bran flavor.

WITH RAISINS
This cereal seemed like a good idea, but the raisins cooked up dry and tough.

FILL 'ER UP

For big, hearty muffins, make sure to fill the muffin cups to the rim. And for nicely domed muffins, mound the batter in the cups and don't level it off.

SOFTENING THE BRAN

When we added the cereal directly to the batter, the muffins were marred by crunchy bits and twigs sticking out of the top. When we processed all of the cereal into a fine powder, the muffins were too dense. By processing just half of the cereal and leaving the other half in twig form, we created muffins with an even, but not heavy, texture.

BLUEBERRY STREUSEL MUFFINS
MAKES 12 MUFFINS

WHAT MAKES THIS A BEST RECIPE: You'd think it would be easy to find plenty of great recipes for something as popular as blueberry muffins, but we know that to be far from the case. Most recipes we have tried produce dry or spongy muffins with an ugly blue (or even green) color and bland blueberry flavor. A streusel topping further adds to the trouble by being tough, sandy, or so heavy it sinks. This recipe, however, solves all the ills in one fell swoop and produces tender, cakey muffins bursting with berries and crowned with chewy nuggets of butter and sugar. While the test kitchen typically prepares muffins with sour cream for a rich, tangy flavor, we found that in this case, sour cream made for a muffin that wasn't sturdy enough to support the weighty blueberries and streusel. We tried replacing the sour cream with heavy cream, yogurt, milk, and buttermilk and found that the latter created muffins with a sturdy-but-light texture. We thought any old blueberry would suffice, but fresh blueberries proved bland and waterlogged. Frozen (wild) berries are smaller and more flavorful, but they weren't perfect either. If allowed to thaw, they stained the batter an unappealing blue; keeping the berries frozen until the last second helped, and tossing them with flour before adding them to the batter prevented the berries from sinking to the bottom of the muffins. Although streusel toppings can include oats, nuts, or dried fruit, tasters preferred a simple mixture of flour, butter, dark brown sugar, granulated sugar, and cinnamon. For a slightly chewy streusel texture, melted butter was a must.

STREUSEL

1¼ cups (6¼ ounces) unbleached all-purpose flour
⅓ cup (2⅓ ounces) packed dark brown sugar
⅓ cup (2⅓ ounces) granulated sugar
½ teaspoon ground cinnamon
   Pinch salt
7 tablespoons unsalted butter, melted

The sweet streusel topping adds appealing, crumbly texture to these tender, berry-filled muffins.

MUFFINS

  1 **large egg**
  1 **teaspoon vanilla extract**
  1 **cup (7 ounces) granulated sugar**
  1 **teaspoon grated lemon zest**
  4 **tablespoons unsalted butter, melted and cooled slightly**
  ½ **cup buttermilk**
  2 **cups (10 ounces) unbleached all-purpose flour**
  1 **tablespoon baking powder**
  ½ **teaspoon salt**
  1½ **cups frozen blueberries**

1. FOR THE STREUSEL: Combine the flour, sugars, cinnamon, and salt in a bowl. Drizzle with the melted butter and toss with a fork until evenly moistened and the mixture forms large chunks with some pea-sized pieces throughout.

2. FOR THE MUFFINS: Adjust an oven rack to the middle position and heat the oven to 375 degrees. Spray a standard muffin tin with nonstick cooking spray. Whisk the egg in a medium bowl until pale and evenly combined, about 30 seconds. Add the vanilla, granulated sugar, and zest and whisk vigorously until thick, about 30 seconds. Slowly whisk in the melted butter; add the buttermilk and whisk until combined.

3. Reserve 1 tablespoon flour. Whisk the remaining flour, baking powder, and salt in a large bowl. Fold in the egg mixture until nearly combined. Toss the blueberries with the reserved 1 tablespoon flour and fold into the batter until just combined.

4. Divide the batter in the prepared muffin tin and top with the streusel. Bake until light golden brown and a toothpick inserted into the center of a muffin comes out with a few dry crumbs attached, 23 to 27 minutes, rotating the pan halfway through baking. Cool the muffins in the tin for 20 minutes, then carefully transfer to a rack to cool completely.

WHERE THINGS CAN GO WRONG: To prevent a streaky batter, leave the blueberries in the freezer until the last possible moment. And resist the urge to add more blueberries than specified in the recipe as the extra moisture creates muffins with fruit-soaked bottoms.

WHAT YOU CAN DO AHEAD OF TIME: The muffins can be stored in an airtight container at room temperature for 3 days.

NOTES FROM THE TEST KITCHEN

SOGGY BOTTOM
Think more blueberries make better muffins? Think again. When more than 1½ cups of berries are used, the extra moisture creates muffins with fruit-soaked bottoms.

MIXING BLUEBERRY MUFFIN BATTER
The timing of adding the berries can make or break a blueberry muffin. If you add them too soon, the berries will break and the batter will turn blue. For perfect muffins every time, gently fold in the flour-coated berries when the dry and wet ingredients are just combined (small streaks of flour will remain).

GINGERBREAD MUFFINS

MAKES 12 MUFFINS

WHAT MAKES THIS A BEST RECIPE: Who says the complex flavors of gingerbread are just for dessert? This recipe takes the spices and molasses that make gingerbread so good and uses them in leaner, breakfast-oriented muffins. As a starting point, we chose our favorite basic muffin recipe (eggs, flour, milk, sugar, and baking powder) and got to work. To keep things simple—and avoid dragging out a standing mixer—we wanted to use the quick-bread mixing method. In this method, which is used for most types of muffins, the dry and wet ingredients are mixed together independently, then blended quickly just before baking. Melted butter lent rich flavor and incorporated easily into the batter; a couple of eggs contributed additional richness and structure. As for the liquid component, plain milk proved boring, but tangy buttermilk perfectly accented the muffin's unique flavors. Content with a base muffin, we tackled the flavorings. Blackstrap, dark, and even light molasses came on too strong in the muffin. (The additional richness of conventional gingerbread tempers all that forceful flavor.) Dark brown sugar, however, proved perfect, contributing the characteristic flavor without all the bitterness. After testing every conceivable combination of spices, we settled on a relatively simple blend of ginger, cinnamon, and allspice. A tablespoon of ground ginger brought its characteristic flavor to the fore and pulled up the earthy flavor of the dark brown sugar. Muffins this good give anyone the perfect reason to linger over a second cup of coffee.

2	cups (10 ounces) unbleached all-purpose flour
½	teaspoon baking soda
½	teaspoon salt
1	tablespoon ground ginger
2	teaspoons ground cinnamon
½	teaspoon ground allspice
2	large eggs
1½	cups (10½ ounces) packed dark brown sugar
1	cup buttermilk
8	tablespoons (1 stick) unsalted butter, melted and cooled slightly

1. Adjust an oven rack to the middle position and heat the oven to 375 degrees. Spray a standard muffin tin with nonstick cooking spray.

2. Whisk the flour, baking soda, salt, ginger, cinnamon, and allspice together in a large bowl. Whisk together the eggs, brown sugar, and buttermilk in a large bowl. Add the melted butter to the egg mixture and whisk vigorously until thick and homogeneous. Whisk half of the dry ingredients into the wet ingredients until the two begin to come together, and then add the remaining dry ingredients and stir with a rubber spatula or wooden spoon until just combined.

3. Divide the batter in the prepared muffin tin. Bake until golden and a toothpick inserted into the center of a muffin comes out clean, 18 to 22 minutes, rotating the pan halfway through baking. Cool the muffins in the tin for 5 minutes, then transfer to a wire rack and cool for 10 more minutes. Serve warm.

WHERE THINGS CAN GO WRONG: Be very careful not to overmix the muffins in step 2, which can lead to excessive gluten development and a dense squat texture.

WHAT YOU CAN DO AHEAD OF TIME: The muffins can be stored in an airtight container at room temperature for 3 days.

NOTES FROM THE TEST KITCHEN

THE BEST MUFFIN TIN

With price tags ranging from $5 to a whopping $26, we wondered if there was a good reason for shelling out the big bucks for a simple muffin tin. It turns out that there are differences in the way the tins performed. The best tins browned the muffins evenly; the worst tins browned the muffins on top, but left them pale and underbaked on the bottom. Darker coated metals, which absorb heat, do the best job of browning baked goods. Heavy-duty (and higher-priced) models did not produce muffins that were any better than those baked in the least expensive model. The supermarket staple Baker's Secret ($6.29) performed well and finished in a respectable second place. But **Wilton Ultra-Bake** ($9.99) was the clear winner, in part because of its generous 2-inch lip.

DOUBLE CORN CORNBREAD

SERVES 8 TO 10

WHAT MAKES THIS A BEST RECIPE: It's funny that something as humble as cornbread can be so polarizing. In the north, cornbread is cakey and sweet, while southerners demand theirs thin, crusty, and utterly savory. Quite frankly, we like something in between—neither too muffin-like nor too austere—tender and slightly sweet, yet dark and crunchy. Most of all, we want our cornbread bursting with bold corn flavor. This recipe for double corn cornbread hits all of our buttons. The recipe starts off conventionally enough, with a blend of equal parts of either white or yellow cornmeal. (Despite regional allegiances, tasters couldn't tell the difference between the two varieties in a blind taste test.) A little baking powder and baking soda leavens the mixture and just two tablespoons of sugar lend a welcome sweetness without making it cloying. But cornmeal alone didn't pack the rich corn flavor we wanted. Some recipes we had found swapped the conventional buttermilk used as the liquid component for a combination of sour cream (for tang) and a can of creamed corn. Tasters loved the added richness imparted by the sour cream but found the canned corn tinny. Not wanting to give up on creamed corn just yet, we made a quick homemade version by pureeing defrosted frozen kernels with the sour cream. This mixture, along with two eggs for moisture and structure, a shot of hot sauce for kick, and a little melted butter, gave the cornbread great flavor. Regardless of region, cornbread fares best in a super-hot oven, and 450 degrees proved the best temperature to form a craggy crust and prompt a high rise from the leavener. For the crunchiest, brownest bottom crust, a preheated pan (preferably cast iron, the traditional southern choice) is a must.

1 cup cornmeal (yellow or white)
1 cup (7 ounces) unbleached all-purpose flour
2 tablespoons sugar
2 teaspoons baking powder
¼ teaspoon baking soda
¾ teaspoon salt
1 cup frozen corn, thawed
1 cup sour cream
2 large eggs
½ teaspoon hot sauce
4 tablespoons unsalted butter, melted
2 teaspoons vegetable oil

1. Adjust an oven rack to the middle position and heat the oven to 450 degrees. Whisk the cornmeal, flour, sugar, baking powder, baking soda, and salt in a large bowl. Pulse the corn, sour cream, eggs, and hot sauce in a food processor until the corn is coarsely chopped and the mixture is combined. Fold the corn mixture into the cornmeal mixture, then stir in the melted butter.

2. Heat the oil in a 10-inch ovensafe skillet over medium-high heat until just beginning to smoke. Take the skillet off the heat; quickly add the batter and place the skillet in the oven. Bake until a toothpick inserted in the center comes out clean, about 25 minutes. Cool the cornbread in the skillet on a wire rack for 20 minutes (the handle will be hot). Serve warm.

NOTES FROM THE TEST KITCHEN

BAKING POWDER FRESHNESS

While we've found no discernible difference in the action or flavor of the national brands of baking powder, we have found that freshness is important and that old powder simply doesn't have the effectiveness of fresh. Check the date on the container and if it's older than 6 months, it should be tested to see if it's still good. Mix 2 teaspoons of baking powder with 1 cup of hot tap water. If there's an immediate reaction of fizzing and foaming, the baking powder is fine. If the reaction is delayed or weak, throw the baking powder away and buy a fresh can. A can of baking powder that has been opened for a year or more should always be replaced.

DON'T HAVE AN OVENSAFE SKILLET?

A cast-iron skillet (or any ovensafe pan) is our first choice for this recipe, but a 9-inch cake pan will also work. Instead of heating it on the stovetop, place the cake pan with the oil in the preheated oven for 5 minutes before adding the batter.

ALMOND RING COFFEE CAKE

MAKES 2, EACH SERVING 6

WHAT MAKES THIS A BEST RECIPE: Don't be tempted by the saccharine boxed versions at the supermarket. You can make a much better yeasted coffee cake at home—one with buttery, tender cake and a rich nut filling. One bite of this rich and almondy yeasted coffee cake and you'll never be satisfied with Entenmann's again. Most yeasted coffee cakes rely on brioche, a dough made with milk, butter, and eggs. Because the almond filling would be rich, we found that a lighter dough (made with one stick of butter and not two, as many recipes directed) was a better bet. Three egg yolks gave the dough good structure, and leaving out the whites made the dough easier to handle. (We saved the whites for gluing the garnish of sliced almonds onto the ring.) After experimenting with various amounts of granulated and brown sugar, we decided to try using honey to sweeten the dough. Tasters loved the light caramel flavor the honey contributed as well as the fact that it made the dough moister, more tender, and easier to handle. As for the filling, most recipes simply enrich cream cheese with ground almonds and sugar for the filling, but we found this combination problematic—the mixture was so soft it leaked out of the dough, and the almonds were barely perceptible. Instead, we favored a stiffer, more flavorful blend of cream cheese and rich almond paste. With the soft, malleable dough and firm filling, assembling the coffee cake couldn't have been easier. And by using a preheated and then turned-off oven as a proofing box, we were able to make the coffee cake in just a couple of hours.

FILLING

- 1 (7-ounce) tube almond paste
- ½ cup confectioners' sugar
- 4 ounces cream cheese, softened

DOUGH

- ⅓ cup warm milk (110 degrees)
- ⅓ cup honey
- 8 tablespoons (1 stick) unsalted butter, melted
- 3 large egg yolks (reserve whites for topping)
- 2 teaspoons vanilla extract
- 4½ cups unbleached all-purpose flour, plus extra for the work surface
- 1 package rapid-rise or instant yeast
- 2 teaspoons salt

TOPPING

- 3 large egg whites
- ½ cup sliced almonds
- 1½ cups confectioners' sugar
- 2 ounces cream cheese
- 2 tablespoons milk
- ½ teaspoon vanilla extract

1. FOR THE FILLING: Fit a standing mixer with the paddle attachment and mix the almond paste, confectioners' sugar, and cream cheese until smooth. Cover with plastic wrap and refrigerate until ready to use.

2. FOR THE DOUGH: Adjust the oven racks to the upper-middle and lower-middle positions and heat the oven to 200 degrees. When the oven reaches 200 degrees, shut the oven off. Lightly grease a large bowl with nonstick cooking spray. Line 2 baking sheets with parchment paper and grease with cooking spray.

3. Mix the milk, honey, melted butter, yolks, and vanilla in a large measuring cup. Mix the flour, yeast, and salt in the bowl of a standing mixer fitted with the dough hook. Turn the mixer to low and slowly add the milk mixture. After the dough comes together, increase the speed to medium and mix until shiny and smooth, 4 to 6 minutes. (Dough will be sticky.) Turn the dough onto

a heavily floured work surface, shape into a ball, and transfer to the greased bowl. Cover the bowl with plastic wrap and place in the turned-off oven until the dough is nearly doubled, about 20 minutes.

4. On a lightly floured work surface, divide the dough into 2 equal pieces. Working with one piece of dough at a time, roll the dough into an 18 by 9-inch rectangle with the long side facing you. Following the photos, spread with half of the filling and roll up the dough. Brush the top edge with water, then press to seal and transfer, seam side down, to one of the parchment-lined baking sheets. Repeat with the remaining dough and filling. Shape each cylinder into a ring. Using a paring knife, make cuts around the outside of the dough and shape as shown in the photos.

5. Cover with plastic wrap coated with cooking spray and return to the oven until the rings have puffed slightly, 30 to 40 minutes. Remove from the oven and heat the oven to 375 degrees.

6. FOR THE TOPPING: Whisk the reserved egg whites in a small bowl, then brush the rings with the beaten whites. Sprinkle with the almonds and bake until deep brown, about 25 minutes, switching and rotating the pans halfway through baking. While the rings are baking, whisk the confectioners' sugar, cream cheese, milk, and vanilla in a small bowl until smooth. Let the rings cool slightly, then drizzle with the icing and serve warm.

WHERE THINGS CAN GO WRONG: While "proofing" the dough in a warmed oven expedites the dough's rise, heating the dough too warm, above 140 degrees, can kill the yeast, so be careful and pay close attention to the oven's temperature.

WHAT YOU CAN DO AHEAD OF TIME: While both rings can be baked at once, they also freeze quite well for up to 1 month. To freeze, transfer the ring (prepared through step 4) to a large plate and wrap in two layers of plastic and then foil. The night before baking, transfer the frozen ring to the refrigerator. The next day, unwrap the ring and transfer it to a baking sheet lined with parchment paper that has been greased with cooking spray. Proceed with step 5, letting the dough rise in an oven that has been heated to 200 degrees and then turned off. Brush with the egg wash, sprinkle with the almonds, bake (on the middle rack), cool, and ice as directed.

NOTES FROM THE TEST KITCHEN

HOW TO MAKE A RING-SHAPED COFFEE CAKE

1. Spread a 1-inch-wide strip of filling about 1 inch above the bottom edge of the dough rectangle.

2. Using both hands, carefully roll the dough into an even cylinder and moisten the top ½ inch of the dough to seal.

3. Shape the dough into a ring. With a paring knife, make 11 cuts around the outside of the ring, spacing them about 1½ inches apart.

4. Rotate each piece of dough cut side up.

FREEZER BISCUITS
MAKES ABOUT 24 BISCUITS

WHAT MAKES THIS A BEST RECIPE: This recipe for freezer biscuits from *The Best Make-Ahead Recipe* produces a cut biscuit that is quick and easy to make and can be frozen and then baked in its frozen state, making it virtually an anytime biscuit, like the bags of frozen biscuits you can buy in the supermarket, only better. We used our basic cream biscuit recipe as our starting point because these biscuits are rich tasting, can be rolled and cut, and don't require cutting butter into flour. The dry ingredients (flour, sugar, baking powder, and salt) are whisked together, combined with cream, kneaded (contrary to most biscuit recipes, these actually require a quick knead to develop a bit of structure; otherwise they slump), cut, and baked. The recipe takes no more than a couple of minutes to prepare. How did our biscuits bake up from the freezer or refrigerator? Those that sat in the refrigerator overnight baked into squat round disks, nothing like those that were made right away. It seemed that the long resting period worked against our kneading, by allowing the gluten in the dough to relax. We tried kneading the dough longer, but after many attempts were forced to give up on refrigerated biscuits. Next up were frozen biscuits. Much to our delight, they baked up beautifully straight from the freezer (which halted any chance that the gluten could relax), and took only a few minutes longer to cook than those baked right away.

- 6 cups (30 ounces) unbleached all-purpose flour, plus extra for the work surface
- 2 tablespoons sugar
- 2 tablespoons baking powder
- 1½ teaspoons salt
- 4½ cups heavy cream

1. Line a rimmed baking sheet with parchment paper (if your baking sheets are small, you may need to use two); set aside. Whisk the flour, sugar, baking powder, and salt together in a large bowl. Stir in the cream with a wooden spoon until a dough forms, about 30 seconds. Turn the dough out onto a lightly floured work surface and gather into a ball. Knead the dough briefly until smooth, about 60 seconds, adding extra flour as needed if the dough is too sticky.

2. Pat the dough into a ¾-inch-thick circle. Cut out biscuits using a 2½-inch round biscuit cutter. Lay the biscuits, spaced about ½ inch apart, on the prepared baking sheet. Gather up the scraps of dough and reknead them briefly to combine, then pat the dough again into a ¾-inch-thick round and cut more biscuits; repeat this process a third time. You can either discard any remaining bits of dough or gently pat them into rustic hand-formed biscuits.

3. Wrap the baking sheet tightly in greased plastic wrap and freeze the biscuits until frozen solid, about 6 hours. Transfer the frozen biscuits to a large zipper-lock bag and freeze for up to 1 month. (Do not thaw before baking.)

4. TO BAKE: Adjust an oven rack to the upper-middle position and heat the oven to 450 degrees. Arrange the frozen biscuits, about 2 inches apart, on a parchment-lined baking sheet and bake until puffed and golden brown, 20 to 25 minutes. (If baking a large amount of biscuits, spread them out over 2 baking sheets and bake the sheets separately; do not bake both sheets at the same time.) Serve hot.

WHERE THINGS CAN GO WRONG: Contrary to most biscuit recipes, it is important to knead the dough a bit to develop some gluten for structure; otherwise the biscuits will slump once baked and fall apart. That said, the dough can be overworked, so it is important to cut out as many biscuits as possible the first time the dough is rolled out.

NOTES FROM THE TEST KITCHEN

TO BAKE IMMEDIATELY
Follow the baking instructions in step 4, but reduce the baking time to 15 to 20 minutes.

MONTE CRISTO SANDWICHES

SERVES 6

WHAT MAKES THIS A BEST RECIPE: A Monte Cristo is a decidedly odd, though thoroughly delicious sandwich. It starts out like any other grilled Swiss cheese, ham, and turkey sandwich before it is dipped in an egg and cream batter and fried—only one or two at a time—in a skillet. This lunch favorite is then served with jam, sugar, and/or syrup to create a sweet and savory combination that's hard to beat. The problem is they are the sort of thing that can be impossible to successfully prepare for a crowd—unless you have the skills of a line cook and can keep three or four skillets going at once. This recipe makes it not only possible, but easy. First of all, we abandoned the limited real estate of a skillet in favor of a broad baking sheet —so we could oven-fry the sandwiches. High heat proved crucial for adequate browning (it took some testing, but we decided 450 degrees was optimal), though heat wasn't the sole solution: The sandwiches were still on the soggy side. Exploring the options—and inspired by a Monte Cristo's close cousin, French toast—we found it necessary to toast the bread first before assembling the sandwiches, thereby eradicating excess moisture. Adding a bit of sugar to the egg coating enhanced browning. The recipe, however, doesn't stop at reinventing the cooking method; the basic formula gets a couple of upgrades as well. In addition to the sugar in the egg coating, we added a bit of dry mustard and a pinch of cayenne to maximize its flavor. And breaking with tradition, we found the unmitigated sweetness of jam simply too much for a savory sandwich. Cutting it with Dijon mustard proved so good that tasters wanted it spread inside the sandwich itself, not just served alongside.

4 large eggs

¼ cup heavy cream

2 teaspoons sugar

½ teaspoon salt

½ teaspoon dry mustard

⅛ teaspoon cayenne pepper

6 tablespoons strawberry or raspberry preserves (see page 116)

2 tablespoons Dijon mustard

12 slices high-quality white sandwich bread, lightly toasted

18 thin slices deli Swiss or Gruyère cheese

12 thin slices deli ham, preferably Black Forest

12 thin slices deli turkey

3 tablespoons vegetable oil

   Confectioners' sugar

1. Adjust an oven rack to the upper-middle position and heat the oven to 450 degrees. Whisk the eggs, cream, sugar, salt, dry mustard, and cayenne in a shallow dish until combined. Stir the jam and Dijon mustard together in a small bowl.

2. Spread 1 teaspoon of the jam mixture on one side of each slice of toast. Layer slices of cheese, ham, and turkey on 6 slices of toast. Repeat with a second layer of cheese, ham, and turkey. Add a final layer of cheese and top with the remaining toast, with the jam side facing the cheese. Using your hands, lightly press down on the sandwiches.

3. Pour the oil onto a rimmed baking sheet and heat in the oven until just smoking, about 7 minutes. Meanwhile, using 2 hands, coat each sandwich with the egg mixture and transfer to a large plate. Transfer the sandwiches to the preheated baking sheet and bake until golden brown on both sides, 4 to 5 minutes per side. Serve immediately with the remaining jam mixture and a sprinkling of confectioners' sugar.

WHERE THINGS CAN GO WRONG: Make sure to choose good-quality, dense-textured sandwich bread such as Arnold Country Classics White or Pepperidge Farm Farmhouse Hearty White; otherwise it may not be sturdy enough to absorb the egg coating. You will likely need to trim the slices of meat and cheese to fit into the bread.

NOTES FROM THE TEST KITCHEN

CRISP MONTE CRISTO SANDWICHES

Here's how we got crisp sandwiches without frying.

TOASTED BREAD
Toasting the bread jump-starts browning and helps keep it from turning soggy when coated with batter.

SWEET BATTER
Coating the sandwiches in an egg batter that contains a bit of sugar encourages browning and crispness.

HOT PAN
Preheating the oil and baking sheet makes the sandwiches sizzle when they hit the pan; they begin to crisp right away.

THE BEST STRAWBERRY PRESERVES

To find out which brand of strawberry preserves we liked best, we rounded up eight nationally available brands and headed into the tasting lab. Our big winners were two familiar names: **Welch's** (left) and **Smucker's** (right). Unlike other brands, they were not too sweet and packed big, distinct strawberry flavor. Oddly enough, they contain more total sugar (from the fruit and corn syrup as well as the sugar) than most of the other brands but we didn't perceive them as too sweet because they have less pure sugar (which tastes sweeter). They also are more acidic (we measured the pH) which helps give them a better, more rounded strawberry flavor.

OLIVE-ROSEMARY BREAD
MAKES TWO 12 BY 3-INCH LOAVES

WHAT MAKES THIS A BEST RECIPE: One of our favorite breads is flavored with olives and the subtle perfume of rosemary, but unless your neighborhood is blessed with a great bread bakery, you're probably stuck with the gummy, bland stuff the supermarkets pass off as "rustic" bread. That is, until you try this recipe. Most hearty-style breads start off with bread flour and very-high moisture content, but we quickly discovered that a wet dough combined with olives yielded an unmanageable, sticky mass of dough that baked into a heavy, gummy bread. Clearly the olives contributed a good deal of extra moisture, so we reduced the standard ratio of water to flour. We kept the bread flour for its high protein level, but added a little whole wheat flour and honey for flavor. While most rustic breads start off with a "sponge," or blend of flour, water, and yeast, we didn't think the extra effort was necessary. Instead, we found autolyse (allowing the mixture of flours, water, and yeast to rest for 20 minutes so that the flour has more time to absorb the water) was instrumental to successful kneading and a great texture. Turning the dough during the first rise, or folding the dough in onto itself, also drastically improved its elasticity and strength, which resulted in larger holes in the bread and a heartier chew. Misting the loaves in the first few minutes they were in the oven guaranteed a thick, well-browned, crunchy crust. But the dough resisted all efforts to incorporate the slippery olives, whether by hand or machine. On the verge of pulling our hair out, we figured that rolling the olives up into the dough before the first and second rises was the answer. We finally had a well-textured loaf with evenly dispersed olives. And the final touch was a whopping 2 tablespoons of chopped fresh rosemary to suffuse the loaves with a rich herbiness.

1¾ cups water, room temperature

2 teaspoons rapid-rise or instant yeast

2 tablespoons honey

3½ cups (19¼ ounces) bread flour, plus extra for the dough and work surface

½ cup (2¾ ounces) whole wheat flour

2 teaspoons salt

2 tablespoons chopped fresh rosemary

1½ cups pitted black olives, rinsed, chopped rough, and patted dry

Crisp crust, chewy crumb, and big olive flavor equal one perfect loaf.

1. Whisk the water, yeast, and honey in the bowl of a standing mixer fitted with a dough hook. Add the flours and mix on low speed until a cohesive dough is formed, about 3 minutes. Cover the bowl with plastic wrap and let sit at room temperature for 20 minutes.

2. Remove the plastic wrap; make a well in the center of the dough and add the salt and rosemary. Knead the dough on low speed for 5 minutes (if the dough creeps up the attachment, stop the mixer and scrape down). Increase the speed to medium and continue to knead until the dough is smooth and slightly tacky, about 1 minute. If the dough is very sticky, add 1 to 2 table-spoons flour and continue mixing for 1 minute. Transfer the dough to a lightly floured work surface and pat into a 12 by 6-inch rectangle. Following the photos on page 118, press the olives evenly into the dough. Starting at the long side, roll the rectangle into a tight log. With the seam side up, roll the log into a coil. Transfer the dough, spiral side up, to an oiled container or bowl, at least 2 quarts in volume, and cover with plastic wrap. Let the dough rise in a warm, draft-free place until it increases in size by 50 percent, about 1 hour.

3. Fold the partially risen dough over itself. Turn the bowl 90 degrees; fold again. Turn the bowl again; fold once more. Cover with plastic wrap and let rise 30 minutes. Repeat the folding, replace the plastic wrap, and let rise until doubled in volume, about 30 minutes.

4. Transfer the dough to a lightly floured work surface, being careful not to deflate it. Divide the dough in half, loosely shape each piece into a ball, and let rest 15 minutes. Flip each ball over and, starting from the top, roll into a tight oval shape. Using your palms, roll each oval (seam side down) from the center outward until a

12-inch loaf is formed. Poke any olives that fall off into the bottom seam, then pinch the seam closed. Transfer each loaf, seam side down, to a 12 by 6-inch piece of parchment and cover with plastic wrap. Let rise until doubled in size, 1 to 1½ hours (the dough is ready when it springs back slowly when pressed lightly with a finger). Meanwhile, adjust an oven rack to the lower-middle position, place a baking stone on the rack, and heat the oven to 450 degrees at least 30 minutes before baking.

5. Slide the parchment sheets with the loaves onto a peel or the back of an inverted baking sheet. Starting and stopping about 1 inch from each side, use a razor blade or sharp knife to cut three ½-inch-deep slashes on the diagonal along the top of each fully risen loaf; spray the loaves lightly with water. Carefully slide the parchment with the loaves into the oven using a jerk-ing motion. Bake 15 minutes, spraying the loaves with water twice more in the first 5 minutes, and then reduce the oven temperature to 375 degrees. Continue to bake until the bread is deep golden brown and an instant-read thermometer inserted into the center of a loaf registers 210 degrees, 25 to 30 minutes. Transfer the loaves to a wire rack, discard the parchment, and cool to room temperature, about 2 hours.

WHAT YOU CAN DO AHEAD OF TIME: The bread can be wrapped tightly in plastic wrap and stored at room temperature for up to 2 days. To recrisp the crust, place the bread in a 450-degree oven for 5 to 10 minutes. The bread can be frozen for several months wrapped in foil and placed in a large zipper-lock bag.

GREAT DISCOVERIES

TURNED, NOT PUNCHED

Most bread recipes call for punching down the dough between the first and second rises. Despite its name, punching down is best accomplished by pressing down gently on the dough. This process exposes the yeast to new food sources, which keeps it going strong longer. Punching also "degasses" the bread, resulting in a loaf with a fairly fine crumb—perfect for sandwich bread, but not for a rustic loaf. To create a coarser crumb with better chew, I discovered that turning the dough (gently folding it over onto itself between the first and second rises) reactivates the yeast without pressing out as much air.

ERIKA BRUCE | ASSOCIATE EDITOR, *COOK'S ILLUSTRATED*

PUNCHED
This bread bakes up with a tight, more regular crumb, better suited to sandwich bread.

TURNED
This bread bakes up with a coarse, open crumb and chewy texture, better suited to rustic bread.

NOTES FROM THE TEST KITCHEN

MAKING OLIVE-ROSEMARY BREAD

1. After patting the dough into a 12 by 6-inch rectangle, press the olives evenly into the dough.

2. With the long side facing you, roll the rectangle into a tight log.

3. Make sure the seam side is facing up, then roll the log into a coil. Place the dough, spiral side up, in an oiled bowl.

4. Cover the bowl with plastic wrap and let the dough rise until doubled in size. Follow the recipe for further rising and shaping.

BENCH SCRAPERS

Bread bakers rely on metal bench scrapers—broad, slightly blunt blades with handles that span the length of the metal—to cut through plump rounds of yeast bread or biscuit dough or to scrape sticky dough loose from the counter. We tested six models and found we most preferred those with flatter plastic, rubber, or nylon grips. While it wasn't the most comfortable one we tested, we most liked the **OXO Scraper** ($7.99) because of its ruler mark-engraved blade and its considerably thinner edge than those of the other models, which was perfectly suited to another common bench scraper task—scooping up chopped herbs and vegetables.

CORN DODGERS

MAKES 22

WHAT MAKES THIS A BEST RECIPE: Abraham Lincoln was raised on these little oval cornmeal cakes, George Washington Carver took them to school, and John Wayne used them for target practice in the movie *True Grit*. Dating back to the 1800s, the first corn dodgers were made from "hot water corn bread," a mixture of cornmeal, pork fat, salt, and boiling water that was formed into small oblong loaves and baked. A recipe with so much heritage really deserves to see the light of day, which was the goal of its inclusion in *America's Best Lost Recipes*. Maybe our tastes have changed through the generations, but most of the nineteenth-century recipes that we tried weren't terribly interesting. We added a bit of sugar to bring out the cornmeal's sweet side and replaced some of the water with buttermilk for a tangy flavor that everyone enjoyed. Baking soda (which reacts with the buttermilk) and baking powder helped to lighten the dodgers considerably, and a single egg provided richness to the lean batter and gave the dodgers a creamy interior. All was well except for the cornmeal, which remained hard and gritty even when mixed with hot water. Some recipes required resting the dough overnight to soften the cornmeal. But, being impatient, we simmered the cornmeal in hot water and buttermilk. Cooled, shaped, and baked, these corn dodgers were crisp on the outside and creamy on the inside.

2	tablespoons corn or vegetable oil
2	cups yellow cornmeal
1½	tablespoons sugar
½	teaspoon baking soda
½	teaspoon salt
2	cups water, plus extra for forming the dodgers
1	cup buttermilk
1	tablespoon unsalted butter
2	teaspoons baking powder
1	large egg

These easy-to-make cornmeal cakes were popular with Civil War soldiers and pioneers heading West.

1. Adjust an oven rack to the middle position and heat the oven to 450 degrees. Spread 1 tablespoon of the oil on a rimmed baking sheet.

2. Whisk the cornmeal, sugar, baking soda, and salt in a medium bowl. Combine the water, buttermilk, and butter in a large saucepan. In a slow, steady stream, whisk the cornmeal mixture into the liquid. Cook the mixture over medium-high heat, whisking constantly, until the water is absorbed and the mixture is very thick, about 6 minutes. Remove from the heat and cool until warm, about 10 minutes.

3. Whisk the baking powder and egg in a small bowl, then stir into the cornmeal mixture. Fill a medium bowl with tap water. Scoop out a generous 2 tablespoons of the mixture and, using wet hands, form into a 4 by 1½-inch loaf shape. Place on the prepared baking sheet and repeat with the remaining mixture, spacing the dodgers about ½ inch apart. Brush with the remaining 1 tablespoon oil. Bake until deep brown on the bottom and golden brown on top, rotating the pan halfway through baking, 25 to 30 minutes. Transfer the corn dodgers to a wire rack to cool slightly. Serve warm.

WHAT YOU CAN DO AHEAD OF TIME: The corn dodgers, wrapped tightly in plastic wrap, can be refrigerated for up to 2 days and reheated on a baking sheet in a 350-degree oven.

BREAD BAKING DEMYSTIFIED

9 BREAD MYTHS YOU SHOULDN'T BELIEVE

MYTH #1:
BREAD FLOUR IS BEST

Unbleached all-purpose flour is the best choice in most bread recipes. Bread flour (which has more protein than all-purpose) is necessary only for rustic breads with a sturdy crumb and thick crust.

MYTH #2:
TAP WATER IS FINE

Water from the tap can contain many minerals and additives that adversely affect the flavor of bread. In our experience, bread made with bottled water has a sweeter, fuller flavor than bread made with tap water.

MYTH #3:
SALT IS OPTIONAL

If salt comes in direct contact with yeast, it will kill the yeast so it should be added to the dough after the yeast has been mixed with the flour. Because salt controls the activity of yeast, strengthens gluten, and accents the bread's flavor, it should never be omitted.

MYTH #4:
YEAST MUST BE PROOFED

Older books tell you to sprinkle yeast over warm water and wait five minutes before proceeding. This process, called proofing the yeast, is no longer necessary. Our test kitchen relies on instant yeast (also labeled rapid-rise yeast) and adds the yeast directly to the dry ingredients.

MYTH #5: ALWAYS START
WITH A SPONGE

A sponge is made by mixing a portion of the flour, water, and yeast before the dough is made. This sponge is then allowed to ferment for several hours or overnight before the dough is prepared. Although a sponge does impart a great deal of flavor to rustic breads, it isn't necessary with higher-fat loaf breads.

MYTH #6:
HAND-KNEADING IS BETTER

Kneading in a standing mixer is our technique of choice. (Use the paddle attachment to combine ingredients, then switch to the dough hook to knead.) A standing mixer is especially suited for kneading wet or sticky dough.

MYTH #7:
YOU CAN'T OVERKNEAD

Prolonged kneading will overoxidize the dough, which leads to flavor loss. When properly kneaded, dough should have a smooth, almost shiny appearance. If you pull the dough, it should feel very stretchy and quickly spring back into place.

MYTH #8:
RISING TIMES ARE FLEXIBLE

While there is some flexibility in the first rise, it is important to pay close attention during the second rise. Underproofed, dough might rise too much when baked, splitting and tearing. Overproofed, dough may collapse when baked. Properly proofed dough will feel spongy when pressed and the indentation will slowly fill in.

MYTH #9: BAKED BREAD
WILL SOUND HOLLOW

Many recipes instruct the baker to tap the bottom of the loaf to check the bread's doneness—if it sounds hollow, then it's done. We have found this technique to be inexact. It is much better to use an instant-read thermometer. Rustic breads should be baked to an internal temperature of 200 to 210 degrees, while richer breads are done at 190 to 195 degrees.

To test a free-form loaf, turn the bread over using an oven mitt or potholder and insert a thermometer through the bottom crust into the center of the loaf.

To test bread baked in a loaf pan, insert a thermometer from the side, just above the edge of the loaf pan, directing it at a downward angle toward the center of the loaf.

BREAD MAKING AT A GLANCE

1. MEASURE

The ratio of flour to water greatly impacts the end result, so we recommend weighing ingredients.

2. MIX

Mixing starts the development of gluten.

3. AUTOLYSE

A rest after mixing (autolyse) allows the flour to completely absorb the moisture and makes kneading quicker and easier.

4. KNEAD

Kneading develops the gluten strands in the dough, which in turn provide the bread's structure.

5. FERMENT

During fermentation the starches in the flour break down to feed the yeast, which then releases carbon dioxide, giving the bread lift. We ferment dough in a clear, straight-sided container, which allows us to easily judge when the dough has properly risen. It is also helpful to mark the height of the dough by placing a rubber band around the container.

6. PUNCH DOWN

Punching down helps redistribute the yeast and allows it to find new food, ultimately leading to bread with a better texture. Pull the edges of the dough toward the center or push down gently on the dough.

7. SHAPE

Form the dough into the desired shape on an unfloured work surface, which allows the dough to grip the counter, thus facilitating shaping.

8. PROOF

Proofing is the dough's final rise before baking which gives the yeast one last burst of activity in the hot oven.

9. SLASH

Slashing the proofed loaf allows the crust to expand and prevents the bread from splitting in the oven.

10. ADD WATER

Misting the loaf right before baking delays the formation of a crust, allowing the bread to fully expand without tearing or splitting, while the steam promotes a crispy, glossy crust.

11. BAKE

A baking stone helps keep the oven temperature steady and promote a thicker, crispier crust on free-form loaves.

12. COOL

Cooling on a rack allows moisture to escape and keeps the bottom crust from becoming soggy. Breads that are baked in a loaf pan should be removed from the pan as soon as possible.

PASTA

SPAGHETTI WITH FRIED EGGS AND BREAD CRUMBS 124

PENNE ALLA VODKA 126

BAKED MANICOTTI 129

CREAMY BAKED PENNE AND CHICKEN WITH ARTICHOKES,
TARRAGON, AND LEMON 131

LOW-FAT MEATY LASAGNA 132

PASTA WITH FRESH TOMATO SAUCE WITH ROSEMARY AND BACON 135

MEATBALLS AND MARINARA 136

SLOW-COOKER ITALIAN SUNDAY GRAVY 138

PASTA SALAD WITH PESTO 140

ANTIPASTO PASTA SALAD 141

SPAGHETTI
WITH FRIED EGGS AND BREAD CRUMBS
SERVES 4

WHAT MAKES THIS A BEST RECIPE: Pasta with fried eggs, sometimes known as Salerno style (Salerno is a town that lies just south of Naples), is a perfect pantry dinner. We love this recipe because it solves a universal dilemma: Just when you think you have nothing to cook for dinner, in minutes you can whip up a warm bowl of garlicky pasta topped with a fried egg. *Presto!* We found out, though, that while this dish is simple, the timing here is important. Using a preheated nonstick skillet, we were able to create perfectly fried eggs with whites that were firm and yolks that were still runny. As for the all-important timing, we had success when we waited to fry the eggs (they cook in 2 to 3 minutes) until just after the spaghetti was drained (we gave the skillet for the eggs a head start by preheating it as the pasta finished cooking). To keep the pasta from sticking together or drying out while waiting on the eggs, we tossed it with the other ingredients along with a splash of the pasta cooking water and held it in the pasta cooking pot (still warm from cooking the pasta) with the lid on. To add flavor to our pasta, we cooked garlic slowly in olive oil until it turned golden and mellow, far more complex in texture and tone than quickly sautéed garlic. Parmesan cheese added a nutty depth of flavor, a little parsley imparted freshness, and a pinch of red pepper flakes provided a spicy kick. For contrasting texture to this otherwise soft-textured dish, we sprinkled crispy homemade bread crumbs on top of the pasta just before adding the eggs. This rustic Italian dish is comfort food at its very best.

2 slices high-quality white sandwich bread, torn into quarters

10 tablespoons extra-virgin olive oil
Salt and pepper

4 garlic cloves, minced

¼–½ teaspoon red pepper flakes

1 pound spaghetti

1 ounce Parmesan cheese, grated (about ½ cup), plus extra for serving

¼ cup minced fresh parsley

4 large eggs, cracked into 2 small bowls (2 eggs per bowl)

1. Adjust an oven rack to the middle position and heat the oven to 375 degrees. Pulse the bread in a food processor to coarse crumbs, about 10 pulses. Toss the bread with 2 tablespoons of the oil and season with salt and pepper. Spread the crumbs out over a rimmed baking sheet and bake, stirring often, until golden brown, 8 to 10 minutes; set aside.

2. Bring 4 quarts water to a boil in a large pot for the pasta. Meanwhile, cook 3 more tablespoons of the oil, garlic, pepper flakes, and ¼ teaspoon salt in a 12-inch nonstick skillet over low heat, stirring constantly, until the garlic foams, is sticky, and straw-colored, 8 to 10 minutes. Transfer the garlic mixture to a small bowl; set aside. Wipe the skillet clean with paper towels and set aside.

3. Add 1 tablespoon salt and the pasta to the boiling water. Cook, stirring often, until the pasta is al dente. A minute or two before draining the pasta, return the skillet to low heat for 5 minutes (for the eggs). Reserve 1 cup of the pasta cooking water, drain the pasta, and return it to the pot. Stir in ½ cup of the reserved pasta cooking water, the garlic mixture, 3 more tablespoons of the oil, Parmesan, parsley, and ¾ teaspoon salt and toss to combine. Cover and set aside to keep warm while cooking the eggs.

4. When the skillet is hot, add the remaining 2 tablespoons oil and swirl to coat the pan. Following the

photo on page 126, quickly add the eggs to the skillet. Season the eggs with salt and pepper, cover, and cook until the whites are set but the yolks are still runny, 2 to 3 minutes. Uncover and remove the pan from the heat.

5. Loosen the pasta with the remaining ½ cup cooking water as needed, then divide the pasta among 4 serving bowls. Sprinkle each bowl with 2 tablespoons of the reserved toasted bread crumbs. Carefully slide 1 fried egg on top of the pasta in each bowl. Serve immediately, passing the Parmesan separately.

WHERE THINGS CAN GO WRONG: Timing is key here—to ensure perfectly cooked pasta and eggs, drain the pasta just moments before cooking the eggs (but make sure the skillet preheats for 5 minutes before adding the eggs). Use a nonstick skillet when cooking the eggs or they will not release easily from the pan.

NOTES FROM THE TEST KITCHEN

GETTING THE EGGS INTO THE PAN

Crack the eggs into two small bowls, before sliding them into the hot skillet simultaneously from opposite sides of the pan.

RESERVING THE PASTA WATER
When draining pasta, it's easy to forget to reserve some of the pasta cooking water (for adding to the sauce or to moisten a dry pasta dish), so try this: Before cooking the pasta, set up the colander in the sink, then place a measuring cup inside the colander. It's sure to nudge your memory at the appropriate moment.

PENNE ALLA VODKA
SERVES 4 TO 6

WHAT MAKES THIS A BEST RECIPE: Penne alla vodka is one of our favorite pasta dishes, yet most versions are absurdly rich, containing more cream than tomatoes; others added too much vodka too late, yielding soupy, boozy sauces. We fine-tuned this modern classic to strike the right balance of sweet, tangy, spicy, and creamy. As with most dishes that look simple on paper, this one finds success in its proportions and timing. The recipe begins with a basic tomato sauce of canned tomatoes— we pureed half and chopped half to achieve the perfect consistency—onion, garlic, tomato paste, and red pepper flakes. While many recipes add the vodka to the tomato sauce along with the heavy cream near the end, we found that no matter how much restraint we mustered, the sauce tasted boozy. Trial and error taught us to add a liberal amount of vodka along with the tomatoes so that the alcohol mostly—but not completely—cooked off. To finish the sauce, we swirled in ½ cup of heavy cream for a luxurious but not over-the-top consistency. Letting the penne finish cooking in the sauce (a standard Italian method) encouraged cohesiveness. We then garnished the pasta with chopped basil and grated Parmesan.

1	(28-ounce) can whole tomatoes, drained and liquid reserved
2	tablespoons extra-virgin olive oil
¼	cup minced onion
1	tablespoon tomato paste
2	garlic cloves, minced
¼–½	teaspoon red pepper flakes
	Salt
⅓	cup vodka
½	cup heavy cream
1	pound penne
2	tablespoons minced fresh basil
	Grated Parmesan cheese, for serving

For our Penne Alla Vodka, a liberal dose of vodka cooks along with the sauce which is then finished with cream.

1. Puree half of the tomatoes in a food processor until smooth, about 20 seconds. Chop the remaining tomatoes into ½-inch pieces, discarding the cores. Combine the pureed and diced tomatoes in a liquid measuring cup (you should have about 1⅔ cups). Add the reserved liquid to equal 2 cups.

2. Heat the oil in a large saucepan over medium heat until shimmering. Add the onion and tomato paste and cook, stirring occasionally, until the onion is light golden around the edges, about 3 minutes. Stir in the garlic and pepper flakes and cook until fragrant, about 30 seconds.

3. Stir in the tomatoes and ½ teaspoon salt. Remove the pan from the heat and add the vodka. Return the pan to medium-high heat and simmer, stirring frequently, until the alcohol flavor is cooked off, 8 to 10 minutes. (Lower the heat to medium if the simmering becomes too vigorous.) Stir in the cream and cook until hot, about 1 minute.

4. Meanwhile, bring 4 quarts water to a boil in a large pot for the pasta. Add 1 tablespoon salt and the pasta to the boiling water. Cook, stirring often, until the pasta is just shy of al dente. Reserve ¼ cup of the pasta cooking water, drain the pasta, and return it to the pot. Stir in the sauce and toss to combine. Cook over medium heat until the pasta absorbs some of the sauce, about 1½ minutes.

Thin the sauce with the reserved pasta cooking water as needed. Stir in the basil and season with salt to taste. Serve, passing the Parmesan separately.

WHERE THINGS CAN GO WRONG: Do not drop the pasta into the boiling water until just after you add the vodka to the sauce, or it will be cooked before the sauce is ready. Make sure to cook your pasta until not quite al dente, as it will cook further (and absorb some of the sauce) when it is combined with the sauce in step 4.

WHAT YOU CAN DO AHEAD OF TIME: The sauce can be made through step 3 and refrigerated in an airtight container for up to 2 days or frozen for up to 1 month.

NOTES FROM THE TEST KITCHEN

OUR FAVORITE VODKA

Does vodka quality matter in our penne recipe? To find out, we conducted a taste test of sauces made with six brands of vodka, ranging in price from $6.99 to $34 per bottle. To our surprise, 9 out of 10 tasters favored the sauce made with the most expensive vodka, noting a "fresher," "cleaner" flavor. It turns out that cheap vodkas are distilled only once to remove harsh tastes, while "premium" and "super-premium" brands are filtered three or more times—and you can taste the difference, even in a tomato sauce. You don't necessarily need to cook with **Grey Goose** (winner of this taste test), but don't ruin your sauce with rotgut vodka you'd never drink on its own.

THE BEST TOMATO PASTE

Tomato paste is basically tomato puree with most of the moisture cooked out. Tomato paste adds body, color, and intensity to many dishes. Here in the test kitchen, we discovered that a tablespoon of tomato paste deepened the tomato flavor in our vodka sauce and improved its color. We simply sautéed the tomato paste with onion, which darkened its color as it intensified its flavor. We find that no-fuss tubes of tomato paste are more convenient than cans, and **Amore** was the hands-down winner in a recent tasting.

BAKED MANICOTTI

SERVES 6 TO 8

WHAT MAKES THIS A BEST RECIPE: We have a love-hate relationship with manicotti here in the test kitchen. Well-made versions—pasta tubes stuffed with rich ricotta filling and blanketed with tomato sauce—can be eminently satisfying, but the preparation is surprisingly fussy: blanching, shocking, draining, and stuffing slippery pasta tubes require more patience (and time) than we usually have. We wanted a simpler, better recipe. To eliminate the assembly problems associated with manicotti tubes, we turned to no-boil lasagna noodles which, when soaked, mimicked fresh pasta. After a quick soak in boiling water, we spread the softened no-boil lasagna noodles with filling, rolled them up in a few minutes, and arranged them seam side down in a baking dish. As for the filling, we used the traditional combination of ricotta, mozzarella, and Parmesan, and boosted the flavor with parsley and basil. We made a bright, fresh, 15-minute tomato sauce with olive oil, garlic, and canned diced tomatoes pureed in a food processor to give the sauce body. We then punched up our quick recipe with fresh basil leaves and a dash of red pepper flakes before spooning it over the stuffed pasta. For a browned, cheesy topping, we added a light sprinkling of Parmesan and passed the casserole under the broiler before serving.

TOMATO SAUCE

- 2 (28-ounce) cans diced tomatoes in juice
- 2 tablespoons extra-virgin olive oil
- 3 garlic cloves, minced
- ½ teaspoon red pepper flakes (optional)
  Salt
- 2 tablespoons chopped fresh basil

CHEESE FILLING AND PASTA

- 3 cups part-skim ricotta cheese
- 4 ounces Parmesan cheese, grated (about 2 cups)
- 8 ounces mozzarella, shredded (about 2 cups)
- 2 large eggs, lightly beaten
- ¾ teaspoon salt
- ½ teaspoon pepper
- 2 tablespoons chopped fresh parsley
- 2 tablespoons chopped fresh basil
- 16 no-boil lasagna noodles (see page 130)

1. FOR THE TOMATO SAUCE: Pulse 1 can of the tomatoes with their juice in a food processor until coarsely chopped, four 1-second pulses. Transfer to a bowl. Repeat with the remaining can of tomatoes.

2. Heat the oil, garlic, and pepper flakes (if using) in a large saucepan over medium heat until fragrant but not brown, about 1½ minutes. Stir in the tomatoes and ½ teaspoon salt and simmer until thickened slightly, about 15 minutes. Off the heat, stir in the basil and season with salt to taste.

3. FOR THE CHEESE FILLING: Combine the ricotta, 1 cup of the Parmesan, mozzarella, eggs, salt, pepper, parsley, and basil in a medium bowl; set aside.

4. TO ASSEMBLE: Adjust the oven racks to the upper-middle and lower-middle positions and heat the oven to 375 degrees. Pour 1 inch of boiling water into a 13 by 9-inch broiler-safe baking dish, then add noodles one at a time. Following the photos on page 130, soak the noodles until pliable, about 5 minutes, separating the noodles with the tip of a sharp knife to prevent sticking. Remove the noodles from the water and place in a single layer on clean kitchen towels; discard the water in the baking dish and wipe the baking dish dry.

5. Spread the bottom of the baking dish evenly with 1½ cups sauce. Spread ¼ cup of the cheese filling evenly onto the bottom three-quarters of each noodle (with the short side facing you), leaving the top quarter of noodle exposed. Roll into a tube shape and arrange in the baking dish seam side down. Top evenly with the remaining sauce, making certain that the pasta is completely covered. Cover the manicotti with foil and bake on the lower-middle rack until bubbling, about 40 minutes.

6. Remove the baking dish from the oven and discard the foil. Turn the oven to broil. Sprinkle the manicotti evenly with the remaining 1 cup Parmesan. Broil on the upper-middle rack until the cheese is spotty brown, 4 to 6 minutes. Cool for 15 minutes before serving.

WHERE THINGS CAN GO WRONG: When soaking the noodles, it is important to add them to the water one at a time, to separate them with the tip of a sharp knife as they soak, and to arrange them in a single layer on clean kitchen towels when removing them from the water, or they will stick together and make rolling the manicotti nearly impossible.

WHAT YOU CAN DO AHEAD OF TIME: The assembled, unbaked manicotti can be wrapped tightly with plastic wrap and then foil and refrigerated for up to 2 days or frozen for up to 1 month. (If frozen, the manicotti must be thawed completely in the refrigerator, about 24 hours.) To bake, heat the oven to 375 degrees and bake the casserole, covered with foil, 1 to 1¼ hours, then proceed with the recipe as directed in step 6.

NOTES FROM THE TEST KITCHEN

MANICOTTI 1, 2, 3
In our streamlined recipe, the ricotta filling is spread onto softened no-boil lasagna noodles, eliminating the slippery task of stuffing parboiled manicotti shells.

1. Soak no-boil lasagna noodles in boiling water for 5 minutes until pliable, using the tip of a paring knife to separate the noodles and prevent sticking.

2. Using a soup spoon, spread about ¼ cup filling onto three-quarters of each noodle, leaving the top quarter of each noodle exposed.

3. Roll each noodle by hand and place in a baking dish, seam side down.

NO SHORTCUT AT ALL

Many manicotti recipes replace the traditional pastry bag used for stuffing the shells with a zipper-lock plastic bag. But using a plastic bag to stuff parboiled pasta tubes is a messy, frustrating job. Our simple recipe requires only a spoon.

THE BEST NOODLE
Over the past few years, no-boil (also called oven-ready) lasagna noodles have become a permanent fixture on supermarket shelves. Much like "instant rice," no-boil noodles are precooked at the factory. The extruded noodles are run through a water bath and then dehydrated mechanically. During baking, the moisture from the sauce softens, or rehydrates the noodles, especially when the pan is covered as the lasagna bakes. For both our lasagna and manicotti recipes, we prefer **Barilla** no-boil lasagna noodles for their delicate texture which resembles fresh pasta. Note that Pasta Defino and Ronzoni brands contain only 12 no-boil noodles per package; the manicotti recipe requires 16 noodles.

OUR FAVORITE RICOTTA CHEESE
Originally crafted from the whey by-product of Romano cheesemaking, ricotta cheese has garnered fame on its own as a white, cushiony filling for baked pasta dishes. As ricotta has gained global popularity, however, preservation methods used by many large-scale manufacturers have turned these once fluffy, buttery, sweet curds into chalky, sour spreads. Seeking at least one noble specimen, we sampled four nationally available brands of part-skim ricotta. All three commercial brands that we tried—Dragone, Sargento, and Sorrento—consistently garnered unfavorable adjectives, such as "grainy," "soggy," and "rancid." Incidentally, they are all packed with gums and other stabilizers to guarantee shelf-stability for weeks. At the other end of the spectrum entirely sat **Calabro**, with its fresh curds—drawn from nothing other than Vermont farm whole milk, skim milk, a starter, and a sprinkle of salt. Granted, the latter's shelf life spans only a matter of days, but one spoonful should be enough to guarantee its quick disappearance from your fridge. If you can't find Calabro, read labels and look for another fresh ricotta without gums or stabilizers.

CREAMY BAKED PENNE AND CHICKEN
WITH ARTICHOKES, TARRAGON, AND LEMON
SERVES 8

WHAT MAKES THIS A BEST RECIPE: Pasta and chicken are such popular ingredients on their own that we figured teaming them up in a casserole would be a smash hit. We wanted a pasta casserole that turned out juicy chunks of chicken and tender (not mushy!) pasta, all bound together with a creamy, well-seasoned sauce. We made a light-tasting, but flavorful cream sauce by sautéing onions and garlic, then adding white wine, chicken broth, and cream, and allowing it to simmer, thicken, and reduce before finishing with an Italian cheese blend. To keep our pasta from being overcooked and mushy, we boiled it for only 5 minutes (at which point the pasta is still quite raw) before tossing it with the remaining ingredients and baking. In the oven, the pasta absorbed some of the sauce and cooked through, but still retained some of its texture. For the chicken, we poached boneless, skinless breasts in the sauce, and then shredded them and stirred them into the casserole—this allowed the chicken to take on some of the sauce's flavor and vice versa. To give the casserole more oomph and elevate it to an elegant, company-worthy dish, we added artichoke hearts, lemon juice, and fresh tarragon.

Salt
1 pound penne
4 tablespoons olive oil
3 (9-ounce) boxes frozen artichokes, thawed, patted dry, and chopped coarse
1 onion, minced (about 1 cup)
8 garlic cloves, minced

¼ teaspoon grated lemon zest, plus 3 tablespoons juice from 2 lemons
¼ cup unbleached all-purpose flour
2 cups low-sodium chicken broth
1 cup dry white wine
1 cup heavy cream
2 pounds boneless, skinless chicken breasts, trimmed
3 bay leaves
8 ounces shredded Italian cheese blend (about 2 cups) (see page 132)
1½ cups frozen peas
Pepper
3 tablespoons minced fresh tarragon

1. Adjust an oven rack to the middle position and heat the oven to 400 degrees. Bring 4 quarts water to a boil in a large pot for the pasta. Add 1 tablespoon salt and the pasta to the boiling water. Cook, stirring often, until the pasta is just beginning to soften, about 5 minutes. Drain the pasta, toss with 1 tablespoon of the oil, and set aside.

2. Wipe the pot dry, then add the remaining 3 tablespoons oil and heat over medium heat until shimmering. Add the artichokes, onion, and 1 teaspoon salt and cook until the artichokes are lightly browned, 8 to 10 minutes.

3. Stir in the garlic and lemon zest and cook until fragrant, about 30 seconds. Stir in the flour and cook, stirring constantly, until golden, about 1 minute. Slowly whisk in the broth, wine, and cream.

4. Add the chicken breasts and bay leaves and bring to a simmer. Reduce the heat to low, cover, and cook until the thickest part of the chicken registers 160 degrees on an instant-read thermometer, 10 to 15 minutes.

5. Remove the pot from the heat and remove and discard the bay leaves. Transfer the chicken to a plate and set aside to cool; keep the sauce covered. When the chicken is cool enough to handle, shred it into bite-sized pieces. Stir the cooked pasta, shredded chicken,

1 cup of the cheese, peas, and lemon juice into the sauce. Season with salt and pepper to taste. Transfer to a 13 by 9-inch baking dish and sprinkle with the remaining 1 cup cheese.

6. Bake until the sauce is bubbling around the edges and the top is browned, 25 to 35 minutes. Sprinkle with the tarragon before serving.

WHERE THINGS CAN GO WRONG: Remember to cook the pasta just until it is beginning to soften or it will become overcooked and mushy when it bakes in the oven.

WHAT YOU CAN DO AHEAD OF TIME: The assembled, unbaked casserole can be wrapped tightly with plastic wrap and then foil and refrigerated for up to 2 days or frozen for up to 1 month. (If frozen, the casserole must be thawed completely in the refrigerator, about 24 hours.) To bake, heat the oven to 400 degrees and bake the casserole, covered with foil, 30 to 40 minutes. Remove the foil and continue to bake until hot throughout and browned on top, 25 to 30 minutes longer. Before serving, sprinkle with the tarragon.

NOTES FROM THE TEST KITCHEN

SHREDDED ITALIAN CHEESE BLEND
The refrigerator section of our local supermarket practically overflows with varieties of preshredded cheese, but the flavorful combination known as Italian cheese blend (a mix of 4 or 5 cheeses, often mozzarella, provolone, Parmesan, fontina, and Asiago) caught our attention. It is certainly convenient, adding flavor dimension to many dishes without the need to buy four types of cheese at the supermarket.

LOW-FAT MEATY LASAGNA
SERVES 8

WHAT MAKES THIS A BEST RECIPE: When it comes to lasagna, our favorite type is lasagna *Bolognese*, which lives up to its fancy name with two sauces—a rich meat sauce simmered for hours with milk or cream as well as a creamy white sauce (called *béchamel*)—and plenty of Parmesan cheese. But at 600 calories and 30 grams of fat per serving, we wondered: Could we lighten this elegant lasagna? Unwilling to make sacrifices in taste and texture, we created a lasagna with big flavor from lean ingredients. Using ground turkey supplemented with a pound of finely chopped mushrooms instead of the traditional beef, pork, or veal, we harnessed that "meaty" flavor and texture without the fat. Instead of simmering the meat in cream or whole milk, we used 2-percent milk, which tenderized the meat and enriched the sauce nicely. For our lighter béchamel sauce, we found success with 2-percent milk and chicken broth thickened with flour. Parmesan added directly to the sauce helped to thicken it further. When building the lasagna, we saved the white sauce for the top, making its flavor more pronounced. At just 360 calories and 11 grams of fat per serving, we could finally tuck into a hefty plate of low-fat meaty lasagna that didn't look, feel, or taste "light."

1 carrot, peeled and cut into chunks
1 pound cremini or white mushrooms
6 garlic cloves, peeled
2 (28-ounce) cans whole tomatoes with juice
2 teaspoons extra-virgin olive oil
1 onion, minced (about 1 cup)
 Salt and pepper
3 tablespoons tomato paste
1¼ pounds 93-percent-lean ground turkey
2 cups 2-percent milk
2 cups low-sodium chicken broth
1 bay leaf
½ cup minced fresh basil
5 tablespoons unbleached all-purpose flour
2 ounces Parmesan cheese, grated (about 1 cup)
12 no-boil lasagna noodles

1. Pulse the carrot, mushrooms, and garlic in a food processor until finely chopped, ten 1-second pulses; transfer to a bowl. Add the tomatoes with their juice to the food processor and process until almost smooth, five 1-second pulses. Combine 1 teaspoon of the oil, onion, ½ teaspoon salt, and ¼ teaspoon pepper in a large Dutch oven. Cover and cook over medium-low heat until the onion is softened, 3 to 4 minutes. Add the chopped vegetable mixture and cook, uncovered, until the mushrooms release their liquid, 5 to 7 minutes. Increase the heat to medium-high and cook until the liquid has evaporated, 3 to 5 minutes.

2. Stir in the tomato paste and cook until it begins to brown, about 2 minutes. Stir in the turkey and 1 cup of the milk. Cook, using a wooden spoon to break up any large chunks, until most of the milk has evaporated, 5 to 7 minutes. Stir in the tomatoes, 1 cup of the broth, and the bay leaf. Bring to a simmer and cook until the sauce has thickened and most of the liquid has evaporated, 45 to 60 minutes. Off the heat, remove and discard the bay leaf and stir in the basil. Season with salt and pepper to taste.

3. Meanwhile, whisk the remaining 1 cup milk, remaining 1 cup broth, and flour together in a medium saucepan until smooth. Bring the mixture to a simmer over medium-high heat and cook, stirring constantly, until thickened, about 2 minutes. Off the heat, stir in the remaining 1 teaspoon oil and the cheese. Season with salt and pepper to taste.

4. Adjust an oven rack to the upper-middle position and heat the oven to 425 degrees. Spread 2 cups of the meat sauce in a 13 by 9-inch baking dish. Lay 3 noodles on top of the sauce, spaced evenly apart. Repeat this layering of sauce and noodles 3 more times. Spread the white sauce evenly on the top layer of noodles, leaving a 1-inch border around the edge. Bake until the lasagna is bubbling around the edges and the top begins to brown, 25 to 30 minutes. Cool on a wire rack for at least 20 minutes before serving.

WHAT YOU CAN DO AHEAD OF TIME: The meat sauce and the white sauce can be refrigerated in separate airtight containers for up to 2 days. Gently reheat the sauces separately before proceeding with step 4.

NOTES FROM THE TEST KITCHEN

THE BEST LASAGNA PAN

When making lasagna, we usually reach for an ordinary 13 by 9 by 2-inch Pyrex baking dish. But do specialized lasagna pans offer any advantages? The first thing we noticed about the five pans we tested was their size: They're big. The Mario Batali extra deep lasagna pan ($79.95) weighed in at 11 pounds—when empty—and holds 1½ batches of our Low-Fat Meaty Lasagna. Second, a pan holding several pounds of pasta, sauce, and cheese needs handles, which the Chicago Metallic Professional ($23.50) and Kaiser La Forme ($40) lacked. These two pans also featured dark nonstick surfaces that scorched the lasagna even at a lower oven temperature. In the end, we liked just one pan. The **Metro 3 Piece Lasagna Pan Set** (top), $19.99, including a spatula and roasting rack, is light colored, double handled, and big (14¼ by 10½ by 4 inches) but not awkward—perfect for super-sized lasagna recipes. But since we don't mind the 2-inch depth of our trusty **Pyrex Bakeware** (bottom), $9.79, it remains the test kitchen standard.

MEATY MUSHROOMS

Sliced mushrooms had the wrong texture for our lasagna. Finely chopping the mushrooms in the food processor gave them a meaty texture similar to that of the ground turkey.

SLICED   FINELY CHOPPED

PASTA WITH FRESH TOMATO SAUCE
WITH ROSEMARY AND BACON
SERVES 4 TO 6

WHAT MAKES THIS A BEST RECIPE: The dog days of summer produce the only fresh tomatoes of the year fit for pairing with pasta. Packed with bracing acidity and sweet fruitiness, they taste the way tomatoes should yet rarely do. Seizing the opportunity, we splurged on several crates of these rare specimens and created a quick pasta sauce that capitalized on their full, robust flavor. We found that the best way to prepare the tomatoes for the sauce was to skin, seed, and chop them into small pieces before simmering them in a skillet with garlic and olive oil. With the skillet's ample cooking surface, it was only a matter of minutes before the excess moisture evaporated and the tomatoes gently slumped into a hearty sauce. Any type of tomato tasted fine cooked this way: Ripeness, not variety, was the key to the recipe. For flavorings, we wanted bold ingredients that would stand up to the liveliness of the tomatoes, namely potent, piney rosemary, spicy red pepper flakes, and smoky bacon. These ingredients pointed up the fresh qualities of these gutsy tomatoes yet gamely shared the spotlight.

- 6 slices bacon, cut crosswise into ½-inch strips
- 2 tablespoons extra-virgin olive oil
- 2 garlic cloves, minced
- ½ teaspoon minced fresh rosemary
- ½–¾ teaspoon red pepper flakes
- 3 pounds ripe round tomatoes, cored, peeled, seeded, and cut into ½-inch pieces (about 3¾ cups)
- 1 tablespoon chopped fresh parsley
- Salt
- Pepper
- Sugar
- 1 pound spaghetti
- 2 ounces Parmesan cheese, shaved thin with a vegetable peeler (about ¾ cup)

1. Bring 4 quarts of water to a boil in a large pot for the pasta.

2. Cook the bacon in a 10-inch skillet over medium heat, stirring occasionally, until crisp, 8 to 10 minutes. Using a slotted spoon, transfer the bacon to a paper towel–lined plate. Pour off the bacon fat from the pan and discard.

3. Heat the oil, garlic, rosemary, and pepper flakes in the now-empty skillet over medium-high heat until fragrant, about 30 seconds. Stir in the tomatoes and cook until the tomato pieces lose their shape and form a chunky sauce, about 10 minutes. Stir in the parsley and season with salt, pepper, and sugar to taste.

4. Meanwhile, add 1 tablespoon salt and the pasta to the boiling water. Cook, stirring often, until the pasta is al dente. Reserve ¼ cup of the pasta cooking water, drain the pasta, and return it to the pot. Stir in the sauce and toss to combine, adding reserved pasta water as necessary. Serve, sprinkling the reserved bacon and Parmesan over individual bowls.

WHAT YOU CAN DO AHEAD OF TIME: The sauce can be refrigerated in an airtight container for up to 2 days or frozen for up to 1 month.

NOTES FROM THE TEST KITCHEN

SUBSTITUTING CANNED TOMATOES FOR FRESH
When fresh tomatoes aren't in season, it's better to use canned tomatoes rather than the pale, mealy tomatoes available most of the year. For every pound of fresh tomatoes needed, simply substitute one 14.5-ounce can of drained diced tomatoes plus 1 tablespoon of the drained liquid. Canned diced tomatoes are firmer than fresh tomatoes, so they should be pressed against the side of the pan with a wooden spoon to help them break down as they cook.

MEATBALLS AND MARINARA

SERVES 8 TO 10 (ENOUGH TO SAUCE 2 POUNDS OF PASTA)

WHAT MAKES THIS A BEST RECIPE: Big, tender meatballs and marinara sauce, served over a bowl of steaming-hot spaghetti or eaten with a slice of crusty bread to sop up the sauce, is Italian-American comfort food at its finest. While making big, "Little Italy"–sized meatballs is easy, making big meatballs that are also flavorful, tender, and moist, with enough structure to hold their shape, is difficult. But in classic test kitchen style, we figured out how to do it. Most meatball recipes call for equal parts of pork and beef and use a soupy panada (bread mashed with milk as a binder) made with upward of 2 cups of liquid. We cut way back on both, using a 5-to-1 ratio of beef to pork and a stiff panada consisting of four slices of bread and only ¾ cup of milk. This drier, leaner mixture held its shape well and cooked up easily in the pan, but losing most of the fat meant we were also losing much of the flavor. Adding sautéed onion, garlic, red pepper flakes, dried oregano, and fresh parsley helped. A handful of Parmesan added richness, but the real secret to our recipe was substituting raw Italian sausage for the ground pork, which added a great flavor boost. When it came to cooking the meatballs, instead of frying them in several batches, we turned to a hot oven (475 degrees) and cooked them all in one batch—no babysitting or messy frying required. For the marinara sauce, we built rich tomato flavor by frying tomato paste with the aromatics before adding crushed tomatoes and red wine. The resulting sauce had a compelling color, a hearty texture, and a flavor that was deep and rich—all in just one hour.

ONION MIXTURE

- ¼ cup olive oil
- 3 onions, minced (about 3 cups)
- 8 garlic cloves, minced
- 1 tablespoon dried oregano
- ¾ teaspoon red pepper flakes

MARINARA

- 1 (6-ounce) can tomato paste
- 1 cup dry red wine
- 1 cup water
- 4 (28-ounce) cans crushed tomatoes
- 1 ounce Parmesan cheese, grated (about ½ cup)
- ¼ cup chopped fresh basil
- Salt
- 1–2 teaspoons sugar

MEATBALLS

- 4 slices high-quality white sandwich bread, torn into pieces
- ¾ cup milk
- ½ pound sweet Italian sausage, casings removed
- 2 ounces Parmesan cheese, grated (about 1 cup)
- ½ cup minced fresh parsley
- 2 large eggs, lightly beaten
- 2 garlic cloves, minced
- 1½ teaspoons salt
- 2½ pounds 80 percent lean ground chuck

1. FOR THE ONION MIXTURE: Heat the oil in a large Dutch oven over medium-high heat until shimmering. Add the onions and cook until golden, 10 to 15 minutes. Stir in the garlic, oregano, and pepper flakes and cook until fragrant, about 30 seconds. Transfer half of the onion mixture to a large bowl and set aside.

2. FOR THE MARINARA: Add the tomato paste to the remaining onion mixture in the pot and cook until fragrant, about 1 minute. Add the wine and cook until thickened slightly, about 2 minutes. Stir in the water and tomatoes and simmer over low heat until the sauce is no longer watery, 45 to 60 minutes. Stir in the cheese and basil and season with salt and sugar to taste.

3. FOR THE MEATBALLS: Meanwhile, adjust an oven rack to the upper-middle position and heat the oven to 475 degrees. Mash the bread and milk in the bowl with the reserved onion mixture until smooth. Add the sausage, Parmesan, parsley, eggs, garlic, and salt and mash to combine. Add the beef and knead with your hands until well combined. Form the mixture into 2½-inch meatballs (you should have about 16 meatballs), place on a rimmed baking sheet, and bake until well browned, about 20 minutes.

4. Transfer the meatballs to the pot with the sauce and simmer for 15 minutes. Serve.

WHAT YOU CAN DO AHEAD OF TIME: The meatballs and marinara sauce can be refrigerated in an airtight container for up to 2 days, or frozen for up to 1 month.

NOTES FROM THE TEST KITCHEN

OUR FAVORITE CRUSHED TOMATOES

Crushed tomatoes, also known as ground tomatoes, are whole peeled tomatoes that are crushed and enriched with tomato puree. Here in the test kitchen, we tasted ten brands of crushed tomatoes, both poured from the can and reduced with olive oil and garlic to a spoonable consistency. We rated the crushed tomatoes on their freshness of flavor, sweetness, acidity, and overall appeal. What did we find out? Brands with less puree have better flavor, and the texture of crushed tomatoes varies greatly among brands; some are chunky, others watery. Overall, our favorite brands were **Tuttorosso Crushed Tomatoes in Thick Puree with Basil** (left)—which tasters declared "chunky with dimensional flavor and bright tomato taste"—and **Muir Glen Organic Crushed Tomatoes with Basil** (right), which had a "balanced, bright tomato flavor."

WHO'S FRYING NOW?

Not us, that's for sure. We found that a super-hot oven was all we needed to get a golden brown crust on these meatballs. Finally, a short dunk in the sauce allows the sauce to season the meat, and vice versa.

1. For a great crust without the hassle of frying, bake the meatballs in a very hot oven.

2. For the best flavor, let the meatballs sit in the simmering sauce for at least 15 minutes before serving.

SLOW-COOKER ITALIAN SUNDAY GRAVY
SERVES 8 TO 10 (ENOUGH TO SAUCE 2 POUNDS OF PASTA)

WHAT MAKES THIS A BEST RECIPE: It's not just a legend that many Italian grandmothers wake up early Sunday morning to begin making the elaborate (and unforgettable) meaty tomato sauce, called "gravy," that will top the pasta of the day. This involves making meatballs, stuffing and rolling up a flank steak to make braciole, and adding whole pork chops and sausage to a vat of simmering sauce. While we love the idea of Sunday gravy, a whole day in the kitchen is just too much. Since this dish is all about long, slow cooking, for this recipe, we streamlined its preparation and used a slow cooker. Meatballs didn't hold up in the slow cooker, and braciole took too long to prepare, so to replace their beefy flavor, we used flank steak, which held up superbly in our long-cooked recipe. Moving on to the pork, regular chops were tough and chewy, but country-style spareribs provided flavorful meat that fell off the bone after eight hours in the slow cooker. In fact, both the steak and the spareribs were tender enough to shred and stir back into the sauce. Sweet and hot Italian sausage, both sliced in half, added kick to the sauce while staying juicy. For the tomatoes, a combination of drained diced tomatoes, canned tomato sauce, and tomato paste gave our sauce the best balance of flavor and texture. When it came to flavorings, we found that cooking onions, lots of garlic (a whopping 12 cloves), wine, and oregano in the sausage drippings at the onset built a rich flavor base that carried through to the end of cooking. And to brighten the finished sauce, we added fresh basil. Here in the test kitchen, we now had our own version of Italian Sunday gravy, worthy of any Italian grandmother's praise.

1 tablespoon vegetable oil
1 pound sweet Italian sausage
1 pound hot Italian sausage
2 onions, chopped medium (about 2 cups)
12 garlic cloves, minced

  2 teaspoons dried oregano

  1 (6-ounce) can tomato paste

  ½ cup dry red wine

  1 (28-ounce) can diced tomatoes, drained

  1 (28-ounce) can tomato sauce

  2 pounds bone-in country-style spareribs, trimmed of excess fat

  1½ pounds flank steak

  3 tablespoons chopped fresh basil

  Pepper

1. Heat the oil in a large Dutch oven over medium-high heat until just smoking. Add the sweet sausage and cook until well browned and the fat begins to render, about 8 minutes. Using a slotted spoon, transfer the sausage to a paper towel–lined plate to drain, then place in a slow-cooker insert. Cook the hot sausage in the pan drippings in the same way, and add to the insert.

2. Cook the onions in the sausage fat over medium heat until well browned, 5 to 7 minutes. Stir in the garlic and oregano and cook until fragrant, about 30 seconds. Add the tomato paste and cook until the paste begins to brown, about 5 minutes. Stir in the wine and simmer, scraping up any browned bits, until it is reduced, about 3 minutes. Transfer to the slow-cooker insert and stir in the diced tomatoes and tomato sauce.

3. Submerge the spareribs and flank steak in the sauce in the slow-cooker insert. Set the slow cooker on low, cover, and cook until the meat is tender, 8 to 10 hours. (Alternatively, cook on high for 4 to 5 hours.)

4. About 30 minutes before serving, transfer the sausages, ribs, and flank steak to a baking sheet and set aside until cool enough to handle. Shred the ribs and flank steak into small pieces, discarding any excess fat and bones; slice the sausages in half crosswise. Use a wide spoon to skim the fat off the surface of the gravy, then stir the sausages and shredded meat back into the sauce. Stir in the basil and season with pepper to taste. Serve.

WHAT YOU CAN DO AHEAD OF TIME: The gravy can be refrigerated in an airtight container for up to 3 days or frozen for up to 1 month.

Italian Sunday Gravy is a hearty, slow-simmered tomato sauce enriched with three kinds of meat.

NOTES FROM THE TEST KITCHEN

THE MEAT MATTERS

Ask a hundred Italian grandmothers what meat they use for Sunday gravy and you'll get a hundred different answers—everything from meatballs to pork chops. For our easy slow-cooker version, we prefer the taste, texture, and convenience of the following combination.

ITALIAN SAUSAGES
Browning the sausage in advance helps build deep flavor.

FLANK STEAK
This lean cut adds beefy flavor without too much grease.

COUNTRY-STYLE SPARERIBS
These meaty ribs become fall-apart tender in a slow cooker.

PASTA SALAD WITH PESTO

SERVES 6 TO 8

WHAT MAKES THIS A BEST RECIPE: We love this recipe because it combines two of our favorite things—pesto and pasta—but with a twist, making it a pasta salad. Punctuated by toasted pine nuts and sweet tomatoes, this is our new summertime standby. At its best, pesto is fresh, green, and full of herbal flavor, but unfortunately, we quickly found out that numerous issues arise once it is added to a pasta salad. The refrigerator dulls the color and flavor of the pesto, which turns greasy and clumpy as the pasta cools. The key to this recipe was to supplement the basil with baby spinach (1 cup added to 3 cups of basil), to provide a lovely bright green color and smooth texture without interfering with the herbal flavor. We also found that while the relatively thin consistency of traditional pesto might be fine for hot noodles, a thicker, creamier pesto was in order for room-temperature pasta. We decided to borrow a standard ingredient used in many American pasta salads: mayonnaise. The creamy, tangy condiment served as the perfect binder. We finessed the dish even more by adding lemon juice to cut through the richness, and an extra ½ cup of toasted pine nuts for a sweet, nutty note as well as textural contrast. A pint of quartered cherry tomatoes or halved grape tomatoes contributed color and small bursts of freshness.

2 garlic cloves, unpeeled
  Salt
1 pound farfalle
¼ cup plus 1 tablespoon extra-virgin olive oil
  Pepper
¾ cup pine nuts, toasted
3 cups packed fresh basil (about 4 ounces)
1 cup packed baby spinach (about 1 ounce)
2 tablespoons fresh lemon juice
1½ ounces Parmesan cheese, grated (about ¾ cup), plus extra for serving
6 tablespoons mayonnaise
1 pint cherry tomatoes, quartered, or grape tomatoes, halved (optional)

1. Bring 4 quarts water to a boil in a large pot for the pasta. When the water boils, add the garlic and cook for 1 minute. Remove the garlic with a slotted spoon and rinse under cold water to stop the cooking; set aside. Add 1 tablespoon salt and the pasta to the boiling water. Cook, stirring often, until the pasta is just past al dente. Reserve ¼ cup of the pasta cooking water, drain the pasta, and return it to the pot. Pour 1 tablespoon oil over the pasta and toss to combine. Season with salt and pepper to taste. Spread the pasta on a rimmed baking sheet and cool to room temperature, about 30 minutes.

2. When the garlic is cool, peel and mince it. Process ¼ cup of the nuts, garlic, basil, spinach, lemon juice, remaining ¼ cup oil, 1 teaspoon salt, and ½ teaspoon pepper in a food processor until smooth, scraping the sides of the bowl as necessary, about 20 seconds. Add the cheese and mayonnaise and process until thoroughly combined, about 20 seconds. Transfer the pesto to a large serving bowl.

3. Add the cooled pasta and toss to combine, adding the reserved pasta water, 1 tablespoon at a time, until the pesto evenly coats the pasta. Fold in the remaining ½ cup nuts and tomatoes (if using). Serve with additional grated Parmesan.

WHAT YOU CAN DO AHEAD OF TIME: The pesto can be refrigerated in an airtight container for up to 1 day—just cook the garlic cloves in a small saucepan of boiling water for 1 minute.

NOTES FROM THE TEST KITCHEN

TWO SECRETS TO BETTER PESTO PASTA SALAD

It's not hard to make a pesto pasta salad taste good. To get the appearance and texture to live up to the vibrant flavors, we came up with two easy tricks.

BRIGHT COLOR
Supplementing the basil with baby spinach helped maintain the pesto's bright green color.

CREAMY TEXTURE
Adding a touch of mayonnaise turned the too-slick pesto creamy and cohesive.

ANTIPASTO PASTA SALAD
SERVES 6 TO 8

WHAT MAKES THIS A BEST RECIPE: This main-course hearty, full-flavored pasta salad is reminiscent of an antipasto platter—it includes a variety of cured meats, cheese, and pickled vegetables. But the recipes we tried for this type of salad were greasy and heavy, with lackluster dressing and not enough flavor in the pasta itself. Turning first to the add-ins, we found that tasters liked pepperoni and sopresatta (a spicy, cured Italian sausage) for the meat component, particularly after we quickly microwaved them to remove excess grease. Strong, aged provolone was preferred over milder cheeses, especially when we grated it into the salad for even distribution. For vegetables, roasted red peppers were favored for sweetness, pepperoncini for heat, and homemade marinated mushrooms for earthy flavor. Next, for the dressing, we found that where pasta salads typically use a 2-to-1 ratio of oil to vinegar, we had to nearly reverse this ratio since the meats and cheese were so rich. Some vinegary brine from the pepperoncini further sharpened the dressing, while a bit of mayonnaise added body and promoted cling. Most pasta salad recipes call for rinsing the cooked noodles, but this method left us with bloated pasta that didn't absorb any flavor from the dressing. Tossing the hot pasta with the dressing and extra vinegar made the pasta an equal partner in this salad, which is anything but boring.

8 ounces sliced pepperoni, cut into ¼-inch strips
8 ounces thick-sliced sopresatta or salami, halved and cut into ¼-inch strips
10 tablespoons red wine vinegar
6 tablespoons extra-virgin olive oil
3 tablespoons mayonnaise
1 (12-ounce) jar pepperoncini, drained (2 tablespoons juice reserved), stemmed, and chopped coarse
4 garlic cloves, minced
¼ teaspoon red pepper flakes
 Salt and pepper
1 pound short, curly shaped pasta, such as fusilli or campanelle
1 pound white mushrooms, quartered
4 ounces aged provolone cheese, grated (about 1 cup)
1 (12-ounce) jar roasted red peppers, drained, patted dry, and chopped coarse
1 cup minced fresh basil

1. Bring 4 quarts water to a boil in a large pot for the pasta. Meanwhile, place the pepperoni in a single layer on a large, paper towel–lined plate. Cover with another paper towel and place the sopresatta on top. Cover with another paper towel and microwave on high for 1 minute. Discard the paper towels and set the pepperoni and sopresatta aside.

2. Whisk 5 tablespoons of the vinegar, olive oil, mayonnaise, pepperoncini juice, garlic, pepper flakes, ½ teaspoon salt, and ½ teaspoon pepper together in a medium bowl.

3. Add 1 tablespoon salt and the pasta to the boiling water. Cook, stirring often, until the pasta is al dente. Drain the pasta and return it to the pot. Pour ½ cup of the dressing and the remaining 5 tablespoons vinegar over the pasta and toss to combine. Season with salt and pepper to taste. Spread the pasta on a rimmed baking sheet and cool to room temperature, about 30 minutes.

4. Meanwhile, bring the remaining dressing to a simmer in a large skillet over medium-high heat. Add the mushrooms and cook until lightly browned, about 8 minutes. Transfer to a large bowl and cool to room temperature.

5. Add the meat, provolone, roasted red peppers, basil, and cooled pasta to the mushrooms and toss to combine. Season with salt and pepper to taste before serving.

WHERE THINGS CAN GO WRONG: Be sure to cool the mushrooms to room temperature before adding the other ingredients, or the cheese will melt and the basil will wilt.

WHAT YOU CAN DO AHEAD OF TIME: The salad can be wrapped tightly with plastic wrap and refrigerated for up to 3 days. Bring to room temperature and adjust the seasonings as needed before serving.

NOTES FROM THE TEST KITCHEN

HOW TO DEGREASE PEPPERONI AND SOPRESATTA
Microwaving the pepperoni and sopresatta eliminates the possibility that it will turn your pasta salad into a grease trap. After microwaving for just 1 minute, you can see how much fat is rendered on the paper towels.

MEAT

STEAK FRITES **144**

HERB-CRUSTED BEEF TENDERLOIN
WITH HORSERADISH CREAM SAUCE **146**

30-MINUTE MEAT LOAVES **148**

CHARCOAL GRILL–ROASTED PRIME RIB **150**

CHARCOAL-GRILLED SKIRT STEAK FAJITAS **153**

CHARCOAL-GRILLED STEAK AND POTATOES
WITH BLUE CHEESE BUTTER **154**

ROAST BEEF TENDERLOIN WITH CARAMELIZED ONION
AND MUSHROOM STUFFING **156**

SLOW-COOKER BEEF STROGANOFF **159**

ITALIAN POT ROAST **160**

CALIFORNIA-STYLE BARBECUED TRI-TIP **162**

CHINESE STICKY RIBS **164**

SLOW-COOKER BRISKET AND ONIONS **167**

AUTHENTIC BEEF ENCHILADAS **169**

CHARCOAL-GRILLED WELL-DONE HAMBURGERS **170**

PHILLY CHEESESTEAKS **174**

CRISP IOWA SKINNY **172**

STROMBOLI WITH SALAMI, CAPOCOLLO, AND PROVOLONE **175**

SLOW-COOKER SMOTHERED PORK CHOPS **176**

HERB-CRUSTED PORK LOIN **179**

SLOW-FRIED SHREDDED PORK **181**

CHINESE BARBECUED PORK **182**

LEXINGTON-STYLE PULLED PORK **185**

STUFFED PORK CHOPS WITH PORT, PECANS, AND DRIED FRUIT **187**

PORK TENDERLOIN MEDALLIONS WITH APPLE-CIDER SAUCE **190**

CHARCOAL-GRILLED LAMB CHOPS
WITH NEAR EAST RED PEPPER PASTE **192**

STEAK FRITES
SERVES 4

WHAT MAKES THIS A BEST RECIPE: When in Paris, the first thing any member of the test kitchen does is head to the nearest bistro for *steak frites*. It might sound like a pedestrian choice, but in Paris, the steak is always perfectly cooked and the fries are fluffy on the inside and crisp on the outside. This recipe successfully recreates the best of the bistros—without a flight to Paris. Recipes agree that high-starch russet potatoes make the best fries and that double-cooking, or a low-temperature "blanch" in oil followed by a high-temperature "fry" yields the crispest exterior and fluffiest interior. We couldn't disagree. Fries cooked in peanut oil were more flavorful and less greasy than those cooked in vegetable oil and shortening, respectively, and cooking multiple small batches of fries ensured that the oil's temperature wouldn't plunge too much. Soaking the potatoes in cold water before they were cooked further improved their crispness, and a "rest" between the first and second frying allowed the fries to develop a thin coating of starch, which even further improved their crispness. Tossing them with additional starch—in the form of cornstarch—made them perfect. In France, steak frites is usually prepared with a cut called entrecôte (literally, "between the ribs"), which is a French cut you won't find in the States, but is actually quite similar to our rib-eye steak. Choosing the right size—or cutting them to fit—meant we could sear four steaks at once in a large skillet. Capped with a quick herb butter, the steaks tasted all the part like the bistro classic.

HERB BUTTER

4	tablespoons unsalted butter, softened
½	shallot, minced (about 1 tablespoon)
1	garlic clove, minced
1	tablespoon minced fresh parsley
1	tablespoon minced fresh chives
¼	teaspoon salt
¼	teaspoon pepper

STEAK AND POTATOES

2½	pounds russet potatoes (about 4 large), sides squared off and cut lengthwise into ¼ by ¼ inch fries (see page 145)
2	tablespoons cornstarch
3	quarts peanut oil
1	tablespoon vegetable oil
2	boneless rib-eye steaks (1 pound each), cut in half (see page 145)
	Kosher salt and pepper

1. FOR THE BUTTER: Combine all the ingredients in a medium bowl; set aside.

2. FOR THE POTATOES: Rinse the cut potatoes in a large bowl under cold running water until the water turns clear. Cover with cold water and refrigerate for at least 30 minutes or up to 12 hours.

3. Pour off the water, spread the potatoes onto kitchen towels, and thoroughly dry. Transfer the potatoes to a large bowl and toss with the cornstarch until evenly coated. Transfer the potatoes to a wire rack set in a rimmed baking sheet and let rest until a fine white coating forms, about 20 minutes.

4. Meanwhile, heat the peanut oil over medium heat to 325 degrees in a large, heavy-bottomed Dutch oven fitted with a clip-on-the-pot candy thermometer.

5. Add half of the potatoes, a handful at a time, to the hot oil and increase the heat to high. Fry, stirring with a mesh spider or large-hole slotted spoon, until the potatoes start to turn from white to blond, 4 to 5 minutes. (The oil temperature will drop about 75 degrees during this frying.) Transfer the fries to a thick paper bag or paper towels. Return the oil to 325 degrees and repeat with the remaining potatoes. Reduce the heat to medium and let the fries cool while cooking the steaks, at least 10 minutes.

6. FOR THE STEAKS: Heat the vegetable oil in a 12-inch skillet over medium-high heat until smoking. Meanwhile, season the steaks with kosher salt and pepper. Lay the steaks in the pan, leaving ¼ inch between them. Cook, without moving the steaks, until well browned, about 4 minutes. Flip the steaks and continue to cook until an instant-read thermometer inserted in the center registers 120 degrees for rare to medium-rare, 3 to 7 minutes. Transfer the steaks to a large plate, top with

For super-crisp fries, we coat the potatoes with an unlikely ingredient.

the herb butter, and tent loosely with foil; let rest while finishing the fries.

7. Increase the heat under the Dutch oven to high and heat the oil to 375 degrees. Add half of the fries, a handful at a time, and fry until golden brown and puffed, 2 to 3 minutes. Transfer to a thick paper bag or paper towels. Return the oil to 375 degrees and repeat with the remaining fries. Season the fries with salt to taste and serve immediately with the steaks.

WHERE THINGS CAN GO WRONG: The proper oil temperature is crucial to achieving crisp fries, and the only foolproof way to gauge that is with a candy thermometer.

WHAT YOU CAN DO AHEAD OF TIME: The herb butter can be refrigerated in an airtight container for up to 1 day.

NOTES FROM THE TEST KITCHEN

SQUARING THE SPUD

The best way to uniformly cut fries is to start by trimming a thin slice from each side of the potato. Once the potato is "squared," you can slice it into ¼-inch planks and then cut each plank into ¼-inch fries.

ONE STEAK BECOMES TWO

In order to have four steaks that fit in a skillet at the same time, it is necessary to buy two 1 pound steaks and cut them in half according to their thickness. If your steaks are 1¼ to 1¾ inches thick, cut them in half vertically into small, thick steaks. If your steaks are thicker than 1¾ inches, cut them in half horizontally into two thinner steaks.

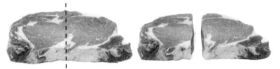

THIN STEAK Cut in half vertically.

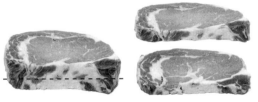

THICK STEAK Cut in half horizontally.

THE BEST SPIDERS

If you peek into a restaurant kitchen, you'll see chefs working over steaming stockpots, using shallow, woven wire baskets on long handles to retrieve blanched vegetables, french fries, and thin-skinned wontons. Most chefs wouldn't part with their "spiders," as they are called, which effortlessly scoop out multiple handfuls of food with one swoop and leave all the hot cooking oil, water, or broth behind. But is one species of spider superior to the others? While cooking skinny french fries and plump cheese ravioli, we noted that several models trapped too much liquid and that sharp wire edges snagged delicate ravioli wrappers. Wood handles soaked up oil and water, discoloring the wood and absorbing odors. One model, the **Typhoon Extra-Large Wire Skimmer** ($15), avoided all these shortcomings and was our clear favorite.

HERB-CRUSTED
BEEF TENDERLOIN
WITH HORSERADISH CREAM SAUCE
SERVES 12 TO 16

WHAT MAKES THIS A BEST RECIPE: Few dishes say holiday quite like a beef tenderloin. Sure it tastes good simply roasted (albeit a bit bland), but gussying it up with an herb crust is like adding a bow to the package. That said, a crust adds a whole extra layer of complexity to cooking the meat. We developed what we think is the perfect recipe for herb-crusted tenderloin—easy, attractive, and virtually foolproof. Early on in testing, we decided that the beef must first be seared before the crust could be applied; we needed to establish a flavor base. Stovetop searing was a messy process, but thankfully we found that a deep-colored, flavorful sear could be developed in a hot oven, especially once we added a little sugar to the salt rub we liberally applied to the exterior. Tucking the skinny "tail" of the tenderloin under and binding the length of the roast with twine ensured even cooking. We experimented with a variety of different crusts and settled on an herb and cheese paste and bread crumb combination. The sticky paste of mixed fresh herbs acted as a "glue" to adhere flavored fresh crumbs to the tenderloin's exterior. The crumbs browned and crisped in the oven's heat. We had the best results when we cooked the roast suspended on a wire rack above a baking sheet, which allowed for even heat circulation. Few flavors complement beef quite as well as horseradish, so we decided to "gild the lily" and serve the roast with a horseradish sauce. We blended peppery, vinegar-laced prepared horseradish with sour cream and heavy cream, which thickened to a luxurious texture if allowed to "culture" on the counter at room temperature for an hour or two.

SAUCE

- ½ cup sour cream
- ½ cup heavy cream
- ¼ cup prepared horseradish, drained
- 2 teaspoons Dijon mustard
- 1 garlic clove, minced
- ¼ teaspoon sugar
- Salt and pepper

BEEF

- 1 whole beef tenderloin (5 to 6 pounds), trimmed and patted dry
- Kosher salt and cracked pepper
- 2 teaspoons sugar
- 2 slices high-quality white sandwich bread, quartered
- ½ cup chopped fresh parsley
- 2 teaspoons plus 2 tablespoons chopped fresh thyme
- 2¼ ounces Parmesan cheese, grated (about 1¼ cups)
- 6 tablespoons olive oil
- 4 garlic cloves, minced

1. FOR THE SAUCE: Mix all the ingredients in a small bowl and season with salt and pepper. Cover and let stand at room temperature for 1 to 1½ hours to thicken.

2. FOR THE BEEF: Following the photos on page 148, tuck the tail of the tenderloin under and tie the roast. Combine 1 tablespoon salt, 1 tablespoon pepper, and sugar in a small bowl and rub the mixture all over the tenderloin. Transfer the tenderloin to a wire rack set on a rimmed baking sheet and let stand at room temperature for 2 hours.

3. Meanwhile, pulse the bread in a food processor to fine crumbs. Transfer the crumbs to a medium bowl and toss in 2 tablespoons parsley, 2 teaspoons thyme, ½ cup Parmesan, and 2 tablespoons oil until evenly combined. Wipe out the food processor and process the remaining 6 tablespoons parsley, 2 tablespoons thyme, remaining ¾ cup cheese, 4 tablespoons oil, and garlic to a smooth paste. Transfer the paste to a small bowl.

4. Adjust an oven rack to the upper-middle position and heat the oven to 400 degrees. Roast the tenderloin 20 minutes and remove from the oven. Using scissors, cut and remove the twine. Coat the tenderloin with the herb paste followed by the crumb topping. Roast until an instant-read thermometer inserted into the thickest part of the meat registers about 125 degrees for medium-rare and the topping is golden brown, 20 to 25 minutes. (If the topping browns before the meat reaches the preferred internal temperature, cover loosely with foil for the balance of the roasting time; remove the foil while the roast rests.) Let the roast rest, uncovered, on a wire rack for 30 minutes. Transfer to a cutting board and carve. Serve accompanied by the sauce.

WHERE THINGS CAN GO WRONG: Begin this recipe 2 hours before you plan to put the roast in the oven; otherwise the meat won't cook evenly.

WHAT YOU CAN DO AHEAD OF TIME: The tenderloin can be trimmed, tied, rubbed with the salt mixture, and refrigerated up to 24 hours in advance Bring the roast back to room temperature before putting it into the oven. The sauce can be refrigerated in an airtight container for up to 2 days.

NOTES FROM THE TEST KITCHEN

PREPARING HERB-CRUSTED BEEF TENDERLOIN

1. To ensure even cooking, fold the thin, tapered end under the roast, then tie the entire roast with kitchen twine every 1½ inches.

2. After the meat has cooked for 20 minutes, use scissors to snip the twine and carefully pull the strings away from the tenderloin.

3. Using a spatula, spread the herb paste evenly over the top and sides of the tenderloin.

4. Press the bread-crumb mixture evenly onto the roast, using the other hand to catch the crumbs and keep them from falling through the rack.

30-MINUTE MEAT LOAVES
SERVES 4

WHAT MAKES THIS A BEST RECIPE: Most meat-loaf recipes call for an hour of baking time in an oven set to 350 or 375 degrees. Add another half-hour to cook the onions and garlic, measure other ingredients, and knead the meat mixture, and you're talking at least 90 minutes to get meat loaf on the table. Not bad considering that most of the time is hands-off, but not good if it's already 6 o'clock and everyone is hungry. This recipe, however, cuts that time by one hour and puts meat loaf on the table in just 30 minutes. How did we cut so much time? First of all, we decided to make individual-size "loaves," thereby doing away with the long bake required of a full-size meat loaf. We also chose to brown the loaves on the stovetop to maximize flavor and color, and then finish them on a broiler tray (heated to hasten things along) in the oven so that excess grease could drain away. As for ingredients, we took some liberties that further trimmed time. While we kept our favorite basic formula for making meat loaf—meat-loaf mix (equal parts ground beef, pork, and veal sold in one package at most supermarkets), crushed saltines, a little milk, and a single egg—we successfully substituted onion powder and garlic powder for their fresh counterparts; fresh herbs, however, were a must. Other seasonings—Worcestershire sauce, Dijon mustard, and cayenne pepper—required just a minute or two to assemble and measure, and a quick ketchup and brown-sugar glaze added valuable flavor. The size of these meat loaves might be unconventional, but they tasted every bit as good as any big loaf, with an even better crust.

Our single-serving meat loaves have a flavorful crust and a tender interior.

MEAT LOAVES

- 17 saltines, crushed fine (about ⅔ cup)
- ¼ cup milk
- 3 tablespoons Worcestershire sauce
- ⅓ cup minced fresh parsley
- 1½ tablespoons Dijon mustard
- 1 large egg
- 1 teaspoon onion powder
- 1 teaspoon garlic powder
- ⅛ teaspoon cayenne pepper
  Salt and pepper
- 1½ pounds meat-loaf mix
- 2 teaspoons vegetable oil

GLAZE

- ½ cup ketchup
- ¼ cup packed light brown sugar
- 4 teaspoons cider vinegar

1. FOR THE MEAT LOAVES: Adjust an oven rack to the middle position, place a broiler pan with a slotted top on the oven rack, and heat the oven to 500 degrees.

2. Mix the cracker crumbs, milk, Worcestershire, parsley, mustard, egg, onion powder, garlic powder, cayenne, ½ teaspoon salt, and ½ teaspoon pepper in a large bowl. Add the meat and mix with your hands until evenly combined. Form into 4 tightly packed loaves, each measuring 4 by 3 inches.

3. Heat the oil in a large nonstick skillet over medium-high heat until just smoking. Cook the loaves until well browned on the top and bottom, 2 to 3 minutes per side.

4. FOR THE GLAZE: While the meat is browning, combine all the ingredients in a bowl.

5. Carefully transfer the loaves to the heated slotted broiler-pan top and spoon 1 tablespoon of the glaze over each loaf. Bake until an instant-read thermometer inserted in the middle of a loaf registers 160 degrees, 7 to 9 minutes. Let the loaves rest on the broiler pan for 3 minutes. Serve, passing the remaining glaze separately.

WHAT YOU CAN DO AHEAD OF TIME: The loaves can be formed, wrapped in plastic, and refrigerated overnight. Let the loaves sit at room temperature for 20 minutes before proceeding with step 3.

NOTES FROM THE TEST KITCHEN

A BETTER MEAT LOAF
Thirty minutes or not, meat loaves suffer the same problems no matter their size—crumbly texture, pale exterior, and excessive greasiness. Here's how we eliminated these problems in our little loaves.

1. Pack the meat-loaf mixture tightly into compact loaves to make sure they don't fall apart.

2. Sear the top and bottom of the loaves to develop a crisp and flavorful exterior.

3. Bake the loaves on the top of a heated broiler pan so excess fat can drip away.

A SUBSTITUTE FOR MEAT-LOAF MIX
If meat-loaf mix is not available, substitute ¾ pound each of ground pork and 85 percent lean ground beef.

CHARCOAL GRILL–ROASTED PRIME RIB

SERVES 6 TO 8

WHAT MAKES THIS A BEST RECIPE: Prime rib of beef is a special-occasion food: It's pricey, it's impressive, and it feeds a crowd. To make the most of it, it's best to sear the exterior and cook it at a low temperature, a messy and cumbersome process for most home cooks (flipping a sputtering seven-pound roast isn't much fun). However, this recipe takes the roast—and the mess—outside and grill-roasts the meat to great effect. Developing a successful grilling method, however, was a long, expensive haul. Simple searing and roasting wouldn't work no matter how we positioned the roast on the grill or the amount of coals we added to the fire: Either the exterior was perfectly seared and the interior overcooked or the exterior was overcooked by the time the center reached medium-rare. Eventually we settled on a unique method in which the seasoned boneless roast was strapped back onto its bones—for protection from the grill's heat—and the two sides were seared, after which the meat was finished over low indirect heat. We left the ends of the roast unseared to minimize the time the meat spent over hot coals. While plain charcoal didn't add much flavor to the meat, adding wood chunks to the coals did. The smoke flavor penetrated only about half an inch into this huge roast—basically, the outer crust—leaving the majority of the pink interior untainted so that each slice provided contrasting flavor. A generous layer of salt applied three hours ahead of time and lots of black pepper was all the added flavor the meat needed— a spice rub unnecessarily complicated things.

1	first-cut (3- or 4-rib) beef standing rib roast (about 7 pounds), meat removed from the bones, bones reserved, exterior fat trimmed to ⅛ inch
1	tablespoon vegetable oil
	Pepper
¼	cup kosher salt
2	(3-inch) wood chunks
	Disposable aluminum roasting pan

Beyond the well-charred, intensely smoky salt crust lies a generous slab of meltingly tender—and perfectly cooked—premium beef.

1. Rub the roast with the oil and season generously with the pepper. Spread the salt on a rimmed baking sheet; press the roast into the salt to coat evenly on all the sides. Tie the meat back onto the bones exactly from where it was cut with four to six 2½-foot lengths of twine, passing two lengths of twine between each set of bones and knotting securely. Refrigerate the roast, uncovered, for 1 hour, then let stand at room temperature for 2 additional hours.

2. Meanwhile, soak the wood chunks in water to cover for 1 hour; drain. About 20 minutes before grilling, open the top and bottom grill vents. Light a large chimney starter filled two-thirds full with charcoal briquettes (about 60 pieces) and allow it to burn until the charcoal is partially covered in a thin layer of fine gray ash, about 15 minutes. Spread the coals over half of the grill bottom, leaving the other half with no coals. Place the disposable aluminum roasting pan on the empty side of the grill. Set the cooking grate over the coals, cover the grill, and heat until hot, about 5 minutes. Use a grill brush to scrape the cooking grate clean.

3. Place the roast on the grate over the hot side of the grill and sear on the fat-covered sides until well browned, turning as needed, 8 to 10 minutes total. (If flare-ups occur, move the roast to the cooler side of the grill until the flames die down.) When thoroughly browned, transfer the roast to the cooler side of the grill, bone side down, with the tips of the bones pointed away from the fire. Place the soaked wood chunks on the coals. Cover the grill, positioning the top vent over the roast to draw the smoke through the grill. Grill-roast (do not remove the lid for at least 1½ hours) until an instant-read thermometer inserted into the center of the roast reads 125 degrees for medium-rare, 2 to 2½ hours.

4. Transfer the roast to a cutting board, tent loosely with foil, and let rest 20 minutes. Remove the strings and bones, cut into ½-inch-thick slices, and serve.

WHERE THINGS CAN GO WRONG: Your butcher can remove the bones and trim the excess fat (⅛-inch layer is perfect and will minimize flare-ups) from the roast; just make sure that the bones are packed up along with the meat, as you need them to protect it from overbrowning. If the only roast you can find is boneless, fashion a protective "bone" from aluminum foil (see photos).

NOTES FROM THE TEST KITCHEN

GAS GRILL–ROASTED PRIME RIB

Follow the recipe for Charcoal Grill–Roasted Prime Rib through step 1. Soak 2 cups wood chips in water for 30 minutes; drain. Place the wood chips in a small disposable aluminum pan; position the pan over the primary burner on a gas grill (the burner that will remain on during cooking). Turn all the burners to high, close the cover, and heat until very hot, about 15 minutes. Use a grill brush to scrape the cooking grate clean. Leave one burner on high heat and turn the remaining burners off. Continue with the recipe from step 3, cooking with the lid down once the roast has been seared and positioned as directed on the cooler side of the grill.

OUR FAVORITE CUT

The first-cut roast consists of ribs 10 through 12 (sometimes rib 9 is included, too). Its large center eye of meat and beefy flavor make this our preferred cut.

IS 'PRIME' PRIME RIB WORTH A PREMIUM?

Originally used to refer to the most desirable portions of the rib section, the term became somewhat confusing once the U.S. Department of Agriculture began using the label "Prime" as one of its beef-grading classifications. The grades classify the meat according to fat marbling and age—as well as by price. Prime is the best, followed by Choice and Select. Prime-grade prime rib costs about $17 a pound, while Choice-grade prime rib goes for about $13 a pound. Additionally, some butchers offer dry-aged prime rib—Prime-grade rib roasts that have been aged for up to a month to tenderize the meat and concentrate its flavors. Dry-aging adds another $2 to $3 per pound. To find out if Prime-grade prime rib is worth the premium, we cooked about $1,500 worth of beef, including several Prime-grade, Choice-grade, and dry-aged rib roasts. In the entire lot, there were no outright losers, but the experiment was telling. First, we don't recommend spending the extra cash on dry-aging: Any distinguishing nuances were lost on the grill. On the other hand, in most cases the Prime cuts beat out the Choice cuts in terms of superior marbling and, thus, superior flavor and texture. Go ahead and splurge on Prime—we think it's worth it.

FOIL "BONE"

If you happen to buy a prime rib without its bones, you will need to fashion a "bone" out of foil to shield the meat from overcooking.

1. Fold a 12- to 14-foot sheet of aluminum foil in half lengthwise and then in half lengthwise again; gently roll and scrunch it into a narrow tube. Coil the foil tube into a tight disk about 6 inches across. Flatten to form a rectangle.

2. Tie the foil "bone" to the roast (where the real bones were removed) and proceed with the recipe.

CHARCOAL-GRILLED SKIRT STEAK FAJITAS
SERVES 4

WHAT MAKES THIS A BEST RECIPE: Skirt steak is the traditional cut of beef used for fajitas, though it has largely been replaced in recent years with flank steak. The reason? Texture—flank steak is typically more tender. That being said, we much prefer the fuller flavor of skirt steak and sought to find a way to tenderize its fibrous texture and make great-tasting fajitas. A marinade seemed like a good solution, though we found adding just the right ingredients crucial to success. The surprise ingredient proved to be an odd one for fajitas: soy sauce. As for other marinade flavors, tasters particularly liked lime juice, Worcestershire sauce (which enhanced the meatiness of the steak), cumin (for its earthy flavor), a fresh chile, and brown sugar. Pricking the steaks with a fork (to break down the muscle fibers) helped the marinade penetrate and flavor the meat (in only 30 minutes) and made the steak quite tender. The best fajitas are grilled, and peppers and onions are a must as accompaniments. We grilled the onions and peppers first over the hot fire (and slid them to the cool side to finish), and then cooked the meat over the cooler coals. The fajitas tasted perfect but for one thing: the smokiness from the grill overpowered the lime flavor. The solution was easy: a second marinade. Drizzling the steaks with some fresh marinade did the trick.

½ cup fresh lime juice from 3 limes
¼ cup vegetable oil
3 garlic cloves, minced
2 tablespoons soy sauce
2 teaspoons ground cumin, toasted
2 teaspoons light brown sugar
1 jalapeño chile, seeds and ribs removed, then minced
1 tablespoon minced fresh cilantro
2 skirt steaks (about ¾ pound each)
2 large onions, cut into ½-inch slices
3 large bell peppers (1 red and 2 green), stemmed, cut in half lengthwise, and seeded
12 (6-inch) flour tortillas

1. Whisk the lime juice, 2 tablespoons of the oil, garlic, soy sauce, cumin, brown sugar, and chile in a bowl. Transfer ¼ cup of the marinade to another bowl, add the cilantro, and set aside. Prick the steaks with a fork about 50 times on each side, then cut each steak in half crosswise. Place the steaks in a large zipper-lock plastic bag, pour in the marinade without the cilantro, seal the bag, and refrigerate at least 30 minutes or up to 2 hours. Remove the steaks from the bag, pat dry with paper towels, and discard the marinade in the bag.

2. Light a large chimney starter filled with charcoal briquettes (about 100 pieces) and allow it to burn until all the charcoal is covered with a layer of fine gray ash, about 20 minutes. Pour the coals into a pile on one side of the grill. Set the cooking grate in place. Cover and let the grill heat up 5 minutes. Use a grill brush to scrape the cooking grate clean.

3. Meanwhile, brush the onions and peppers with the remaining 2 tablespoons oil. Grill the onions and peppers, turning occasionally, until lightly charred and softened, 8 to 12 minutes. (The peppers will cook more quickly.) Move the vegetables to the cool side of the grill. Grill the steaks directly over the coals until seared on both sides but still pink in the center, 4 to 6 minutes per side. Transfer the steak and vegetables to a serving platter, pour the cilantro marinade over them, cover with foil, and let rest 5 minutes.

4. Meanwhile, toast the tortillas over the hot fire, about 10 seconds per side. Wrap in aluminum foil to keep warm. Following the photo on page 154, slice the steak across the grain into thin pieces and cut the vegetables into finger-length pieces. Serve immediately with the warm tortillas.

WHERE THINGS CAN GO WRONG: Toasting intensifies the flavor of cumin, but it burns easily. Toast in a dry skillet over medium heat about 1 minute only, until fragrant. Remove the pan from the heat.

NOTES FROM THE TEST KITCHEN

GAS-GRILLED SKIRT STEAK FAJITAS
Follow the recipe for Charcoal-Grilled Skirt Steak Fajitas through step 1. Turn all the burners on a gas grill to high, close the cover, and heat until very hot, about 15 minutes. Use a grill brush to scrape the cooking grate clean. Grill the vegetables, with the lid down, as directed in step 3. Turn off one burner, then move the vegetables to the cool side of the grill. Proceed as directed, grilling the steaks on the hot side of the grill.

SUBSTITUTING STEAKS
Although we prefer the beefier flavor of skirt steak , it's not as widely available as flank steak, which will also work well in this recipe. How can you tell the two apart? Skirt steak is narrower, and the grains run crosswise. Flank steak is wider, and the grain runs lengthwise. If using flank steak, cut the meat into thirds lengthwise.

FLANK STEAK
The grain runs lengthwise

SKIRT STEAK
The grain runs crosswise

THE RIGHT SLICE

Once the steak has rested, slice the meat across the grain into thin pieces.

GREAT DISCOVERIES

MYSTERY MARINADE INGREDIENT
While developing a marinade for our skirt steak fajitas, I tried all manner of Latin ingredients I thought would both tenderize and flavor the tough skirt steak, but nothing seemed to do the trick. Throwing convention to the wind, I added soy sauce, an ingredient that has worked well for me in Asian-style marinades. The results were the best to date: the meat was as tender as I could have hoped for and deeply flavored, though the particular flavor of the soy sauce wasn't evident. Why was it so successful? After some research, I realized that the soy sauce acted like a brine—a salt-water solution that helps meat hold on to its natural moisture and makes it more tender.

KATIE HENDERSON | TEST COOK, *COOK'S COUNTRY*

CHARCOAL-GRILLED STEAK AND POTATOES
WITH BLUE CHEESE BUTTER
SERVES 4

WHAT MAKES THIS A BEST RECIPE: Steak and potatoes are a classic pairing for good reason. The slightly bitter charred crust of the steak balances the rich, juicy interior, and the sweet, tender potatoes soak up the meat's juices and complement the chewy meat. However, cooking the two together on the grill for several people at once requires the skill and timing of a restaurant grill cook. Or does it? We found, with a little forethought and organization, it was a breeze to master. After trying everything from cheap sirloin to premium filet mignon, we found we most liked the beefy flavor, tender texture, and pronounced grain of strip steaks. And as an added bonus, they are a little less fatty than many other types, which means less fat melts onto the hot coals to generate arm-singeing flare-ups. (Should you not be able to find "strip steaks" at your market, look for them under one of many aliases: hotel steak, Kansas City strip, New York strip, shell steak, or sirloin strip steak.) The next question was how to best cook our cut of choice. A two-level fire—one side quite hot and the other more moderate—was imperative for developing a rich crust and a medium-rare interior. We seared both sides of the steaks, after which we slid them over to the cooler side of the grill to cook through. Initially we thought that we could simply slice potatoes, oil them lightly, and put them alongside the steaks on the grill, but no such luck—they tasted slightly raw and had an unpleasant mealy texture. Parcooking the potatoes was a must. We simmered them until just tender, coated them with oil, and finished them over the hot side of the grill. Thick-sliced planks of Red Bliss potatoes proved the most flavorful and the sturdiest. As for the blue cheese butter, it's just that: crumbled blue cheese mashed with softened butter. A bit of minced shallot and garlic adds a contrasting bite, and fresh parsley brings some welcome color.

Partially cooked potatoes can be finished on the grill—alongside the steaks—so that the potatoes pick up a smoky flavor and attractive char.

2   pounds Red Bliss potatoes (about 6 medium), cut crosswise into ½-inch-thick rounds
    Salt
2   tablespoons vegetable oil
    Pepper
4   tablespoons unsalted butter, softened
3   tablespoons crumbled blue cheese
1   shallot, minced (about 3 tablespoons)
1   teaspoon chopped fresh parsley
1   garlic clove, minced
4   strip steaks, 1¼ to 1½ inches thick (12 to 16 ounces each)

1. Bring the potatoes, 1 teaspoon salt, and 1½ quarts cold water in a large pot to a boil over high heat. Reduce the heat to medium and simmer until the potatoes are barely tender, about 6 minutes. Drain the potatoes in a colander, being careful not to break them. Transfer the potatoes to a rimmed baking sheet coated with 1 tablespoon of the oil. Drizzle the remaining 1 tablespoon oil over the potatoes and season with salt and pepper.

2. While the potatoes are cooking, light a large chimney starter filled with charcoal (about 100 pieces) and allow it to burn until all the charcoal is covered with a layer of fine gray ash, about 20 minutes. Stack most of the coals on one side of the grill bottom and arrange the remaining coals in a single layer on the other side of the grill.

Set the cooking grate in place. Cover and let the grill heat up 5 minutes. Use a grill brush to scrape the cooking grate clean.

3. Meanwhile, beat the butter with a fork until light and fluffy in a bowl. Add the cheese, shallot, parsley, garlic, ¼ teaspoon salt, and ⅛ teaspoon pepper; set aside.

4. Generously sprinkle both sides of the steaks with salt and pepper. Cook, uncovered, over the hotter part of the grill until well browned on one side, about 3 minutes. Turn the steaks; grill the second side until well browned, 3 minutes. Once browned, move the steaks to the cooler side of the grill. Continue grilling, uncovered, to the desired doneness, 7 to 8 minutes more for rare (120 degrees on an instant-read thermometer), 9 to 10 minutes for medium-rare on the rare side (125 degrees), 11 to 12 minutes for medium-rare on medium side (130 degrees), or 12 to 13 minutes for medium (135 to 140 degrees). Transfer the steaks to a cutting board and let rest 5 minutes.

5. Once the steaks are moved to the cooler side of the grill, place the potatoes on the hotter side. Cook, turning once, until grill marks appear and the potato slices are cooked through, 6 to 8 minutes.

6. To serve, place one steak and some of the potatoes on each plate and top each steak with 2 tablespoons of the blue cheese butter. Serve immediately.

WHERE THINGS CAN GO WRONG: Watch the potatoes closely as they are blanching; it is important to take them out of the water before they are tender. Trying to grill potatoes that are already fully cooked is nearly impossible.

NOTES FROM THE TEST KITCHEN

GAS-GRILLED STEAK AND POTATOES WITH BLUE CHEESE BUTTER
Follow the recipe for Charcoal-Grilled Steak and Potatoes through step 1. While the potatoes are cooking, turn all the burners on a gas grill to high, close the cover, and heat until very hot, about 15 minutes. Use a grill brush to scrape the cooking grate clean. Leave one burner on high and turn the other burners to medium. Proceed with the recipe from step 3, cooking with the lid down.

ROAST BEEF TENDERLOIN
WITH CARAMELIZED ONION AND MUSHROOM STUFFING
SERVES 4 TO 6

WHAT MAKES THIS A BEST RECIPE: While there's nothing wrong with plain beef tenderloin, a rich stuffing invests it with special meaning—it's the ultimate holiday centerpiece. A stuffing, however, further complicates an already difficult cut to cook. We wasted a lot of beef—and money—perfecting this one. The thin, tapered shape simply isn't designed for even cooking or thorough browning, much less fitting into a skillet to be seared. A perfectly cylindrical Châteaubriand (the front two-thirds of a whole tenderloin), however, fits comfortably into a 12-inch skillet, roasts at an even rate, and accommodates plenty of stuffing. The higher per-pound price was well worth it. Searing the roast stovetop and finishing in a hot (450 degrees) oven on a wire rack raised above a baking sheet ensured thorough browning and even cooking. Butterflying the roast open like a book didn't yield much surface area for the filling, though double butterflying, or cutting the meat so that it resembled a three-fold business letter, did and was easy enough for the most amateur cook to perform. As for a stuffing, tasters favored a mushroom-based filling from the start. Grinding the mushrooms—cremini for maximum flavor—in a food processor minimized their volume. Caramelized onion contributed sweetness and bound the mushrooms into a thick, slightly sticky jam that was easy to spread across the surface of the butterflied beef—and helped it stay put upon carving. Minced garlic and a splash of Madeira rounded out the flavors, and, for a bit of color, we included a layer of baby spinach before rolling and tying the roast. For a finishing touch, we slathered on a rich, herb-studded compound butter.

STUFFING

- 8 ounces cremini mushrooms, broken into rough pieces
- 1 tablespoon unsalted butter
- 1 teaspoon olive oil
- 1 onion, halved and sliced ¼ inch thick (see page 24)
- ¼ teaspoon salt
- ⅛ teaspoon pepper
- 1 garlic clove, minced
- ½ cup Madeira or sweet Marsala wine

BEEF ROAST

- 1 beef tenderloin center-cut Châteaubriand (2 to 3 pounds), trimmed of fat and silver skin Kosher salt and pepper
- ½ cup lightly packed baby spinach
- 3 tablespoons olive oil

HERB BUTTER

- 4 tablespoons unsalted butter, softened
- 1 tablespoon chopped fresh parsley
- ¾ teaspoon chopped fresh thyme
- 1 garlic clove, minced
- 1 tablespoon whole grain mustard
- ⅛ teaspoon salt
- ⅛ teaspoon pepper

1. FOR THE STUFFING: Process the mushrooms in a food processor until coarsely chopped, about six 1-second pulses. Melt the butter and oil in a 12-inch nonstick skillet over medium-high heat; add the onion, salt, and pepper; cook, stirring occasionally, until the onion begins to soften, about 5 minutes. Add the mushrooms and cook, stirring occasionally, until all the moisture has evaporated, 5 to 7 minutes. Reduce the heat to medium and continue to cook, stirring frequently, until the vegetables are deeply browned and sticky, about 10 minutes. Stir in the garlic and cook until fragrant, 30 seconds. Slowly stir in the Madeira and cook, scraping the bottom of the skillet to loosen any browned bits, until the liquid has evaporated, 2 to 3 minutes. Transfer the onion-mushroom mixture to a plate and cool to room temperature.

2. FOR THE ROAST: Following the photos on page 158, butterfly the roast. Season the cut side of the roast liberally with kosher salt and pepper. Spread the cooled stuffing mixture over the interior of the roast, leaving a ½-inch border on all sides; lay the spinach on top of the stuffing. Roll the roast lengthwise and tie.

3. Stir together 1 tablespoon of the oil, 1½ teaspoons kosher salt, and 1½ teaspoons pepper in a small bowl. Rub the roast with the oil mixture and let stand at room temperature for 1 hour.

4. Adjust an oven rack to the middle position and heat

the oven to 450 degrees. Heat the remaining 2 tablespoons oil in a 12-inch skillet over medium-high heat until smoking. Add the beef to the pan and cook until well browned on all sides, 8 to 10 minutes total. Transfer the beef to a wire rack set in a rimmed baking sheet and place in the oven. Roast until an instant-read thermometer inserted into the thickest part of the roast registers 120 degrees for rare, 16 to 18 minutes, or 125 degrees for medium-rare, 20 to 22 minutes.

5. FOR THE BUTTER: While the meat roasts, combine all the ingredients in a small bowl. Transfer the tenderloin to a cutting board; spread half of the butter evenly over the top of the roast. Tent the roast loosely with foil; let rest for 15 minutes. Cut the roast between the pieces of twine into thick slices. Remove the twine and serve with the remaining butter passed separately.

WHERE THINGS CAN GO WRONG: This recipe calls for a Châteaubriand-cut tenderloin, which is only a portion of a whole tenderloin. Be sure to remove the silver skin on the exterior, which will turn tough and fibrous once cooked, marring the otherwise tender texture of the meat.

WHAT YOU CAN DO AHEAD OF TIME: The stuffed, rolled, and tied roast, wrapped tightly in plastic wrap, can be refrigerated for up to 1 day. Do not season the exterior until you are ready to cook it. Let the roast sit at room temperature for an hour before roasting.

GREAT DISCOVERIES

SALT AND TIME

While tenderloin is one of the most expensive cuts of beef, it has a pretty mild flavor that needs all the help it can get. I was trying everything I could to maximize the meat's flavor and eventually seized on a technique the test kitchen has used to great effect with other cuts of meat. I liberally coated the exterior of the roast with coarse kosher salt and allowed the roast to sit for one hour—at room temperature—before I commenced cooking. In that time, the salt broke down the protein fibers of the outermost layer of meat, desiccating it to the point that it browned quickly for maximum flavor.

SANDRA WU | ASSOCIATE EDITOR, *COOK'S ILLUSTRATED*

STUFFING AND TYING A TENDERLOIN

1. Insert a chef's knife about 1 inch from the bottom of the roast and cut horizontally, stopping just before the edge. Open the meat like a book.

2. Make another cut diagonally into the thicker portion of the roast. Open up this flap, smoothing out the butterflied rectangle of meat.

3. Spread the filling evenly over the entire surface, leaving a ½-inch border on all the sides. Press the spinach leaves evenly on top of the filling.

4. Using both hands, gently but firmly roll up the stuffed tenderloin, making it as compact as possible without squeezing out the filling.

5. Evenly space 8 pieces of kitchen twine (each about 14 inches) beneath the roast. Tie each strand tightly around the roast, starting with the ends.

SLOW-COOKER BEEF STROGANOFF

SERVES 6 TO 8

WHAT MAKES THIS A BEST RECIPE: A classic comfort food, beef Stroganoff combines tender slices of beef and earthy mushrooms with a creamy sauce. It's typically cooked in a skillet on the stovetop, but we wanted a version that could be conveniently prepared in a slow cooker. We replaced the conventional (and expensive) tenderloin with more robust chuck-eye roast, which we cut into chunks instead of the more typical strips so that the meat would better withstand the simmering. We knew from previous testing undertaken for a slow-cooker beef stew, we could get away with not browning the meat if we thoroughly sautéed the onions with tomato paste and an unexpected ingredient, soy sauce. We also found that the same held true for the mushrooms: we could add them raw if we compensated for the lack of flavorful browning with rich-tasting dried porcini mushrooms. Even after nine hours of simmering, the mushrooms held their shape and tasted great. Flour is the usual thickener for Stroganoff, but it wouldn't do in this case. After trying the options, we turned to Minute Tapioca, which dissolved into the sauce and was virtually impossible to detect, outside of its highly effective thickening power. Dry white wine, Dijon mustard, and chicken broth rounded out the stew's flavors. Sour cream lends Stroganoff its characteristic richness and velvety texture, but we found that it must be added with care. When we stirred it directly into the sauce just before serving, the cream curdled; "tempering," or slowly bringing it up to temperature by blending in a bit of the hot broth before stirring it into the stew, was the solution.

- 2 tablespoons vegetable oil
- 3 onions, minced
- ¼ cup tomato paste
  Salt
- ¾ cup dry white wine
- 1 boneless beef chuck-eye roast (5 pounds), trimmed and cut into 1½-inch chunks
- 10 ounces white button mushrooms, quartered
- 2 cups low-sodium chicken broth
- ⅓ cup soy sauce
- ¼ cup Minute Tapioca
- ½ ounce dried porcini mushrooms, rinsed and minced
- ½ cup sour cream
- 2 teaspoons Dijon mustard
  Pepper

1. Heat the oil in a 12-inch nonstick skillet over medium heat until shimmering but not smoking. Add the onions, tomato paste, and ¼ teaspoon salt and cook until the onions are softened and lightly browned, 10 to 15 minutes. Stir in the wine, scraping up any browned bits on the bottom of the pan.

2. Transfer the onion mixture to a slow cooker insert and stir in the meat, white mushrooms, broth, soy sauce, tapioca, and porcini mushrooms until evenly combined. Cover and cook on low until the meat is tender, 9 to 11 hours. (Alternatively, cover and cook on high for 5 to 7 hours.)

3. Gently tilt the slow-cooker insert and degrease as much fat as possible off the surface of the stew with a large flat spoon. Stir 1 cup of the stewing liquid into the sour cream to temper, then stir the sour cream mixture back into the stew. Stir in the mustard, season with salt and pepper to taste, and serve.

WHERE THINGS CAN GO WRONG: Don't be tempted to simply add the sour cream to the hot mixture without first mixing in a portion of the stewing liquid or you'll end up with a curdled mess.

NOTES FROM THE TEST KITCHEN

THE BEST SOY SAUCE

We never gave soy sauce much thought until we gathered 12 brands and tested them. We were struck by their varying colors and widely different flavors—from subtle and delicate to pungent and assertive. Tasters fell for the "salty, sweet, roasted" flavors of the commercially produced **Lee Kum Kee Tabletop Soy Sauce** (left), $1.99 for 5.1 ounces. The other winner was artisan-made **Ohsawa Nama Shoyu Organic Unpasteurized Soy Sauce** (right), $6.49 for 10 ounces, which was cited for its "clean" and "caramel" flavors, as well as for being "rich and nuanced."

ITALIAN POT ROAST

SERVES 4 TO 6

WHAT MAKES THIS A BEST RECIPE: Italian pot roast (sometimes called *stracotto*) replaces the potatoes, carrots, and thin gravy of its American cousin with mushrooms, onions, and a thick sauce based on tomatoes, red wine, garlic, and herbs. Changing the vegetables was as easy as it sounds, but getting the sauce just right proved to be a real challenge. Pot roast, of course, starts with the meat. Beefy flavored, fat-ribboned chuck-eye roast is the test kitchen's favorite cut for American pot roast, and we found no reason to change course here. We browned the meat and the vegetables to intensify their flavors—an easy start—before braising them until tender in the oven. After trying every likely tomato product, we preferred a mixture of canned diced tomatoes, tomato sauce, and tomato paste. The diced tomatoes added a fresh tomato flavor missing in recipes that called for just tomato sauce, while the tomato paste lent backbone. Too much red wine added at the outset overpowered the other flavors in the pot, so we scaled it back a bit and added a splash at the end for brightness. Minced garlic (the traditional choice) lost its punch during the long simmer, so borrowing a trick we use when making soup, we cut a whole head of garlic in half and dropped it right into the pot, where it gently perfumed the meat and sauce. The softened cloves could also be squeezed right back into the pot for extra kick and additional thickening. As for herbs, tasters preferred rosemary (added at the end of cooking so it didn't overpower everything) along with woodsy thyme (mellow enough to add at the start).

1   **boneless chuck-eye roast (3½ to 4 pounds), tied**
    Salt and pepper
2   **tablespoons vegetable oil**
1   **onion, chopped (about 1 cup)**
1   **celery rib, chopped**
1   **pound cremini or white mushrooms, quartered**
2   **tablespoons tomato paste**
1   **(14.5-ounce) can diced tomatoes**
½   **cup canned tomato sauce**

To ensure even cooking, we simmer pot roast in the oven rather than on the stovetop, where the sauce can scorch.

2   **teaspoons sugar**
½   **cup water**
1   **cup red wine**
1   **large garlic head, outer papery skins removed, then halved**
1   **large sprig fresh thyme**
1   **sprig fresh rosemary**

1. Adjust an oven rack to the middle position and heat the oven to 300 degrees. Pat the roast dry with paper towels and season with salt and pepper.

2. Heat the oil in a Dutch oven over medium-high heat until just smoking. Brown the roast on all sides, 8 to 12 minutes. Transfer the roast to a large plate. Reduce the heat to medium and cook the onion, celery, mushrooms, and tomato paste until the vegetables begin to soften, about 8 minutes. Add the diced tomatoes, tomato sauce, sugar, water, ½ cup of the wine, garlic, and thyme. Return the roast and the accumulated juices to the pot and bring to a simmer over medium-high heat. Place a piece of foil over the pot, cover with the lid, and transfer the pot to the oven.

3. Cook until the roast is just fork-tender, 2½ to 3½ hours, flipping the roast after 1 hour. Uncover the pot and let the roast rest in its juices for 30 minutes, skimming the surface fat after 20 minutes. Transfer the roast to a carving board and tent with foil. Remove and reserve the garlic head and skim the remaining fat from the pot. Add the remaining ½ cup wine to the pot, bring to a boil over medium-high heat, and cook until the sauce begins to thicken, about 12 minutes. Meanwhile, carefully squeeze the garlic from the halves and mash into a paste. Add the rosemary to the pot and simmer until fragrant, about 2 minutes. Remove and discard the rosemary and thyme sprigs, stir in the mashed garlic, and season the sauce with salt and pepper to taste.

4. Remove the twine from the roast and cut the meat against the grain into ½-inch-thick slices, or pull apart into large pieces. Transfer the meat to a serving platter and pour ¾ cup sauce over the meat. Serve with the remaining sauce.

WHERE THINGS CAN GO WRONG: Every piece of meat cooks differently, so start checking the roast after 2 hours. If there is a little resistance when prodded with a fork, it's done.

WHAT YOU CAN DO AHEAD OF TIME: The pot roast can be refrigerated in an airtight container for up to 3 days.

NOTES FROM THE TEST KITCHEN

ALL TIED UP

A tied roast will cook evenly and won't fall apart during the long cooking time. If your supermarket hasn't already done so, tie pieces of kitchen twine around the roast every inch or so. Make sure to use food-safe cotton twine (often sold as butcher's twine).

PUT A LID ON IT

Cooking the pot roast with just a lid on the pot wasn't enough to prevent moisture loss—we also had to make a second lid out of aluminum foil. Here's how we did it: After you return the meat to the Dutch oven, tent a sheet of foil loosely over the roast and cover the pot with the lid. When it's time to flip the roast, carefully remove the foil, give the roast a flip, and tent again. The foil harnesses the moisture around the meat, which ensures a moist and tender roast.

GETTING THE GARLIC RIGHT

Here's how we infuse our Italian Pot Roast with mellow garlic flavor.

1. Slice a whole head of garlic in half and add it to the pot.

2. Once the roast is done, squeeze the garlic cloves from their skins and mash the garlic with a fork.

3. Stir the mashed garlic back into the sauce.

THE BEST KITCHEN SHEARS

While you can make do with regular scissors or poultry shears, we are fond of the versatility and hygienic nature of "take-apart" kitchen shears. We tested seven models, focusing on core tasks—snipping chives, cutting butcher's twine and parchment paper, trimming pie pastry, and butterflying chicken. Our favorite shears, **Messermeister's Take-Apart Shears** ($23.99), are precise and super-sharp. A slip-resistant handle and slim blades make these shears agile without sacrificing their brute force. The only downside is a definite right-hand bias.

CALIFORNIA-STYLE BARBECUED TRI-TIP

SERVES 4 TO 6

WHAT MAKES THIS A BEST RECIPE: In California's Santa Maria Valley lies a barbecue tradition all its own. There they grill a garlic-, salt-, and pepper-seasoned tri-tip (a large, boomerang-shaped cut of beef from the bottom sirloin) over red oak embers until it's lightly charred on the outside and rosy on the interior. It's sliced thin and served with tangy barbecued beans, fresh salsa, and buttered French bread. Simple, perhaps, but a dish not without its problems. Tri-tip is usually referred to as a steak, but at its size, we knew it needed to be cooked like a roast. Following the test kitchen's method for grilling large cuts, we pushed all the coals to one side of the grill to create a hot and cool side. We seared the steak over the hot fire and then finished it slowly on the cooler side, leaving it with a flavorful char and a juicy interior. We thought we could simply toss a handful of wood chips onto the fire to flavor the meat, but searing the tri-tip directly above the smoldering wood chips left it tasting unpleasantly smoky. Revisiting technique, we withheld adding the chips until after the meat was seared. This allowed the smoke to dissipate slightly before contacting the meat, perfuming—but not overpowering—the tri-tip with a subtle smoke flavor. As for flavor, we combined a fresh garlic spice rub (brushed off before grilling to prevent burning) and garlic salt for a double kick of flavor. Liberally pricking the roast with a fork before applying the garlic rub ensured that its flavor effectively penetrated the interior of the meat.

  1 tri-tip roast (about 2 pounds), trimmed
  6 garlic cloves, minced
  2 tablespoons olive oil
  ¾ teaspoon salt
  2 cups wood chips, preferably oak
  1 teaspoon pepper
  ¾ teaspoon garlic salt

1. Pat the roast dry with paper towels. Using a fork, prick the roast about 20 times on each side. Combine the garlic, oil, and salt and rub over the roast. Cover with plastic wrap and refrigerate for 1 hour.

2. Soak the wood chips in cold water to cover for 15 minutes; drain. Open the bottom grill vents. Light a large chimney starter filled with charcoal briquettes (about 100 pieces) and allow it to burn until the charcoal is covered in a layer of fine gray ash. Spread the coals over half of the grill bottom, leaving the other half with no coals. Set the cooking grate in place, cover, open the lid vents completely, and heat until hot, about 5 minutes. Use a grill brush to scrape the cooking grate clean.

3. Using paper towels, wipe the garlic paste off the roast. Rub the pepper and garlic salt all over the meat. Grill directly over the coals until well browned, about 5 minutes per side. Carefully remove the roast and cooking grate from the grill and scatter the soaked wood chips over the coals. Replace the cooking grate and place the roast on the cooler side of the grill. Cover, positioning the lid vents directly over the meat, and cook until an instant-read thermometer inserted into the thickest part of the roast registers about 130 degrees for medium-rare, about 20 minutes. Transfer the meat to a cutting board, tent loosely with foil, and let rest for 20 minutes. Slice thinly across the grain. Serve.

WHAT YOU CAN DO AHEAD OF TIME: The roast may be prepared through step 1 and refrigerated for up to 24 hours.

NOTES FROM THE TEST KITCHEN

GAS-GRILLED CALIFORNIA-STYLE BARBECUED TRI-TIP
Follow the recipe for California-Style Barbecued Tri-Tip through step 1. Soak the wood chips in a bowl of water to cover for 15 minutes, seal in a foil packet, and place over the primary burner on a gas grill. Turn all the burners to high, close the cover, and heat until the chips smoke heavily, about 15 minutes. Use a grill brush to scrape the cooking grate clean. Wipe the garlic paste off the roast. Rub pepper and garlic salt all over the meat. Place the roast on the side of the grate opposite the primary burner and grill, covered, until well browned, about 5 minutes per side. Leave the primary burner on high and turn the remaining burners off; cook until an instant-read thermometer inserted into the thickest part of the roast registers about 130 degrees for medium-rare, about 20 minutes. Let rest and slice as directed.

CALIFORNIA-STYLE BARBECUED TRI-TIP

WHAT IS A TRI-TIP?

Also known as a "bottom sirloin roast," "bottom sirloin butt," or "triangle roast," tri-tip is cut from the bottom sirloin primal, an area near the rear leg of the cow, adjacent to the round and flank. Before being "discovered" as a steak, this cut was thought to be extremely tough and was typically ground into hamburger or cut into stew meat.

IF YOU CAN'T FIND TRI-TIP

Since tri-tip can be hard to find in some parts of the country, we looked for a widely available substitute. We tried flank steak (too thin), shoulder steak (too tough), and strip steak (too pricey) before we arrived at bottom round steak. Aside from being similar to tri-tip in thickness and weight (and therefore cooking time and yield), bottom round also has the big, beefy flavor of tri-tip at a modest price. Unfortunately, the long muscle fibers of this cut can make it extremely tough. We found that thinly slicing the steak straight down on a 45-degree angle shortened the muscle fibers and dramatically reduced the chewiness.

THE BEST CHARCOAL CHIMNEY STARTERS

We've long considered a chimney starter to be the best way to light charcoal. Shaped like oversized coffee mugs, these simple metal contraptions are divided into two chambers, the lower of which holds a few sheets of crumpled newspaper that, once lit, ignite the charcoal in the upper chamber. Recently, many new models have appeared on the market and we wanted to see if there was really much difference among them. After testing six popular models, we favored the **Weber Rapid Fire Chimney Starter** ($16.99), which easily ignited six quarts of coals (the perfect amount for high-heat endeavors) and had two handles for easy—and safe—handling.

CHINESE STICKY RIBS
SERVES 6

WHAT MAKES THIS A BEST RECIPE: With their glossy glaze, complex flavor, and fork-tender meat, Chinese sticky ribs are the perfect appetizer for any Asian meal. But order them at most restaurants and you're brought out a plate of sugary, neon-red bones sparsely covered with gristly meat. No thanks. We knew we could do better and with this recipe, we did. After trying a dozen-odd recipes and a variety of cooking methods, we had the best results with braising the ribs, or simmering them slowly in a flavorful sauce in the oven. The moist heat tenderized the tough meat, rendered the excess fat, and the meat absorbed the sauce's Asian flavors: ginger, garlic, cilantro, scallion, and orange peel sweetened with hoisin sauce, sugar, and sherry. Reducing the braising liquid (with the fat skimmed away) to a thick sauce and brushing the ribs before broiling didn't produce the classic sticky glaze we sought (though it certainly tasted good). We whisked in sweeteners like honey, but the results were cloying—more candy than appetizer. Spicy red pepper jelly proved to be the magic bullet, the chile heat of which cut the overall sweetness. After a few minutes under the broiler and several coats of glaze, the ribs were a rich mahogany color and as sticky as a lollipop—and not too sweet.

RIBS

- 2 racks pork ribs (2½ to 3½ pounds each), preferably St. Louis–cut or baby back ribs
- 1 cup hoisin sauce
- 1 cup sugar
- ½ cup soy sauce
- ½ cup dry sherry
- 1 (6-inch) piece ginger, peeled and sliced into rounds
- 6 garlic cloves, smashed
  Strips of peel from 1 orange
- 1½ teaspoons cayenne pepper
- 30 sprigs fresh cilantro, stems chopped coarse (reserve leaves for glaze)
- 8 scallions, white parts cut into 1-inch pieces (reserve green parts)

GLAZE

1 (10-ounce) jar hot red pepper jelly
½ cup cider vinegar
¼ cup minced fresh cilantro
¼ teaspoon cayenne pepper
  Minced scallion greens, for garnish

1. FOR THE RIBS: Adjust an oven rack to the middle position and heat the oven to 350 degrees. Following the photos, loosen the membrane on the underside of each rack of ribs with the tip of a paring knife. Grab the membrane with a paper towel and pull it off slowly in a single piece. Combine the remaining ingredients in a large roasting pan. Add the spareribs to the pan, turning to coat both sides, and arrange meaty side down. Cover the pan tightly with foil and cook until just tender, 2½ to 3 hours. Transfer the ribs to a large plate.

2. FOR THE GLAZE: Strain 3 cups of the cooking liquid from the roasting pan into a large nonstick skillet (do not wash the roasting pan) and discard the solids and the remaining liquid. Skim the fat from the liquid. Stir in the jelly and vinegar. Bring to a simmer over medium-high heat and cook until syrupy and reduced to 2 cups, 15 to 20 minutes. Off the heat, stir in the minced cilantro and cayenne.

3. Heat the broiler (do not raise the oven rack). Pour enough water into the roasting pan to cover the bottom and fit the pan with a flat roasting rack. Reserve ½ cup glaze for serving. Arrange the ribs on the rack meaty side down and brush with the glaze. Place the roasting pan back on the middle rack in the oven and broil until beginning to brown, 2 to 4 minutes. Flip the ribs over, brush with more glaze, then broil, brushing the ribs with glaze every 2 to 4 minutes, until the ribs are a deep mahogany color, 9 to 12 minutes (watch the broiler carefully). Transfer the ribs to a cutting board, tent with foil, and let rest 10 minutes. Slice between the bones, transfer the ribs to a platter, and brush with the reserved glaze. Sprinkle with the scallions and serve.

WHERE THINGS CAN GO WRONG: Regular, full-size spareribs will not work in this recipe; they are too large and fatty.

WHAT YOU CAN DO AHEAD OF TIME: The ribs and glaze can be prepared through step 2 up to 2 days in advance. Wrap the ribs tightly in foil and refrigerate. Transfer the glaze to a microwave-safe bowl, cover, and refrigerate. Before serving, allow the ribs to stand at room temperature for 1 hour. Heat the glaze in the microwave on high power until warm, about 1 minute. Proceed with step 3 as directed.

NOTES FROM THE TEST KITCHEN

REMOVING THE MEMBRANE
It's easy to remove the tough membrane from the underside of each rack of St. Louis–cut spareribs. Here's how:

1. At one end of the rack, loosen the membrane with the tip of a paring knife.

2. Grab the membrane with a paper towel to keep it from slipping. Pull slowly—it should come off in one piece.

OUR SECRET SAUCE INGREDIENT
In the test kitchen, we've discovered that hot red pepper jelly is good for something other than spreading on a buttered biscuit or eating with cheddar cheese—it makes a great base for glazes. Aside from its bold flavor, there are two reasons why hot red pepper jelly works so well in this application: It's thickened with pectin, meaning that it will stick to the ribs (or other meats), and it contains sugar, so it caramelizes nicely. If you can't find hot red pepper jelly, substitute red currant or apple jelly.

SLOW-COOKER BRISKET AND ONIONS

SERVES 8

WHAT MAKES THIS A BEST RECIPE: While cooking tough beef brisket in a slow cooker until tender seems to make perfect sense, most recipes fail to accommodate the large amount of liquid—and fat—shed by the meat, and the results are typically bland and watery at best, gross and greasy at worst. How, then, do you successfully braise a brisket in a slow cooker? First of all, we significantly limited the amount of liquid we added. We found that we could start the brisket with very little liquid at all and that by the time it was tender (after nine hours), the meat would be submerged in liquid, which could then be strained and reduced to serve as the sauce. To maximize the beef's flavor, we coated it with an assertive spice rub and let it sit overnight to absorb the flavors. For the braising liquid—the little we added at the start—we combined chicken broth with red wine vinegar, which was more potently flavored than red wine. A little tomato paste further boosted the dish's flavors. Brisket without onions is simply unthinkable in our opinion. We browned them with a little brown sugar and garlic before adding them to the sauce. For timing's sake, we prepped everything the night before and assembled the mix in the slow cooker the next morning, where it could stew away all day.

- 1 tablespoon vegetable oil
- 3 large onions (about 2 pounds), halved and sliced ½ inch thick (see page 24)
- 1 tablespoon light brown sugar
  Salt
- 1 tablespoon tomato paste
- 2 tablespoons unbleached all-purpose flour
- 3 garlic cloves, minced
- 1¾ cups low-sodium chicken broth
- 2 tablespoons plus 1 teaspoon red wine vinegar
- 1 tablespoon paprika
- 2 teaspoons onion powder
- 1 teaspoon garlic powder
- ⅛ teaspoon cayenne pepper
- 1 flat-cut beef brisket (5 pounds), trimmed of excess fat

- 3 sprigs fresh thyme
- 3 bay leaves

1. Heat the oil in a large skillet over medium-high heat until shimmering. Cook the onions, brown sugar, and ¼ teaspoon salt until the onions are golden, 10 to 12 minutes. Stir in the tomato paste and flour and cook until darkened, about 2 minutes. Add the garlic and cook until fragrant, about 30 seconds. Stir in the broth and cook until the sauce thickens, about 4 minutes. Off the heat, stir in 2 tablespoons vinegar and transfer the mixture to a bowl.

2. Combine 1 teaspoon salt, paprika, onion powder, garlic powder, and cayenne in a bowl. Using a fork, prick the brisket all over. Rub the spice mixture over the brisket and wrap tightly in plastic. Cover the bowl with the onion mixture with plastic wrap. Refrigerate the brisket and the bowl with the onion mixture overnight.

3. The next morning, add half of the onion mixture to a slow-cooker insert. Add the thyme and bay leaves and place the brisket, fat side up, on top. Spread the remaining onion mixture over the brisket. Set the slow cooker to low, cover, and cook until the brisket is fork-tender, 9 to 10 hours. (Alternatively, cover and cook on high for 5 to 6 hours.) Turn the cooker off and allow the brisket to rest for 30 minutes.

4. Transfer the brisket to a cutting board, cut across the grain into ½-inch slices, and transfer to a serving platter. Tent with foil. Pour the sauce into a large skillet, discard the herbs, and simmer over high heat until slightly thickened, 8 to 10 minutes. Skim the fat, add the remaining 1 teaspoon vinegar, then pour half of the sauce over the brisket. Serve with the remaining sauce on the side.

WHERE THINGS CAN GO WRONG: Don't use the thicker point-cut brisket in this recipe as it is much fattier, and, in a slow cooker, the fat will make the sauce greasy.

NOTES FROM THE TEST KITCHEN

THE INCREDIBLE SHRINKING BRISKET

The edges of the brisket will sit above the liquid in the slow-cooker insert. As the brisket cooks, it will shrink and the edges will become submerged in the liquid.

AUTHENTIC BEEF ENCHILADAS

SERVES 4 TO 6

WHAT MAKES THIS A BEST RECIPE: Traditional beef enchiladas—corn tortillas stuffed with silky, slow-cooked meat and baked under a blanket of hearty chile sauce and cheese—are the ultimate in Mexican comfort food. Too bad they take so long to make. While there are dozens of "quick" beef enchilada recipes out there, we weren't pleased with any, so we created our own—a recipe that captures all the authentic flavor of long-cooked traditional recipes but with a shortened method.

Enchiladas are nothing without a great-tasting, complexly flavored sauce. We chose canned tomato sauce to serve as the base, and store-bought chili powder sufficed for flavoring, especially when spiked with cumin, coriander, and a little sugar for balance. Sautéing the spices along with onions and garlic revived their volatile oils, and their flavors bloomed. Traditionally, the beef for the filling is "stewed" in the sauce until tender, after which the two are separated, the meat is rolled in the tortillas, and the sauce is ladled on top. While we saw no reason to mess with a good thing, we needed to find a cut of meat that cooked quicker than the tough chuck roast typically used. After numerous batches with different types of beef, we settled on full-flavored blade steak, which we cut into small chunks to hasten things along. Within 1½ hours of simmering—half the time required by most recipes—we had a complex sauce and the basic filling for our enchiladas, to which we added fresh cilantro, spicy-tart pickled jalapeños, and cheese. Microwaving the tortillas softened them enough to roll into tight cylinders around the filling, and, after a quick bake topped with the sauce and more cheese, our enchiladas were ready to go in timely fashion.

3 garlic cloves, minced

3 tablespoons chili powder

2 teaspoons ground coriander

2 teaspoons ground cumin

1 teaspoon sugar

   Salt

1¼ pounds top blade steaks, trimmed

1 tablespoon vegetable oil

2 onions, chopped (about 2 cups)

1 (15-ounce) can tomato sauce

½ cup water

8 ounces Monterey Jack or mild cheddar cheese, shredded (about 2 cups)

⅓ cup chopped fresh cilantro

¼ cup chopped canned pickled jalapeños

12 (6-inch) corn tortillas

1. Combine the garlic, chili powder, coriander, cumin, sugar, and 1 teaspoon salt in a small bowl. Pat the meat dry with paper towels and sprinkle with salt. Heat the oil in a Dutch oven over medium-high heat until shimmering. Cook the meat until browned on both sides, about 6 minutes. Transfer the meat to a plate. Add the onions to the pot and cook over medium heat until golden, about 5 minutes. Stir in the garlic mixture and cook until fragrant, about 1 minute. Add the tomato sauce and water and bring to a boil. Return the meat and juices to the pot, cover, reduce the heat to low, and gently simmer until the meat is tender and can be broken apart with a wooden spoon, about 1½ hours.

2. Adjust an oven rack to the middle position and heat the oven to 350 degrees. Strain the beef mixture over a medium bowl, breaking the meat into small pieces; reserve the sauce. Transfer the meat to a bowl and mix with 1 cup of the cheese, cilantro, and jalapeños.

3. Spread ¾ cup of the sauce in the bottom of a 13 by 9-inch baking dish. Microwave 6 tortillas on a plate on high power until soft, about 1 minute. Spread ⅓ cup of the beef mixture down the center of each tortilla, roll the tortillas tightly, and set in the baking dish, seam side down. Repeat with the remaining tortillas and beef mixture (you may have to fit 2 or more enchiladas down the sides of the baking dish). Pour the remaining sauce over the enchiladas and spread to coat evenly. Sprinkle the remaining 1 cup cheese evenly over the enchiladas, wrap with foil, and bake until heated through, 20 to 25 minutes. Remove the foil and continue baking until the cheese browns slightly, 5 to 10 minutes. Serve.

WHAT YOU CAN DO AHEAD OF TIME: Although it's best to roll and bake the enchiladas right before serving, the beef filling and sauce can be prepared through step 2 and refrigerated in separate containers for up to 2 days.

NOTES FROM THE TEST KITCHEN

TRIMMING BLADE STEAKS

After testing various beef cuts, we found that blade steaks (which are cut from the chuck) had enough marbling to produce silky, flavorful shredded beef for our enchiladas. The only trick is to cut away the center strip of gristle, which is very easy to do because the strip is in plain sight in the middle of each steak. Simply halve each steak lengthwise and then slice away the gristle, as shown here.

THE BEST TOMATO SAUCE

Tomato sauce is made from cooked tomatoes that have been strained of seeds and skins and lightly seasoned. Don't confuse it with heat-and-serve jarred tomato sauces, which are much more flavorful. After testing a fair share of what most supermarkets stock, we found our favorite: **Hunt's Tomato Sauce.**

FREEZING TORTILLAS

Corn tortillas are smaller and richer in flavor than their flour cousins, and they are often sold in packages of 24 or more. To freeze corn tortillas, gently peel individual tortillas from the stack and place them between pieces of waxed or parchment paper, then freeze up to 12 tortillas in a zipper-lock freezer bag. When you're ready to use them, defrost stacks of four to six tortillas in the microwave at 50-percent power until thawed, 10 to 20 seconds per stack.

CHARCOAL-GRILLED WELL-DONE HAMBURGERS
SERVES 4

WHAT MAKES THIS A BEST RECIPE: While we often disagree with the recommendations for cooking temperatures of pork, beef, and lamb that the U.S. Department of Agriculture suggests (their temperatures typically leave meat dry and flavorless), we recognize that many backyard cooks grill their burgers to medium-well and beyond to be on the safe side. The problem is, cooking most burgers beyond medium results in tough, desiccated hockey pucks with a diminished flavor. There's a real trick to making burgers that can be thoroughly cooked, and this recipe has mastered it. We examined each and every element—from ingredients to the science of making a hamburger—to find the solution. Our first important finding regarded the beef. The richer the beef, the longer it could be grilled without drying out. Eighty-percent-lean ground beef (or 20-percent fat) proved the best starting point for our burgers. Adding additional fat, as butter, bacon fat, or cheese, produced some interesting results, though no definite solutions. The science suggested that burgers dry out because the collagen in the meat seizes and squeezes out the juices. For a successful well-cooked burger you needed to trap that moisture. Once we thought about it, the solution seemed obvious: bread crumbs—like those used in meat loaf and meatballs—would be the key to moist well-done burgers. Instead of adding dry bread crumbs, we mashed fresh bread with a little milk to a stiff paste, folded it into the beef, and were rewarded with the best burgers yet. To keep the beef flavor clear, we limited seasonings to just minced garlic and the subtle tang of steak sauce. These burgers could easily be cooked over a moderately hot fire for flavorful searing and cooked through without any detriment to flavor.

1 slice high-quality white sandwich bread, crust removed and discarded, bread chopped into ¼-inch pieces

2 tablespoons whole milk

¾ teaspoon salt

¾ teaspoon pepper

1 garlic clove, minced

2 teaspoons steak sauce, such as A.1.

1½ pounds 80-percent-lean ground chuck

 Vegetable oil for the cooking grate

6 ounces sliced cheese (optional)

4 rolls or buns

1. Light a large chimney starter filled with charcoal briquettes (about 100 pieces) and allow it to burn until all the charcoal is covered with a layer of fine gray ash, about 20 minutes. Spread the hot coals out over half of the grill bottom, leaving the other half with no coals. Set the cooking grate in place. Cover and let the grill heat up for 5 minutes. Use a grill brush to scrape the cooking grate clean. The grill is ready when the coals are medium-hot (you can hold your hand 2 inches above the grate for 3 to 4 seconds).

2. Meanwhile, mash the bread and milk in a large bowl with a fork until homogeneous (you should have about ¼ cup). Stir in the salt, pepper, garlic, and steak sauce.

3. Break up the beef into small pieces over the bread mixture. Using a fork or your hands, lightly mix together until the mixture forms a cohesive mass. Divide the meat into 4 equal portions. Gently toss one portion of the meat back and forth between your hands to form a loose ball. Gently flatten into a ¾-inch-thick patty that measures about 4½ inches in diameter. Press the center of the patty down with your fingertips until it is about ½ inch thick, creating a slight depression in each patty. Repeat with the remaining portions of meat.

4. Lightly dip a wad of paper towels in vegetable oil; holding the wad with the tongs, wipe the cooking grate. Grill the burgers on the hot side of the grill, uncovered, until well seared on the first side, 2 to 4 minutes. Flip the burgers and continue grilling, about 3 minutes for medium-well or 4 minutes for well-done. (Add the cheese, if using, about 2 minutes before reaching the desired doneness, covering the burgers with a disposable aluminum pan to melt the cheese.) While the burgers grill, toast the buns on the cooler side of the grill. Serve the burgers on the buns.

NOTES FROM THE TEST KITCHEN

GAS-GRILLED WELL-DONE HAMBURGERS

Turn all the burners on a gas grill to high, close the cover, and heat until very hot, about 15 minutes. Use a grill brush to scrape the cooking grate clean. Lightly dip a wad of paper towels in vegetable oil; holding the wad with long-handled tongs, wipe the cooking grate. Leave the primary burner on high heat and turn the remaining burners to low. Follow the recipe for Charcoal-Grilled Well-Done Hamburgers from step 2, grilling the patties with the lid down.

PRESLICED CHEDDAR CHEESE

Tangy, salty cheddar is the test kitchen's favorite cheese for topping a hamburger. Beckoned by the ease and convenience of presliced cheese, we rounded up nine packages from the supermarket dairy case. Whether tasted straight up, in grilled-cheese sandwiches, or on burgers, the "sharp" cheddars carried the day over their "mild" and "medium" counterparts. Aged for at least nine months, sharp cheddar cheese has a strong tanginess that tasters preferred in every application. Mild and medium cheddars—aged for days rather than months—tasted more like mild Monterey Jack. Our favorites included the bolder versions from **Tillamook** and **Cabot**, and the milder, though creamier, rendition produced by **Cracker Barrel.**

THE BEST HAMBURGER BUNS

In a tasting of supermarket hamburger buns, we were surprised by the differences in flavor and texture. Sunbeam and Wonder were so airy that they all but deflated if grasped too indelicately, while heartier brands stood up well to wet condiments. But the deal breaker was size: Of eight products, six measured less than 3½ inches across—a tight fit for most patties. Our favorite, **Pepperidge Farm Premium Bakery Rolls** (not the smaller "Classic" variety), had a generous 4½-inch diameter, hearty texture, "wheaty" taste, and the least amount of sugar in the lineup.

PHILLY CHEESESTEAKS
SERVES 4

WHAT MAKES THIS A BEST RECIPE: The Philly cheesesteak, a hoagie of thin-sliced beef, sautéed onions, and cheese, was born in 1930 at Pat's King of Steaks, located in an Italian-American neighborhood in South Philadelphia. Today you can find a cheesesteak joint on almost every corner in Philly and at delis throughout the country, though few beyond the city's limits really taste all that authentic. We know: We sent a test cook on a tasting tour of Philadelphia so that we could develop a genuine recipe. First and foremost, cheesesteaks are about the beef, which must be tender and deeply flavored. After sampling rib-eye, top sirloin, top round, blade, chuck, flank, and sirloin tips, we most liked inexpensive sirloin tips. Slicing the meat ultra-thin by hand—even when frozen—was nearly impossible; pounding small chunks of meat with a mallet proved a more successful way to replicate the thin, tender sheets of steak cut by special slicers in Philadelphia. Aside from the beef, the most important element in a true Philly cheesesteak is the cheese, and tasters had strong opinions on the subject. We tried sandwiches made not only with the traditional Cheez Whiz but also with two other Philly favorites, provolone and American. In the end, the test kitchen voted for the provolone. But whichever cheese you end up using, don't go overboard—a real Philly cheesesteak is all about the beef.

    6   teaspoons vegetable oil
    1   onion, chopped (about 1 cup)
    1½ pounds sirloin tips, cut into 1-inch cubes and pounded
        until paper-thin
        Salt and pepper
    8   thin slices provolone cheese, cut in half
    4   (6-inch) sub rolls, slit partially open lengthwise

1. Heat 2 teaspoons of the oil in a large nonstick skillet over medium-high heat until shimmering. Add the onions and cook until softened and golden, about 5 minutes. Transfer to a small bowl.

2. Heat an additional 2 teaspoons oil in the now-empty skillet over high heat until smoking. Place half of the steak slices in the skillet (don't worry if they overlap) and season with salt and pepper. Cook until the meat is no longer pink, about 1 minute per side. Remove the pan from the heat, layer 4 half-slices of the cheese over some meat, top with more of the cooked meat, and finally 4 more half-slices of cheese. Cover the pan with a lid to melt the cheese, about 1 minute. Divide the meat and cheese between 2 rolls, top with half of the onions, and pour the juices accumulated in the skillet over the meat. Wrap each sandwich tightly in foil and set aside while preparing the remaining sandwiches.

3. Wipe the skillet clean with paper towels and repeat step 2 with the remaining 2 teaspoons oil, meat, cheese, and onions. Wrap the sandwiches in foil and let sit for about 1 minute to let the flavors come together. Serve.

NOTES FROM THE TEST KITCHEN

THE SECRET TO PAPER-THIN SLICES
Sirloin tips, tasty and much cheaper than the rib-eye steak used in Philly sandwich shops, are often sold in long strips, making slicing against the grain difficult. We found it much easier to cut the meat into cubes and then pound them into paper-thin pieces.

1. Cut each sirloin tip with the grain into 1-inch cubes.

2. Stagger the beef cubes in a single layer 6 inches apart between two sheets of plastic wrap.

3. Using a meat pounder, pound the cubes until paper-thin. You should be able to almost see through the slices.

CRISP IOWA SKINNY
SERVES 4

WHAT MAKES THIS A BEST RECIPE: Iowa is home to the "skinny," a fried pork sandwich that's as simple as it gets. It starts with a chunk of pork tenderloin that is pounded to platter size before being lightly breaded and fried. The cutlet is then served on a soft bun topped with lettuce, tomato, and a slather of mayo. There's not much room for things to go wrong, though they do. We've had "skinnies" with mushy, bland crusts, or with pork so thick and tough that it requires a serious chew. Such simple things really should be perfect and this recipe is just that. One tenderloin proved more than adequate for four sandwiches when quartered and pounded to a ¼-inch thickness (any thicker and the coating burned before the pork was cooked through). To get the requisite golden brown, crunchy coating, we tried a number of batters and breadings before settling on a basic flour, egg, and fresh bread crumb approach. Adding crushed saltines to the bread crumbs provided a welcome saltiness and even more crispness, but the flavor was still a bit bland for us. In previous similar instances, we'd had luck using mayonnaise as part of a breading, and it worked perfectly here. A combination of eggs and mayo added a pleasing richness and sweet tang that enhanced the flavor of the pork without weighing down the crust.

1   pork tenderloin (about 1 pound), cut into 4 equal pieces and pounded into ¼-inch-thick cutlets
    Salt and pepper
½   cup unbleached all-purpose flour
2   large eggs
¼   cup mayonnaise, plus extra for serving
3   slices high-quality white sandwich bread, quartered
16 saltines
1   cup vegetable oil
4   soft hamburger buns
¼   head iceberg lettuce, shredded
1   tomato, sliced

1. Adjust an oven rack to the middle position and heat the oven to 200 degrees. Pat the pork cutlets dry with paper towels and season with salt and pepper.

2. Place the flour in a shallow dish. Beat the eggs and mayonnaise in a second shallow dish. Combine the bread and saltines in a food processor and pulse to fine crumbs; transfer to a third shallow dish.

3. Coat the cutlets in the flour, shaking off the excess. Dip both sides of the cutlets in the egg mixture, then dredge in the crumbs, pressing on the crumbs to adhere. Place the cutlets on a wire rack set over a baking sheet and let dry for 5 minutes (or refrigerate up to 1 hour).

4. Heat ½ cup of the oil in a large nonstick skillet over medium heat until shimmering. Lay 2 cutlets in the skillet and fry until crisp and deep golden, about 2 minutes per side. Transfer to a large paper towel–lined plate and place in the oven. Discard the oil, wipe out the skillet, and repeat with the remaining oil and cutlets. Place 1 cutlet on each bun and top with the lettuce, tomato, and mayonnaise. Serve.

NOTES FROM THE TEST KITCHEN

PREPARING PORK CUTLETS

1. Use a paring knife to remove any silver skin or extraneous fat from the tenderloin.

2. Cut the tenderloin into 4 equal pieces.

3. Arrange the pieces cut side up on a cutting board. Cover with plastic wrap and pound into ¼-inch-thick cutlets.

STROMBOLI

WITH SALAMI, CAPOCOLLO, AND PROVOLONE

SERVES 4

WHAT MAKES THIS A BEST RECIPE: An omnipresent staple in Italian pizzerias, stromboli—a close cousin of the calzone—seemed to us like an ideal make-ahead entrée for a busy weeknight. With their crunchy, golden-brown exterior and flavorful layered meat and cheese fillings, stromboli pair well with salad for a welcome change-of-pace dinner. Less doughy than calzones, stromboli typically rely on a sturdy filling of layered deli meats and mozzarella or provolone cheese and therefore hold up well enough to be made ahead of time. Never made stromboli? Neither had we—until we developed this recipe. The first step was the dough. From previous testing, we knew that pizza dough (suitable for stromboli too) can be whipped up in a couple of minutes (with the aid of a food processor); if this is too time consuming, there's always store-bought dough. To save on time and effort, we quickly decided to make just one large stromboli, which could be sliced into individual servings. For the filling, we tried all manner of Italian deli specialties and eventually settled on a combination of salami, capocollo, roasted peppers, provolone cheese, and a dusting of Parmesan. We assumed that a hot oven was the key to a crispy crust, but at temperatures above 400 degrees the exterior verged on burning long before the interior had cooked through; at temperatures below that the crust became hard and crunchy. Covering the stromboli with aluminum foil for the first half of the baking gave the interior a sufficient headstart, and, after 25 minutes, we removed the foil to allow the exterior to brown. Brushed with an egg wash and coated with sesame seeds, our stromboli looked just like those made at our local Italian deli. Tasters could hardly keep their hands off the slices as we served stromboli in the test kitchen—a good indication of how well this recipe can fit into your repertoire. Serve with tomato sauce, if desired.

DOUGH

- 2 cups (11 ounces) bread flour, plus extra for the work surface
- 1 teaspoon rapid-rise or instant yeast
- ¾ teaspoon salt
- 2 tablespoons olive oil, plus extra for the bowl
- 1 cup warm water

STROMBOLI

- Olive oil
- 4 ounces thinly sliced deli salami
- 4 ounces thinly sliced deli capocollo
- 4 ounces thinly sliced deli provolone cheese
- 4 ounces jarred roasted red bell peppers, sliced thin, rinsed, and patted dry (about ½ cup)
- 1 ounce Parmesan cheese, grated (about ½ cup)
- 1 large egg, lightly beaten
- 1 teaspoon sesame seeds
- Kosher salt (optional)

1. FOR THE DOUGH: Pulse the flour, yeast, and salt in a food processor (fitted with a dough blade if possible) to combine. With the food processor running, pour the oil, then the water, through the feed tube and process until a rough ball forms, 30 to 40 seconds. Let the dough rest in the bowl for 2 minutes, then process for 30 seconds longer.

2. Turn the dough out onto a lightly floured work surface and knead by hand to form a smooth, round ball, about 5 minutes, adding additional flour as needed to prevent the dough from sticking. Transfer to a lightly oiled bowl, cover with plastic wrap, and let rise in a warm place until doubled in size, 1 to 1½ hours.

3. Adjust an oven rack to the middle position and heat the oven to 400 degrees. Gently deflate the dough with your fist and turn it out onto an unfloured work surface. Gently reshape the dough into a ball and cover with plastic wrap lightly sprayed with vegetable oil spray. Let the dough rest 15 minutes, but no more than 30 minutes.

4. FOR THE STROMBOLI: Brush a rimmed baking sheet lightly with oil. On a lightly floured work surface, roll the dough into a 12 by 10-inch rectangle, about ¼ inch thick. Place the meat and provolone over the dough, leaving a 1-inch border along the edges. Top with the roasted red bell peppers and Parmesan.

5. Brush the edges of the dough with water. Starting from a long side, roll the dough tightly into a long cylinder, pressing the edges to seal. Transfer the stromboli to the prepared baking sheet, seam side down.

6. Brush the top with the egg wash, and sprinkle with the sesame seeds and kosher salt (if using). Cover the stromboli lightly with aluminum foil that has been sprayed with vegetable oil spray (or use nonstick foil) and bake for 20 minutes. Remove the foil and continue to bake until the crust is golden, about 25 minutes. Transfer the stromboli to a wire rack and let cool 5 minutes. Transfer to a carving board and slice into 2-inch pieces.

WHAT YOU CAN DO AHEAD OF TIME: The stromboli can be prepared through step 5, wrapped tightly in plastic wrap, and refrigerated for up to 24 hours. Increase the baking time by about 5 minutes.

NOTES FROM THE TEST KITCHEN

QUICK DOUGH
If time is tight, feel free to pick up prepared dough from the supermarket or your local pizzeria (you will need 1 pound of dough). One 12-ounce or 13.8-ounce pop-up canister of pizza dough (Pillsbury brand) also works well here.

SLOW-COOKER SMOTHERED PORK CHOPS
SERVES 6

WHAT MAKES THIS A BEST RECIPE: The best smothered pork chops are fall-off-the-bone tender, covered with caramelized onions, and enriched with a deeply flavored onion gravy. They are typically prepared in a skillet, but we successfully adapted them to the slow cooker. The test kitchen's favorite skillet smothered chop recipe uses relatively thin ¾-inch rib chops, but eight hours in a slow cooker made them dry and stringy. Thicker rib chops didn't fair any better, so we tested different types of chops. Blade chops, which are cut from the shoulder end of the loin and contain a lot of fat and connective tissue, proved to be the solution. Best of all, there was no need to special-order extra-thick chops, since readily available ¾-inch blade chops worked perfectly. The fat melted into the meat, keeping it moist and tender, and the connective tissue all but disappeared over the course of eight hours. Unfortunately the "dump and cook" approach to slow-cooker cuisine failed to impress here and we found it necessary to brown the chops on the stovetop. The pan developed a flavorful fond from the meat, so it made sense to capitalize on that flavor and brown the onions as well. Garlic, thyme, and a bay leaf rounded out the flavors; a little brown sugar boosted the pork's earthiness and soy sauce deepened the gravy's color and intensity. The last challenge was to perfect the texture of the gravy, which the slow cooker left too watery. More onions thickened it, but they also threw off the balance. Fortunately, our solution was sitting next to the slow cooker: the blender. Pureeing the onions with the cooking liquid—and a bit of cornstarch—gave us just the gravy we wanted. With a splash of vinegar and a garnish of crispy bacon and parsley, we had chops every bit as good as the skillet original.

4 slices bacon, chopped fine
  Vegetable oil (if necessary)
6 bone-in blade-cut pork chops, about ¾ inch thick
  Salt and pepper
3 onions, halved and sliced into ½-inch-thick pieces
1 teaspoon plus 1 tablespoon light brown sugar
¼ cup plus 2 tablespoons water
3 garlic cloves, minced
2 teaspoons minced fresh thyme
3 cups low-sodium chicken broth
1 tablespoon soy sauce
2 bay leaves
1 tablespoon cornstarch
1 tablespoon cider vinegar
1 tablespoon minced fresh parsley

1. Fry the bacon in a large skillet over medium heat until lightly browned, about 8 minutes. Transfer the bacon to paper towels with a slotted spoon, leaving the fat in the pan (you should have 2 tablespoons fat; if not, supplement with the oil). Refrigerate the bacon.

2. Heat the fat over high heat until smoking. Meanwhile, pat the pork chops dry with paper towels and sprinkle with salt and pepper. Cook 3 chops until golden brown on both sides, about 3 minutes per side. Transfer the chops to a slow-cooker insert. Repeat with the remaining chops and transfer to the slow-cooker insert.

3. Pour off all but 1 teaspoon of fat from the skillet; add the onions, 1 teaspoon brown sugar, ¼ teaspoon salt, and ¼ cup water to the now-empty skillet. Using a wooden spoon, scrape the browned bits from the pan bottom and cook over medium-high heat until the onions are soft, about 6 minutes. Stir in the garlic and thyme and cook until fragrant, about 30 seconds longer. Pour the onion mixture over the chops in the slow-cooker insert. Add the broth, soy sauce, and the remaining 1 tablespoon brown sugar to the skillet, bring to a boil, and add the bay leaves. Pour the mixture over the onions in the slow cooker.

4. Cover the slow cooker and cook on low until the pork is very tender, about 8 hours. (Alternatively, cover and cook on high for 4 hours.)

5. When ready to serve, reheat the bacon in a large saucepan until crisp and transfer to a small bowl. Carefully transfer the chops to a platter with a large spoon and tent with foil. Remove and discard the bay leaves and pour the liquid through a mesh strainer into a saucepan. Transfer the solids to a blender with 1 cup of the liquid and blend until smooth. Stir back into the remaining liquid in the saucepan. Mix the cornstarch and remaining 2 tablespoons water together in a small bowl and stir into the sauce. Cook over medium heat until thickened, about 8 minutes. Add the vinegar, and season with salt and pepper to taste. Pour the sauce over the chops, and sprinkle with the bacon and parsley. Serve.

WHERE THINGS CAN GO WRONG: Be very careful when removing the chops from the slow cooker; otherwise they can fall apart.

NOTES FROM THE TEST KITCHEN

CHOP SHOP

The secret to great slow-cooked smothered pork chops is choosing the right chop. The excess fat on a blade chop melts away after eight hours in the slow cooker.

HERB-CRUSTED PORK LOIN

SERVES 4 TO 6

For flavor in every bite, we spread an herb paste in the middle and on top of the roast. A cheesy crust is the crowning touch.

WHAT MAKES THIS A BEST RECIPE: While a center-cut pork roast's uniform shape and compact eye of meat make it an attractive, easy-to-slice roast, it's the leanest part of the pig and, consequently, very bland. It needs help. Usually that help comes via a rich sauce or stuffing, but this recipe takes a different approach entirely: an herb crust. First we had to cook the pork just so; the best crust couldn't remedy overcooked meat. Usually, we brine center-cut pork loins to keep them moist and flavorful—we followed that protocol here. As for roasting, we seared the meat on the stovetop first—for flavor and coloring—after which we slid it into the oven to cook through at a moderate 325 degrees. To avoid burning the crust, we put it on top of the meat after searing, just before it went into the oven. Scoring a crosshatch pattern into the roast's fat cap before searing gave the crust something to grip and helped further unify the crust and meat. Following the lead of one of the best recipes we tested, we decided to make the crust from two components: an herb paste prepared from a handful of fresh herbs and olive oil, and a shallot and Parmesan cheese-flavored fresh bread crumb mixture that we packed into the paste. We couldn't add enough crust to the meat to make every taster happy (outside of encasing the roast in the rub), so we cut a pocket into the center of the roast and stuffed more of the paste inside. The meat was moist to a fault and shot through with rich flavor—no sauce needed here.

1 **boneless center-cut pork loin roast (2½ to 3 pounds)**
  Salt
¼ **cup sugar**
1 **slice high-quality white sandwich bread, quartered**
1 **ounce Parmesan or pecorino cheese, grated (about ½ cup)**
1 **shallot, minced (about 3 tablespoons)**
4 **tablespoons plus 2 teaspoons olive oil**
  Pepper
⅓ **cup packed fresh parsley or basil**
2 **tablespoons minced fresh thyme**
1 **teaspoon minced fresh rosemary or ½ teaspoon dried**
1 **garlic clove, minced**

1. Following the photos on page 180, lightly score the fat cap on the pork, making a ¼-inch crosshatch pattern, then cut a pocket in the roast. Dissolve ½ cup salt and the sugar in 2 quarts water in a large container; submerge the roast, cover with plastic wrap, and refrigerate for 1 hour. Rinse the roast under cold water and dry thoroughly with paper towels.

2. Meanwhile, adjust an oven rack to the lower-middle position and heat the oven to 325 degrees. Pulse the bread in a food processor until coarsely ground, about sixteen 1-second pulses. Transfer the crumbs to a medium bowl (do not wash the food processor bowl) and add 2 tablespoons of the Parmesan, the shallot, 1 tablespoon of the oil, ⅛ teaspoon salt, and ⅛ teaspoon pepper. Using a fork, toss the mixture until the crumbs are evenly coated with oil.

3. Add the parsley, thyme, rosemary, garlic, remaining 6 tablespoons Parmesan, 3 tablespoons oil, ⅛ teaspoon salt, and ⅛ teaspoon pepper to the now-empty food processor and process until smooth, about twelve 1-second pulses. Transfer the herb paste to a small bowl.

4. Following the photos, spread ¼ cup of the herb paste inside the roast and tie. Season the roast with pepper (and salt, if using enhanced pork).

5. Heat the remaining 2 teaspoons oil in a 12-inch skillet over medium-high heat until just smoking. Add the roast fat side down and brown on all sides, 8 to 10 minutes, lowering the heat if the fat begins to smoke. Transfer the roast to a wire rack set in a rimmed baking sheet lined with aluminum foil.

6. Using scissors, snip and remove the twine from the roast; discard the twine. Spread the remaining herb paste over the roast and top with the bread crumb mixture. Transfer the baking sheet with the roast to the oven and cook until the thickest part of the roast registers 145 degrees on an instant-read thermometer, 50 to 75 minutes. Remove the roast from the oven and let rest 10 minutes. (The internal temperature should rise to 150 degrees.)

7. Transfer the roast to a carving board, taking care not to squeeze the juices out of the pocket in the roast. Cut the roast into ½-inch slices and serve immediately.

WHERE THINGS CAN GO WRONG: If only "enhanced" pork is available (the label will state that the pork was injected with a water-salt solution), do not brine the roast. Instead, simply season the stuffed and tied roast with salt before browning. Note that you should not trim the pork of its layer of fat. The roasting time will vary widely depending on the thickness of the meat.

WHAT YOU CAN DO AHEAD OF TIME: The roast can be brined, stuffed, and tied, wrapped tightly in plastic wrap, and refrigerated for up to 1 day. Do not prepare the bread crumb topping until you are ready to cook the roast.

NOTES FROM THE TEST KITCHEN
PREPARING HERB-CRUSTED PORK LOIN

1. SCORE THE FAT: Using a sharp boning knife, lightly score the fat cap on the roast to make ¼-inch crosshatch pattern.

2. MAKE THE FIRST INCISION: Starting ½ inch from the end of the roast, insert the knife into the middle of the roast, with the blade parallel to the work surface.

3. MAKE THE POCKET: Cut along the side of the pork, stopping ½ inch short of the other end. Pull open the roast and use gentle strokes to cut the pocket deeper.

4. STUFF THE ROAST: Spread ¼ cup of the herb paste evenly into the pocket, making sure the paste reaches the corners of the pocket.

5. TIE THE ROAST: Fold the roast over to the original shape and tie at even intervals along its length with 3 pieces of kitchen twine.

6. APPLY THE PASTE: After browning the roast in the skillet and removing the kitchen twine, spread the remaining herb paste evenly over the top of the roast.

7. AFFIX THE CRUMBS: Sprinkle the crumbs on the top of the roast, gently pressing them on with your hands. Finish cooking the roast in the oven.

SLOW-FRIED SHREDDED PORK

SERVES 4 TO 6

WHAT MAKES THIS A BEST RECIPE: Spanish for "little meats," *carnitas* is pork slowly fried until it's meltingly tender with crispy, caramelized edges. The meat is then shredded and can be eaten on its own or stuffed into tacos or burritos. Our recipe brings this authentic Mexican fare into the home kitchen without skipping a beat. Most recipes simmer the pork in water until the fat is rendered (after which it fries in its own fat), or they poach the pork in oil. We thought each method had its flaws. A third technique, a hybridization of the first two, involves slow-cooking the pork in oil supplemented with a small amount of water. Essentially, the water helps prevent the oil temperature from rising, ensuring gentle slow cooking, like poaching, but with the added flavor and richness of frying. The results? Browned, tasty, fork-tender pork. Drained in a colander and shredded with forks, it was ready to go. To flavor the pork, we tried including citrus fruit and spices in the oil. The acid of fresh lime cut through the rich flavor of the meat and added just a hint of tanginess to the pork. Next, we added cinnamon sticks and bay leaves to the oil, and seasoned the pork with salt and cumin before placing it in the pot. We also uncovered one interesting substitute for the water in some recipes: cola. The change in flavor was minor, but the phosphoric acid in the cola acted as a tenderizer, and the sugar further browned the pork, giving the crust a noticeable sweetness. When the pork was done, we drained it in a colander to remove the excess fat, and shredded it with forks.

CARNITAS

- 1 **boneless pork shoulder roast (Boston butt) (3 pounds),** trimmed and cut into 2-inch chunks
- 1 **teaspoon ground cumin**
  Salt
- 4 **cups peanut oil**
- ¼ **cup water or cola**
- 2 **cinnamon sticks**
- 2 **bay leaves**
- 1 **lime, halved**
  Pepper

TORTILLAS AND ACCOMPANIMENTS

- 12 **(6-inch) corn tortillas, warmed**
  Sour cream
  Minced white or red onion
  Fresh cilantro sprigs
  Lime wedges

1. Adjust an oven rack to the lower-middle position and heat the oven to 375 degrees. Pat the pork dry with paper towels, season with the cumin and 1 teaspoon salt, and transfer to a large Dutch oven. Add the oil, water, cinnamon sticks, and bay leaves. Juice the lime directly into the pot, then add the spent lime halves.

2. Bring the mixture to a simmer over medium-high heat, then transfer the pot to the oven and cook, uncovered, until the edges of the pork are well browned and the meat falls apart when prodded with a fork, about 2½ hours.

3. Remove the pot from the oven and, with a slotted spoon, transfer the pork to a colander set over a bowl; let drain about 10 minutes. Discard the oil. Shred the pork with two forks and season with salt and pepper to taste. Serve with warm corn tortillas, sour cream, minced onion, cilantro, and lime wedges.

GREAT DISCOVERIES

MAINTAINING A STEADY OIL TEMPERATURE

Oil and water don't mix, right? Well, that was the premise behind this unique cooking method for carnitas. I found that slow-cooking the pork in oil supplemented with a small amount of water prevented the oil temperature from rising, ensuring gentler, slower cooking, like poaching, but with the added flavor and richness of frying. How? As long as there is water present in the oil, the temperature of the oil cannot exceed the boiling point of water, 212 degrees. This keeps the oil temperature low enough to render the tough pork tender. As the last bit of water evaporates, the temperature of the oil begins to climb, browning and crisping the exterior of the now tender pork.

BRYAN ROOF | TEST COOK, BOOKS

CHINESE BARBECUED PORK

SERVES 6

WHAT MAKES THIS A BEST RECIPE: With its ruby-red color, deeply browned and crusty edges, and sticky glazed exterior, Chinese barbecued pork (aka *char siu*) is eye candy for meat lovers. It's Boston butt that has been marinated, cut into strips (to help render fat quickly), hung from hooks, and blast-cooked in a hot oven. Normally we make the trek to Chinatown to pick it up and serve it alongside rice and spicy greens, but this recipe brings it on home and produces an entirely authentic version requiring no trip beyond your local grocery store. While suspending the meat on hooks in the oven was out (burned forearms and a messy oven were our rewards for our experiments with "hanging" the meat), we were able to mimic the method by roasting the meat on a wire rack above a baking sheet. Covering the meat tightly with foil and adding a little water to the pan for the first part of the cooking kept it moist; finishing it uncovered gave the strips of pork the slightly chewy texture that characterizes the authentic version. As for flavor, marinating the pork in a mixture of soy sauce and dry sherry enlivened with ginger, garlic, toasted sesame oil, and white pepper guaranteed deep flavor. A glaze of honey and ketchup perfectly mimicked that of the pork we bought in Chinatown (which is usually colored with red food coloring), especially once we ran the pork under the broiler to crisp it.

1 boneless pork shoulder roast (Boston butt) (4 pounds), cut into 8 strips and excess fat removed (see page 183)

½ cup sugar

½ cup soy sauce

6 tablespoons hoisin sauce

¼ cup dry sherry

¼ teaspoon ground white pepper

1 teaspoon five-spice powder

1 tablespoon toasted sesame oil

2 tablespoons grated fresh ginger

2 garlic cloves, minced

¼ cup ketchup

⅓ cup honey

This oven-barbecue recipe relies on a sweet glaze to create a lacquered crust.

1. Prick the pork 10 to 12 times on each side. Place the pork in a large plastic zipper-lock bag. Combine the sugar, soy sauce, hoisin, sherry, pepper, five-spice powder, sesame oil, ginger, and garlic in a medium bowl. Measure out ½ cup of the marinade and set aside. Pour the remaining marinade into the bag with the pork. Press out as much air as possible; seal the bag. Refrigerate for at least 30 minutes or up to 4 hours.

2. While the meat marinates, combine the ketchup and honey with the reserved marinade in a small saucepan. Cook the glaze over medium heat until syrupy and reduced to 1 cup, 4 to 6 minutes.

3. Adjust an oven rack to the middle position and heat the oven to 300 degrees. Line a rimmed baking sheet with aluminum foil and set a wire rack on the pan; spray the foil and the rack with vegetable oil spray.

4. Remove the pork from the marinade, letting any excess drip off, and place on the wire rack. Pour ¼ cup water into the bottom of the pan. Cover the pan with heavy-duty aluminum foil, crimping the edges tightly to seal. Cook the pork for 20 minutes. Remove the foil and continue to cook until the edges of the pork begin to brown, 40 to 45 minutes.

5. Turn on the broiler. Broil the pork until evenly caramelized, 7 to 9 minutes. Remove the pan from the oven and brush the pork with half of the glaze; broil until deep mahogany color, 3 to 5 minutes. Flip the meat and broil until the other side caramelizes, 7 to 9 minutes. Brush the meat with the remaining glaze and continue to broil until the second side is deep mahogany, 3 to 5 minutes. Cool for at least 10 minutes, then cut into thin strips and serve.

WHERE THINGS CAN GO WRONG: Pay close attention to the meat when broiling—you are looking for it to darken and caramelize, not blacken. Do not use a drawer broiler—the heat source will be too close to the meat. Instead, increase the oven temperature in step 5 to 500 degrees and cook for 8 to 12 minutes before glazing and 6 to 8 minutes once the glaze has been applied; flip the meat and repeat on the second side.

NOTES FROM THE TEST KITCHEN

BUTCHERING PORK BUTT
Pork butts are usually about 4 inches thick. If using a pork butt that is thinner than 4 inches, cut into 6 pieces instead of 8.

1. Cut the roast in half lengthwise.

2. Turn each half on its cut side and slice lengthwise into 4 equal pieces.

3. Trim the excess hard, waxy fat, leaving some fat to render while cooking.

CHINESE BBQ AT A GLANCE

1. PRICK: Using a fork, prick the pork 10 to 12 times on each side.

2. MARINATE: Place the pork and marinade in a bag and refrigerate for 30 minutes.

3. ROAST: Place the pork on a rack set in a foil-covered baking sheet; add water.

4. GLAZE: Turn the oven to broil and brush the pork with the glaze.

HOISIN SAUCE
Hoisin sauce is a thick, reddish brown mixture of soybeans, sugar, vinegar, garlic, and chiles used in many classic Chinese dishes, including barbecued pork, Peking duck, and moo shu pork. Spoonfuls of six hoisin sauces and forkfuls of our hoisin-basted barbecued pork indicated that no two brands of this staple condiment are identical; in fact, they vary dramatically in flavor, consistency, and even color—from gloppy and sweet, like plum sauce, to grainy and spicy, like Asian chili paste. According to our tasters, the perfect hoisin sauce balances sweet, salty, pungent, and spicy elements so that no one flavor dominates. **Kikkoman** came closest to this ideal, with tasters praising its initial "burn," which mellowed into a harmonious blend of sweet and aromatic flavors. Two other brands also fared well in our tasting. Koon Chun was described as "fruity" (if a bit grainy), and Lee Kum Kee was deemed "plummy" (but salty).

LEXINGTON-STYLE PULLED PORK

SERVES 8 TO 10

WHAT MAKES THIS A BEST RECIPE: The Carolinas are Balkanized by the style of barbecue served in the different regions. We should be nonpartisan about such things, but we have our favorite: Lexington-style pulled pork. It's sweet and smoky, and served with a simple peppery sauce. The professionals cook the meat for a day over barely smoking coals, but we wanted a recipe that was faster and could easily be accomplished by the dilettante pitmaster. This is it. While some recipes use such dubious methods as indoor smokers or liquid smoke to invest the meat with "smoke" flavor in a hurry, we're not impressed; instead we prefer starting the meat on the grill with wood chips and finishing it in the oven once the meat is richly flavored with smoke. After numerous tests, we decided that leaving the meat on the grill for two hours—with a hefty four cups of wood chips for flavor (twice what we would normally use)—followed by two to three hours in the oven (covered) produced falling-apart tender meat every bit as good as that cooked completely over coals. To bump up the flavor, we coated the pork with a basic barbecue rub before placing it on the grill. As for the sauce, it's nothing more than vinegar, sugar, pepper, and ketchup. But even with so few ingredients, it still took some testing to get the balance of flavors just right. As a base, cider vinegar was the clear favorite for its fruity taste, especially when cut with an equal amount of water to curb its harshness. Granulated sugar and a moderate amount of ketchup tempered the acidity and the peppery bite provided by black pepper and some red pepper flakes.

PORK

- 2 tablespoons paprika
- 2 tablespoons pepper
- 2 tablespoons brown sugar
- 1 tablespoon salt
- 1 boneless pork shoulder roast (Boston butt) (4 to 5 pounds)
- 4 cups wood chips

SAUCE

- 1 cup water
- 1 cup cider vinegar
- ½ cup ketchup
- 1 tablespoon sugar
- ¾ teaspoon salt
- ½ teaspoon pepper
- ½ teaspoon red pepper flakes

1. FOR THE PORK: Combine the spices, brown sugar, and salt in a small bowl, breaking up any lumps as necessary. Massage the entire pork roast with the spice rub.

2. Soak the wood chips in a bowl of water to cover for 15 minutes; drain. Open the bottom grill vents. Light a large chimney starter filled halfway with charcoal briquettes (about 50 pieces) and allow it to burn until the charcoal is covered with a layer of fine gray ash. Pour the coals into a pile on one side of the grill and scatter the soaked wood chips over the coals. Set the cooking grate in place, cover the grill, and heat 5 minutes. Use a grill brush to scrape the cooking grate clean.

3. Following the photo on page 186, position the pork on the cooler side of the grill. Cover, positioning the half-open lid vents directly over the meat, and cook until the meat has a dark, rosy crust and the charcoal is spent, about 2 hours.

4. Meanwhile, adjust an oven rack to the lower-middle position and heat the oven to 325 degrees. Transfer the pork to a large roasting pan, wrap the pan and pork tightly in foil, and roast in the oven until a fork inserted into the pork can be removed with no resistance, 2 to 3 hours. Remove from the oven and allow to rest, still wrapped in the foil, for 30 minutes.

5. FOR THE SAUCE: Whisk together all the ingredients until the sugar and salt are dissolved. Using your hands, pull the pork into thin shreds, discarding the fat if desired. Toss the pork with ½ cup of the sauce, serving the remaining sauce at the table.

WHERE THINGS CAN GO WRONG: Choosing the right cut of pork is half the battle. Pork butt, which is usually sold off the bone and wrapped in netting, is a richly marbled, "working" cut of meat laced with collagen, which guarantees a rich flavor—once broken down via slow heat. If barbecuing a bone-in roast, or if your pork butt weighs more than 5 pounds, plan on an extra 30 to 60 minutes of oven cooking time.

WHAT YOU CAN DO AHEAD OF TIME: The roast can be prepared through step 1, wrapped tightly in plastic wrap or aluminum foil, and refrigerated for up to 1 day.

NOTES FROM THE TEST KITCHEN

GAS-GRILLED LEXINGTON-STYLE PULLED PORK

Seal 4 cups drained soaked wood chips in a foil packet (see the following photos). Place the packet on the primary burner of a gas grill, turn all the burners to high, cover, and heat with the lid down until the chips are smoking heavily, about 15 minutes. Turn the primary burner to medium and turn the remaining burners off, adjusting the temperature of the primary burner as needed to maintain an average temperature of 275 degrees. Position the pork over the cool part of the grill. Proceed with the recipe as directed.

MAKING A FOIL PACKET

1. Place the soaked and drained chips on an 8-inch square piece of heavy-duty aluminum foil. Fold the foil over the chips and crimp all the sides to seal well.

2. Using a paring knife, cut slits in the top of the foil packet and place it directly on the primary burner (the burner that will remain on during the entire cooking time). When protected in this fashion, the chips should smoke for 30 to 40 minutes.

HOW TO SET UP THE GRILL

Indirect heat is the key to low and slow BBQ. Place the roast on the side of the grill opposite the lit coals.

HOW TO FINISH THE PORK

1. After taking the pork off the grill, transfer it to a roasting pan, cover the pan with foil, and finish in a heated 325-degree oven.

2. Wearing kitchen gloves to protect your hands from the heat, shred (or "pull") the pork into thin strands, adding sauce as you go.

THE BEST CIDER VINEGARS

Cider vinegar is a staple ingredient in everyone's pantry that is rarely given little consideration at all, though, after a recent tasting, we think it really should. We chose 10 different brands—both national brands and a couple from France and Canada—and right off the bat, it was clear that those we picked were not identical products. The colors ranged from pale straw to deep gold, flavors were sweet to puckeringly tart, and some were crystal clear and others were clouded with particulate matter. After tasting the vinegars in four different ways—straight, a vinaigrette, a cooked sauce, and a vinegar-based barbecue sauce—one thing was clear: Sweet vinegars stole the show. Scientific analysis backed up our tasters' palates and proved that the two winners were the sweetest of the 10 tested. Our favorite, French-produced **Maille Apple Cider Vinegar** (left, $4.00 for 16.9 ounces), won raves for its "deep, warm" flavor profile and complex notes of honey, caramel, and sweet, "definite apple" taste. California-made **Spectrum Naturals Organic Apple Cider Vinegar** (right, $2.89 for 16 ounces) came in a close second for its "distinct apple flavor," "floral" aroma, and "assertive, tangy" qualities.

STUFFED PORK CHOPS
WITH PORT, PECANS, AND DRIED FRUIT
SERVES 4 TO 6

WHAT MAKES THIS A BEST RECIPE: Stuffing a pork chop is not a bad idea—today's lean pork needs all the help it can get—but it is rarely well executed. Most recipes insist on cramming the chops full of bulky bread stuffing, which does little to improve the chop's flavor. This recipe, however, packs a rich-tasting stuffing into a thick, juicy pork chop and—an added bonus—can be assembled the night before. What's not to love? For the best flavor and juiciest texture, we knew bone-in pork chops were a must. The best option we found was a chop cut from the rib cage, which has a wide, unbroken "eye" of meat and a curved rib bone off to the side and out of the way. And while most recipes butterfly the chop to stuff it and sew or pin it closed, we prefer a less invasive technique, in which a sharp paring knife is used to cut a wide pocket whose opening is actually quite small. To keep the meat moist, we found brining was essential. The brined meat could be deeply seared on the stovetop and finished in a moderate oven without fear of the meat drying out. We sought fillings that incorporated moisture, fat, and assertive flavors to enhance the lean, mild pork. Along the way, we discovered that creamy, even sticky, stuffings were much easier to pack into a chop. We settled on a red onion and fruit jam stuffing with dates, sour cherries, orange, pecans, and a topping of blue cheese—a perfect foil to the juicy pork.

4   **bone-in pork rib chops, 1½ inches thick (12 to 14 ounces each)**
¾   **cup packed light brown sugar**
    Salt
2   **tablespoons olive oil**
1   **large red onion, halved and sliced ⅛ inch thick**
1   **tablespoon granulated sugar**
¾   **cup ruby port**
⅓   **cup chopped pitted dates**
⅓   **cup dried sour cherries**
1   **orange, cut into 4 wedges**
3   **tablespoons white wine vinegar**
2   **teaspoons minced fresh thyme**
⅓   **cup pecans, toasted**
    Pepper
3   **ounces blue cheese, crumbled (about ¾ cup), for serving**

1. Following the photos on page 188, cut a 1-inch opening into the side of each pork chop, then cut a pocket for the stuffing. Dissolve the brown sugar and ¼ cup salt in 6 cups of water in a large bowl or container. Submerge the chops in the brine, cover with plastic wrap, and refrigerate for 1 hour.

2. While the chops brine, heat 1 tablespoon of the oil in a medium saucepan over medium heat until shimmering. Add the onion and granulated sugar and cook, stirring occasionally, until browned, 20 to 25 minutes.

3. Meanwhile, combine the port, dates, and cherries in a microwave-safe bowl, cover with plastic wrap, and microwave on high power until simmering, about 1 minute. Set aside. Squeeze ¼ cup of juice from the orange wedges into a small bowl, reserving the juiced wedges for sealing the stuffing pockets in the chops.

4. When the onions are browned, stir in the dried fruit mixture, orange juice, 2 tablespoons of the vinegar, and thyme. Cook, stirring occasionally, until thickened and jam-like, 10 to 12 minutes. Stir in the remaining 1 tablespoon vinegar and the pecans. Season with salt and pepper. Cool until just warm, about 15 minutes.

5. Remove the chops from the brine, rinse, and pat dry with paper towels. Place one-quarter of the stuffing (about ⅓ cup) in the pocket of each chop. Trim the reserved orange wedges from the stuffing recipe to 2-inch lengths. Insert 1 orange wedge into each pocket to contain the stuffing. Season the chops with pepper to taste.

6. Adjust an oven rack to the lower-middle position, place a rimmed baking sheet on the rack, and heat the oven to 450 degrees. Heat the remaining 1 tablespoon oil in a heavy-bottomed large skillet over medium-high heat until just smoking. Add the chops and brown well on both sides, 5 to 6 minutes.

7. Transfer the chops to the preheated sheet in the oven. Cook until an instant-read thermometer inserted into the center of the stuffing registers 140 degrees, 10 to 15 minutes, flipping the chops halfway through the cooking time. Transfer the chops to a platter, tent loosely with foil, and let rest for 10 minutes. Sprinkle with the blue cheese before serving. Serve whole or, to serve 6, slice into ½-inch-thick slices.

WHERE THINGS CAN GO WRONG: If using enhanced pork, do not brine the pork in step 1. Manufacturers don't use the terms "enhanced" or "natural" on package labels, but if the pork has been enhanced it will have an ingredient list. Natural pork contains pork and no other ingredients. Care must be taken not to poke straight through the edge of the chop when enlarging the pocket, however. After making this mistake half a dozen times, we learned to guard against it by leaving the thin layer of fat and connective tissue around the edge of the chop untrimmed.

WHAT YOU CAN DO AHEAD OF TIME: The chops can be prepared through step 5, wrapped tightly in plastic wrap, and refrigerated for up to 24 hours.

NOTES FROM THE TEST KITCHEN

BUYING THE RIGHT CHOP
Stuffed pork chops depend on purchasing the right chop. Note that even within the rib chop category, there are good ones cut from close to the center of the loin and not-so-good ones cut from the shoulder or blade end of the loin.

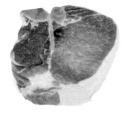

LOIN CHOP
The bone running through this chop makes it difficult to stuff.

BLADE-END CHOP
This chop contracts during cooking and squeezes out the stuffing.

RIB CHOP
The unbroken eye of meat makes this chop perfect for stuffing.

STUFFING A PORK CHOP

1. Using a sharp boning or paring knife, trim away the excess fat and connective tissue around the edge of the meat.

2. With the knife positioned as shown, insert the blade through the center of the side of the chop until the tip touches the bone.

3. Swing the tip of the blade through the middle of the chop to create a pocket (the opening should be about 1 inch wide).

4. With your fingers, gently press the stuffing mixture into the pocket, without enlarging the opening.

ENHANCED OR UNENHANCED PORK?
Because modern pork is remarkably lean and therefore somewhat bland and prone to dryness if overcooked, a product called "enhanced" pork has overtaken the market. In fact, it can be hard to find unenhanced pork. Enhanced pork has been injected with a solution of water, salt, sodium phosphates, sodium lactate, potassium lactate, sodium diacetate, and varying flavor agents to bolster flavor and juiciness, with enhancing ingredients adding 7 to 15 percent extra weight. After several taste tests, we have concluded that while enhanced pork is indeed juicier and more tender than unenhanced pork, the latter has more genuine pork flavor. Some tasters picked up artificial, salty flavors in enhanced pork. It can also leach juices that, once reduced, will result in overly salty sauces. We prefer natural pork, but the choice is up to you.

STUFFED PORK CHOPS

PORK TENDERLOIN MEDALLIONS
WITH APPLE-CIDER SAUCE
SERVES 4 TO 6

WHAT MAKES THIS A BEST RECIPE: With no bones, minimal fat, and wide availability, pork tenderloin has plenty going for it. When cooked properly, it has a tenderness rivaling that of beef tenderloin, the deluxe roast that gives us filet mignon. On the downside, this ultra-lean cut has an ultra-mild flavor that needs a major boost. There are a lot of options to improve its flavor, like brining and marinades, but all that takes lots of time. We like this recipe, however, because it's quick, putting a meal on the table in minutes, not hours. For the best flavor, we knew we had to deeply brown the meat, yet keep it moist too—a tall order. Whole tenderloins cooked unevenly because of their oblong shape and it was hard to thoroughly brown them. Instead, we opted to cut the tenderloins crosswise into individual "filets"; each side could be browned for maximum flavor. If cut too thin, the meat overcooked before it adequately browned; if cut too thick, the pork had to be finished in the oven after browning to cook the center through—a complicated process. At 1½ inches, the interior was cooked through but still juicy and the top and bottom surfaces were beautifully browned. Binding the circumference of each medallion with twine ensured a consistent shape and even cooking. A quick pan sauce prepared with the rich fond left in the skillet after cooking the meat seemed like the obvious way to further boost the meat's flavor. Apples and pork pair perfectly, so we whipped up a sauce flavored with diced apples, apple cider, apple brandy, cinnamon, shallots, and thyme. Reducing the sauce's liquid components in a separate pan while the meat browned helped keep timing tight.

PORK

- 2 pork tenderloins (1 to 1¼ pounds each), trimmed of fat and silver skin, cut crosswise into 1½-inch pieces, and tied; thinner end pieces removed and tied together
  Kosher salt and pepper
- 2 tablespoons vegetable oil

Taking a cue from the more famous filet mignon, our "pork mignons" are thick-cut to keep them juicy and moist.

SAUCE

- 1½ cups apple cider
- 1 cup low-sodium chicken broth
- 2 teaspoons cider vinegar
- 1 cinnamon stick
- 4 tablespoons unsalted butter, cut into 4 pieces
- 2 shallots, minced (about 6 tablespoons)
- 1 Granny Smith apple, peeled, cored, and diced small
- ¼ cup Calvados or apple-flavored brandy
- 1 teaspoon minced fresh thyme
  Salt and pepper

1. FOR THE MEAT: Season the pork with salt and pepper. Heat the oil in a 12-inch skillet over medium-high heat until shimmering. Add the pork cut side down and cook, without moving the pieces, until well browned, 3 to 5 minutes. Turn the pork and brown the second side, 3 to 5 minutes more. Reduce the heat to medium. Using tongs, stand each piece on its side and cook, turning the pieces as necessary, until the sides are well browned and the internal temperature registers 145 to 150 degrees on an instant-read thermometer, 8 to 12 minutes. Transfer the pork to a platter and tent loosely with foil.

2. FOR THE SAUCE: While the pork cooks, combine the cider, broth, vinegar, and cinnamon stick in a medium saucepan; simmer over medium-high heat until the liquid is reduced to 1 cup, 10 to 12 minutes. Remove the cinnamon stick and discard. Set the sauce aside until the pork is cooked.

3. Pour off any fat from the skillet in which the pork was cooked. Melt 1 tablespoon of the butter over medium heat; add the shallots and apple and cook, stirring occasionally, until softened and beginning to brown, 1 to 2 minutes. Remove the skillet from the heat and add the Calvados. Return the skillet to the heat and cook about 1 minute, scraping the bottom of the pan with a wooden spoon to loosen the browned bits. Add the reduced cider mixture, any juices from the resting meat, and thyme; increase the heat to medium-high and simmer until thickened and reduced to 1¼ cups, 3 to 4 minutes. Off the heat, whisk in the remaining 3 tablespoons butter and season with salt and pepper to taste. Pour the sauce over the pork and serve immediately.

WHAT YOU CAN DO AHEAD OF TIME: The pork can be sliced, tied, wrapped tightly in plastic wrap, and refrigerated for up to 1 day. The cider mixture reduction in step 2 can also be refrigerated in an airtight container for up to 1 day.

NOTES FROM THE TEST KITCHEN

GOOD PORK, BAD PORK

While developing our recipe for pork tenderloin medallions, we struggled to achieve a deeply seared exterior without overcooking the interior. Our solution? Cut thicker medallions, which can spend more time in the pan.

GOOD
Great browning, moist interior

BAD
Good browning, dry interior

TURNING THE END PIECE INTO A MEDALLION

After cutting the tenderloins into symmetrical 1½-inch medallions, you will inevitably have a few irregularly shaped pieces left over. The tapered end pieces can be scored, folded, and tied into medallions. Tie any remaining smaller pieces together into a medallion shape, making sure the top and bottom surfaces are flat.

1. Score the tenderloin's tapered end piece.

2. Fold in half at the incision.

3. Tie the medallion with twine, making sure the top and bottom surfaces are flat.

BUTCHER'S TWINE

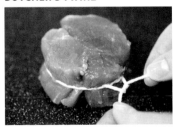

Thick medallions allow for more browning, but they can flop over in the pan. To prevent this, tie each piece with twine.

CHARCOAL-GRILLED LAMB CHOPS
WITH NEAR EAST RED PEPPER PASTE
SERVES 4

WHAT MAKES THIS A BEST RECIPE: A smoky charcoal fire can bring out the very best in full-flavored lamb—that is, when the dripping fat from the rich meat doesn't create a blazing inferno. Lamb chops aren't cheap, and we wanted a foolproof method for cooking them. The first step was choosing the right cut. Lamb chops are available from the loin, rib, and shoulder. Loin and rib chops are by far the more expensive choices; shoulder chops can cost two-thirds less and, as we found, have a gutsier flavor and are less temperamental. They can be cooked to medium without adverse effect to flavor or texture. Cheaper and easier to cook? What's not to love? Slightly thicker chops, about ¾ to 1 inch thick, allowed for a thicker, more flavorful crust to develop and slightly more carefree cooking—grilling times should always be a little flexible to take the variables into consideration. Lamb chops cooked over direct heat from start to finish scorched terribly; searing them over a hot side and then finishing them over a cooler fire cooked them more evenly and precluded some—but not all—of the flare-ups. A squirt bottle filled with water will take care of the few that do occur. Cumin and cinnamon serve to complement the assertive flavor of lamb, and adding these spices to a paste prepared from sautéed peppers (both hot and sweet), garlic, and mint not only added depth but also prevented the dried spices from burning over the hot fire.

RED PEPPER PASTE

- 3 tablespoons extra-virgin olive oil
- ½ red bell pepper, stemmed, seeded, and chopped coarse (see page 45)
- ½ serrano or jalapeño chile, stemmed, seeded, and chopped coarse

Bargain-priced shoulder chops pack a rich flavor and juicy texture that is perfect for grilling.

- 2 teaspoons fresh lemon juice
- 1 garlic clove, minced
- 1½ teaspoons chopped fresh mint
- ½ teaspoon ground cumin
- ½ teaspoon dried summer savory
- ¼ teaspoon ground cinnamon

CHOPS

- 4 shoulder lamb chops (blade or round-bone), ¾ to 1 inch thick
  Salt and pepper

1. FOR THE PASTE: Heat 1 tablespoon of the oil in a small skillet over medium-high heat until shimmering. Add the red bell pepper and chile and cook, stirring frequently, until just beginning to soften, about 2 minutes. Reduce the heat to medium-low and continue to cook until softened, about 5 minutes.

2. Transfer the contents of the skillet to a food processor. Add the lemon juice, garlic, mint, cumin, summer savory, cinnamon, and remaining 2 tablespoons oil and process until almost smooth (there will still be some chunky pieces of pepper).

3. FOR THE CHOPS: Rub the chops with the paste and sprinkle with salt and pepper; marinate at room temperature for 20 minutes.

4. Light a large chimney starter filled with charcoal briquettes (about 100 pieces) and allow it to burn until all the charcoal is covered with a layer of fine gray ash, about 20 minutes. Stack most of the coals on one side of the grill bottom and arrange the remaining coals in a single layer on the other side of the grill. Set the cooking grate in place. Cover and let the grill heat up 5 minutes. Use a grill brush to scrape the cooking grate clean.

5. Grill the chops, uncovered, over the hotter part of the grill, turning them once, until well browned, about 4 minutes. (If the chops start to flame, drag them to the cooler part of the grill and/or extinguish the flames with a squirt bottle.) Move the chops to the cooler part of the grill and continue grilling, turning once, to the desired doneness, about 5 minutes for rare (about 120 degrees on an instant-read thermometer), about 7 minutes for medium (about 130 degrees), or about 9 minutes for well-done (140 to 150 degrees).

6. Remove the chops from the grill to a platter and let rest 5 minutes. Serve.

WHERE THINGS CAN GO WRONG: If you purchase shoulder lamb chops that are less than ¾ inch thick, they are likely to overcook. If you can only find chops that are ½ inch thick, reduce the cooking time over the medium-low fire by about 30 seconds on each side. While this method largely precludes flare-ups, they are still a concern; keep a squirt bottle filled with water handy to extinguish them.

WHAT YOU CAN DO AHEAD OF TIME: The lamb chops can be prepared through step 3, wrapped in plastic wrap, and refrigerated for up to 24 hours. Bring to room temperature before grilling, about 30 minutes.

NOTES FROM THE TEST KITCHEN

GAS-GRILLED LAMB CHOPS
WITH NEAR EAST RED PEPPER PASTE

To make sure the lamb chops aren't flaming up under the grill cover, watch for any substantial amount of smoke coming through the vents. This indicates that flare-ups are occurring and need to be extinguished. Turn all the burners on a gas grill to high, close the cover, and heat until very hot, about 15 minutes. Use a grill brush to scrape the cooking grate clean. Leave one burner on high and turn other burners down to medium. Proceed with step 5, cooking with the lid down. After moving the chops to the cooler side of the grill and turning, cook to the desired doneness, about 6 minutes for rare (about 120 degrees on an instant-read thermometer), about 8 minutes for medium (about 130 degrees), or about 10 minutes for well-done (140 to 150 degrees). Remove the chops from the grill to a platter and let rest for 5 minutes. Serve.

BUY THE RIGHT LAMB CHOPS

Lamb shoulder is sliced into two different cuts, blade and round-bone chops. Blade chops are roughly rectangular in shape, and some are thickly striated with fat. Each blade chop includes a piece of the chine bone (the backbone of the animal) and a thin piece of the blade bone (the shoulder blade of the animal). Round-bone chops, also called arm chops, are more oval in shape and as a rule are substantially leaner than blade chops. Each contains a round cross-section of the arm bone so that the chop looks a bit like a small ham steak. In addition to the arm bone, there's also a tiny line of riblets on the side of each chop.

ROUND-BONE CHOP

BLADE CHOP

KNOWING WHEN FOOD IS DONE

KNOWING WHEN FISH, MEAT, AND POULTRY ARE DONE

This chart presents ideal serving temperatures. Since the temperature of meat will continue to rise as it rests, it should be taken off the heat just before it reaches the desired temperature. (This phenomenon doesn't occur with poultry and fish.) These temperatures (in degrees Fahrenheit) reflect our opinions regarding optimal flavor and juiciness. The U.S. Department of Agriculture recommends cooking beef, lamb, veal steaks and roasts, and fish to 145 degrees, pork and all ground meat to 160 degrees, and poultry to 180 degrees to eliminate potential food-borne pathogens.

	RARE	MEDIUM-RARE	MEDIUM	WELL-DONE
Fish	110	120	140	*
Red Meat (beef, lamb, veal)	125	130	140	160**
Pork	*	*	145	160**
Poultry (white meat)	*	*	*	160 to 165
Poultry (dark meat)	*	*	*	175

* Not recommended
** Recommended only for ground meat dishes, such as meat loaf

CARRYOVER EFFECT

When it comes to red meat and pork, judging doneness, even with a thermometer, involves some guesswork. That's because sometimes you aren't judging whether the food is ready to eat but whether it will be ready to eat once it has cooled or rested. For instance, to allow for juices to distribute themselves evenly, steaks, chops, and roasts should rest five to 20 minutes. (A steak needs less time than a big roast.) As meat rests, its temperature will climb. The thicker the cut, the more the temperature will rise. Also, food coming out of a very hot oven will have more residual heat than food coming out of a cooler oven.

JUDGING THE DONENESS OF FISH

You can use an instant-read thermometer to check doneness in thick fillets, but in most cases you have to resort to nicking the fish with a paring knife and then peeking into the interior to judge color and flakiness. White fish should be cooked to medium (the flesh should be opaque but still moist and just beginning to flake). Salmon and scallops are best cooked to medium-rare (the center should still be translucent), while tuna is best cooked rare (only the outer layer is opaque while the rest of the fish is translucent).

TAKING THE TEMPERATURE OF A ROAST

For many roasts, it's possible to slide the probe right through the meat and into the pan, which will give you a false reading. To make sure that the probe stays in the meat, insert the thermometer at an angle. Push the probe deep into the roast and then slowly draw it out, looking for the lowest temperature to find the center of the meat.

TAKING THE TEMPERATURE OF A CHICKEN OR TURKEY

Check the thickest part of the thigh and the breast. For a stuffed bird, insert the thermometer into the center of the cavity as well to make sure the stuffing has reached a safe temperature of 165 degrees.

TAKING THE TEMPERATURE OF A STEAK OR CHOP

Hold the steak or chop with tongs and insert the thermometer through the side of the meat. Use this method with burgers and chicken.

INSTANT-READ THERMOMETER

WHAT TO BUY: Our test kitchen winner is fast (it registers temperatures from –58 to 572 degrees in seconds), accurate, and perfectly proportioned. A recent test of nine inexpensive models found several with the features we like, although all were slower than our winner.

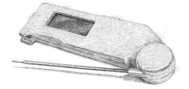

TEST KITCHEN WINNER
★ Thermoworks Super-Fast Thermapen, $85

BEST BUY
★ CDN ProAccurate DTQ450, $17.95

KNOWING WHEN BAKED GOODS ARE DONE

COOKIES

We think most cookies are best when they are chewy. This means taking them out of the oven when they are slightly underdone—in fact, the cookies are often so soft they will droop over the end of a spatula. Bake cookies on parchment and cool on the baking sheet for a few minutes; after they have set up slightly, slide the parchment onto a cooling rack. If the cookies have crevices, the crevices should appear moist. When baking smooth cookies, look at the edges, which should be lightly browned; the center should be set but not fully dry.

PUDDINGS AND CUSTARDS

Egg-based puddings and custards can curdle if cooked beyond 185 degrees. We take crème anglaise off the heat when the mixture registers 175 to 180, but when making the base for ice cream we push the temperature to 180 to 185 for maximum thickness. Baked custards, such as flan and crème brûlée, should jiggle (but not slosh) when gently shaken. This will occur between 170 and 175 degrees.

CAKES, MUFFINS, AND QUICK BREADS

There are two ways to judge doneness in cakes, muffins, and quick breads.

1. Fully baked items should feel springy and resilient when the center is gently pressed. If your finger leaves an impression—or the center jiggles—the item is not done.

2. A skewer or toothpick should emerge fairly clean, with perhaps just a few crumbs attached. If you see moist batter, the item needs to bake longer.

CHEESECAKE

Cheesecake is ready to come out of the oven when the center just barely jiggles and the internal temperature reaches 150 degrees. (At higher temperatures, the texture will suffer.) If possible, insert the thermometer into the side of the cheesecake where it rises above the pan (otherwise, insert it into the center of the cake).

PIES AND PASTRIES

For pies and pastries, it's all about color. A well-browned crust is more flavorful than a blond one, and it won't be doughy in the middle. We bake all pies in glass pie plates so we can examine the bottom of the crust to determine doneness. When working with puff pastry or other flaky doughs, lift up the bottom of individual pieces and look for even browning.

BROWNIES

Use the skewer test to determine doneness, but look for moist, sticky crumbs.

TIPS FOR USING A THERMOMETER

- Regularly check accuracy by leaving the probe in a bucket of ice water for a minute or two. If the temperature doesn't register 32 degrees Fahrenheit, use the calibration button to reset the thermometer.

- Slide the probe deep into the center of foods, making sure that the tip does not exit the food.

- Avoid bones, cavities (say, in a turkey), and pan surfaces, all of which will throw off the reading.

- Take more than one reading, especially in large roasts and turkeys.

YEAST BREADS

Lean breads are done when the internal temperature measures 210 degrees. Richer loaves made with eggs and butter are done when the internal temperature measures 190 degrees. Breads with a modest amount of fat fall in between; they are done at 195 to 200 degrees.

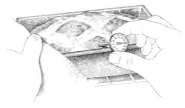

For free-form loaves, tip the loaf up and insert the probe through the bottom crust.

For bread baked in a loaf pan, insert the thermometer from the side, just above the pan edge.

POULTRY

CHICKEN MARSALA 198

ITALIAN CHICKEN WITH SAUSAGE AND PEPPERS 200

MODERN COQ AU VIN 202

MODERN CHICKEN DIVAN 204

PARMESAN-CRUSTED CHICKEN CUTLETS 206

LATINO-STYLE CHICKEN AND RICE 207

PECAN-CRUSTED CHICKEN CUTLETS 209

KING RANCH CASSEROLE 211

MARYLAND FRIED CHICKEN 212

COBB CHICKEN SALAD 214

ROAST CHICKEN WITH ROOT VEGETABLES 216

FIRECRACKER CHICKEN 219

SPICE-RUBBED PICNIC CHICKEN 220

GRILL-ROASTED TURKEY BREAST 222

CLASSIC BARBECUED CHICKEN 224

CHARCOAL-GRILLED BUTTERFLIED LEMON CHICKEN 227

ROAST SALTED TURKEY 230

CHARCOAL-GRILLED DUCK BREASTS
WITH PEACH-HABAÑERO CHUTNEY 232

CHICKEN MARSALA

SERVES 4

WHAT MAKES THIS A BEST RECIPE: Chicken Marsala is a well-loved Italian classic in which sautéed chicken cutlets are blanketed with a Marsala wine and mushroom-flavored pan sauce. Simple, yes, but not always successful. We've had our fair share of mediocre, even miserable versions at purportedly authentic Italian restaurants. We decided to make our own and stay true to the dish's roots. Preparation starts with sautéing the chicken, after which the sauce is constructed in the same pan to capitalize on the fond, or the flavorful browned bits left behind by the chicken. For the thin cutlets typically used in this dish, we found it best to cook them quickly over high heat so that they browned a bit and stayed moist; dusting them with flour before cooking also helped prevent them from drying out. With the chicken resting, we built the sauce in the skillet. The first step in building a complex-tasting sauce was browning the mushrooms along with onions and garlic. Next, we deglazed the pan with Marsala and simmered it until slightly thickened. Sliding the cutlets back into the pan warmed them and married sauce to meat. But we weren't done yet—we still had a problem: the mushrooms sucked up the sauce and tasted of little but the Marsala. The simple solution was to remove them from the pan, reduce the sauce, and, just before serving, return the mushrooms to the sauce along with a knob of butter for richness and a little lemon juice and parsley to freshen the whole. This great-tasting chicken Marsala is well balanced and easy to make.

8 chicken cutlets (about 1½ pounds)
   Salt and pepper
¼ cup unbleached all-purpose flour
2 tablespoons vegetable oil
3 tablespoons unsalted butter
½ small onion, chopped fine
8 ounces white mushrooms, quartered
1 garlic clove, minced

¾ cup sweet Marsala wine
½ cup low-sodium chicken broth
2 teaspoons fresh lemon juice
1 tablespoon minced fresh parsley

1. Pat the cutlets dry with paper towels and season with salt and pepper. Dredge the cutlets in the flour to coat and shake to remove excess. Heat 1 tablespoon of the oil in a large nonstick skillet over high heat until just smoking. Add 4 cutlets and cook until golden brown, 2 to 2½ minutes on each side. Transfer to a large plate and tent with foil. Repeat with the remaining oil and cutlets.

2. Melt 1 tablespoon of the butter in the now-empty skillet over medium-high heat. Cook the onion and mushrooms until browned, about 5 minutes. Add the garlic and cook until fragrant, about 30 seconds. Transfer the mushroom mixture to a medium bowl and tent with foil.

3. Add the Marsala and broth to the empty skillet, bring to a boil over high heat, and cook until reduced to ½ cup, about 5 minutes. Reduce the heat to medium-low, return the chicken and accumulated juices to the skillet, and turn the chicken to heat through, about 1 minute. Transfer the chicken to a serving platter. Off the heat, whisk in the remaining 2 tablespoons butter, lemon juice, parsley, and mushroom mixture. Pour the sauce over the chicken. Serve.

WHERE THINGS CAN GO WRONG: To ensure even cooking, make sure to purchase cutlets between ¼ and ½ inch thick, or cut your own from boneless, skinless chicken breasts.

NOTES FROM THE TEST KITCHEN

MARSALA WINE

Marsala is a fortified wine that originally hailed from Sicily. Like vermouth or sherry, Marsala starts with regular table wine that is then fortified with extra alcohol (often in the form of brandy) to increase its shelf life. An open bottle of fortified wine will keep in the pantry for several months (if not longer), making it the perfect choice for the cook who uses small quantities for recipes. Marsala comes in sweet and dry varieties; we like the sweet for Chicken Marsala.

ITALIAN CHICKEN WITH SAUSAGE AND PEPPERS

SERVES 4 TO 6

WHAT MAKES THIS A BEST RECIPE: Just how this Italian-American skillet dish (*chicken scarpariello*) came about is debatable, but its use of bright, flavorful ingredients is indisputable. This Little Italy specialty combines crisp, browned chicken pieces with sweet onions, Italian sausage, red bell peppers, and spicy pickled cherry peppers in a tart, vinegary sauce. If not prepared properly, it's the stuff of heartburn and indigestion; our version is blessedly balanced—no antacid necessary. Most recipes start by browning the sausage and then the chicken in a large skillet before sautéing the onions, bell peppers, jarred cherry peppers, and garlic. Once the vegetables have softened, the cooking liquid (typically the brine from the jar of cherry peppers supplemented by white wine vinegar) is added, followed by the browned chicken and sausage. By the time the chicken finishes cooking, the liquid has reduced into a sauce. To streamline the process—and ensure even cooking—we opted to use split bone-in, skin-on chicken breasts cut into pieces—the sausage contributed enough fat to keep the chicken moist. Using sweet, not hot, Italian sausage helped moderate the dish's heat. And to prevent excessive greasiness, we wiped the skillet clean in between steps and used a minimum of mixed chicken and sausage fat to sauté the peppers. As for the liquid, we eschewed the cherry pepper brine in favor of chicken broth tarted up with white wine vinegar and tempered with a couple pinches of sugar. Traditionally, the dish is entirely prepared on the stovetop, but we found the chicken's skin became unpalatably flabby when prepared in this fashion. We chose to slide the skillet into the oven and raise the chicken above the liquid—by resting it on top of the peppers—so that the skin crisped. Once the chicken was done, we let it rest, and thickened the sauce with a little cornstarch.

Little Italy's "shoemaker" chicken is traditionally prepared entirely on the stovetop. To ensure crisp skin, we put the skillet in the oven to finish cooking.

1	tablespoon vegetable oil
8	ounces sweet Italian sausage, casings removed
2	pounds bone-in, skin-on chicken breast halves, trimmed and cut crosswise into 2 or 3 pieces
	Salt and pepper
1	onion, halved and sliced ¼ inch thick
1	large red bell pepper, stemmed, seeded, and cut into ¼-inch strips
3–5	pickled hot cherry peppers, stemmed, seeded, and cut into ¼-inch strips (about ¼ cup)
3	garlic cloves, minced
2	teaspoons sugar
⅓	cup plus 2 tablespoons white wine vinegar
¾	cup plus 1 tablespoon low-sodium chicken broth
1	teaspoon cornstarch
1	teaspoon minced fresh thyme
1	tablespoon minced fresh parsley

1. Adjust an oven rack to the middle position and heat the oven to 350 degrees. Heat 1 teaspoon of the oil in a 12-inch ovensafe skillet over medium-high heat until shimmering. Add the sausage and cook, stirring to break the sausage into ½-inch pieces, until browned, about

3 minutes. Transfer the sausage to a paper towel–lined plate. Remove the skillet from the heat; pour off the fat into a small bowl and reserve; wipe out the skillet with paper towels.

2. Return the skillet to medium-high heat and heat the remaining 2 teaspoons oil until smoking. Pat the chicken dry and liberally season with salt and pepper. Add the chicken skin side down and cook without moving until well browned, 3 to 5 minutes. Using tongs, turn the chicken and brown on the other side, about 3 minutes. Transfer the chicken to a large plate. Remove the skillet from the heat and pour off the fat into the bowl with the sausage fat; wipe out the skillet with paper towels.

3. Return the skillet to medium-high heat and heat 1 tablespoon of the reserved fat until shimmering. Add the onion and cook until beginning to soften, about 2 minutes. Add the bell pepper and cherry peppers and cook, stirring occasionally, until the bell pepper begins to soften, about 4 minutes. Add the garlic and cook, stirring frequently, until fragrant, about 30 seconds. Add the sugar, ⅓ cup vinegar, and ¾ cup broth; bring the mixture to a boil, scraping up any browned bits from the pan bottom.

4. Add the sausage, chicken, and any accumulated juices to the skillet, arranging the chicken pieces in a single layer, skin side up, on top of the peppers and onion. Transfer the skillet to the oven and cook until an instant-read thermometer inserted into the thickest part of the chicken registers 160 degrees, 18 to 22 minutes, removing the smaller pieces sooner if necessary. Meanwhile, combine the cornstarch, thyme, and remaining tablespoon broth in a small bowl.

5. Carefully remove the skillet from the oven (the handle will be very hot) and transfer the chicken skin side up to a platter or individual serving plates. Place the skillet over medium-high heat and stir in the cornstarch mixture. Simmer the sauce mixture until slightly thickened, 2 to 3 minutes. Off the heat, taste the sauce and add up to 2 tablespoons of the remaining vinegar. Season with salt and pepper to taste. Spoon the sauce around the chicken, being careful not to pour it directly over the chicken, and sprinkle with the parsley. Serve immediately.

WHERE THINGS CAN GO WRONG: This dish is inherently spicy but you can control the heat level by adjusting the amount of cherry peppers as desired. Also, this recipe requires an ovensafe skillet. If you don't have one, make the following adjustments: Add the cornstarch mixture to the skillet in step 3 (instead of step 5) along with the vinegar and simmer until slightly thickened, 3 to 4 minutes. Stir in the sausage and transfer the mixture to a 13 by 9-inch baking dish. Arrange the chicken over the mixture and bake as directed.

NOTES FROM THE TEST KITCHEN

SPLITTING A BONE-IN CHICKEN BREAST
To make bone-in chicken breasts faster cooking and more manageable to eat, we cut them into smaller pieces. If using large chicken breasts (about 1 pound each), cut each breast into three pieces. If using smaller breasts (10 to 12 ounces each), cut each breast into two pieces.

Using a sharp chef's knife, cut into the breast until the knife hits the bone. Rock the knife back and forth through the bone.

CHILE PEPPER HEAT
Most of a chile's heat is contained within its seeds and ribs. So, if you prefer things on the hotter side, include all or a portion of the seeds and ribs; otherwise diligently remove them.

CHERRY PICKING
Cherry peppers are often found in the international section of the supermarket rather than in the pickle aisle. Most jars feature a combination of the red and green peppers, which are equally hot. Don't confuse cherry peppers with roasted red peppers.

TO SUBSTITUTE CHICKEN THIGHS
To make this dish with chicken thighs, increase the cooking time in the oven to about 25 minutes, or until an instant-read thermometer inserted into the thickest part of the thigh registers 175 degrees.

MODERN COQ AU VIN

SERVES 4 TO 6

WHAT MAKES THIS A BEST RECIPE: Originally made with roosters past their prime, *coq au vin* (chicken stewed in red wine) began life as provincial peasant fare. Simmered for hours with mushrooms, herbs, and pearl onions, the tough, old fowl soaked up the wine's rich flavor as the acidic liquid gently broke down the sinewy fibers. So what do you do when you don't have a rooster or hours to spare to tend the pot? Think modern—as this recipe does. It has all the flavor of the classic dish and can be ready in half the time. First things first, we switched from a whole bird to quick-cooking boneless, skinless chicken thighs. For maximum flavor, we sautéed them in bacon fat before simmering. We also swapped fuller flavored cremini mushrooms for the more classic white mushrooms and simmered the bacon in the stew, rather than using it as a garnish. Within 25 minutes of simmering, the chicken was fork-tender. But without the chicken bones, our basic recipe tasted boring—and another problem reared its head: With such a short simmer all that wine tasted boozy and astringent. Tomato paste and garlic improved the flavor, but did little for the booziness. That was solved by simmering the wine with some chicken broth in a separate pan until reduced before adding it to the stew. And, finally, while traditional recipes thicken the stew with chicken blood, we settled for something a bit less sanguine: a simple flour and butter roux.

1	bottle medium-bodied red wine
2	cups low-sodium chicken broth
10	sprigs fresh parsley plus 2 tablespoons minced fresh parsley

Red wine, mushrooms, and bacon transform chicken thighs into a rich, hearty stew. Serve with mashed potatoes to soak up every drop of the sauce.

2	sprigs fresh thyme
1	bay leaf
4	ounces bacon, preferably thick-cut, cut crosswise into ¼-inch pieces
2½	pounds boneless, skinless chicken thighs, trimmed and cut in half crosswise
	Salt and pepper
5	tablespoons unsalted butter
24	frozen pearl onions, thawed, drained, and patted dry
8	ounces cremini mushrooms, halved if small and quartered if large
2	garlic cloves, minced
1	tablespoon tomato paste
2	tablespoons unbleached all-purpose flour

1. Bring all but 1 tablespoon of the wine (reserve for later use), broth, parsley sprigs, thyme, and bay leaf to a simmer in a large saucepan over medium-high heat. Cook until reduced to 3 cups, about 25 minutes. Discard the herbs.

2. Meanwhile, cook the bacon in a large Dutch oven over medium heat until browned, 7 to 8 minutes. Transfer the bacon to a paper towel–lined plate. Reserve 2 tablespoons of the fat in a small bowl; discard the remaining fat.

3. Lightly season the chicken with salt and pepper. Heat 1 tablespoon of the reserved bacon fat in the Dutch oven over medium-high heat until just smoking. Add half of the chicken in a single layer and cook until lightly browned, about 2 minutes per side. Transfer to a plate and repeat with the remaining chicken and 1 tablespoon bacon fat.

4. Melt 3 tablespoons of the butter in the now-empty Dutch oven over medium-high heat; add the pearl onions and mushrooms; cook, stirring occasionally, until lightly browned, 5 to 8 minutes. Reduce the heat to medium, add the garlic, and cook until fragrant, about 30 seconds. Add the tomato paste and flour; cook, stirring frequently, until well combined, about 1 minute.

5. Add the reduced wine mixture, scraping the bottom of the pot with a wooden spoon to loosen any browned bits; add ¼ teaspoon pepper. Return the chicken, any accumulated juices, and the reserved bacon to the pot; increase the heat to high and bring to a boil. Reduce the heat to medium-low, cover the pot, and simmer until the chicken is tender, about 25 minutes, stirring halfway through the cooking time.

6. Transfer the chicken to a large bowl and tent with foil. Increase the heat to medium-high and simmer the sauce until thick and glossy and measures 3¼ cups, about 5 minutes. Off the heat, stir in the remaining 2 tablespoons butter and reserved 1 tablespoon wine. Season with salt to taste. Return the chicken to the pot and sprinkle with the minced parsley. Serve.

WHAT YOU CAN DO AHEAD OF TIME: The wine and broth mixture can be refrigerated in an airtight container for up to 2 days.

NOTES FROM THE TEST KITCHEN

COQ AU VIN IN 90 MINUTES
Butchering, chopping, browning, straining, simmering, thickening . . . most coq au vin recipes require almost 3 hours from start to finish. We came up with some shortcuts to keep this simple stew under control.

NO BONES
Opting for boneless thighs rather than bone-in legs shaved more than 30 minutes from the cooking time.

TWO POTS
We reduced the wine, stock, and herb mixture in a separate saucepan while browning the chicken and vegetables.

THE BEST WINE OPENERS
In a wine opener testing conducted nearly ten years ago by the test kitchen, we decided that the lever-style bottle openers were the best bet, but at $150, our winning Le Creuset Screwpull Lever LX was also very expensive. Since that time, other lever-style options have flooded the market—some at much more attractive price points. We gathered 13 contenders (ranging in price from $12.95 to $134.95) to see just how low you can go and still get great performance. Our favorite model, the **Screwpull Trigger**, $79.95, has an ingenious slip-over sleeve design, which helps center the screw over the bottle opening—you squeeze the "trigger" to secure the bottle. This new feature streamlines an already speedy process, making this model our new "ultimate" choice. That said, the more reasonably priced Wine Enthusiast QuickSilver Deluxe Corkscrew Set, $34.95, has a heavy chrome crank and handles and sleek lever that make it easy to use (plus it comes with a display stand, bottle opener, foil cutter, and wax remover).

MODERN CHICKEN DIVAN
SERVES 4

WHAT MAKES THIS A BEST RECIPE: Despite its current reputation as a cheesy chicken and broccoli casserole doused in hollandaise sauce that you pick up in the frozen-food aisle, chicken Divan has a fabled history tracing back to New York's famed (and now defunct) Divan Parisien restaurant. While the original recipe takes scads of effort—and pots—to prepare, we wanted to reclaim this once luxury dish and rejuvenate it as a modernized skillet supper. There were three components to tackle: the broccoli, the chicken, and the sauce. To keep the dish limited to just one pan, batch-cooking was in order. It was easy enough to sauté the broccoli and steam it in a little chicken broth, after which it emerged flavorful, tender, and emerald green. Boneless, skinless chicken breasts got a similar treatment in the empty pan (minus the steam), after being dusted with flour to maximize browning. Briefly simmering them in the sauce's liquid components cooked the chicken breasts through without the chance of drying them out the way dry heat cooking would. Mimicking the original sauce took some kitchen trickery. Simmering chicken broth with heavy cream gave the sauce a rich mouthfeel, and sherry, Worcestershire, and a full cup of grated Parmesan warmed up the flavors. And instead of preparing a separate hollandaise sauce, we whisked egg yolks and lemon juice together, then tempered the mixture with a little of the hot pan sauce. Once returned to the pan (off the heat so as not to curdle the eggs), along with some butter, the sauce thickened to pure luxury. We poured the sauce over the waiting chicken and broccoli, topped everything with more Parmesan, and slid the dish under the broiler for a few minutes. We now had chicken Divan that was as opulent as the original but didn't require anywhere near the effort.

3 tablespoons vegetable oil
1½ pounds broccoli, stalks discarded, florets cut into bite-sized pieces
2½ cups low-sodium chicken broth

1½ pounds boneless, skinless chicken breasts
 Salt and pepper
¼ cup unbleached all-purpose flour
2 shallots, minced (about 6 tablespoons)
1 cup heavy cream
½ cup dry sherry
2 teaspoons Worcestershire sauce
3 ounces grated Parmesan cheese (about 1½ cups)
3 large egg yolks
1 tablespoon fresh lemon juice
3 tablespoons unsalted butter

1. Adjust an oven rack to the lower-middle position and heat the broiler. Heat 1 tablespoon of the oil in a large skillet over medium-high heat until just smoking. Add the broccoli and cook until spotty brown, about 1 minute. Add ½ cup of the broth, cover, and steam until the broccoli is just tender, about 1½ minutes. Remove the lid and cook until the liquid has evaporated, about 1 minute. Transfer the broccoli to a paper towel–lined plate; rinse and wipe out the skillet.

2. Season the chicken with salt and pepper and dredge in the flour to coat. Meanwhile, heat the remaining 2 tablespoons oil in the now-empty skillet over medium-high heat until smoking. Cook the chicken until golden brown, 2 to 3 minutes per side. Transfer the chicken to a plate.

3. Off the heat, add the shallots to the skillet and cook until just beginning to color, about 1 minute. Add the remaining 2 cups broth and cream and scrape the browned bits from the bottom of the pan. Return the chicken to the skillet and simmer over medium-high heat until cooked through, about 10 minutes. Transfer the chicken to a clean plate and continue to simmer the sauce until reduced to 1 cup, about 10 minutes. Add the sherry and Worcestershire and simmer until reduced again to 1 cup, about 3 minutes.

4. Stir in 1 cup of the cheese. Whisk the yolks and lemon juice in a small bowl, then whisk in about ¼ cup of the hot sauce. Off the heat, whisk the egg yolk mixture into the sauce in the skillet, then whisk in the butter.

5. Cut the chicken into ½-inch-thick slices and arrange on a broiler-safe platter. Scatter the broccoli over the chicken and pour the sauce over the broccoli. Sprinkle with the remaining ½ cup cheese and broil until golden brown, 3 to 5 minutes. Serve.

PARMESAN-CRUSTED CHICKEN CUTLETS

SERVES 4

WHAT MAKES THIS A BEST RECIPE: If you order chicken Parmesan at one of those questionably authentic "Italian" chain restaurants, you'll likely be served a gummy-breaded, overcooked chicken breast buried under a blanket of melted cheese. It's a far cry from what the dish should be: juicy, flavorful meat encased in a crisp, wafer-thin Parmesan cheese–flavored coating. This recipe makes such great results easy. After some initial tests, we knew a few things for sure. First, the chicken would have to be pan-fried, not baked. While baking simply melted the cheese, pan-frying showed potential to deliver the crisp crust we wanted. Second, the chicken would have to be cooked in a nonstick skillet to keep the crust from fusing to the bottom of the pan, and it would have to be cooked quickly to prevent the cheese from burning**.** Boneless, skinless chicken breasts, therefore, were a given, and they had to be fairly thin. For chicken that cooked through in just 3 minutes, we used ¼-inch-thick cutlets. Traditionally, the cutlets are coated with flour followed by beaten egg and a final bread crumb-and-cheese mixture. Blending fine-ground Parmesan with the flour in the first layer added our first level of flavor, and grating more Parmesan coarsely for the outer crust (skipping any crumbs entirely) created just the shaggy, potently flavored crust we were after. Tossing a mere tablespoon of flour with the outermost layer of shredded cheese filled in any gaps between the cheese and egg-white layers, creating a crispier exterior. The final touch was removing the yolks from the egg wash, which made the crust even crisper and the flavor cleaner.

2 boneless, skinless chicken breasts (8 ounces each), tenderloins removed, trimmed, and halved horizontally
Salt and pepper
¼ cup plus 1 tablespoon unbleached all-purpose flour
½ ounce Parmesan cheese, grated (about ¼ cup) (see note on page 207)
3 large egg whites
2 tablespoons minced fresh chives (optional)
6 ounces Parmesan cheese, shredded (about 2 cups) (see note on page 207)
4 teaspoons olive oil
Lemon wedges, for serving

1. Adjust an oven rack to the middle position and heat the oven to 200 degrees. Place the chicken between sheets of plastic wrap and pound to an even ¼-inch thickness. Pat dry with paper towels and season both sides with salt and pepper.

2. Set a wire rack on a rimmed baking sheet. Whisk together ¼ cup flour and the grated cheese in a pie plate. In a medium bowl, whisk the egg whites and chives (if using) together until slightly foamy. In a second pie plate, combine the shredded cheese and remaining 1 tablespoon flour.

3. Working with 1 cutlet at a time, coat the chicken in the flour mixture, shaking off any excess. Transfer the chicken to the egg-white mixture; coat evenly and let the excess run off. Coat the chicken with the shredded Parmesan mixture, pressing gently so that the cheese adheres. Place on the wire rack.

4. Heat 2 teaspoons of the oil in a 12-inch nonstick skillet over medium-high heat until shimmering. Place 2 cutlets in the skillet and reduce the heat to medium. Cook until the cheese is pale golden brown, about 3 minutes. While the chicken is cooking, use a thin nonstick spatula to gently separate any cheesy edges that have melted together. Carefully flip the cutlets and continue to cook until the cheese is pale golden brown on the second side and the meat is no longer pink in the center, about 3 minutes. Transfer the chicken to the wire rack on the baking sheet and keep warm in the oven. Wipe out the skillet with paper towels and return it to medium heat. Repeat with the remaining 2 teaspoons oil and cutlets. Serve immediately with the lemon wedges.

NOTES FROM THE TEST KITCHEN

TWO WAYS TO CUT THE PARMESAN

An ideal crust requires cheeses of two different textures. A base layer of finely grated Parmesan cut on the smallest holes of a box or Microplane grater (left) is paired with an exterior layer of coarsely shredded Parmesan cut on the largest holes of a box grater (right).

GRATED

SHREDDED

GREAT DISCOVERIES

BITTER BROWNED CHEESE

During development for our Parmesan-Crusted Chicken Cutlets, I was plagued by a bitter flavor in the finished dish that I couldn't seem to overcome. Whenever I cooked the chicken until it looked gorgeous—a deep, dark brown—it tasted burnt. When I underbrowned the chicken (a counterintuitive move), it tasted fine. After some head scratching, I traced the problem back to the Maillard reaction. This chemical effect occurs when amino acids (building blocks for proteins) and sugars in foods are heated, causing them to combine and form new flavor compounds. Most cheeses undergo very little of this reaction when heated, because they don't contain much sugar. Parmesan cheese, however, contains fairly high levels of the sugar galactose, which undergoes the reaction quite readily. As the galactose reacts with sizable amounts of glutamic acid (an amino acid), the formation of bitter-tasting substances happens as soon as the cheese starts to brown. Turning the heat down to medium once the cutlets were in the pan—thus keeping browning at bay—allowed the chicken and cheese to cook through without tasting burnt.

SANDRA WU | ASSOCIATE EDITOR, *COOK'S ILLUSTRATED*

LATINO-STYLE CHICKEN AND RICE
SERVES 4 TO 6

WHAT MAKES THIS A BEST RECIPE: The bold-flavored cousin of American-style chicken and rice, *arroz con pollo* is Latino comfort food at its most basic. The sad truth is that authentic recipes take a long time to prepare: "Comfort" is one thing, "convenience" something else entirely. The "quick" recipes we tried didn't come close to capturing the original dish's charm, so we decided to split the difference and develop a streamlined method that wouldn't disappoint. Which comes first, the chicken or the rice? In this case, the chicken. While the dish is typically prepared with a whole hacked-up chicken, we switched to well-trimmed dark meat thighs. We cooked the chicken briefly with the vegetables—a *sofrito* of onion and green pepper—before simmering it with the rice in chicken broth. A brief marination in a garlic, oregano, and vinegar slurry before cooking hugely improved its flavor, as did a second soak in an olive-oil-and-vinegar-laced "marinade" after we shredded the cooked meat off the bone. As for the rice, creamy medium-grain rice easily beat out more austere long-grain rice. Stirring it a couple of times as it simmered ensured even cooking. Arroz con pollo is typically colored crimson with achiote (a seed), which can be hard to find, so we switched to tomato as a coloring agent, which worked just fine. Arroz con pollo wouldn't be right without capers, red pepper flakes, pimientos, and briny olives, so we stirred them into the cooked rice. With fresh cilantro and lemon wedges on the side, our "streamlined" recipe was packed with flavor and definitely quicker and more convenient than the original.

6 garlic cloves, minced
  Salt
½ teaspoon dried oregano
1 tablespoon plus 2 teaspoons distilled white vinegar
  Pepper
8 bone-in, skin-on chicken thighs (3½ to 4 pounds), trimmed
2 tablespoons olive oil
1 onion, chopped fine (about 1 cup)
1 green bell pepper, stemmed, seeded, and chopped fine
¼ teaspoon red pepper flakes
¼ cup minced fresh cilantro
1 (8-ounce) can tomato sauce
1¾ cups low-sodium chicken broth
¼ cup water
3 cups medium-grain rice
½ cup green manzanilla olives, pitted and halved
1 tablespoon capers
½ cup jarred pimientos, cut into 2 by ¼-inch strips
  Lemon wedges, for serving

1. Adjust an oven rack to the middle position and heat the oven to 350 degrees. Place the garlic and 1 teaspoon salt in a large bowl and mix to a smooth paste with a rubber spatula. Add the oregano, 1 tablespoon vinegar, and ½ teaspoon pepper to the garlic paste and stir to combine. Add the chicken to the marinade and stir to coat evenly; set aside for 15 minutes.

2. Heat 1 tablespoon of the oil in a large Dutch oven over medium heat until shimmering. Add the onion, bell pepper, and pepper flakes; cook, stirring occasionally, until the vegetables begin to soften, 4 to 8 minutes. Add 2 tablespoons of the cilantro; stir to combine. Push the vegetables to the sides of the pot and increase the heat to medium-high. Place the chicken skin side down in an even layer in the clearing in the pot. Cook, without moving the chicken, until the outer layer of meat becomes opaque, 2 to 4 minutes. (If the chicken begins to brown, reduce the heat to medium.) Flip the chicken and cook on the second side until opaque, 2 to 4 minutes more. Add the tomato sauce, broth, and water; stir to combine. Bring to a simmer; cover, reduce the heat to medium-low, and simmer for 20 minutes.

3. Add the rice, olives, capers, and ¾ teaspoon salt; stir well. Bring to a simmer, cover, and place the pot in the oven. After 10 minutes, remove the pot from the oven and stir the chicken and rice once from the bottom up.

Return the pot to the oven. After another 10 minutes, stir once more, adding ¼ cup water if the rice appears dry and the bottom of the pot is beginning to burn. Cover and return the pot to the oven; cook until the rice has absorbed all the liquid and is tender but still holds its shape and an instant-read thermometer inserted in the thickest part of a thigh registers 175 degrees, about 10 minutes longer.

4. Remove the chicken from the pot, replace the lid, and set the pot aside. Remove and discard the chicken skin; using 2 spoons, pull the meat off the bones into large chunks. Using your fingers, remove any remaining fat and dark veins from the chicken pieces. Place the chicken in a large bowl and toss with the remaining 1 tablespoon olive oil, remaining 2 teaspoons vinegar, remaining 2 tablespoons cilantro, and pimientos; season with salt and pepper to taste. Place the chicken on top of the rice, cover, and let stand until warmed through, about 5 minutes. Serve, passing the lemon wedges separately.

NOTES FROM THE TEST KITCHEN

THE RICE IS RIGHT
For arroz con pollo, we prefer the sticky-yet-firm consistency of medium-grain rice. Although there are brands available from many places, we found that Hispanic brands of rice had the best texture for this dish. That said, if you want to use long-grain rice, increase the water to ¾ cup in step 2.

TAKING THE MEAT OFF THE BONE
Removing the meat from the bones isn't hard when there's plenty of time for it to cool, but we wanted it fast. We tried using a fork, but it tended to shred the meat rather than pull it apart intact. Our solution? Two spoons, which were much more gentle—and just as effective.

PECAN-CRUSTED CHICKEN CUTLETS

SERVES 4

WHAT MAKES THIS A BEST RECIPE: Adding a pecan-flavored crust to chicken breasts sounds like a great idea, but ground nuts don't readily adhere to chicken, and, when they do, they usually burn long before the chicken is cooked through. We, however, found the secret to golden-hued, crisp-crusted chicken breasts. After testing several recipes, it was easy to see that beaten eggs alone weren't tacky enough to effectively "glue" the crust to the meat. We tried a slew of different options and eventually hit upon a solution—Dijon mustard, which turned the eggs thick and sticky. While we were at it, we mixed minced garlic, salt, pepper, and a little tarragon (to complement the sweetness of the pecans) into the mustard-and-egg slurry. Letting the chicken repose for a few minutes in the flavored egg wash allowed the flavors to penetrate the meat. While the nuts stayed put on the meat, they were burning. Some recipes solved this burning issue by baking the coated chicken cutlets, but no one in the test kitchen liked the pallid, soggy results. For a really crisp coating, we knew pan-frying was the only option. After unsuccessfully testing different pan temperatures and pan-frying methods, we realized that mixing the nuts with neutral-flavored, fresh bread crumbs effectively shielded the nuts and prevented burning. Adding a few teaspoons of moisture-absorbing cornstarch to the crumbs ensured an ultra-crisp crust, and a pinch each of cinnamon and brown sugar highlighted the subtle sweetness of the pecans.

2 large eggs
4 teaspoons Dijon mustard
3 garlic cloves, minced
2 teaspoons dried tarragon
  Salt and pepper
4 boneless, skinless chicken breasts (about 1½ pounds), halved horizontally
2 cups pecans
2 slices high-quality white sandwich bread, torn in half
4 teaspoons cornstarch
1 tablespoon dark brown sugar
⅛ teaspoon ground cinnamon
1 cup vegetable oil

1. Adjust an oven rack to the middle position and heat the oven to 250 degrees. Line a rimmed baking sheet with a wire rack. Whisk the eggs, mustard, garlic, tarragon, ½ teaspoon salt, and ½ teaspoon pepper in a large bowl. Add the chicken, coat well, cover with plastic wrap, and refrigerate while preparing the nut mixture.

2. Pulse the pecans in a food processor until finely chopped, with some pebble-sized pieces, 10 to 12 seconds. Transfer to a pie plate or shallow rimmed dish. Pulse the bread in the food processor until finely ground, about 12 pulses. Add the bread crumbs to the nuts and stir in the cornstarch, brown sugar, ½ teaspoon pepper, ¼ teaspoon salt, and cinnamon.

3. Working one at a time, remove the cutlets from the egg mixture, letting the excess drip back into the bowl. Thoroughly coat the chicken with the nut mixture, pressing on the coating to help it adhere, and transfer to a large plate.

4. Heat ½ cup of the oil in a large nonstick skillet over medium-high heat until shimmering. Place 4 cutlets in the skillet and cook until golden brown on both sides, 3 to 4 minutes per side (lower the heat if the crust is browning too quickly). Transfer the chicken to the rack on the baking sheet and keep warm in the oven. Discard the oil and solids from the skillet and repeat with the remaining ½ cup oil and cutlets. Season the cutlets with salt and pepper to taste. Serve immediately.

WHERE THINGS CAN GO WRONG: Do not process the pecans too finely or their natural oils will be released and you'll end up with pecan paste.

NOTES FROM THE TEST KITCHEN

PRODUCING PERFECT CUTLETS

Chicken breasts are too thick to use in this recipe (the outside will burn long before the meat cooks through), and packaged cutlets are often too thin (the meat overcooks before the coating browns). For crisp, browned cutlets that are perfectly cooked through, it's best to buy chicken breasts and cut them in half horizontally yourself. Each breast should yield two pieces that are about ½ inch thick.

KING RANCH CASSEROLE

SERVES 6 TO 8

WHAT MAKES THIS A BEST RECIPE: With its layers of tender chicken, corn tortillas, and spicy tomatoes bound together in a rich, cheesy sauce, King Ranch Casserole might be the most famous casserole in Texas. Favored by home cooks and Junior Leaguers, this subtly spicy casserole dates back to the 1950s and the recipes are usually as dated, calling for "a can of this," or "a package of that." This modernized recipe captures the classic flavors with "scratch" ingredients. Starting with the sauce, we cooked onions and chiles in butter, then added ground cumin and Ro-Tel tomatoes, the Texas brand of spicy canned tomatoes that are the hallmark of this recipe. Instead of draining the tomatoes and discarding the flavorful juice (as most recipes instructed), we reduced the liquid to intensify the tomato flavor. Then went in flour for thickening, cream for richness, and chicken broth for flavor. Twenty minutes of kitchen work yielded a silky, flavorful sauce that put canned soup to shame. Things went sideways at that point. When we layered pre-cooked chicken into the casserole with raw corn tortillas and cheese, the chicken came out stringy and the tortillas turned to mush. Partially poaching the chicken in the sauce before assembly kept it moist and flavorful. As for the tortillas, crisping them in the oven pre-assembly proved to be the easy solution. And for the regulation crunchy topping, the kitchen stuck to the traditional choice: Fritos chips. Our King Ranch Casserole was *almost* from scratch.

12 (6-inch) corn tortillas
1 tablespoon unsalted butter
2 onions, chopped fine
2 jalapeño chiles, seeds and ribs removed, then minced
2 teaspoons ground cumin
2 (10-ounce) cans Ro-Tel tomatoes
5 tablespoons unbleached all-purpose flour
1 cup heavy cream
3 cups low-sodium chicken broth
1½ pounds boneless, skinless chicken breasts, halved lengthwise and cut crosswise into ½-inch slices
2 tablespoons minced fresh cilantro

1 pound Monterey Jack cheese, shredded (about 4 cups)
Salt and pepper
2¼ cups Fritos corn chips, crushed

1. Adjust the oven racks to the upper-middle and lower-middle positions and heat the oven to 450 degrees. Lay the tortillas on two baking sheets, lightly coat both sides with cooking spray, and bake until slightly crisp and browned, about 12 minutes. Cool slightly, then break into bite-sized pieces. Using potholders, adjust the top oven rack to the middle position.

2. Melt the butter in a large Dutch oven over medium-high heat. Cook the onions, chiles, and cumin until lightly browned, about 8 minutes. Add the tomatoes with their juice and cook until most of liquid has evaporated, about 10 minutes. Stir in the flour and cook 1 minute. Add the cream and broth, bring to a simmer, and cook until thickened, 2 to 3 minutes. Stir in the chicken and cook until no longer pink, about 4 minutes. Off the heat, add the cilantro and cheese and stir until the cheese is melted. Season with salt and pepper to taste.

3. Scatter half of the tortilla pieces in a 13 by 9-inch baking dish set over a rimmed baking sheet. Spoon half of the filling evenly over the tortillas. Scatter the remaining tortilla pieces over the filling, then top with the remaining filling.

4. Bake until the filling is bubbling, about 15 minutes. Sprinkle the Fritos evenly over the top and bake until the Fritos are lightly browned, about 10 minutes. Cool the casserole 10 minutes. Serve.

THINGS YOU CAN DO AHEAD OF TIME: The casserole can be assembled through step 3 and refrigerated, covered with plastic wrap, for up to 1 day. When ready to bake, remove the plastic, cover the casserole with foil, and bake until the filling is bubbling, about 30 minutes. Remove the foil, top with the crushed Fritos, and proceed as directed with the rest of step 4.

NOTES FROM THE TEST KITCHEN

RO-TEL TOMATOES
Ro-Tel tomatoes are canned chopped tomatoes blended with chiles. If you can't find them, substitute one 14.5-ounce can diced tomatoes and one 4-ounce can drained chopped green chiles.

MARYLAND FRIED CHICKEN

SERVES 4 TO 6

WHAT MAKES THIS A BEST RECIPE: In Maryland, fried chicken is traditionally made by simply seasoning chicken pieces and dusting them with flour prior to frying rather than dipping them in a buttermilk batter (and then frying them). This old-fashioned cooking method results in crisp, mahogany chicken that, with a gentle tug, sheets off the bone with its deliciously brittle skin still intact. But what really sets Maryland fried chicken apart is the creamy, black pepper–spiked pan gravy that's equally fit for drumstick dunking or mopping up with a biscuit. It's a tried-and-true approach that we wanted to master. While we liked the texture of the recipes we tried, the bland flavor left us bored. We wanted to add a few spices to the chicken, but when we mixed them into the flour before dusting the chicken, they scorched and tasted bitter. Applying the spices directly to the chicken proved a better option as the flour shielded them from burning. We added salt, dry mustard, and garlic powder—all time-tested fried chicken seasonings. Once the chicken was cooked, we dusted it with Maryland's signature seasoning, Old Bay, for another flavor boost. Resting the seasoned and floured chicken in the fridge for 30 minutes improved it even further, allowing the seasonings and flour to take hold for an extra-crispy coating. As for the gravy, most recipes start with a roux made from pan drippings and flour, and we weren't about to argue with that. As for the liquid base of the gravy, tasters found straight cream too rich, but cut with chicken broth and enlivened with a hefty shot of black pepper, it was perfect.

FRIED CHICKEN

- 4 **pounds bone-in, skin-on chicken pieces, trimmed**
- 1 **tablespoon dry mustard**
- 1 **tablespoon garlic powder**
- 1 **teaspoon salt**

This simple, traditional fried chicken is dressed up with a peppery cream gravy.

- 2 **cups unbleached all-purpose flour**
- 1 **teaspoon baking powder**
- 3 **cups peanut oil or vegetable shortening**
  Old Bay seasoning

CREAM GRAVY

- ¼ **cup pan drippings (from frying the chicken)**
- ¼ **cup unbleached all-purpose flour**
- 2 **cups low-sodium chicken broth**
- 1 **cup heavy cream**
- 1 **teaspoon pepper**
  Salt

1. FOR THE CHICKEN: Pat the chicken dry with paper towels. Combine the mustard, garlic powder, and salt in a small bowl and sprinkle evenly over the chicken. Combine the flour and baking powder in a shallow dish and, working with one piece at a time, dredge the chicken parts until well coated, shaking off the excess. Refrigerate on a plate for 30 minutes (or up to 2 hours).
2. Adjust an oven rack to the middle position and heat the oven to 200 degrees. Heat the oil in a large Dutch oven over medium-high heat to 375 degrees. Arrange half of the chicken in the pot, skin side down, cover, and cook until well browned, about 5 minutes per

side. Lower the temperature to medium, adjusting the burner as necessary to maintain the oil temperature between 300 and 325 degrees. Cook uncovered, turning the chicken as necessary, until cooked through, about 5 minutes. (The internal temperature should register 160 degrees for white meat and 175 degrees for dark meat.) Transfer the chicken to a wire rack set over a baking sheet, season with Old Bay, and transfer to the oven. Bring the oil back to 375 degrees and repeat with the remaining chicken.

3. **FOR THE GRAVY:** Pour off all but ¼ cup of the oil in the pot. Stir in the flour and cook until golden, about 2 minutes. Slowly whisk in the broth, cream, and pepper. Simmer until thickened, about 5 minutes. Season with salt and serve with the hot chicken.

WHERE THINGS CAN GO WRONG: The chicken will not cook evenly unless the breasts are halved crosswise and the leg quarters separated into thighs and drumsticks.

NOTES FROM THE TEST KITCHEN

WHOLE LOT OF SHAKIN' GOING ON

1. Instead of coating the chicken by hand, try using a brown paper grocery bag. Pat the chicken dry with paper towels, then place it in the bag.

2. After shaking the chicken with seasonings, add the flour to the bag.

3. Tightly close the bag and shake until all the chicken pieces are well coated with flour.

FRYING WITHOUT FEAR

While developing our recipe for Maryland Fried Chicken, batch after batch of the chicken was marred by an odd "fishy" flavor. To find the culprit, we tried adjusting every variable in the recipe, but nothing worked. As a last resort, we switched from vegetable oil (our usual frying medium) to peanut oil (another commonly used frying oil), and the problem was solved. As it turns out, after a total frying time of roughly 30 minutes, the vegetable oil was beginning to break down and impart a spoiled, fishy flavor to the chicken. Peanut oil (which has a higher smoke point) fared better and didn't break down, resulting in no off flavors in the chicken. We also tried safflower oil, canola oil, and vegetable shortening. The peanut oil was still best, but the vegetable shortening was the runner-up, winning praise for its "clean" flavor.

THE BEST INSTANT-READ THERMOMETERS

When cooking meat, we highly recommend using an instant-read thermometer to accurately gauge its temperature. They are also valuable for judging the temperature of everything from bread and caramel to hot oil. Our favorite model is the **ThermoWorks Super-Fast Thermapen** (left), a true workhorse that quickly provides accurate readings across a broad range of temperatures. But at $85, the Thermapen isn't cheap. Recently, cheaper instant-read thermometers have come on the market and we wondered if any of them could approach the performance of the Thermapen. We purchased eight models and put them through their paces in the kitchen. While none of the cheaper models could match the speed, temperature range, or accuracy of the Thermapen, we were pleased with the performance of the **CDN ProAccurate Quick Tip Digital Cooking Thermometer DTQ450** (right), $17.95. While not as fast as the Thermapen, it performed admirably enough to earn our endorsement.

COBB CHICKEN SALAD
SERVES 6

WHAT MAKES THIS A BEST RECIPE: Most chicken salad recipes start off with steamed or poached plain, white chicken, which makes little sense to us. Bland chicken begets bland chicken salad. This recipe for Cobb chicken salad, however, puts the flavor of the chicken first and foremost, and then captures the flavors of Cobb salad in a quick salad perfect for convenient sandwiches. For maximum flavor, we thought we'd start with a whole chicken, but we were quickly turned off by the soft texture of the dark meat in the chicken salad, much less the bird's lengthy cooking time (60-plus minutes for a four-to-five-pound bird). Switching to white meat, we tried roasting whole chicken breasts, but this still took a good bit of time. Quickly cooking boneless, skinless chicken breasts on the stovetop proved to be a better option. Not only did they cook in mere minutes, but, sautéed to a golden brown, they were every bit as tasty as the roasted chicken. Mayonnaise is usually the primary ingredient in any chicken salad dressing, but we found that too much mayo made the dressing bland and dulled the chicken's flavor. We opted to cut the mayonnaise with tart sour cream and a fair amount of lemon juice. And, for true Cobb salad flavor, we folded in crumbled blue cheese, diced avocado, and bits of hard-boiled egg, topping it all off with the requisite crisp bacon bits. In mere minutes, we had a perfect chicken salad with a robust chicken flavor.

- 4   boneless, skinless chicken breasts (about 1½ pounds), trimmed
  Salt and pepper
- 2   tablespoons vegetable oil
- ½   cup mayonnaise
- 2   ounces crumbled blue cheese (about ½ cup)
- 2   tablespoons sour cream
- 2   tablespoons fresh lemon juice
- 2   hard-cooked eggs, chopped fine
- 1   avocado, pitted, skinned, and diced
- 4   slices bacon, cooked and crumbled

1. Pat the chicken dry with paper towels and season with salt and pepper. Heat the oil in a large nonstick skillet over medium heat until shimmering. Cook the chicken until golden brown and cooked through, about 6 minutes per side. Transfer to a plate and refrigerate until chilled, about 30 minutes. Cut into ½-inch chunks.
2. Mix the mayonnaise, cheese, sour cream, and lemon juice in a large bowl until combined. Add the eggs, avocado, and chicken; toss gently until coated. Season with salt and pepper. Sprinkle with the crumbled bacon. Serve on toasted white bread or a baguette.

WHERE THINGS CAN GO WRONG: Make sure that the chicken is fully cooled before mixing with the other ingredients; otherwise, the residual heat can make the dressing runny, melt the blue cheese, and/or turn the avocado mushy.

THINGS YOU CAN DO AHEAD OF TIME: The salad (minus the bacon and avocado) can be refrigerated in an airtight container for up to 2 days. Add the cooked bacon and diced avocado just before serving.

NOTES FROM THE TEST KITCHEN

MANUAL KNIFE SHARPENERS
Even the best knife grows dull with use and will require maintenance to bring back its edge. While we take heavily worn or damaged blades to the professionals, electric sharpeners can work wonders for average wear and tear. But the best electric sharpeners cost over $100. A cheaper option—perfect for fine-tuning knives—is a manual sharpener. These hand-held gizmos typically rely on a diamond, steel, ceramic, or tungsten carbide surface to grind the blade sharp again. After testing a dozen models—all of varying styles—our favorite model happened to be one of the simplest and least expensive. **The Accusharp Knife and Tool Sharpener** ($11.71) established a sharp edge both quickly and easily. While its design requires that the sharpener must be drawn over the exposed blade, we quickly overcame our initial trepidation. Its compact shape, far smaller than the rest of the sharpeners we tested, was an added bonus.

ROAST CHICKEN
WITH ROOT VEGETABLES
SERVES 4 TO 6

WHAT MAKES THIS A BEST RECIPE: In theory, roasting a chicken and root vegetables together sounds like a no-brainer, but practice proves otherwise. The vegetables suck up the rendered chicken fat like little sponges and overcook during the long roast required of the chicken. However, this recipe trumps the problems and delivers a perfect crisp-skinned chicken and tender but firm vegetables invested with rich chicken flavor—not chicken grease. To serve a crowd (or at least six), we started with a big six- to eight-pound bird. To maximize the chicken's flavor, we chose to brine it before roasting in a salt-and-sugar solution powerfully flavored with crushed garlic and crumbled bay leaves. Despite the bird's size, we found we could simply adapt our small-bird roasting method, which requires roasting at 400 degrees and rotating the chicken at intervals for even browning. As for the vegetables, we knew roasting them separately was a must, but how would they pick up the chicken's flavor? After trying to use the chicken fat in several fashions without success, we had a moment of clarity: The fond, or browned bits left behind in the roasting pan by the chicken, packed the fullest chicken flavor. Once the chicken was cooked, we deglazed the pan, then roasted the vegetables in the same pan to minimize the number of dishes (and the chicken benefited from the rest). Once the vegetables were almost done, we tossed them with the defatted drippings and finished them under the high, direct heat of the broiler to evaporate their moisture and crisp their exteriors. Who would have thought that the secret to ultra-chickeny chicken and roast vegetables was to make sure the chicken and vegetables never met at all—at least not until they hit the plate?

For roasted vegetables that are dripping with chicken flavor—not chicken grease—make sure the serving platter is the first place the chicken and vegetables meet.

CHICKEN AND BRINE

- 1½ cups table salt
- 1½ cups sugar
- 2 heads garlic, outer papery skins removed, cloves separated, unpeeled, and crushed
- 6 bay leaves, crumbled
- 1 (6- to 8-pound) chicken, giblets discarded
  Pepper
- 1 cup low-sodium chicken broth, plus more as needed

VEGETABLES

- 1 pound small red potatoes (about 6 potatoes), scrubbed and unpeeled
- 1 pound carrots, peeled, cut into 2- to 3-inch pieces, tapered ends left whole, large upper portions halved lengthwise
- ½ pound parsnips, peeled, cut into 2- to 3-inch pieces, tapered ends left whole, large upper portions halved lengthwise
- 3 small onions, peeled, root ends left intact, and quartered
- 3 tablespoons vegetable oil
- ½ teaspoon salt
- ⅛ teaspoon pepper

1. FOR THE CHICKEN AND BRINE: Dissolve the salt and sugar in 1 gallon of cold water in a large container. Stir in the garlic and bay leaves; immerse the chicken and refrigerate until fully seasoned, about 2 hours.

2. Adjust an oven rack to the middle position and heat the oven to 400 degrees. Set a V-rack in a large flameproof roasting pan and lightly spray with nonstick cooking spray. Remove the chicken from the brine and thoroughly pat dry with paper towels.

3. Season the chicken on all sides with pepper; set the chicken wing side up on the prepared V-rack and roast for 30 minutes. Remove the roasting pan from the oven and, using 2 wads of paper towels, rotate the chicken so the other wing side faces up; continue to roast for 30 minutes.

4. Remove the roasting pan from the oven and, using 2 large wads of paper towels, rotate the chicken breast side up. Add the broth to the roasting pan and continue to roast until the chicken is golden brown and an instant-read thermometer inserted in the thickest part of the breast registers 160 degrees, and 175 degrees in the thickest part of the thigh, about 40 minutes. (If necessary, add more broth to maintain a thin layer of broth on the bottom of the roasting pan.) Transfer the chicken to a cutting board and let rest, uncovered, while roasting the vegetables; remove the V-rack from the roasting pan.

5. FOR THE VEGETABLES: While the chicken is resting, adjust an oven rack to the middle position and increase the oven temperature to 500 degrees. Using a wooden spoon, scrape the browned bits in the roasting pan and pour the liquid into a fat separator. Return the now-empty roasting pan to the oven and heat until the oven reaches 500 degrees, about 5 minutes. Toss the vegetables with the oil, salt, and pepper.

6. Scatter the vegetables in a single layer in the heated roasting pan, arranging the potatoes and onions cut side down. Roast, without stirring, for 25 minutes.

7. While the vegetables are roasting, pour off ½ cup liquid from the fat separator; discard the remaining liquid and fat. Remove the roasting pan from the oven and heat the broiler. Drizzle the liquid over the vegetables and broil for 5 minutes. Stir the vegetables, coating them well with the reducing liquid, and continue to broil until tender and deep golden brown, about 5 minutes. Transfer the vegetables to a serving platter.

8. While the vegetables are broiling, carve the chicken. Transfer to the platter with the vegetables and serve.

NOTES FROM THE TEST KITCHEN

WANT TO ROAST A SMALLER BIRD?
The times given in the recipe are designed to work with a 6- to 8-pound chicken. It's possible to roast a slightly smaller bird (around 5 pounds) by reducing the roasting time in step 4 to about 25 minutes. Begin carving the chicken as soon as the vegetables are placed underneath the broiler.

BOOSTING A BLAND BIRD'S FLAVOR
Mass-produced chickens are notoriously bland, and their more flavorful "boutique" counterparts aren't widely available in larger sizes. We solved the problem by adding two full heads of garlic and six bay leaves to the brine, along with the usual salt and sugar.

THE BEST ROASTING RACKS
A roasting rack is as unglamorous as it is essential. It raises poultry and roasts out of the drippings, while giving the oven's heat easy access to the whole surface—a good start toward a well-rendered exterior. We picked up a handful of different models to see if any were really all that different. Right away, we noted that not all V-racks are actually V-shaped; some had slight bends, others were more trough-like. In addition to shape, handles were a decisive factor. Tall, vertical handles make removing the rack easy, even with bulky oven mitts. Horizontal handles, or no handles at all, make removal nearly impossible. In our tests, we also noticed that handle position matters. When located on the short sides of a rectangular rack they can get in the way of the roasting pan's handles. We prefer handles positioned on the long side of the rack. The **All-Clad Non-Stick Roasting Rack**, $24.95, easily bested the rest as it's large enough to hold two small chickens and has the features we like. If you're in the market for a new roasting pan, you should consider our favorite roaster, the Calphalon Contemporary Stainless All Season Pan ($99), which includes a rack that's just as good as the All-Clad model.

FIRECRACKER CHICKEN

SERVES 6

WHAT MAKES THIS A BEST RECIPE: Essentially, firecracker chicken is "tenders" of fried chicken first marinated in and then coated with a fiery, mustard-based sauce. To be honest, the chicken is really just a vehicle for the sauce. This recipe produces a spicy-hot, complexly flavored sauce and great-tasting, crunchy chicken that would taste good even without the sauce. How did we do it? Well, first of all, we decided that plain yellow mustard had the right consistency and bright flavor to be a perfect sauce base. To the mustard, we added sinus-clearing powdered mustard, chili sauce, and fresh habañero chile for its unapologetic heat. Pickled banana peppers (plus some of their pickling juices) provided a nice acidic tang, which brown sugar balanced. A bit of garlic rounded everything out. We marinated the chicken in a portion of the sauce and reserved the remainder to drizzle over the finished chicken. In classic fried chicken, the coating adheres to the cut-up chicken parts because the skin is tacky, but we wanted to use strips of boneless, skinless breasts, which were slick to the touch. Borrowing a trick from our buttermilk fried chicken recipe, we added a dribble of the fiery sauce to the flour, cornstarch, and baking powder coating, which took on the texture of wet sand and stuck to the chicken in irregular clumps. When fried, this lumpy texture created thick, crispy pockets of coating that tasters loved. To ensure that the coating stayed stuck to the meat, we found it best to dip the chicken strips in beaten egg white (adding the yolks made the chicken taste too "eggy"), then set the coated chicken to dry in the refrigerator for 15 minutes.

SAUCE

- ½ cup sliced pickled banana peppers, chopped fine, plus ¼ cup pickling liquid
- ¼ cup fresh lemon juice
- ¼ cup vegetable oil
- ¼ cup yellow mustard
- 3 tablespoons dry mustard
- 2 tablespoons chili sauce
- 2 tablespoons brown sugar
- 3 garlic cloves, minced
- 1 habañero chile, stemmed, seeded, and minced
- 4 scallions, sliced thin

CHICKEN

- 6 boneless, skinless chicken breasts (about 2½ pounds), trimmed
- 2 cups unbleached all-purpose flour
- ½ cup cornstarch
- 1 tablespoon salt
- 1 teaspoon baking powder
- 4 large egg whites
- 1 cup vegetable oil

1. FOR THE SAUCE: Whisk all the ingredients together in a large bowl; set aside.

2. FOR THE CHICKEN: Cover the chicken breasts with plastic wrap and pound lightly with a meat mallet until roughly ½ inch thick. Slice the breasts in half lengthwise and transfer to a large zipper-lock storage bag. Add ¼ cup sauce to the bag, seal, and gently squeeze the bag to coat the chicken with the sauce. Refrigerate for 30 minutes (or up to 2 hours).

3. Meanwhile, combine the flour, cornstarch, salt, and baking powder in a large bowl. Add 6 tablespoons of the sauce and, using your hands, blend until the mixture resembles coarse, wet sand.

4. In another large bowl, whisk the egg whites until foamy. Remove the chicken from the marinade and pat dry with paper towels. Following the photos on page 220 and working with one strip at a time, dip the chicken in the egg whites and transfer to the flour mixture, pressing lightly to adhere. Place the chicken pieces on a wire rack set on a rimmed baking sheet and refrigerate 15 minutes (or up to 4 hours).

5. Adjust an oven rack to the middle position and heat the oven to 200 degrees. Line a baking sheet with paper towels. Heat the oil in a large skillet over medium-high heat until shimmering. Carefully place half of the chicken strips in the oil and fry until golden brown and cooked through, 2 to 4 minutes per side. Transfer to the lined baking sheet and place in a warm oven. Repeat with the remaining chicken strips. Transfer the chicken to a platter, drizzle with the remaining sauce, and serve.

WHAT YOU CAN DO AHEAD OF TIME: The sauce can be refrigerated in an airtight container for up to 3 days.

NOTES FROM THE TEST KITCHEN

THE SECRETS OF CRUNCHY CHICKEN

1. Dip the chicken in the foamy egg whites to anchor the coating.

2. Pat the moistened coating mixture onto the chicken to ensure adhesion.

3. Let the breaded chicken strips rest in the refrigerator for 15 minutes and then pan-fry them in oil until very crisp.

SOME LIKE IT HOT

We use four elements of heat—bottled mustard, dry mustard, pickled peppers, and fresh hot chiles—to give our firecracker sauce its spicy kick.

SPICE-RUBBED PICNIC CHICKEN

SERVES 8

WHAT MAKES THIS A BEST RECIPE: While cold barbecued chicken may be a picnic classic, it makes little sense. Covered with a sticky sauce, the chicken is hard to eat with a fork and impossibly messy eaten out of hand. And because the chicken has been cooked and then chilled, the skin is flabby and the meat is so dry it squeaks. This recipe, however, works wonders in that it produces chicken with well-seasoned, moist meat and spice-covered skin designed to be consumed chilled. Given that soggy skin was one of the biggest issues to overcome, we quickly ruled out barbecue sauce in favor of a dry spice rub. After fiddling with simple combinations of chili powder, black pepper, paprika, cayenne, and a little brown sugar, we were able to mimic the flavors of a good sauce. Rubbing the spice mixture both under and over the skin guaranteed robust flavor. Diligently trimming the fat from the chicken pieces further improved the skin, and, once roasted (at 425 degrees), the skin was *almost* edible, though the meat was dry and bland. We turned to what we thought was the obvious solution, brining, but this made the skin flabbier than ever. Flummoxed, we returned to the library and came across a technique from Judi Rodgers (chef of Zuni Café in San Francisco). She salts her chicken up to several days in advance of cooking, the thought being that the salt initially draws moisture out, then, after a few hours, the reverse happens, and the salt and moisture flow back into the flesh. We followed the technique and were rewarded with near-perfect chicken. Best of all, the skin was flavorful, delicate, and definitely not flabby. To streamline things, we combined the salt with the spice mixture and the chicken was the best yet.

5   **pounds bone-in, skin-on chicken parts, trimmed, breasts halved**
3   **tablespoons brown sugar**
2   **tablespoons kosher salt**

2   tablespoons chili powder

2   tablespoons sweet paprika

2   teaspoons pepper

¼–½   teaspoon cayenne pepper

1. Use a sharp knife to make 2 or 3 short slashes in the skin of each piece of chicken, taking care not to cut into the meat. Combine the sugar, salt, and spices in a small bowl and mix thoroughly. Coat the chicken pieces with the spices, gently lifting the skin to distribute the spice rub underneath but leaving it attached to the chicken. Transfer the chicken skin side up to a wire rack set over a rimmed baking sheet, tent with foil, and refrigerate 6 to 24 hours.

2. Secure the skin of each breast piece with 2 or 3 toothpicks placed near the edges of the skin.

3. Adjust an oven rack to the middle position and heat the oven to 425 degrees. Roast the chicken until the thickest part of the smallest piece registers 140 degrees on an instant-read thermometer, 15 to 20 minutes. Increase the oven temperature to 500 degrees and continue roasting until the chicken is browned and crisp and the thickest parts of the breast pieces register 160 degrees, 5 to 8 minutes longer, removing the pieces from the oven and transferring them to a wire rack as they finish cooking. Continue to roast the thighs and/or drumsticks, if using, until the thickest part of the meat registers 170 to 175 degrees, about 5 minutes longer. Remove from the oven; transfer the chicken to the rack and let cool completely before refrigerating or serving.

WHERE THINGS CAN GO WRONG: The skin on the breast pieces will shrink considerably in the oven (leaving the meat exposed and prone to dry out), so we think the extra effort required to secure the skin with toothpicks is justified.

WHAT YOU CAN DO AHEAD OF TIME: The chicken can be prepared through step 1 and refrigerated anywhere from 6 to 24 hours before proceeding with the recipe. The chicken can be cooked and refrigerated in an airtight container for up to 2 days. If you plan to serve the chicken later on the same day that you cook it, refrigerate it immediately after it has cooled, then let it come back to room temperature before serving.

GREAT DISCOVERIES

SALTING: BETTER THAN BRINING?

In the test kitchen, we're strong advocates of brining—soaking meat in a solution of salt and water before cooking. The meat absorbs water as well as salt, with the latter helping the meat retain the moisture as it cooks. With our Spice-Rubbed Picnic Chicken, however, brining made the skin soggy. To solve this problem, we turned to salting the chicken overnight, which helped the meat retain moisture as it cooked—and it didn't harm the skin. Chicken naturally contains some salt and lots of water, which coexist in a happy balance. In coating the chicken with salt, we threw off that balance. To restore order, or equilibrium, water in the meat moved to the surface, where it dissolved the salt. But wouldn't drawing all that water out of the chicken make the situation worse, causing the meat to dry out? It certainly did—until I figured out the timing. When I tried cooking chicken that had been salted for three hours, the chicken cooked up drier than if I hadn't salted it. (The juices that had made it to the exterior simply evaporated in the oven.) But when I cooked the chicken after six hours, the story changed entirely. By that point, the exterior salt had pulled so much water to the surface that the balance of the salt concentration had changed. To restore equilibrium, the water simply changed directions, flowing back into the meat. But this time—and here's the key—the dissolved salt went along for the ride. Essentially, I had "brined" the chicken using its own juices instead of a bucket of water. Once I successfully tapped into this means of delivering salt to the interior, I wondered if it was possible to deliver other flavors the same way. As it turns out, it all comes down to whether the flavoring agent is water soluble (like salt) or fat soluble. With the rub I used for our picnic chicken, the salt and brown sugar, which dissolve easily in water, flowed right in, as did some of the distinguishing flavor compounds of the black pepper, cayenne, chili powder, and paprika. But the spiciness was waylaid at the surface. Capsaicin, the compound that gives chile peppers their spicy heat, is soluble only in fat, so it was unable to join the caravan.

SARAH WILSON | ASSOCIATE EDITOR, *COOK'S ILLUSTRATED*

GRILL-ROASTED TURKEY BREAST

SERVES 6 TO 8

WHAT MAKES THIS A BEST RECIPE: When you want grilled turkey without the rigmarole required of a whole bird (or *all* that meat), a bone-in, skin-on turkey breast is the way to go. However, the lean white meat can overcook easily and taste bland as can be. After a bit of trial-and-error, we developed a "best" recipe for a simple grill-roasted turkey breast. While we usually brine whole turkeys destined for the grill (and oven too), we don't think it's necessary for the breast alone, as long as it's removed from the grill as soon as the internal temperature reaches 160 degrees. Proper cooking, however, didn't remedy the flavor problem. We've had good luck in the test kitchen applying salt rubs to grilled meat and, in this case, a combination of salt and dark brown sugar rubbed under and over the skin worked wonders, especially when applied the night before so that the flavors penetrated the meat. Wiping the night's condensation off the turkey and reapplying the rub—now augmented with black pepper—was necessary to crisp the skin, as was lancing the skin so that excess fat could flow free. Adding a handful of hickory chips contributed a mild smokiness that accented—not overpowered—the turkey's flavor. For convenience's sake, we also altered our usual grill-roasting method by placing small piles of coals on either side of the turkey, effectively sandwiching the turkey between the heat sources—no turning or flipping required.

1 whole, bone-in, skin-on turkey breast (about 5 pounds)
3 tablespoons dark brown sugar
1 tablespoon salt
2 teaspoons pepper
½ cup wood chips, preferably hickory

1. Rinse the turkey and pat dry with paper towels. Mix 2 tablespoons of the brown sugar and the salt in a small bowl. Following the photos on page 224, loosen the skin from the turkey and rub with the sugar and salt mixture. Tightly wrap the turkey in plastic wrap, place on a plate, and refrigerate for at least 8 hours or overnight.

2. Unwrap the turkey and pat dry with paper towels. Mix the remaining 1 tablespoon brown sugar and the pepper in a small bowl. Rub the mixture under and over the turkey breast skin. Using a skewer, pierce the turkey skin all over.

3. Soak the wood chips in water to cover for 15 minutes. Open the bottom grill vents. Light a large chimney starter filled with charcoal briquettes (about 100 pieces) and allow it to burn until all the charcoal is covered with a layer of fine gray ash, about 20 minutes. Place a 13 by 9-inch disposable aluminum roasting pan in the center of the grill. Pour half of the coals into a pile on one side of the grill and the remaining coals on the other side, leaving the pan in the center. Scatter the wood chips evenly over the coals. Set the cooking grate in place, cover, open the lid vent completely, and let the grill heat up 5 minutes. Use a grill brush to scrape the cooking grate clean.

4. Place the turkey skin side up on the center of the grate. Cover and grill until the skin is well browned and crisp and an instant-read thermometer inscrted in the thickest part of the meat registers 160 degrees, about 1½ hours. Wearing oven mitts or using a wad of paper towels, transfer the breast to a cutting board, tent loosely with foil, and let rest for 20 minutes. Carve and serve.

WHERE THINGS CAN GO WRONG: Resist the urge to open the grill as the turkey breast cooks, which will prolong the cooking time.

NOTES FROM THE TEST KITCHEN

GOOD WOOD

You can use any hardwood as fuel for grilling or smoking (soft woods like pine contain too much resin and give foods an unpleasant flavor), but most stores carry only hickory and mesquite. In the test kitchen, we've found that mesquite is too assertively flavored for smoking applications, but it can give good, musky flavor to meats that don't spend too much time on the grill. Our favorite all-purpose wood for grilling and smoking is hickory, which gives food a subtle, slightly sweet flavor.

GRILL-ROASTED TURKEY BREAST

GAS-GRILLED ROASTED TURKEY BREAST

Follow the recipe for Grill-Roasted Turkey Breast through step 2. Soak the wood chips in water to cover for 15 minutes, seal in a foil packet (see page 186), and place over a burner that will remain on. Turn all the burners to high, close the lid, and heat the grill until the chips smoke heavily, about 20 minutes. (If the chips ignite, extinguish the flames with water from a squirt bottle.) Use a grill brush to scrape the cooking grate clean. Turn off the burner(s) without the wood chips. Place the turkey breast on the cool part of the grill and proceed with the recipe from step 4, rotating the breast, still skin side up, halfway through cooking. Adjust the burner as necessary to maintain a temperature of 350 to 375 degrees.

SECRETS TO CRISPY SKIN

Don't be tempted to rub the turkey breast with both salt and pepper at the outset. The salt rub is left on overnight to fully season the turkey, but it dissolves and causes moisture to bead up on the skin that will inhibit crisping. Wiping away the moisture avoids this problem, but you wouldn't want to wipe away the pepper. Wait to pepper the turkey until it has been patted dry and is ready for the grill.

1. Using your hands, carefully loosen the skin from the meat.

2. Apply the brown sugar/salt mixture on and under the skin. Refrigerate the bird overnight, then wipe off moisture; repeat with brown sugar/pepper mixture.

3. Use a skewer to poke numerous holes in the skin so the fat can render easily.

CLASSIC BARBECUED CHICKEN
SERVES 4 TO 6

WHAT MAKES THIS A BEST RECIPE: Smoky grilled chicken slicked in thick barbecue sauce is one of America's favorite summer meals. But despite its popularity, this recipe causes backyard grillers plenty of headaches. Who hasn't been served barbecued chicken that was nearly blackened on the outside yet bloody near the bone? This recipe takes all the issues into consideration and makes perfect barbecued chicken easy. While most recipes call for searing the chicken quickly over high heat to render the fat in the skin and then finishing it over lower heat, we found just the opposite approach delivered far better chicken. We started the pieces over indirect heat (what we call grill-roasting) and then once they were lightly browned, we moved them closer to the coals and lacquered them with barbecue sauce (a store-bought sauce jazzed up with extra seasonings to boost its flavor). Constant turning and moderate heat allowed us to add multiple layers of the sauce to the pieces, which glazed in flavorful layers. Wanting to finish this chicken with a bang, we moved the pieces directly over the coals, which were fading but still relatively hot, and continued to flip them and slather them with sauce for the final five minutes of cooking. This created a robust, crusty char that our tasters loved.

QUICK BBQ SAUCE

    3   cups bottled barbecue sauce
    ½   cup molasses
    ½   cup ketchup
    ¼   cup cider vinegar
    3   tablespoons brown mustard
    2   teaspoons onion powder
    1   teaspoon garlic powder

CHICKEN

1 teaspoon salt

1 teaspoon pepper

¼ teaspoon cayenne pepper

3 pounds bone-in, skin-on chicken pieces, trimmed and breasts halved

Vegetable oil for the grill grate

1. FOR THE SAUCE: Whisk all the ingredients together in a medium saucepan and bring to a boil over medium-high heat. Reduce the heat to medium and cook until the sauce is thick and reduced to 3 cups, about 20 minutes.

2. FOR THE CHICKEN: Mix the salt, pepper, and cayenne in a small bowl. Pat the chicken dry with paper towels and rub the spice mixture all over the chicken pieces.

3. Open the bottom grill vents. Light a large chimney starter filled with charcoal briquettes (about 100 pieces) and allow it to burn until all the charcoal is covered with a layer of fine gray ash, about 20 minutes. Place a 13 by 9-inch disposable aluminum roasting pan on one side of the grill bottom and spread the hot coals in an even layer over the other side of the grill. Set the cooking grate in place. Cover, open the lid vents completely, and let the grill heat up for 5 minutes. Use a grill brush to scrape the cooking grate clean.

4. Dip a wad of paper towels in the oil and, holding the paper towels with long-handled tongs, wipe the grill grate. Following the photos, place the chicken skin side down over the cooler side of the grill. Cover, with half-opened lid vents positioned over the chicken, and cook until the chicken begins to brown, 30 to 35 minutes. Move the chicken into a single line close to the coals. Begin flipping the chicken and brushing with 2 cups of the sauce every 5 minutes until sticky, about 20 minutes. Slide the chicken pieces over the coals and continue to brush the chicken until the sauce on the chicken becomes crusty and the internal temperature of the breast meat registers 160 degrees on an instant-read thermometer and the legs, thighs, and drumsticks register 175 degrees, about 5 minutes.

5. Transfer the chicken to a platter, tent with foil, and let rest 10 minutes. Remove the foil and serve, passing the remaining sauce at the table.

WHAT YOU CAN DO AHEAD OF TIME: The sauce can be refrigerated in an airtight container for up to 1 week.

NOTES FROM THE TEST KITCHEN

GAS-GRILLED CLASSIC BARBECUED CHICKEN
Follow the recipe for Classic Barbecued Chicken through step 2. Turn all the burners on a gas grill to high, close the cover, and heat until very hot, about 15 minutes. Use a grill brush to scrape the cooking grate clean. Oil the cooking grate. Leave one burner on high heat and turn the remaining burners off. Place the chicken pieces over the cooler side of the grill, cover, and proceed with the recipe as directed in steps 4 and 5.

BARBECUED CHICKEN, SLOW AND LOW
First grill-roasting, then basting over moderate heat, and finally finishing with more basting over higher heat ensures rendered, saucy, perfectly cooked chicken. Here's how we do it.

1. Start the chicken skin side down on the cool side of the grill.

2. After about 30 minutes, move the chicken into a single line close to the coals. Begin basting with the sauce and turning the pieces.

3. Once a nice glaze has formed on the chicken, move the pieces directly over the coals to caramelize the sauce.

THE BEST KETCHUP
After a tasting of eight of the most popular brands of ketchup, both "blind" straight off spoons and on French fries, a few things quickly became clear: The best ketchups were those that were tangy, sweet, and salty, not to mention thick enough to keep buns and fries from turning soggy. Most of us assumed that Heinz—it owns 60 percent of the market—would be the hands-down winner, but that wasn't the case. **Hunt's Ketchup** scored the highest marks across the board and was the overall winner. Tasters praised the "inviting, smooth" texture and "tangy," "fresh" flavor. A close runner-up was Heinz Organic Ketchup. Tasters cited its "vinegary tang" and noted that its "color and texture were perfect."

CHARCOAL-GRILLED BUTTERFLIED LEMON CHICKEN

SERVES 8

WHAT MAKES THIS A BEST RECIPE: The advantages of grilling a butterflied chicken are multifold: The two-dimensional bird cooks in half the time of a whole chicken, flavorings can easily be slid under the skin before grilling, and the skin becomes exceptionally crisp. This recipe provides a foolproof approach for grilling a butterflied chicken simply, but powerfully, flavored with lemon. While the Italians weight their butterflied birds with bricks and cook them over direct heat, we found that this approach—and many others—leads to scorching flare-ups as expelled juices hit the hot coals. We had better luck with grill-roasting, or cooking the chicken over indirect heat on the opposite side of the grill from hot coals. Positioning the legs, which are dark meat, closest to the coals enabled the white and dark meat to come up to temperature (160 degrees for white and 175 degrees for dark) at the same time without rotating or flipping. A final sear directly over the dying coals at the end of cooking crisped and browned the skin nicely—without the risk of flare-ups. For the fullest lemon flavor, we added the citrus in layers. For a pregrill spice rub, we tried all manner of seasonings and finally settled on a simple mixture of lemon zest, salt, and pepper. Dousing the cooked chicken in a lemon-juice-based vinaigrette infused the chicken with a bright lemoniness, especially after we decided to grill the lemons (briefly over the hot coals) before juicing them, which concentrated the flavor and—serendipitously—muted the harsh acidity.

CHICKEN AND RUB

- 2 teaspoons grated lemon zest (reserve the lemon for vinaigrette)
- 2 teaspoons salt
- 1 teaspoon pepper
- 2 (3½- to 4-pound) chickens, butterflied (see page 228) Vegetable oil for the grill grate

VINAIGRETTE

- 4 lemons, halved; plus the reserved zested lemon from the rub, halved
- 1 garlic clove, minced
- ½ teaspoon salt
- 2 teaspoons Dijon mustard
- 1 teaspoon sugar
- ½ teaspoon pepper
- 2 tablespoons minced fresh parsley
- ⅔ cup extra-virgin olive oil

1. FOR THE CHICKEN AND RUB: Combine the lemon zest, salt, and pepper in a bowl. Rub the zest mixture under the skin of the chickens. Transfer the chickens to a rack set over a rimmed baking sheet and refrigerate, uncovered, for 30 minutes.

2. Open the bottom grill vents completely. Light a large chimney starter filled with charcoal briquettes (about 100 pieces) and allow it to burn until all the charcoal is covered with a layer of fine gray ash, about 20 minutes. Place a 13 by 9-inch disposable aluminum roasting pan on one side of the grill bottom and pour the hot coals into a pile on the other side of the grill. Evenly scatter 20 unlit briquettes on top of the hot coals and set the cooking grate in place. Cover, with the lid vents positioned over the cooler side of the grill and opened fully. Let the grill heat up for 5 minutes. Use a grill brush to scrape the cooking grate clean.

3. Dip a wad of paper towels in the oil and, holding the paper towels with long-handled tongs, wipe the grill grate. Place the lemon halves cut side down over the hot side of the grill. Place the chickens skin side down over the cooler side of the grill, with the legs positioned closest to the coals. Cover, with opened lid vents positioned over the chicken.

4. Grill the lemons until deep brown and caramelized, 5 to 8 minutes. Transfer to a bowl. Grill the chickens until the skin is well browned and the breast meat registers 160 degrees on an instant-read thermometer, 45 to 55 minutes. Move the chickens to the hot side of the grill and sear, uncovered, until deep brown, 2 to 4 minutes longer.

5. FOR THE VINAIGRETTE: While the chickens are grilling, squeeze ⅓ cup juice from the grilled lemons into a bowl. Using the flat side of a knife, mash the garlic and salt into a paste and add to the bowl with the lemon juice. Stir in the mustard, sugar, pepper, and parsley, then slowly whisk in the olive oil until emulsified.

6. Transfer the chickens to a cutting board and let rest 10 to 15 minutes. Carve, transfer to a serving platter, and pour ⅓ cup of the vinaigrette over the chicken. Serve, passing the remaining vinaigrette at the table.

WHERE THINGS CAN GO WRONG: Don't try moving the chicken earlier than recommended in the recipe because the skin will likely stick fast and rip.

WHAT YOU CAN DO AHEAD OF TIME: The chickens can be prepared through step 1 up to 24 hours in advance and refrigerated, wrapped tightly in plastic wrap. Allow the chickens to sit at room temperature 30 minutes before grilling.

NOTES FROM THE TEST KITCHEN

GAS-GRILLED BUTTERFLIED LEMON CHICKEN
Follow the recipe for Charcoal-Grilled Butterflied Lemon Chicken through step 1. Turn all the burners on a gas grill to high, close the cover, and heat until very hot, about 15 minutes. Use a grill brush to scrape the cooking grate clean. Oil the cooking grate. Leave one burner on high heat and turn the remaining burners to low. Place the lemons over the hot burner; place the chickens skin side down over the cooler part of the grill, with the legs positioned closest to the heat; cover and proceed with the recipe from step 4, adjusting the hot burner as necessary to maintain the temperature between 350 and 375 degrees. When the chickens are cooked, transfer to the hot part of the grill and sear, uncovered, until deep brown, 2 to 4 minutes. Proceed with the recipe from step 5.

HOW TO BUTTERFLY A CHICKEN
With a few scissor snips and a little leveling from a meat pounder, whole chickens can be quickly flattened to promote even cooking on the grill.

1. Cut through the bones on either side of the backbone and trim any excess fat or skin at the neck.

2. Flip the chicken over and use the heel of your hand to flatten the breast-bone.

3. Cover the chicken with plastic wrap. Using a meat pounder or rubber mallet, pound the breast to the same thickness as the leg and thigh meat.

4. Slip your hand between the skin and meat to loosen the skin. Rub the zest mixture under the skin and into the breast and leg meat.

ROAST SALTED TURKEY

SERVES 10 TO 12

WHAT MAKES THIS A BEST RECIPE: Brining is the best way to guarantee a moist turkey, but it isn't always the most practical as it requires a great deal of refrigerator space. We began to rethink our brine-at-all-costs philosophy while developing our recipe for Spice-Rubbed Picnic Chicken (page 220), where we found that a salt rub could accomplish almost the same end as brining. If it worked with small pieces of chicken, might it also work with a whole turkey? The short answer was yes, and quite well at that. From the previous testing, we knew that the best results came when the salt made direct contact with the flesh, not just the skin. With the aid of a wooden spoon handle or a chopstick, it was easy to loosen the skin all over the bird and insert a thick layer of kosher salt. (We settled on 5 tablespoons as ideal.) After testing birds salted to varying intervals, we decided that 24 hours was minimum, 48 hours maximum for salting. Most of the meat was nicely seasoned, and it was pretty moist. Blotting up the excess moisture ensured that the roasted bird would emerge from the oven crisp and brown. While the turkey tasted good, it wasn't nearly as moist as a brined bird. We had been following our standard cooking method in which the turkey is roasted at 425 degrees and flipped midway through, but we wondered if a "salted" bird demanded a different treatment. After trying a few novel methods with little improvement, we found our answer. Inspired by food scientist Harold McGee, we cooled the bird's breast on ice packs, so that it would cook more slowly than the dark meat parts and thus retain more moisture. This worked really well. Our salted and iced turkey was now on par with our conventional brined bird.

1 (12- to 14-pound) turkey, giblets and neck reserved for gravy, if desired
5 tablespoons kosher salt
1 (5-pound) bag ice cubes
4 tablespoons unsalted butter, melted

1. Following the photos on page 231, carefully separate the turkey skin from the meat on the breast, legs, thighs, and back; avoid breaking the skin. Rub 2 tablespoons of the salt evenly inside the cavity of the turkey, 1 tablespoon salt under the skin of each breast half, and 1½ teaspoons salt under the skin of each leg. Wrap the turkey tightly in plastic wrap; refrigerate 24 to 48 hours.

2. Remove the turkey from the refrigerator. Rinse off the excess salt between the meat and skin and in the cavity, then pat the cavity and outside of the turkey dry with paper towels. Add ice to two 1-gallon zipper-lock bags until each is half full. Place the bags in a large roasting pan and lay the turkey breast side down on top of the ice. Add ice to two 1-quart zipper-lock bags until each is one-third full; place one bag of ice in the cavity of the turkey and the other bag in the neck cavity. (Make sure that ice touches the breast only, not the thighs or legs.) Keep the turkey on ice for 1 hour (the roasting pan should remain on the counter).

3. Meanwhile, adjust an oven rack to the lowest position and heat the oven to 425 degrees. Line a large V-rack with heavy-duty foil and use a paring knife or skewer to poke 20 to 30 holes in the foil.

4. Remove the turkey from the ice and pat dry with paper towels; discard the ice. Tuck the tips of the drumsticks into the skin at the tail to secure, and tuck the wingtips behind the back. Brush the turkey breast with 2 tablespoons of the butter. Set the prepared V-rack in the roasting pan; set the turkey breast side down on the V-rack; brush the back and legs with the remaining 2 tablespoons butter. Roast for 45 minutes.

5. Remove the roasting pan with the turkey from the oven (close the oven door to retain the heat); reduce the oven temperature to 325 degrees. Using clean potholders or kitchen towels, rotate the turkey breast side up; continue to roast until the breast meat registers 160 degrees on an instant-read thermometer and the dark meat registers 170 to 175 degrees, 1 to 1½ hours longer. Transfer the turkey to a carving board; let rest 30 minutes. Carve and serve.

WHERE THINGS CAN GO WRONG: Make sure to notice the brand of kosher salt you are using—it makes a difference. This recipe was developed and tested using Diamond Crystal Kosher Salt. If you have Morton's Kosher Salt, which is denser than Diamond Crystal, use only 4½ teaspoons of salt in the cavity, 2¼ teaspoons of salt per each half of the breast, and 1 teaspoon of salt per leg. Table salt is too fine and not recommended for this recipe. If you are roasting a kosher or self-basting turkey (such as a frozen Butterball), do not salt it; it already contains a good amount of sodium.

NOTES FROM THE TEST KITCHEN

ICING IT DOWN

Cooling the breast down with ice ensures that it will cook more slowly than the legs and thighs, preventing the meat from drying out. Place bags of ice underneath the breast and inside both the large cavity and the neck area.

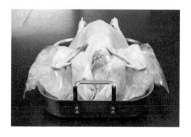

THE BEST CARVING BOARD

While everyone likes the romantic notion of carving the holiday bird at the table for all to see, seasoned cooks know that turkey carving is best done in the kitchen—and requires a sturdy board. We tested eight carving boards to determine which should be entrusted with the important job. A modest 15-pound turkey measures roughly 16 inches long, a fact that put two 18-inch boards out of the running. After half an hour's rest, our birds shed roughly half a cup of liquid, which flooded the shallow channels on two other boards. The deep, wide trench on the **Williams-Sonoma Medium Reversible Carving Board** ($58) easily held any liquid the turkey shed and, what's more, featured a deep, oval-shaped central well in which the turkey rested snugly. And for versatility's sake, the flip side was flat for carving steaks and roasts.

HOW TO SALT A TURKEY

1. Use a chopstick or thin wooden spoon handle to separate the skin from the meat over the breast, legs, thighs, and back.

2. Rub 2 tablespoons kosher salt inside the main cavity.

3. Lift the skin and apply 1 tablespoon kosher salt evenly over each breast half, placing half of the salt on each end of each breast.

4. Apply 1½ teaspoons kosher salt to each leg, adding half the salt while the bird is breast side up; flip and apply remaining salt to the underside of the thigh.

5. After 24 to 48 hours, rinse the bird well to remove excess salt trapped under the skin and in the cavity.

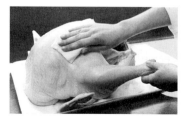

6. Use paper towels to blot excess moisture from the skin so it will crisp and brown in the oven.

CHARCOAL-GRILLED DUCK BREASTS
WITH PEACH-HABAÑERO CHUTNEY
SERVES 4

WHAT MAKES THIS A BEST RECIPE: Rich and flavorful, duck breasts are perhaps the best part of the bird and take just minutes to cook. While quick, duck breasts are tricky to prepare because of their fatty, thick skin that scorches easily and their lean meat that is best cooked to medium-rare. This combination of fat and lean creates a real culinary conundrum: How do you render the fat from the skin and crisp it without overcooking the meat? After burning our way through several batches at varying grill temps, it became clear that some of the fat had to be removed before cooking. We removed the excess fat and skin and, following a tip in several recipes we had collected, we scored the skin, which allowed excess fat to render free. Cooking the breast skin side down over a medium-hot fire for most of the cooking time guaranteed that the skin crisped and the meat remained a ruddy medium-rare. The skin, in fact, was so good that it stole center stage from the meat itself; we trimmed the skin back into a 2-inch strip across the center of each breast, making for a more appropriate balance between crisp skin and succulent meat. To match the duck's assertive flavor, we favored a spicy peach and habañero chile chutney. Subtly laced with spices and mellowed by the fruit's sweetness, it was the perfect accompaniment.

CHUTNEY

- 1½ tablespoons vegetable oil
- 1 medium red onion, chopped fine
- 2 ripe but firm peaches, halved, pitted, and chopped
- ½ medium habañero chile, stemmed, seeded, and minced
- ¼ teaspoon ground ginger

Duck fat is so rich that we remove the majority of the skin before grilling.

- Pinch ground allspice
- Pinch ground cloves
- ¼ cup packed light brown sugar
- ¼ cup red wine vinegar
- 1 tablespoon thinly slivered fresh mint

DUCK

- 2 whole boneless duck breasts (about 12 ounces each), split and trimmed; skin scored 3 or 4 times diagonally (see page 233)
- Salt and pepper

1. FOR THE CHUTNEY: Heat the oil in a medium saucepan over medium heat until shimmering. Add the onion and cook until soft, about 7 minutes. Add the peaches and cook until soft but still intact, about 4 minutes. Add the chile and spices and cook until fragrant, about 1 minute. Stir in the brown sugar and vinegar and bring to a simmer. Reduce the heat to low and simmer until the liquid is very thick and syrupy, about 9 minutes. Transfer the mixture to a small bowl and cool to room temperature. Stir in the mint; set aside.

2. FOR THE DUCK: Light a large chimney starter filled with charcoal briquettes (about 100 pieces) and allow it to burn until all the charcoal is covered with a layer of fine gray ash, about 20 minutes. Spread the coals out into an even layer over the grill bottom. Set the cooking grate in place. Cover and let the grill heat up for 5 minutes. Use a grill brush to scrape the cooking grate clean.

3. Liberally season the duck breasts with salt and pepper. Place the duck breasts skin side down on the grill. Grill the duck breasts, uncovered, until the skin is nicely browned, about 8 minutes. Using tongs, turn the duck breasts and continue grilling until an instant-read thermometer inserted into the thickest part registers 140 degrees, 3 to 4 minutes more.

4. Transfer the breasts to a cutting board, tent loosely with foil, and let rest 5 minutes. Slice the breasts diagonally into 8 slices, ½ inch thick, and fan 1 sliced breast half on each dinner plate. Serve immediately, with the chutney.

WHAT YOU CAN DO AHEAD OF TIME: The chutney can be refrigerated in an airtight container for up to 3 days.

NOTES FROM THE TEST KITCHEN

GAS-GRILLED DUCK BREASTS
Turn all the burners on a gas grill to high, close the cover, and heat until very hot, about 15 minutes. Use a grill brush to scrape the cooking grate clean. Turn the burners down to medium-high. Follow the recipe for Charcoal-Grilled Duck Breasts from step 3, grilling with the cover down.

HOW TO BUY DUCK BREASTS
The duck breasts and whole ducks sold in supermarkets are usually Pekin, or Long Island, ducks. Once raised on Long Island, these birds are now grown on farms around the country, and the largest producer is in Indiana, a long way from New York. Most duck breasts are sold whole, with the skin on but without the bones. They can be split nicely into two halves, each weighing about 6 ounces. Other duck species are available if you are willing to order by mail or can shop at a specialty butcher. The Muscovy is a South American bird that is less fatty than the Pekin and has a stronger game flavor. The Moulard is the sterile offspring of a Muscovy and a Pekin duck and is popular in France. Because these birds are so much leaner, the breasts require a different cooking method. Since the Pekin duck is the breed found in supermarkets, we decided to stick with this variety when developing our recipe for Charcoal-Grilled Duck Breasts with Peach-Habañero Chutney.

PREPARING DUCK BREASTS

1. To prepare a whole boneless duck breast for grilling, first split the breast into two halves.

2. Trim overhanging skin and fat. Slide your fingers under remaining skin to loosen. Slice off the skin so that only a 1½- to 2- inch strip of fat remains.

3. Using a paring knife, score the skin on each breast diagonally 3 to 4 times to allow the fat to melt during cooking.

ESSENTIAL SPICES

NUTMEG

WHAT YOU NEED TO KNOW: Nutmeg is the dried seed-like kernel of an evergreen tree. Its warm, spicy flavor accentuates sweetness in recipes.

HOW TO USE IT: Nutmeg loses its aroma when ground, so it's best to buy whole nutmeg and grate it when needed.

CUMIN

WHAT YOU NEED TO KNOW: Cumin is a highly aromatic spice that comes from a plant in the parsley family.

HOW TO USE IT: If time allows, we like to toast and grind whole cumin seeds; this gives the spice a more complex peppery flavor than when purchased ground.

TEST KITCHEN FAVORITE
★ McCormick Gourmet Collection Ground Cumin

CORIANDER

WHAT YOU NEED TO KNOW: Coriander is the seed of the plant that produces the herb cilantro. Whole seeds provide a more vibrant, complex flavor than ground.

HOW TO USE IT: Toasting whole coriander releases its flavor and aroma.

CAYENNE PEPPER

WHAT YOU NEED TO KNOW: Originally made from cayenne peppers, this spice is now made from a variety of ground dried chiles. It is rich with volatile oils, making it susceptible to flavor loss within a few months.

HOW TO USE IT: Intensity varies from brand to brand, so add a small amount, taste, and adjust seasoning.

CHILI POWDER

WHAT YOU NEED TO KNOW: Most brands are a blend of 80 percent ground dried chiles with garlic powder, oregano, and cumin. Chili powders made solely from chiles can be found in ethnic markets and are usually labeled by type of chile.

HOW TO USE IT: Because chili powder is a blend of spices, it should be "bloomed" in hot oil to bring out its complex flavors.

TEST KITCHEN FAVORITE
★ Spice Islands Chili Powder

CINNAMON

WHAT YOU NEED TO KNOW: True cinnamon is made from the dried bark of a tropical evergreen tree. What most cooks think of as cinnamon is actually cassia, made from the bark of a similar evergreen. Cassia has a darker color and a more pungent flavor than true cinnamon, which we find too mild and not worth seeking out.

HOW TO USE IT: Cinnamon is one of the few spices that we prefer to buy ground. Save whole cinnamon sticks for infusing flavor into hot liquids.

TEST KITCHEN FAVORITE
★ Penzeys China Cassia Cinnamon

CURRY POWDER

WHAT YOU NEED TO KNOW: Curry powder is a blend of spices. Most formulas include cardamom, chiles, cumin, fennel, fenugreek, nutmeg, and turmeric, which gives curry its characteristically yellow color.

HOW TO USE IT: For general cooking, we prefer a mild curry powder; hot curry powder, which contains more chiles, can be overpowering. It should be sautéed in hot oil to "bloom" its flavor.

TEST KITCHEN FAVORITE
★ Penzeys Curry Powder

CLOVES

WHAT YOU NEED TO KNOW: Cloves are the dried unopened flower buds of a species of evergreen tree and boast a sweet, peppery flavor.

HOW TO USE IT: Cloves are potent and should be used sparingly. Because whole cloves are difficult to grind, we buy them ground. Reserve whole cloves for infusing flavor into hot liquids.

PAPRIKA

WHAT YOU NEED TO KNOW: Paprika is a fine powder made by grinding dried red peppers. Its flavor and pungency can range from mild to hot, depending on what type of pepper is used and how much of the placenta (the white veins) is ground with the pepper.

HOW TO USE IT: We prefer the complexity of sweet paprika.

TEST KITCHEN FAVORITE
★ Penzeys Hungary Sweet Paprika

SAFFRON

WHAT YOU NEED TO KNOW: The world's most expensive spice is the hand-harvested stigma of crocus. Buy red saffron threads that are devoid of yellow and orange. Saffron can also be purchased powdered, but it is often mixed with other ingredients and should be bought from a reputable source.

HOW TO USE IT: To release flavor, crush saffron threads with your fingers before adding them to a dish. Use sparingly; too much will impart a metallic taste.

ALL ABOUT SPICES

BUYING AND STORING SPICES

In most cases, purchasing whole spices and grinding them is preferable to buying ground spices. Whole spices have a longer shelf life, and most fresh-ground spices also have superior aroma and flavor. Whether whole or ground, spices should be bought in the smallest quantities available.

Heat and moisture quickly shorten the shelf life of spices, leaving them dull; keep spices in a cool, dark, dry place in a well-sealed container.

Using stick-on dots, write the name and purchase date on top of the spice jar. This will tell you how long you've had the spice.

SPICE GRINDERS

We've determined that the best tool for grinding whole spices to an even, fine powder is an inexpensive blade coffee grinder. If possible, keep one grinder for coffee, another for spices.

TEST KITCHEN FAVORITE
★ Krups Fast-Touch Coffee Mill, Model 203, $17.95

HOW TO CLEAN A SPICE GRINDER

A quick wipe with a brush or cloth is usually sufficient to clean a grinder. Sometimes, however, spice residues remain even after wiping. Because most grinders can't be immersed in water, we developed a technique for "dry cleaning."

Add several tablespoons of raw white rice to the grinder and pulverize to a fine powder. The rice powder will absorb residual spice particles and oils.

PUMPING UP THE FLAVOR

We often toast or bloom spices to release their volatile oils and fullest flavor.

TOASTING

The process of dry-toasting spices is normally reserved for whole spices that are then ground into a fine powder. To toast spices, put them in a small skillet without any oil and set over medium heat. Shake the skillet occasionally to prevent scorching and toast until they are fragrant, 1 to 3 minutes. Cool slightly before grinding.

BLOOMING

To intensify the flavor of commercially ground spices, cook them for a minute or two in a little butter or oil—before any liquid is added to the recipe. This step is particularly important with spice mixtures, such as chili powder and curry powder, where it's crucial to develop their complex flavors. (Whole spices can also be bloomed in oil or butter. The spices should be discarded before the dish is served.)

ALL ABOUT PEPPER

BLACK PEPPER

Black pepper is the most important spice in your pantry. This berry grows in a spike-like cluster on a climbing vine that is indigenous to the tropics. The berries are picked when green and then sun-dried until they become the dry, hard, blackish kernels we know as peppercorns.

WHAT YOU NEED TO KNOW: As soon as peppercorns are cracked, they begin losing the volatile compounds that give them bold aroma and subtle flavor; soon enough, all that's left is a nonvolatile compound called piperine, which gives the sensation of "hotness" but little else. For that reason, we consider whole peppercorns—ground to order in a pepper mill—the only viable option.

TEST KITCHEN FAVORITE
★ McCormick/Schilling Whole Black Pepper

WHITE PEPPER

The berries used to make white pepper are the same as those used to make black pepper, but they are harvested at a riper stage. The hulls are then removed and with them goes some of the heat characteristic of black pepper. White peppercorns are often used when the appearance of a dish would be marred by flecks of black. We use white pepper so infrequently that we can't justify purchasing a pepper mill for the sole purpose of grinding it. Instead, we buy ground white pepper and replenish our stock when the pepper loses its fragrance.

PEPPER MILLS

Our favorite pepper mill has a huge capacity, is easily adjustable, and works with astonishing speed.

TEST KITCHEN FAVORITE
★ Unicorn Magnum Plus Peppermill, $45

SEAFOOD

MUSSELS IN WHITE WINE WITH PARSLEY **238**

CEVICHE **239**

CHARCOAL-GRILLED SHRIMP SKEWERS
WITH SPICY LEMON-GARLIC SAUCE **240**

FLAMBÉED SHRIMP WITH TOMATOES, FETA, AND OUZO **242**

CHARCOAL-GRILLED SWEET AND SAUCY SALMON **245**

CHARCOAL-GRILLED BLACKENED SNAPPER **246**

BROILED SCALLOPS WITH CREAMY MUSHROOM SAUCE **249**

FAMILY-STYLE SHRIMP SCAMPI **250**

CATFISH IN SALTY-SWEET CARAMEL SAUCE **252**

CREOLE-STYLE SHRIMP AND SAUSAGE GUMBO **253**

CHARCOAL-GRILLED LOBSTERS **256**

MUSSELS IN WHITE WINE
WITH PARSLEY
SERVES 6

WHAT MAKES THIS A BEST RECIPE: The most traditional of all French mussel dishes, mussels in white wine, or *moules à la marinière,* includes only a few ingredients, but their combination yields a dish far greater than the sum of its parts. While we didn't want (or need) to reinvent the wheel with this classic, we did want to finesse the flavors and come up with a faultless rendition. The cooking method couldn't be simpler: Shallots and garlic are sautéed in butter, to which wine and the mussels are added and simmered until the shells open. Crème fraîche or cream and parsley are stirred in, and the dish is ready for the table. For the best flavor—and the richest-tasting broth—we found that a good deal of butter was necessary and that a substantial volume of shallots and garlic was important. As for the steaming liquid, a dry white wine proved best as its bright acidity cut through the butter's richness and highlighted the brininess of the mussels. Simmering the wine with the sautéed aromatics, plus a bay leaf, married the flavors well. The mussels (a pound per person) cooked in just a few minutes, after which we stirred in a bit of heavy cream—to lend velvety body to the otherwise thin broth—and chopped fresh parsley. In minutes, we had a one-pot meal that's as simple as can be. Make sure to have a loaf of crusty bread to soak up every last drop of the broth.

- 6 tablespoons (¾ stick) unsalted butter
- 3 shallots, minced (about 9 tablespoons)
- 6 garlic cloves, minced
- 2 cups dry white wine
- 1 bay leaf
- 6 pounds mussels, scrubbed and debearded if necessary
- ¼ cup heavy cream
- ½ cup minced fresh parsley
- Salt and pepper

1. Melt 2 tablespoons of the butter in a large Dutch oven over medium-high heat. Add the shallots and cook until softened, about 2 minutes. Stir in the garlic and cook until fragrant, about 30 seconds. Stir in the wine and bay leaf and simmer until the flavors have blended, about 3 minutes.

2. Increase the heat to high and add the mussels. Cover and cook, stirring occasionally, until the mussels open, 4 to 9 minutes.

3. Transfer the mussels with a slotted spoon to a large serving bowl, leaving the liquid in the pot; discard any mussels that have not opened. Remove and discard the bay leaf. Stir the remaining 4 tablespoons butter and the cream into the broth and simmer over medium-high heat until the butter is melted and the liquid is slightly thickened, about 2 minutes. Stir in the parsley and season with salt and pepper to taste. Pour the sauce over the mussels and serve immediately.

WHERE THINGS CAN GO WRONG: Begin checking the mussels for doneness after 4 minutes of cooking time. Overcooked mussels are tough and rubbery.

NOTES FROM THE TEST KITCHEN

HOW TO BUY AND STORE MUSSELS
Most mussels are now farmed either on ropes or along seabeds. (You may also see "wild" mussels at the market. These mussels are caught the old-fashioned way—by dredging along the sea floor. In our tests, they were extremely muddy and not worth the bother.) Rope-cultured mussels can be as much as twice the cost of wild or bottom-cultured mussels, but we found them to be free of grit and since mussels are generally inexpensive (no more than a few dollars a pound), we think clean mussels are worth the extra money. Before purchasing, ask your fishmonger how and where the mussels you are considering have been grown. The mussels should be tightly closed (do not use any that are even slightly open, a sign that they may be dying or dead and should not be eaten). Store mussels in a bowl in the refrigerator and use within a day or two. (Do not store in a sealed container, as this will cause them to die.) Mussels may need scrubbing as well as debearding, which simply means pulling off the weedy bit protruding from between the shells. Debearding should be done just before you are ready to cook the mussels.

CEVICHE

SERVES 6 AS AN APPETIZER

WHAT MAKES THIS A BEST RECIPE: *Ceviche*, considered the national dish of Peru (most food historians agree that it was first served in northern Peru), is a simple seafood dish that is also served in many other seafaring regions around the world. Recently, ceviche has become wildly popular as one of the best ways to highlight the flavors of fresh seafood. Rather than using conventional heat to cook the seafood, citrus juices are used to "cook" the seafood in ceviche. (The acidic liquid denatures protein in much the same way that heat does.) The result is a refreshing, summery dish that highlights the flavors of the fresh seafood and seasonal local flavors. Ceviche is simple to prepare but, as with most simple dishes, requires careful attention to the details. Starting with the ceviche's acidic medium, we tested several liquids based on recipes we researched including lime juice, lemon juice, white wine vinegar, and cider vinegar, as well as various combinations of these. The vinegars turned out to be bad both on their own and in combination with the fresh juices—they added harsh, stale flavors to the otherwise fresh-tasting dish. Tasters preferred the flavor of lime to lemon when the juices were used on their own (and lime is more traditional), but neither was perfect. The lime juice was too sour and bitter, while the lemon was a tad bland. A 50/50 combination of lime and lemon juice was a nice compromise with a well-rounded, balanced flavor. Unfortunately, the lime-lemon combination still tasted a little generic to some tasters who missed the traditional lime flavor. To remedy this, we simply added a little lime zest, which helped bring the lime flavor to the foreground without making the ceviche taste overly tart. For the sake of saving time, we tried using bottled lime and lemon juice—and ruled this option out. The sweet, artificial flavor of these juices ruined the flavor of the seafood. Next we tested the types of seafood most commonly used for ceviche. Firm-textured, sweet-flavored shrimp and scallops fared

well, as did mild-tasting halibut, sea bass, and sole. (Tuna and salmon tasted good too, though tuna took on a bluish tinge.) As with the citrus juices, freshness was imperative—no frozen fish. Slicing the seafood (all types, including the shrimp and scallops) into ⅓-inch-thick, bite-sized pieces ensured that all of the seafood would be evenly "cooked" in no more than 60 minutes. Draining the ceviche prior to serving emboldened the flavor of the seafood, and a touch of minced garlic, sweet and hot peppers, scallions, cilantro, and a pinch of sugar added just the right textural and colorful notes.

1 pound extra-large shrimp (21 to 25 per pound), large sea scallops, skinless fish fillets, or a combination

1 teaspoon grated zest, plus ½ cup juice from 4 limes

½ cup juice from 4 lemons

1 small red bell pepper, stemmed, seeded, and chopped fine

1 small jalapeño chile, stemmed, seeded, and minced

1 garlic clove, minced

Salt

¼ cup extra-virgin olive oil

4 scallions, sliced thin

3 tablespoons minced fresh cilantro

½ teaspoon sugar

Pepper

1. If using shrimp, peel, devein, and slice each shrimp in half lengthwise (through the deveined groove along the back). If using scallops, remove the side tendon and slice into ⅓-inch-thick rounds. If using fish, remove any bones and slice into 1-inch squares, each about ⅓ inch thick.

2. Stir the lime zest and juice, lemon juice, bell pepper, jalapeño, garlic, and ½ teaspoon salt together in a medium nonreactive bowl. Gently stir in the seafood, cover with plastic wrap, and refrigerate until the seafood is firm and opaque and appears cooked, 45 to 60 minutes, stirring halfway through the marinating time.

3. Drain the mixture briefly in a fine-mesh strainer, leaving the ceviche a little wet, then return to the bowl. Gently stir in the oil, scallions, cilantro, and sugar. Season with salt and pepper to taste. Serve immediately.

CHARCOAL-GRILLED SHRIMP SKEWERS
WITH SPICY LEMON-GARLIC SAUCE
SERVES 4

WHAT MAKES THIS A BEST RECIPE: It's no secret that shrimp can turn from moist and juicy to rubbery and dry in the blink of an eye, a consequence of their small size and lack of fat. Add the unpredictability of cooking over a live fire, and the challenge is magnified. Grilling shrimp in their shells is one method to shield them from the coals' scorching heat, but it can be hard to add much flavor through the shell. We wanted a recipe for grilled shelled shrimp with maximum flavor and a moist texture. Initial testing reaffirmed the obvious: Larger shrimp remained juicier and picked up more flavorful charring than smaller shrimp did because of their broader surface area. We didn't want to pay the prohibitive price for jumbo shrimp, though, and found that we could create "jumbo" shrimp out of smaller shrimp by threading them tightly—head to tail—on a skewer. In this fashion, we could grill the shrimp over a hot fire for maximum flavor without the risk of the shrimp drying out or turning tough. When we applied spice rubs, herbs, garlic, and the like directly to the shrimp, the flavorings burned. Instead, we simply seasoned the shrimp themselves with salt, pepper, and a little sugar (to maximize browning) and prepared a quick lemon-butter sauce with garlic and hot pepper flakes added in a pan on the grill. Once the shrimp were almost cooked through, we dunked them into the sauce to soak it up and finish cooking in the gentle heat.

SHRIMP

1½ pounds extra-large shrimp (21 to 25 per pound), peeled and deveined (see page 250), tails intact
2–3 tablespoons olive oil for brushing skewers
    Salt and pepper
¼ teaspoon sugar

SAUCE

4 tablespoons unsalted butter, cut into 4 pieces
4 tablespoons juice from 2 lemons
½–¾ teaspoon red pepper flakes
3 garlic cloves, minced
⅛ teaspoon salt
    Disposable aluminum pan or pie plate
⅓ cup minced fresh parsley
    Lemon wedges, for serving

1. FOR THE SHRIMP: Pat the shrimp dry with paper towels. Following the photo on page 242, thread the shrimp onto 3 skewers, alternating the direction of heads and tails. Brush both sides of the shrimp with the oil and season lightly with salt and pepper. Sprinkle one side of each skewer evenly with the sugar.

2. Light a large chimney starter filled with charcoal briquettes (about 100 pieces) and allow it to burn until the charcoal is partially covered with a thin layer of gray ash, about 20 minutes. Spread the coals over half of the grill bottom, set the cooking grate in place, cover the grill, and heat until hot, about 5 minutes. Use a grill brush to scrape the cooking grate clean.

3. FOR THE SAUCE: Combine all the sauce ingredients but the parsley in the disposable aluminum pan, set on the hot side of the grill, and cook until the butter melts, about 1½ minutes; transfer the pan to the cooler side of the grill.

4. Place the shrimp skewers, sugared sides down, on the hot side of the grate; use tongs to push the shrimp together on the skewer if they have separated. Grill the shrimp, uncovered, until lightly charred, 4 to 5 minutes. Flip the skewers and grill until the second side is pink and slightly translucent, 1 to 2 minutes longer.

5. Using a potholder or oven mitt, carefully lift each skewer from the grill; use tongs to slide the shrimp off the skewers, into the pan with the sauce. Toss the shrimp and sauce to combine and transfer the pan to the hot side of the grill; cook, stirring, until the shrimp are opaque and fully cooked, about 30 seconds. Remove from the grill, add the parsley, and toss to combine. Transfer to a serving platter and serve immediately with the lemon wedges.

WHERE THINGS CAN GO WRONG: If not threaded tightly together, actually touching, on the skewers, the shrimp can easily overcook.

NOTES FROM THE TEST KITCHEN

GAS-GRILLED SHRIMP SKEWERS WITH SPICY LEMON-GARLIC SAUCE

Follow step 1 of the recipe for Charcoal-Grilled Shrimp Skewers with Spicy Lemon-Garlic Sauce. Turn all the burners on a gas grill to high, close the cover, and heat until very hot, about 15 minutes. Use a grill brush to scrape the cooking grate clean. Proceed with step 3 of the recipe, removing the pan of sauce from the grill once hot and grilling the shrimp with the lid down, checking occasionally to make sure the shrimp are not burning. (The timing may be a few minutes longer than in the charcoal grill recipe.) Finish the recipe as directed in step 5, placing the pan of sauce back on the grill after adding the shrimp to it.

CROWDING SHRIMP ON A SKEWER

Pass the skewer through the center of each shrimp. As you add shrimp to the skewer, alternate the directions of the heads and tails for a compact arrangement of about 12 shrimp. The shrimp should be crowded and touching each other.

THE BEST SKEWERS

How much "performance" difference could there really be between one pointed stick and another? Once we'd surveyed the field—and tried out the designs of different skewers with our recipes for grilled shrimp (and grilled onions too)—our attitude changed. It really is possible to buy bad skewers. Our conclusions? Skip bamboo skewers on the grill: They will burn and break. Go with reusable metal skewers and flat skewers in particular, which grip food tightly and allow for easy turning. Our choice: Any flat, thin metal skewer will do. We particularly like **Norpro's 12-inch Stainless Steel Skewers** (six skewers for $10), which are just ³⁄₁₆ inch thick.

FLAMBÉED SHRIMP
WITH TOMATOES, FETA, AND OUZO
SERVES 4 TO 6

WHAT MAKES THIS A BEST RECIPE: The combination of shrimp, tomatoes, and feta cheese appears in home kitchens, tavernas, and restaurants all over Greece, under a proliferation of names and styles. Sometimes the shrimp are baked or simmered in a sauce, often they are fried in olive oil, and other times they are pan-seared. Whatever form this dish takes, there are a few things that remain constant—plump shrimp are complemented by sweet, fruity tomatoes and briny feta cheese, and there is always enough sauce left over to sop up with bread. With a basic idea of what this dish should be, we set out in the kitchen to figure out the specifics. The challenges here were twofold: cooking the shrimp until succulent and fashioning a sauce that was fresh-tasting and sunny, even after being flambéed. Our research showed that there were several ways to approach cooking the shrimp. Traditional recipes simmered them in the finished sauce, fried them in olive oil, or pan-seared them. The latter option delivered the best results—giving the shrimp a caramelized exterior and juicy interior—and was also the easiest, quickest method (although we did opt to cook the shrimp in two batches to be on the safe side). Moving on, the traditional sauce for this renowned Greek combination typically combines olive oil, tomato, and onion, with garlic, chile peppers, and fresh herbs added. We could find little to argue with there and discovered that making the sauce in the same pan in which the shrimp were seared gave it great flavor from the fond left behind by the shrimp and kept dishes to a minimum. Last, but certainly not least, was the feta cheese. While many recipes simmer the feta in the sauce so it breaks down, we preferred it crumbled and scattered over the finished dish so it melted slightly yet remained distinct. The cheese's salty, briny bite was a great foil to the sweetness of the shrimp and the fruitiness of the tomato. We normally shy away from combining cheese and fish, but, in this instance, it was a perfect pairing. We were now finished with our dish, but a few tasters thought it was still missing a little something. A healthy shot of ouzo—a licorice-flavored spirit popular throughout Greece—sprinkled over the finished dish and then flambéed was the perfect accent.

¼	cup extra-virgin olive oil
2	pounds extra-large shrimp (21 to 25 per pound), peeled and deveined (see page 250)
	Salt and pepper
⅛	teaspoon sugar
1	onion, minced (about 1 cup)
6	garlic cloves, minced
1	tablespoon minced fresh oregano or ½ teaspoon dried
¼–½	teaspoon red pepper flakes
1	(28-ounce) can diced tomatoes, drained, ½ cup juice reserved
¼	cup ouzo (see note)
4	ounces feta cheese, crumbled (about 1 cup)
2	tablespoons minced fresh parsley

1. Heat 1 tablespoon of the oil in a 12-inch skillet over high heat until just smoking. Meanwhile, pat the shrimp dry with paper towels and season with salt and pepper and the sugar. Add half of the shrimp to the skillet in a single layer and cook, without stirring, until the bottoms of the shrimp turn spotty brown, about 30 seconds. Off the heat, flip the shrimp over, then transfer to a medium bowl and repeat with 1 more tablespoon oil and the remaining shrimp.

2. Add the remaining 2 tablespoons oil, the onion, and ½ teaspoon salt to the skillet, and cook over medium heat until the onion is softened, 5 to 7 minutes. Stir in the garlic, oregano, and pepper flakes, and cook until fragrant, about 30 seconds. Stir in the tomatoes and ½ cup juice and cook until thickened slightly, about 2 minutes.

3. Stir the reserved shrimp and accumulated juices and ouzo into the skillet. Remove the skillet from the heat and carefully ignite the ouzo with a long match and shake the skillet until the flames subside (for more information on flambéing safely, see page 38). Sprinkle with the feta and parsley. Serve immediately.

NOTES FROM THE TEST KITCHEN

OUZO

Ouzo is a licorice-flavored liqueur that is served as an aperitif throughout Greece in sidewalk cafes and special ouzo bars with meze called *ouzeria*. It is distilled from grapes, raisins, figs, and sugar, and then infused with various herbs and spices, such as coriander, anise, and mastic (a woodsy, musty, and vanilla-flavored spice made from the crystallized resinous sap of a tree in the pistachio family). Ouzo can vary greatly from bottle to bottle in terms of sweetness and complexity, as well as in color—it can range from clear liquid to black. You will almost never see anything but the clear variety, and although ouzo—like most any liqueur—can vary greatly in price, we have found you do not need to spend a fortune for a quality bottle.

BUYING SHRIMP

FRESH OR FROZEN?

Because nearly all shrimp are frozen at sea, you have no way of knowing when those "fresh" shrimp in the fish case were thawed (unless you are on very personal terms with your fishmonger). We found that the flavor and texture of thawed shrimp deteriorate after a few days, so you're better off buying frozen.

PEELED OR UNPEELED?

If you think you can dodge some work by buying frozen shrimp that have been peeled, think again. Someone had to thaw those shrimp in order to remove their shells, and they can get pretty banged up when they are refrozen.

CHECK THE INGREDIENTS

Finally, check the ingredient list. Frozen shrimp are often treated or enhanced with additives such as sodium bisulfate, STP (sodium tripolyphosphate), or salt to prevent darkening (which occurs as the shrimp ages) or to counter "drip loss," the industry term referring to the amount of water in the shrimp that is lost as it thaws. We have found that treated shrimp have a strange translucency and an unpleasant texture and suggest that you avoid them. Look for the bags of frozen shrimp that list shrimp as the only ingredient.

CHARCOAL-GRILLED SWEET AND SAUCY SALMON

CHARCOAL-GRILLED SWEET AND SAUCY SALMON

SERVES 4

WHAT MAKES THIS A BEST RECIPE: The assertive flavor and meaty texture of salmon is perfect for glazing and for grilling, but try to do both things at once and the fish desperately wants to stick to the grate. So how do you do it? This recipe solves the cooking problems with a unique trick and produces great-flavored, grill-streaked salmon. We tried every glazed salmon recipe we could find and every trick we could think of, but to no avail: Each glazed fillet stuck fast to the grill or flaked apart when we tried removing it. Eventually, we had a brainstorm: Why not cook the salmon in a foil "pan," to insulate it from the grate? Success—great grill marks, full smoke flavor, no sticking, and, if we removed the skin (which most people discard anyway), we could glaze both sides of the salmon. The extra glaze even caramelized in the foil "pan," adding another great dimension. As for the flavor of that glaze, we tried all manner of combinations and found that jalapeño jelly proved the perfect base, as it was a bit sweet, definitely spicy, and it had a consistency that clung to the fish. To the jelly, we added such Latin flavors as cilantro, lime (both zest and juice), and garlic; pureeing the mixture in a food processor smoothly emulsified it and a quick simmer "tightened" the texture and blended the flavors. A bit of butter boosted the flavor of the glaze and lent it a glossy sheen.

- 1 teaspoon grated lime zest, plus 2 tablespoons fresh lime juice
- 2 garlic cloves, minced
- 2 scallions, chopped
- ½ cup packed fresh cilantro leaves and stems
- ½ cup jalapeño jelly

- 2 tablespoons unsalted butter
  Cooking spray for the trays
- 4 salmon fillets, 6 to 8 ounces each (1¼ inches thick), skin removed
  Salt and pepper

1. Process the lime zest and juice, garlic, scallions, cilantro, and jelly in a food processor or blender until smooth. Heat the glaze in a small saucepan over medium heat until just bubbling, 2 to 3 minutes. Remove from the heat and transfer ¼ cup of the glaze to a small bowl to cool slightly. Stir the butter into the glaze remaining in the saucepan, cover, and set aside.

2. Light a large chimney starter filled with charcoal briquettes (about 100 pieces) and allow it to burn until all the charcoal is covered with a layer of fine gray ash, about 20 minutes. Spread the coals over three-quarters of the grill bottom; set the cooking grate in place, cover the grill, and heat until hot, about 5 minutes. Use a grill brush to scrape the cooking grate clean.

3. Following the photos on page 246, use heavy-duty aluminum foil to make four 7 by 5-inch trays. Coat the trays with cooking spray. Season the salmon with salt and pepper, brush each side of each fillet with ½ tablespoon of the reserved glaze (without butter), and place skinned side up on the trays.

4. Place the trays with the salmon over the hot fire and grill until the glaze forms a golden brown crust, 6 to 8 minutes. (Move the trays to the cooler part of the grill if the fillets darken too quickly.) Using tongs, flip the salmon and cook 1 minute. Spoon half of the buttered glaze over the salmon and cook until the center of each fillet is still just translucent, about 1 minute. Transfer the salmon to a platter and spoon the remaining buttered glaze over it. Serve.

NOTES FROM THE TEST KITCHEN

GAS-GRILLED SWEET AND SAUCY SALMON
Follow the recipe for Charcoal-Grilled Sweet and Saucy Salmon, omitting step 2. Turn all the burners on a gas grill to high, close the cover, and heat until very hot, about 15 minutes. Use a grill brush to scrape the cooking grate clean. Proceed with the recipe from step 3, leaving the burners on high and cooking with the lid down.

HOW TO SKIN SALMON FILLETS

1. Insert a sharp boning knife just above the skin about 1 inch from the end of the fillet. Cut through the nearest end, keeping the blade just above the skin.

2. Rotate the fish and grab the loose piece of skin. Run the knife between the flesh and the skin, keeping the knife just above the skin.

STICK-FREE SALMON

Few culinary pitfalls are as irksome as fish that sticks to the grill. Fish baskets leave no attractive grill marks, and, worse, the fish often sticks to the basket. We had better luck with homemade foil trays coated with cooking spray.

1. Cut out four rectangles of heavy-duty aluminum foil and crimp the edges until each tray measures 7 by 5 inches.

2. Place one seasoned and glazed salmon fillet, skinned side up, on each foil tray that has been coated with cooking spray.

3. After the glaze forms a golden brown crust around the edges of the fish, use tongs to flip each fillet.

4. Spoon half the buttered glaze over the salmon in the trays and allow the glaze to thicken slightly on the grill.

CHARCOAL-GRILLED BLACKENED SNAPPER
SERVES 4

WHAT MAKES THIS A BEST RECIPE: Paul Prudhomme popularized his signature dish of blackened redfish in the 1980s and, ever since, it has been a staple on restaurant menus. Essentially, it's a fish fillet coated thickly in spices and butter, and fried in a cast-iron skillet at an extraordinarily high temperature so that the skin and spices crisp (and darken) and the meat remains moist. Sadly, the billowing smoke produced by the cooking method means that it is virtually impossible to produce at home, unless you cook it outside on the grill so that the smoke can dissipate. This recipe keeps the mess outside and makes Prudhomme's classic easy. Before we even approached the stove, we decided to replace Prudhomme's favorite redfish with more readily available snapper and ditched the skillet in favor of the grill grate so that we could cook four fillets at once. Unfortunately, with all the spices, the fish stuck fast to the grate. We tried every trick we could find to make it release easily, though nothing seemed to work. Then it occurred to us that we needed to get the grill hotter and cleaner, which we accomplished by inverting a disposable pan above the grate. With such a hot cooking surface—and a swipe of oil—the fish released easily. While you can buy prepared Cajun spice rubs, we much preferred the flavor of a freshly blended mix of spice cabinet staples like cayenne, black and white pepper, coriander, paprika, and garlic and onion powders. (Fresh garlic and/or onion burned and tasted acrid.) To bring out the best in the spices, we toasted them briefly in melted butter in a skillet. As an added benefit, the butter helped the spices adhere to the snapper as it contributed a toasted, rich flavor to the fish.

2   **tablespoons sweet paprika**
2   **teaspoons onion powder**
2   **teaspoons garlic powder**
¾   **teaspoon ground coriander**
¾   **teaspoon salt**
¼   **teaspoon cayenne pepper**

¼ teaspoon ground black pepper
¼ teaspoon ground white pepper
3 tablespoons unsalted butter
13 by 9-inch disposable aluminum roasting pan
4 red snapper fillets, 6 to 8 ounces each, ¾ inch thick, or striped bass, halibut, or catfish fillets of the same size
Vegetable oil for the cooking grate

1. Combine the paprika, onion powder, garlic powder, coriander, salt, and peppers in a small bowl. Melt the butter in a 10-inch skillet over medium heat. Stir in the spice mixture and cook, stirring frequently, until fragrant and the spices turn dark rust color, 2 to 3 minutes. Transfer the mixture to a pie plate and cool, stirring occasionally, to room temperature, about 10 minutes. Once it is cooled, use a fork to break up any large clumps.

2. Light a large chimney starter filled ⅔ full with charcoal briquettes (about 65 pieces) and allow it to burn until all the charcoal is covered with a thin layer of gray ash, about 20 minutes. Spread the coals over half of the grill bottom, leaving the other half with no coals. Set the cooking grate in place, place the disposable roasting pan upside down on the grate directly over the coals, cover the grill, and heat until hot, about 5 minutes. Remove the roasting pan. Use a grill brush to scrape the cooking grate clean.

3. Meanwhile, pat the fillets dry on both sides with paper towels. Using a sharp knife, make shallow diagonal slashes every inch along the skin side of the fish, being careful not to cut into the flesh. Place the fillets skin side up on a rimmed baking sheet or large plate. Using your fingers, rub the spice mixture in a thin, even layer on the top and sides of the fish. Flip the fillets and repeat on the other side (you should use all of the spice mixture). Refrigerate until needed.

4. Lightly dip a wad of paper towels in the oil and, holding the paper towels with long-handled tongs, wipe the grill grate. Place the fish perpendicular to the grill grate, skin side down, on the hot side of grill. Grill uncovered until the skin is very dark brown and crisp, 3 to 4 minutes. Using a thin metal spatula, carefully flip the fish and continue to grill until dark brown and beginning to flake and the center is opaque but still moist, about 5 minutes longer. Serve immediately.

WHERE THINGS CAN GO WRONG: If using fillets that are ½ inch thick or thinner, reduce the cooking time to 3 minutes per side. If using fillets that are 1 inch or thicker, increase the cooking time on the second side by 2 minutes, moving the fish to the cooler side of the grill after the second side has browned. Making the slashes in the skin requires a sharp knife. If your knife isn't sharp enough, try cutting through the skin with a serrated knife. However, cut in one direction (don't saw) and be careful to not cut into the flesh. If you choose not to eat the skin, be sure to remove it after cooking rather than beforehand.

NOTES FROM THE TEST KITCHEN

GAS-GRILLED BLACKENED SNAPPER
Follow the recipe for Charcoal-Grilled Blackened Snapper, omitting step 2. Turn all the burners on a gas grill to high, close the cover, and heat until very hot, about 15 minutes. Use a grill brush to scrape the cooking grate clean. Proceed with the recipe from step 3, leaving the burners on high and cooking with the lid up.

UNBUCKLING
Skin-on fillets will buckle when grilled because the skin will shrink, pulling the flesh along with it (left). They remain flat if the skin is scored first (right), which prevents it from contracting more quickly than the flesh.

GREAT DISCOVERIES

DON'T GET STUCK
I knew that preheating the grill grate before scraping it with a grill brush was the most effective way to keep food from sticking. When it came to delicate fish, the grates had to be spotless. Thinking how the self-cleaning cycle in an oven transforms caked-on gunk into fine gray ash by superheating the interior, I decided to replicate the process with an inverted aluminum pan. This boosted the grill temperature to 818 degrees: Residue and stuck-on bits didn't stand a chance. This simple trick will allow you to grill most any fish without it sticking.
SANDRA WU | ASSOCIATE EDITOR, *COOK'S ILLUSTRATED*

BROILED SCALLOPS
WITH CREAMY MUSHROOM SAUCE
SERVES 4

WHAT MAKES THIS A BEST RECIPE: In France, this dish, called *coquilles St. Jacques bonne femme*, falls into the category of simple, family-style dishes. (*Bonne femme* means "good wife," or "good woman," in French.) Typically, a dish made in the style of a bonne femme involves a protein topped with a white wine, cream, and mushroom sauce that is cooked quickly under the broiler until browned. Sweet, meaty scallops are a natural choice for such preparation and really shine in this recipe. First we addressed the main ingredient and quickly decided that large sea scallops were the best bet on account of their flavor and availability. They also don't overcook as easily as smaller varieties (such as bay scallops) do. That said, we still found keen timing was imperative for successful results. The sauce for the dish classically starts with white wine and heavy cream cooked together until thickened. Mushrooms are added and cooked until they have released their moisture and the sauce has again cooked down until thickened. But as the sauce still tasted a bit bland to us, we added fresh thyme, shallots, and a splash of chicken broth and lemon juice. The crowning touch was a tip we picked up from an old French cookbook, which folded stiffly beaten whipped cream into the finished sauce. We broiled the scallops until almost done, spooned on the sauce, and, within a minute, the dish was browned and ready to serve. What could be better than tender, sweet sea scallops napped in a luxurious sauce?

2 cups heavy cream

1 cup dry white wine

½ cup low-sodium chicken broth

1 pound white mushrooms, sliced thin

1 shallot, minced (3 tablespoons)

1 teaspoon minced fresh thyme

Salt and pepper

1 teaspoon fresh lemon juice

Unsalted butter for the baking dish

1¼ pounds large sea scallops (about 16 scallops), tendons removed

1. Bring 1½ cups of the cream, the wine, broth, mushrooms, shallot, thyme, ½ teaspoon salt, and pepper to taste to a boil in a 12-inch nonstick skillet over high heat. Reduce the heat to a simmer and cook until the mixture has thickened and measures between 2 and 2½ cups, 20 to 25 minutes; add the lemon juice off the heat. Transfer the mixture to a large bowl and let cool slightly.

2. Meanwhile, adjust an oven rack 6 inches from the broiler element and heat the broiler. Thoroughly butter the inside of a 2-quart broiler-safe baking dish; set aside. Using an electric mixer, whip the remaining ½ cup heavy cream on medium-low speed until small bubbles form, about 30 seconds. Increase the speed to medium-high and continue to whip until stiff peaks form, about 1 minute longer; set aside.

3. Pat the scallops dry with paper towels, season with salt and pepper, and arrange in a single layer in the prepared baking dish. Broil the scallops until the exterior looks opaque but the interior remains translucent, 4 to 7 minutes.

4. While the scallops cook, gently fold the whipped cream into the cooled mushroom sauce until almost no white streaks remain (a few streaks are okay). Spoon the sauce over the broiled scallops and continue to broil until the sauce is nicely browned and the scallops are cooked through, about 1 minute. Serve immediately.

WHERE THINGS CAN GO WRONG: The cooking time of the scallops here will depend on the strength of your broiler and the size of the scallops; we found that extra-large scallops (about 2 inches in diameter and 1 inch thick) took about 7 minutes, while smaller scallops (about 1 inch in diameter and ½ inch thick) took only 4 minutes.

NOTES FROM THE TEST KITCHEN

BUYING SCALLOPS
When buying sea scallops, look first at their color. Scallops are naturally ivory or pinkish tan; processing (dipping them in a phosphate and water mixture to extend shelf life) turns them bright white. Processed scallops are slippery and swollen and are usually sitting in a milky white liquid at the store. You should look for unprocessed scallops (also called dry scallops), which are sticky and flabby; they will taste fresher than processed scallops and will develop a nice crust when browned because they are not pumped with water.

FAMILY-STYLE SHRIMP SCAMPI

SERVES 6

WHAT MAKES THIS A BEST RECIPE: Shrimp scampi is a quick dish in which shrimp are sautéed in garlicky butter and flavored with white wine, lemon juice, and parsley. It could hardly get any easier, right? Well, it's a method that works fine for two or three servings, but double that and the shrimp overcook because of pan crowding. Consequently, the shrimp themselves are tough and the sauce is watery and bland—no amount of garlic can remedy it. How do you successfully make scampi for more than two people? Right away, we realized high-heat cooking wasn't a prerequisite for good scampi; lower, moister cooking actually delivered very flavorful, tender shrimp. We ditched the conventional skillet in favor of a large Dutch oven, which was large enough to contain all the shrimp in one batch. We sautéed minced garlic in olive oil—saving the butter for the end so that it kept its fresh flavor—and added the shrimp along with white wine and clam juice, which furthered the shrimp's flavor. Once the shrimp were cooked through, we pulled them out of the pan with a slotted spoon and "tightened" the cooking liquid a bit with a brief simmer. Following a restaurant trick, we whisked cold butter piece-by-piece into the cooking liquid to both thicken and enrich it. With a handful of chopped parsley and a splash of lemon juice, all the scampi needed was bread or pasta to soak up all that flavorful sauce.

1   tablespoon olive oil
4   garlic cloves, minced
¼   cup dry white wine
¼   cup bottled clam juice
    Salt and pepper

2   pounds extra-large shrimp (21 to 25 per pound), peeled and deveined
4   tablespoons cold unsalted butter, cut into 4 pieces
2   tablespoons fresh lemon juice
2   tablespoons chopped fresh parsley
    Lemon wedges, for serving

1. Heat the oil in a large Dutch oven over medium-high heat until shimmering. Add the garlic and cook until fragrant, about 30 seconds. Add the wine, clam juice, ¼ teaspoon salt, and ⅛ teaspoon pepper; bring to boil. Add the shrimp, cover, and cook until the shrimp are slightly translucent, about 2 minutes. Reduce the heat to medium, stir, cover, and cook until the shrimp are just cooked through, about 2 minutes.

2. Using a slotted spoon, transfer the shrimp to a serving bowl. Bring the sauce to a boil over medium-high heat and cook until reduced by half, about 1 minute. Whisk the butter, 1 piece at a time, into the sauce; stir in the lemon juice and parsley. Season with salt and pepper to taste and pour the sauce over the shrimp. Serve immediately with the lemon wedges.

NOTES FROM THE TEST KITCHEN

DEVEINING SHRIMP

1. After removing the shell, use a paring knife to make a shallow cut along the back of the shrimp so that the vein is exposed.

2. Use the tip of the knife to lift the vein out of the shrimp. Discard the vein by wiping the blade against a paper towel.

CATFISH IN SALTY-SWEET CARAMEL SAUCE

SERVES 4 TO 6

WHAT MAKES THIS A BEST RECIPE: One of the most popular southern Vietnamese "home-style" dishes is catfish simmered in a peppery caramel sauce. And while it is the essence of simplicity, this dish has a rich complexity that belies its few ingredients. Adding caramel to a savory dish may sound odd, but it is in fact common practice in Vietnamese cooking, where it is used to add deep, rich color and a bittersweet base note to counter assertive ingredients like garlic, chiles, and fermented fish. In this dish, meaty catfish is simmered in a caramel-based sauce (a simple mixture of water and sugar) laced with fish sauce, pepper, and garlic. To get our bearings, we looked at the landscape of traditional recipes, settling, after much testing, on the simplest approach: making a caramel in the skillet in which we would cook the fish. We tested using dark brown sugar, light brown sugar, and white sugar. Both of the brown sugars left a cloyingly sweet aftertaste, and never led to a sauce with a nutty caramel flavor. We chose white sugar for its clean and nutty flavor when caramelized. To prevent crystallization of the sugar, we poured the water into the skillet first, and then gently sprinkled the sugar evenly over the water. To the hot caramel, we added a mix of garlic and oil to sauté briefly and "bloom," before adding pungent fish sauce, boiling water, and a generous dose of black pepper. Next we looked at the catfish. Most traditional recipes suggest using catfish steaks, but catfish is not typically cut into steaks in this country. So we settled on using the more available skinless catfish fillets, which worked just fine (and while we liked the flavor of catfish in this recipe, any thin, medium-firm white fish fillets can be substituted). We simmered them in the cooking liquid from five minutes to two hours; contrary to what we would have thought, the fish cooked for two hours was mealy but acceptable. That said, the fish cooked for 25 to 30 minutes were best; the fillets remained tender and moist and the cooking liquid thickened to a glossy sauce. With just a sprinkling of cilantro leaves, one of our favorite new fish dishes was ready to serve.

	Water
¼	cup vegetable oil
5	garlic cloves, minced
⅓	cup sugar
¼	cup fish sauce
1½	teaspoons pepper
2	pounds boneless, skinless catfish fillets (about 5 medium), sliced crosswise into 2-inch-wide pieces
1	cup loosely packed cilantro leaves
3	scallions, green parts only, sliced thin on the diagonal

1. Bring a kettle of water to a boil. Mix the oil and garlic in a small bowl and set aside.

2. Pour ¼ cup cold water into a 12-inch nonstick skillet, then sprinkle the sugar evenly into the water. Cook the sugar mixture over medium heat, gently swirling the pan occasionally (do not stir), until the sugar melts and the mixture turns the color of maple syrup, about 10 minutes. While the sugar mixture cooks, measure out 2 cups of boiling water, cover to keep warm, and set aside.

3. When the sugar mixture is browned, stir in the garlic mixture and cook until fragrant, about 30 seconds. Off the heat, slowly whisk in the reserved 2 cups of boiling water (the sauce may bubble and sizzle slightly).

4. Return the skillet to medium heat and stir in the fish sauce and pepper. Lay the catfish in the skillet (without overlapping), and turn to coat evenly with the sauce. Bring to a simmer, then reduce the heat to medium-low and cook uncovered until the fish is tender and the sauce has thickened to a thick, syrupy consistency, about 25 minutes.

5. Transfer the fish to a platter and pour the sauce over the top. Sprinkle with the cilantro and scallions and serve.

CREOLE-STYLE SHRIMP AND SAUSAGE GUMBO

SERVES 6 TO 8

WHAT MAKES THIS A BEST RECIPE: Few dishes are as classically Cajun as thick, meat-studded gumbo. While it can be prepared with all manner of meats and vegetables, our favorite version combines spicy andouille sausage and shrimp. We sent a test cook to Louisiana to eat his way across the Bayou and investigate the details that make gumbo great. First of all, there's the roux—deep, dark, flavorful roux. While traditional versions take upwards of 45 minutes and constant stirring to prepare, we found we could shorten the work a little—to just 20 minutes—without any ill effect to the flavor by preheating the oil and cooking the oil and flour over medium heat. Constant stirring, however, was unavoidable. From there, we sautéed Cajun cooking's typical aromatics, bell pepper, celery, onion, and garlic (lots of it), in the roux and added broth. For maximum flavor, we decided to whip up a quick stock from the leftover shrimp shells augmented with bottled clam juice. A couple of bay leaves, thyme, and cayenne pepper rounded everything out. While most recipes sauté the meats before adding it to the gumbo, we found we actually preferred the flavor and texture of the sausage and shrimp when we simply slid them into the simmering broth. We added the sausage fairly early so that it could lend its flavor; we reserved the shrimp, however, until the end so that they would remain moist and tender. Shot through with complex flavor and richly colored by the mahogany roux, our gumbo tastes every bit as authentic as any served in the Bayou.

1½ pounds small shrimp (51 to 60 per pound), peeled and deveined (see page 250), shells reserved

1 (8-ounce) bottle clam juice

3½ cups ice water

½ cup vegetable oil

½ cup unbleached all-purpose flour

2 onions, minced (about 2 cups)

1 red bell pepper, stemmed, seeded, and chopped fine

1 celery rib, chopped fine

6 garlic cloves, minced

1 teaspoon dried thyme

Salt

¼ teaspoon cayenne pepper

2 bay leaves

¾ pound smoked sausage, such as andouille or kielbasa, sliced ¼ inch thick

½ cup minced fresh parsley

4 scallions, white and green parts sliced thin

Pepper

1. Bring the reserved shrimp shells and 4½ cups water to a boil in a large saucepan over medium-high heat. Reduce the heat to medium-low; simmer 20 minutes. Strain the stock and add the clam juice and ice water (you should have about 2 quarts of tepid stock, 100 to 110 degrees); discard the shells. Set aside.

2. Heat the oil in a large Dutch oven or large, heavy-bottomed saucepan over medium-high heat until it registers 200 degrees on an instant-read thermometer, 1½ to 2 minutes. (If necessary, tilt the pot so the oil is deep enough to take its temperature.) Reduce the heat to medium and stir in the flour gradually with a wooden spoon, working out any small lumps. Continue stirring constantly, reaching into the corners of the pan, until the mixture has a toasty aroma and is deep reddish brown, about the color of an old copper penny or between the colors of milk chocolate and dark chocolate, about 20 minutes. (The roux will thin as it cooks; if it begins to smoke, remove from the heat and stir constantly to cool slightly.)

3. Add the onions, bell pepper, celery, garlic, thyme, 1 teaspoon salt, and cayenne; cook, stirring frequently, until the vegetables soften, 8 to 10 minutes. Add 1 quart of the reserved stock mixture in a slow, steady stream, stirring vigorously. Stir in the remaining quart stock mixture. Increase the heat to high; bring to a boil. Reduce the heat to medium-low, skim off the foam on the surface, add the bay leaves, and simmer uncovered, skimming the foam as it rises to the surface, about 30 minutes.

4. Stir in the sausage; continue simmering to blend the flavors, about 30 minutes longer. Stir in the shrimp; simmer until cooked through, about 5 minutes longer. Off the heat, remove and discard the bay leaves, stir in the parsley and scallions, and season with salt, black pepper, and cayenne to taste. Serve.

WHERE THINGS CAN GO WRONG: Making a dark roux can be dangerous. The mixture reaches temperatures in excess of 400 degrees. Therefore, use a deep pot for cooking the roux and long-handled utensils for stirring it, and be careful not to splash it on yourself. For a stock that is at the right temperature when the roux is done, start preparing it before you tend to the vegetables and other ingredients, strain it, and then give it a head start on cooling by immediately adding ice water and clam juice. So that your constant stirring of the roux will not be interrupted, start the roux only after you've made the stock. Alternatively, you can make the stock well ahead of time and bring it back to room temperature before using it.

WHAT YOU CAN DO AHEAD OF TIME: The shrimp stock can be prepared and refrigerated in an airtight container for up to 1 day. Before proceeding with the recipe, heat the stock to lukewarm (about 100 degrees) on the stove or in the microwave. The peeled shrimp should be wrapped tightly in plastic wrap and refrigerated. Fully cooked gumbo can be refrigerated in an airtight container for up to 3 days. Warm gently over medium-low heat.

GREAT DISCOVERIES

A SMOOTH ROUX

Throughout the roux testing, the occasional separation of the flour and oil upon the addition of simmering liquid continued to perplex me. All along, I had followed the instructions in most of the recipes I'd studied to add simmering stock to a hot roux-vegetable mixture, both about 200 degrees. But there is another, if less popular, school of thought. Food scientist Harold McGee, *Cook's* consulting editor, legendary restaurateur Jasper White, as well as New Orleans restaurateur Leah Chase all had advised cooling either the roux or the stock before combining them. Sure enough, cooling the stock (which took less time than cooling the roux) did the trick, and warm stock mixed in very well.

ADAM REID | SENIOR EDITOR, *COOK'S ILLUSTRATED*

NOTES FROM THE TEST KITCHEN

TESTING: ROUX GONE RIGHT . . . AND WRONG

Lukewarm stock and constant stirring are keys to the right consistency. The roux in the spoonful of gumbo at left is dispersed smoothly in the liquid. The spoonful of roux at the right has broken, with globs of browned flour floating in oil.

UNDERSTANDING ROUX

When the flour is just added to the oil, the roux will be very light in color.

After about 10 minutes of cooking, the mixture will brown to about the color of peanut butter.

After about 20 minutes of cooking, the completed dark roux will be a deep reddish brown, almost the color of dark chocolate.

FILÉ POWDER

To some, gumbo just isn't gumbo without filé powder, or ground sassafras leaves. It both thickens the gumbo and lends a distinctly woodsy, vaguely herby flavor. We had mixed reactions to gumbo flavored with filé powder in the test kitchen, so we chose to make it optional. If you want to give it a whirl, add 1½ teaspoons along with the herbs in step 4 and allow the gumbo to sit for at least 5 minutes to allow it to thicken before serving.

CHARCOAL-GRILLED LOBSTERS

SERVES 2

WHAT MAKES THIS A BEST RECIPE: We love this recipe because it reminds us of summertime at the beach. There are quite a few recipes out there for grilled lobsters, and we can see why: The smoky fire maximizes the sweetness of the tender lobster meat, and there are no huge pots of boiling water to worry about. The recipes we uncovered in our research grilled the lobster in a variety of ways. After much testing, we found that it was best to simply split the lobsters in half lengthwise before grilling. We then grilled the lobsters cut-side down, and flipped them after two minutes to keep moisture loss to a minimum. A little bit browned and thoroughly moist, the meat was quite flavorful. Because the claws were not cut in half, as was the rest of the lobster, they took longer to cook. To speed up their cooking, we cracked one side of each claw (cracking just one side of the claws minimizes the loss of juices), and covered the claws with a disposable aluminum pie plate to ensure that they got cooked through. We learned that when you split a lobster for grilling, it's important to remove the stomach sac, intestinal tract, and tomalley. The first two should be discarded; the tomalley, however, is something of a delicacy, and we incorporated it into the final dish. We blended the tomalley with bread crumbs, garlic, parsley, and seasonings and packed it into each of the split lobster halves after we flipped them. By the time the meat was done, the crumbs were crisp and the tomalley cooked through. The stuffing lent valuable flavor and texture to the lobster. Lastly, we slathered melted butter onto the meat prior to grilling and were quite pleased with the meat's even richer flavor. Mixing a little garlic into the butter further improved things.

A smoky fire, garlic butter, and tomalley-and-bread crumb stuffing lend grilled lobster valuable flavor.

1 slice high-quality sandwich bread, torn into quarters

6 tablespoons (¾ stick) unsalted butter, melted

2 garlic cloves, minced

2 live lobsters (1½ to 2 pounds each)

2 tablespoons minced fresh parsley

Salt and pepper

Vegetable oil for the cooking grate

2 disposable aluminum pie plates or small roasting pans

Lemon wedges, for serving

1. Light a large chimney starter filled with charcoal briquettes (about 100 pieces) and allow it to burn until all the charcoal is covered with a layer of fine gray ash, about 20 minutes. Spread the coals evenly over the grill bottom. Set the cooking grate in place, cover the grill, and heat until hot, about 5 minutes. Use a grill brush to scrape the cooking grate clean.

2. Meanwhile, pulse the bread in a food processor to coarse crumbs, about 8 pulses. Reserve ¼ cup of the crumbs and discard the remainder (or save for another use); set aside. Combine the butter and garlic in a small bowl; set aside.

3. Following the photos, split the lobsters in half lengthwise, removing the stomach sac and intestinal tract. Scoop out the green tomalley and place in a medium bowl. Using the back of a chef's knife, whack one side of each claw to crack. Stir the bread crumbs, parsley, 2 tablespoons of the melted garlic butter, ¼ teaspoon salt, and a pinch of pepper into the tomalley. Season the tail meat with salt and pepper. Brush the cut side of the lobster halves with some of the remaining garlic butter.

4. Grill the lobsters, flesh side down, for 2 minutes. Transfer the lobsters to a platter, shell side down. Spoon the tomalley mixture evenly into the open cavities of the lobster halves. Return the lobsters to the grill, shell side down. Baste the lobsters with the remaining garlic butter and cover the claws with the disposable aluminum pie plates. Grill until the tail meat turns an opaque creamy white color and the tomalley mixture is bubbly and has begun to brown on top, 4 to 6 minutes.

5. Serve the lobsters immediately with the lemon wedges. Use lobster picks to get the meat from inside the claws and knuckles.

WHERE THINGS CAN GO WRONG: Don't halve the lobsters until the charcoal has been lit. And be sure not to overcook the lobster; like other shellfish, lobster meat gets tough when cooked for too long. The lobsters are done when the tomalley mixture is bubbling and the tail meat has turned an opaque creamy white.

NOTES FROM THE TEST KITCHEN

GAS-GRILLED LOBSTERS
Turn all the burners on a gas grill to high, close the cover, and heat until very hot, about 15 minutes. Scrape the cooking grate clean with a grill brush. Follow the recipe for Charcoal-Grilled Lobsters from step 2, cooking with the lid down and cooking the lobsters for 5 to 7 minutes once flipped in step 4.

PREPARING LOBSTERS FOR GRILLING
To make the lobsters easier to handle you can put them in the freezer for 10 minutes right before you prepare them.

1. Firmly drive the tip of a chef's knife through the back of the lobster's head, then swing the knife through the head to split.

2. Flip the lobster over and finish cutting the lobster in half through the body and tail.

3. Using a spoon, scoop out and reserve the green tomalley.

4. Scoop out and discard the stomach sac and intestinal tract.

5. So that the claws cook at the same rate as the tail (the tail cooks quickly), use the back of a chef's knife to crack one small opening in the shell of each claw.

A GUIDE TO ESSENTIAL KITCHEN KNIVES

Do you really need $400 worth of forged German steel? Manufacturers try to trap you into buying blocks with a dozen knives, but sharp shoppers invest only in the essentials. Here's our guide to choosing (and using) the essential knives.

3½-INCH PARING KNIFE

WHAT WE USE IT FOR: A paring knife is essential for tasks that require more dexterity and precision than a chef's knife can provide: peeling and coring apples, deveining shrimp, cutting citrus segments, and more.

WHAT TO LOOK FOR: The blade should be somewhat flexible for easy maneuvering into tight spots (such as tomato cores) and for handling curves when peeling and paring. Weight and balance are less important than a sharp, agile blade and a firm, comfortable grip.

TEST KITCHEN FAVORITE
★ FORSCHNER FIBROX, $5.95

10-INCH BREAD KNIFE

WHAT WE USE IT FOR: The pointed serrations of a good bread knife glide through crusty breads, bagels, and tomato skins to produce neat slices, while a poorly designed bread knife slips, stutters, and shreds its way through food.

WHAT TO LOOK FOR: A slightly curved blade keeps knuckles from scraping the cutting board, allowing a rocking motion to cut through tough crusts. Pointed serrations give the blade a good grip on the food right away, while wavy serrations slide around before digging in. Knives should be at least 10 inches and the blade should be rigid for stable cutting through tough crusts.

TEST KITCHEN FAVORITE
★ FORSCHNER FIBROX, $36

8-INCH CHEF'S KNIFE

WHAT WE USE IT FOR: From chopping an onion to mincing herbs and butchering a chicken, this one knife will handle 90 percent of your kitchen cutting work.

WHAT TO LOOK FOR: Conventional wisdom dictates that forged blades—made by pouring molten steel into molds—are superior to cheaper stamped blades, which are punched out of a sheet of steel. Forged blades also have a thick collar of metal near the handle called a bolster to help balance the weight of the blade. But we found these distinctions to be less important than weight. In our tests the lighter, stamped knives came out slightly ahead for their maneuverability and quick motion. In addition, we found a bolster does not necessarily improve balance.

We prefer blades made from high-carbon stainless steel, a hard metal that, once sharpened, tends to stay that way. We find that carbon steel knives don't stay sharp for long, while ceramic blades are sharp but fragile. Look for a knife with a long, gently sloping blade, which makes tasks such as mincing and chopping much easier. And we prefer molded plastic handles over wood (which collect grease) or metal (which can get slippery), as well as a handle with a simple shape. The handle should balance the weight of the blade, making a tight, comfortable seal with your hand.

TEST KITCHEN FAVORITE
★ FORSCHNER FIBROX, $22.95

CLEAVER

WHAT TO LOOK FOR: About the only time we reach for a meat cleaver is when making chicken stock—the best way to release flavor from the bones is to hack them up. If you tackle this task regularly, consider adding one to your collection.

TEST KITCHEN FAVORITES
★ GLOBAL, $106
★ LAMSONSHARP, $40

SLICING/CARVING KNIFE

WHAT TO LOOK FOR: A good carving knife does one thing only: cut thin, uniform slices from large cuts of meat. Look for a straight, nonserrated edge with a uniform width (at least 1½ inches) from handle to rounded tip and a rigid 10-inch blade.

TEST KITCHEN FAVORITE
★ CHEF CUTLERY LEGEND 10-inch Granton Slicer, $45

BONING KNIFE

WHAT TO LOOK FOR: The slim, flexible blade of a boning knife is invaluable for sliding through joints, between bones, and under silver skin. Choose a blade between 5 and 7 inches, with a tapered tip and an easy-to-grip handle.

TEST KITCHEN FAVORITE
★ FORSCHNER FIBROX, $18

ELECTRIC KNIFE

WHAT TO LOOK FOR: Aside from carving large holiday roasts, electric knives do an excellent job cutting into foods that are made up of layers with distinctly firm and soft textures—such as pecan pie and quesadillas—which can get mashed by a regular chef's knife. (For perfectionists, admittedly.)

TEST KITCHEN FAVORITE
★ BLACK AND DECKER EK800 Slice Right, $24.99

SHARPENING AND HOLDING KITCHEN KNIVES

A knife loses its sharpness when the fine tip of the cutting edge gets knocked slightly out of alignment, which can happen anytime the blade makes contact with food or a cutting board. The knife may "act dull" even though the edge is still quite sharp—it's just pointed in the wrong direction. This can happen very quickly if you are doing a lot of heavy cutting work, but the edge can be just as quickly restored by using a sharpening steel, which realigns the edge and removes slight irregularities.

Two ways to protect your knife's edge are to avoid hard cutting surfaces such as glass or acrylic (stick to wood and plastic cutting boards) and to keep them out of the dishwasher, where getting knocked around might damage their edge.

SHARPENING

There are two options for grinding a new edge on a knife at home:

SHARPENING STONE
This method is effective but takes some practice, and it's more work than many home cooks want to do. It involves a double-sided sharpening stone, some elbow grease, and about 15 minutes per blade.

KNIFE SHARPENER
An electric home sharpener can restore the edge of even a seriously neglected blade, provided you buy one with a coarse regrinding wheel, such as our favorite, the Chef's Choice 130 ($139). Some less-expensive models feature only medium- and fine-grade slots, good for perking up a dull blade but unable to grind a completely new edge. These machines do remove a certain amount of metal from the blade with each use, so use them no more than necessary.

IS IT SHARP?

To determine if your knife needs to be sharpened, put it to the paper test.

1. Hold a folded, but not creased, sheet of newspaper by one end.
2. Lay the blade against the top edge at an angle and slice outward. If the knife fails to slice cleanly, try steeling it. If it still fails, it needs sharpening.

TWO BASIC KNIFE GRIPS

HANDLE GRIP
With the handle grip, the thumb rests on the side of the handle opposite the index finger. This grip is favored by test cooks with smaller hands. For those who work long hours with a knife, it also causes fewer calluses.

BLADE GRIP
Cooks with larger hands often prefer the blade grip, in which the thumb and index finger actually grip the heel of the blade. While this grip requires a bit more hand strength, it also provides more control over the tip of the blade.

CHOOSING—AND USING—A STEEL

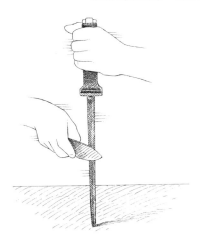

You should steel your knives regularly, before each use if possible, but sharpen them only when necessary. Traditional steels are lightly grooved, magnetized iron rods, but we prefer the newer diamond steels—hollow oval tubes coated with diamond dust. These grind trace amounts of metal from the knife with each swipe, partially sharpening the blade while straightening it and extending the period between sharpenings. However, keep in mind that steeling will only realign a fairly sharp blade; a dull knife has to be sharpened.

1. Hold the steel perpendicular to the work surface, with the tip resting on a cutting board.
2. Place the heel of the blade against the steel, with the blade at a 20-degree angle away from it.
3. With a locked wrist and light pressure, slide the blade down the length of the steel in a sweeping motion, pulling the back of the blade toward you so that the entire length of the blade comes in contact with the steel.
4. Repeat the motion on the other side of the blade. Four or five strokes per side should realign the edge.

CHOCOLATE BLACKOUT CAKE

DESSERTS

RASPBERRY CHIFFON PIE 262

NO-FEAR PIE CRUST 264

PUMPKIN-PRALINE PIE 267

RUSTIC FREE-FORM APPLE TARTLETS 270

ITALIAN-STYLE FIG-WALNUT TART 273

PEACH CRUMBLE 275

TROPICAL CARROT CAKE 278

CRANBERRY-APPLE CRISP 280

STRAWBERRY POKE CAKE 283

RED VELVET CAKE 284

ITALIAN ALMOND CAKE 287

LEMON LAYER CAKE 288

CHOCOLATE BLACKOUT CAKE 291

HOT FUDGE PUDDING CAKE 292

SOUR CREAM COFFEE CAKE 294

INDIVIDUAL FALLEN CHOCOLATE CAKES 296

BLUEBERRY BOY BAIT 297

CLASSIC POUND CAKE 298

NEW ORLEANS BOURBON BREAD PUDDING WITH BOURBON SAUCE 300

BLACK-BOTTOM CUPCAKES 303

NEW YORK–STYLE CRUMB CAKE 305

CHOCOLATE POTS DE CRÈME 307

BIG AND CHEWY LOW-FAT CHOCOLATE CHIP COOKIES 308

FRENCH-STYLE MACAROONS 311

BROWN SUGAR COOKIES 314

JOE FROGGERS 316

KEY LIME BARS 318

PECAN BARS 320

SEVEN-LAYER BARS 322

15-MINUTE CHOCOLATE WALNUT FUDGE 323

BEST-EVER HOT COCOA MIX 325

RASPBERRY CHIFFON PIE

SERVES 8 TO 10

WHAT MAKES THIS A BEST RECIPE: At its best, raspberry chiffon is light, billowy, and creamy. Rarely, however, is it intensely flavored. That's because the filling doesn't contain much fruit—it's mostly whipped egg whites and/or heavy cream, sugar, and gelatin (which allows the filling to set, without baking, in the refrigerator). Our recipe, on the other hand, is full of fruit flavor. Instead of just a chiffon filling, we added an additional layer of fruit to our pie. We cooked frozen berries (one-quarter the price of fresh berries) until they started to break down and then added pectin (a thickener used to make jelly), followed by the sugar. The mixture thickened beautifully and the flavor was intense. We set aside some of this smooth puree to flavor the chiffon filling and poured the rest (with fresh fruit added for texture and flavor) into our prebaked pie shell. After about 10 minutes on the counter, this jam-like mixture set into a thin, dark red layer of pure raspberry flavor. Next we prepared the chiffon filling using the reserved berry mixture and raspberry-flavored gelatin, which bumped up the fruit flavor and gave the filling a vibrant color. We spooned the mixture over the fruit layer and let the gelatin work its magic in the refrigerator. Three hours later, we had a perfectly set, sliceable pie with great color and notable raspberry flavor. With a crown of lightly sweetened whipped cream, this pie tastes as good as it looks.

FRUIT LAYER

- 1 (12-ounce) bag frozen raspberries (2 cups)
- 3 tablespoons pectin (Sure-Jell)
- 1½ cups (10½ ounces) sugar
  Pinch salt
- 1 cup (5 ounces) fresh raspberries
- 1 (9-inch) pie shell, baked and cooled (see page 264)

CHIFFON LAYER

- 3 tablespoons raspberry-flavored gelatin
- 3 tablespoons boiling water
- 3 ounces cream cheese, softened
- 1 cup heavy cream, chilled

WHIPPED CREAM TOPPING

- 1¼ cups heavy cream, chilled
- 2 tablespoons sugar

1. FOR THE FRUIT LAYER: Cook the frozen berries in a medium saucepan over medium-high heat, stirring occasionally, until the berries begin to release their juice, about 3 minutes. Stir in the pectin and bring to a boil, stirring constantly. Stir in the sugar and salt and return to a boil. Cook, stirring constantly, until slightly thickened, about 2 minutes. Pour through a fine-mesh strainer into a medium bowl, pressing on the solids to extract as much puree as possible. Scrape the puree off the underside of the strainer into the bowl.

2. Transfer ⅓ cup of the raspberry puree to a small bowl and cool to room temperature. Gently fold the fresh raspberries into the remaining puree. Spread the fruit mixture evenly over the bottom of the pie shell and set aside.

3. FOR THE CHIFFON LAYER: Dissolve the gelatin in the boiling water in a large bowl. Add the cream cheese and reserved ⅓ cup raspberry puree and, with an electric mixer, beat on high speed until smooth, about 2 minutes, scraping down the sides of the bowl as needed. Add the cream and beat on medium-low speed until incorporated, about 30 seconds. Scrape down the sides of the bowl. Beat on high speed until stiff peaks form, 1 to 2 minutes. Spread evenly over the fruit in the pie shell. Cover the pie with plastic wrap and refrigerate until set, at least 3 hours.

4. FOR THE TOPPING: When ready to serve, with an electric mixer, beat the cream and sugar on medium-high speed in a large bowl until stiff peaks form. Spread or pipe over the chilled filling. Cut into wedges and serve immediately.

WHERE THINGS CAN GO WRONG: Do not whip the heavy cream until ready to serve the pie. The heavy cream must be ice-cold; if not, it won't hold stiff peaks, no matter how long or hard you beat it. Note that cream cheese softened in the microwave will separate; soften it at room temperature.

WHAT YOU CAN DO AHEAD OF TIME: The pie can be made through step 3, wrapped tightly in plastic wrap, and refrigerated for up to 2 days. When ready to serve, proceed with step 4.

NOTES FROM THE TEST KITCHEN

TWO LAYERS, TWO THICKENERS

For the fruit layer on the bottom of the pie, we used Sure-Jell (pectin) to achieve a concentrated raspberry flavor and texture. There are two formulations of Sure-Jell. We found that the original formula (sold in the bright yellow box) made the smoothest, thickest bottom layer of fruit. A few tablespoons of raspberry gelatin made for great stability and color in the creamy chiffon layer and reinforced the berry flavor.

OUR FAVORITE PIE SERVER

Without a sharp and sturdy pie server, dessert can go from flawless to fractured in moments. We sliced up and served dessert with 13 of the latest designs, priced from $1.99 to $32.99. Nearly 100 pies later, we found that what appeared to be minute differences in design actually determined the success or failure of each tool. Blunt edges crushed—rather than cut—crusts. Thin, serrated blades sliced pies more nimbly than thicker blades with custard-marring teeth. And gimmicks, such as an extra-long neck, lethal swordlike blade, or finger-pushing mechanism, are best avoided. In the end, only the sleek (and reasonably priced) **Oxo Steel Pie Server** ($7.95) combined the best blade traits with a comfy grip.

NO-FEAR PIE CRUST
MAKES ONE 9-INCH PIE SHELL

WHAT MAKES THIS A BEST RECIPE: We love the rich flavor and flaky texture of a homemade pie crust, but making one can be frustrating. There are so many places that pie dough can go wrong—from making the dough to rolling it out, to fitting it into the pie plate and baking it. For this recipe, we developed a totally reliable pie dough that baked up flaky and full of buttery flavor. We threw out the rolling pin and made a pat-in-the-pan dough. The secret to our recipe was to supplement the butter with cream cheese, which made the dough easy to manipulate and the crust tender. We also found that this dough could handle a whopping 10 tablespoons of fat, almost twice as much as a standard pie dough. This dough also relies on an unconventional mixing method that beats the butter and cream cheese together, with the flour, sugar, and salt mixture added to that. One more unexpected benefit: To bake the crust, there's no need for foil and pie weights. As long as the dough is chilled when it goes into the oven, it won't shrink. Finally, a dough that was easy to work with, that baked up flaky, and that tasted great!

1¼ cups (6¼ ounces) unbleached all-purpose flour
2 tablespoons sugar
¼ teaspoon salt
8 tablespoons (1 stick) unsalted butter, softened but still cool
2 ounces cream cheese, softened but still cool

1. Lightly coat a 9-inch glass pie plate with vegetable oil spray. Whisk the flour, sugar, and salt together in a medium bowl.

2. With an electric mixer, beat the butter and cream cheese on medium speed in a large bowl until combined, about 2 minutes, scraping down the sides of the bowl as needed. Add the flour mixture and beat on medium-low speed until the mixture resembles coarse cornmeal, about 20 seconds. Scrape down the sides of the bowl. Increase the speed to medium-high and beat until the dough begins to form large clumps, about 30 seconds. Reserve 3 tablespoons of the dough. Turn the remaining dough out onto a lightly floured counter, gather into a ball, and flatten into a 6-inch disk. Transfer the dough to the prepared pie plate.

3. Press the dough evenly over the bottom of the pie plate toward the sides, using the heel of your hand. Hold the plate up to the light to ensure that the dough is evenly distributed. With your fingertips, continue to work the dough over the bottom of the plate and up the sides until evenly distributed.

4. Following the photos, roll the reserved 3 tablespoons dough on a lightly floured surface into three 8-inch ropes, and form a fluted edge. Wrap the pie shell in plastic wrap and refrigerate for at least 1 hour.

5. Meanwhile, adjust an oven rack to the middle position and heat the oven to 325 degrees. Lightly prick the bottom of the crust with a fork. Bake until golden brown, 35 to 40 minutes. Transfer the crust to a wire rack to cool.

WHERE THINGS CAN GO WRONG: If large bubbles form while the crust is in the oven, do not touch them until the crust is fully baked, then gently press on the bubbles with a kitchen towel. The bubbles will settle as the crust cools.

WHAT YOU CAN DO AHEAD OF TIME: The baked pie shell can be cooled completely, wrapped tightly in plastic wrap, and stored at room temperature for up to 1 day. The dough can be pressed into the pie plate, wrapped tightly in plastic wrap, and refrigerated for up to 2 days, or frozen for up to 1 month. Thaw frozen dough in the refrigerator.

NOTES FROM THE TEST KITCHEN

EASY AS PIE

1. Hold the pie plate up to the light to check the thickness of the dough; it should be translucent, not opaque. Pay attention to the curved edges.

2. Roll the reserved dough into three 8-inch ropes. Arrange the ropes around the perimeter of the pie plate, leaving small (about 1-inch) gaps between them.

3. Squeeze the ropes together.

4. Create a fluted edge, dipping your fingers in flour if the dough is sticky.

WHAT TO LOOK FOR IN A PIE PLATE

A pie plate's rim should be wide and sturdy enough to support a fluted edge. We found that pie plates with rims narrower than ½ inch were not up to the task. Of all the pie plates we have tested, the classic **Corning Pyrex Original** ($4.95) was our favorite, delivering a solid performance across the board, a budget price, and a see-through bottom so you can tell when the bottom is nicely browned.

PUMPKIN-PRALINE PIE
SERVES 8 TO 10

WHAT MAKES THIS A BEST RECIPE: We love this pie because it combines the familiar spiced custard of pumpkin pie with the praline-like crunch of pecan pie. Some recipes for this type of pie have a wimpy pumpkin filling, while others skimp on the praline, or, worse, they hide it under the pumpkin, making it soggy. Our recipe starts out with silky and sturdy pumpkin pie as the base and adds a healthy layer of pecan praline on top. To fortify the pumpkin base and make it firm enough to support the praline, we added three eggs (one more than usual) to a can of plain pumpkin puree. Tasters preferred the richness of evaporated milk to either heavy cream or milk, and the caramel flavor of dark brown sugar to granulated sugar. To make the filling smooth and creamy, we gave it a whirl in the food processor, and cooked it on the stovetop to evaporate the excess moisture. For the topping, we tossed chopped pecans with dark brown sugar and a bit of corn syrup—just enough to make the topping clump like streusel—and scattered the uncooked mixture on top of the still-hot, baked pumpkin pie. To keep the filling from sagging under the weight of the topping, we baked it until it was puffed and cracked around the edges before adding the topping. The filling was then perfectly set to receive the topping, and we'd covered the cracks. Then we returned the pie to the oven and the topping bubbled enticingly around the edges. To crisp the topping further, we sprinkled on 2 teaspoons of granulated sugar. We now had a pie that would satisfy everyone gathered around the holiday table.

CRUST

1¼ cups (6¼ ounces) unbleached all-purpose flour
2 tablespoons dark brown sugar
½ teaspoon salt
8 tablespoons (1 stick) unsalted butter, cut into ¼-inch pieces and chilled
3–4 tablespoons ice water

FILLING

1 (15-ounce) can plain pumpkin puree
¾ cup (5¼ ounces) packed dark brown sugar
2 teaspoons ground cinnamon
1 teaspoon ground ginger
½ teaspoon ground allspice
Pinch ground cloves
½ teaspoon salt
1 cup evaporated milk
3 large eggs
2 teaspoons vanilla extract

TOPPING

1 cup pecans, chopped fine
½ cup (3⅓ ounces) packed dark brown sugar
Pinch salt
2 teaspoons dark corn syrup
1 teaspoon vanilla extract
2 teaspoons granulated sugar

1. FOR THE CRUST: Process the flour, brown sugar, and salt in a food processor until combined. Add the butter and pulse until the mixture resembles coarse cornmeal, about ten 1-second pulses. Turn the mixture into a medium bowl.

2. Sprinkle 3 tablespoons of the ice water over the mixture. Stir and press the dough together using a stiff rubber spatula until the dough sticks together. If the dough does not come together, stir in the remaining 1 tablespoon water until the dough forms large clumps and no dry flour remains. Turn the dough out onto the counter and flatten into a 4-inch disk. Wrap the disk in plastic wrap and refrigerate for at least 1 hour before rolling.

3. Remove the disk of dough from the refrigerator. Following the photos on page 268, roll the dough out on a lightly floured surface or between 2 large sheets of parchment paper or plastic wrap to a 12-inch circle ⅛ inch thick. (If the dough becomes soft and/or sticky, return it to the refrigerator until firm.) Transfer the dough to a 9-inch pie plate. Working around the circumference, ease the dough into the plate by gently lifting the edge of the dough with one hand while pressing it into the plate bottom with the other hand. Trim and flute the edges; refrigerate until the dough is firm, about 30 minutes, then freeze for 20 minutes.

4. Meanwhile, adjust an oven rack to the middle position and heat the oven to 375 degrees. Line the chilled dough-lined pie plate with a double layer of aluminum foil and fill with pie weights. Bake until the pie dough dries out, 25 to 30 minutes. Carefully remove the pie weights and foil and continue to bake until the crust is firmly set and lightly browned, 5 to 6 minutes. Transfer to a wire rack.

5. FOR THE FILLING: Adjust an oven rack to the middle position and heat the oven to 350 degrees. Meanwhile, process the pumpkin, brown sugar, spices, and salt in a food processor until smooth, about 1 minute. Cook the mixture in a large saucepan over medium-high heat until thickened, about 4 minutes. (Meanwhile, if necessary, put the pie shell back in the oven to warm.)

6. Off the heat, whisk the evaporated milk into the pumpkin mixture, then whisk in the eggs and vanilla. Pour the filling into the warmed pie shell and bake until the filling is puffed and cracked around the edges and the center barely jiggles when the pie is shaken, about 35 minutes.

7. FOR THE TOPPING: While the pie is baking, combine the pecans, brown sugar, and salt in a medium bowl. Add the corn syrup and vanilla, using your fingers to combine.

8. Scatter the topping evenly over the puffed filling and sprinkle with the granulated sugar. Bake until the pecans are fragrant and the topping is bubbling around the edges, about 10 minutes. Transfer the pie to a wire rack to cool completely, at least 2 hours. Cut into wedges and serve.

WHERE THINGS CAN GO WRONG: Be sure that the pumpkin filling is beginning to crack around the edges before scattering the praline topping over the top, or the topping will sink into the filling and become soggy.

WHAT YOU CAN DO AHEAD OF TIME: The pie can be cooled completely, wrapped tightly in plastic wrap, and refrigerated for up to 2 days. Let the pie come to room temperature before serving. The baked pie shell can be cooled, wrapped tightly in plastic wrap, and stored at room temperature for up to 1 day. The disk of dough can be wrapped tightly in plastic wrap and refrigerated for up to 2 days, or frozen for up to 1 month. Thaw frozen dough in the refrigerator. Before rolling, let the dough stand at room temperature for 15 minutes to soften.

NOTES FROM THE TEST KITCHEN

HOW TO ROLL AND FIT THE DOUGH

1. Lay the dough on a lightly floured surface (or between sheets of parchment paper or plastic wrap), and roll it outward from its center into a 12-inch circle.

2. As you roll the dough, give it a quarter turn every few strokes, adding more flour as needed to keep the dough from sticking to the counter.

3. Loosely roll the dough around the rolling pin. Then gently unroll the dough over the pie plate.

4. Gently press the dough into the corners of the pie plate. Trim and flute the edges, then refrigerate until needed.

BLIND BAKING A PIE CRUST

The crusts for many pies and tarts are baked before filling (this is called blind baking) so that they are golden brown, crisp, and flaky. Here are instructions for successful blind baking:

1. Line the chilled pie crust with a double layer of aluminum foil, covering the edges to prevent burning.

2. Fill the crust with pie weights or pennies and bake for 25 to 30 minutes.

3. Remove the pie weights and foil. For a partially baked crust, continue baking until light golden brown, 5 to 6 minutes; for a fully baked crust, continue baking until deep golden brown, about 12 minutes more.

THE BEST CANNED PUMPKIN

Aside from its status as a Thanksgiving classic, pumpkin pie gets points for taking a plain canned good and dressing it up. To be sure we were opening the best canned pumpkin, we asked 10 tasters to sample pies made from three brands: One-Pie, Libby's, and Farmer's Market Organic. **Libby's** and **One-Pie** ended up in a dead heat. While some tasters favored the "creamy" texture and "mild sweetness" of Libby's, others preferred the slightly "denser" texture and "sharper" pumpkin flavor of One-Pie. Farmer's Market was disqualified for its unpleasantly "vegetal" and "chalky" flavor. Whichever brand you choose, study the label carefully. Our supermarket stocks canned pumpkin from both Libby's and Farmer's Market that's already been spiced and sweetened. These products, marked as "pie mix" but looking very much like the cans of plain pumpkin, are a recipe for a soupy and overly sweet disaster. Read the labels to make sure that you're buying plain pumpkin (left), not pumpkin pie mix (right).

PERFECT PUMPKIN-PRALINE PIE

1. Puree the pumpkin with the brown sugar and spices to break up any fibers.

2. Cook the pumpkin mixture to remove excess moisture.

3. Pour the hot filling into a warmed pie crust to minimize the baking time and promote even cooking.

4. Wait for the filling to crack on top. Usually the sign of a problem, in our recipe the cracking is the cue that tells you exactly when to add the praline topping.

RUSTIC FREE-FORM APPLE TARTLETS

MAKES 6 TARTLETS

WHAT MAKES THIS A BEST RECIPE: Made in the shape of a thin, flat round, the free-form tart is perhaps the oldest of all pastries. And these individual free-form tartlets may be counted among some of the easiest too, requiring little more than a sheet of dough, apples, and sugar. A look at recipes for this classic dessert reminded us that we needed to ensure a rich apple flavor, a moist filling, and a tender but sturdy crust. For the filling, we achieved the best balance of taste and texture using a combination of thinly sliced soft, sweet McIntosh apples and crisp, tart Granny Smiths. A little sugar, cinnamon, and lemon juice seasoned the apples and kept them from drying out as they baked. In search of the perfect dough, we settled on a moist, rich, and tender rugelach-like combination, made with cream cheese. The tartlets turned out perfectly—they were the ideal marriage of pastry to filling. The dough was moist and very tender, and added great flavor to the dessert.

DOUGH

- 1¼ cups (6¼ ounces) unbleached all-purpose flour
- 2 tablespoons sugar
- ¼ teaspoon salt
- 8 tablespoons (1 stick) unsalted butter, cut into ½-inch pieces and chilled
- 4 ounces cream cheese, cut into ½-inch pieces and chilled
- 1–2 tablespoons ice water
- 2 teaspoons fresh lemon juice

FILLING

- 1¼ pounds Granny Smith apples (about 3 small), peeled, cored, and cut into ¼-inch-thick slices
- 1¼ pounds McIntosh apples (about 3 small), peeled, cored, and cut into ¼-inch-thick slices

Cream cheese is the secret ingredient for moist, tender pastry.

- 2 tablespoons fresh lemon juice
- ¼ cup plus 2 tablespoons sugar
- ¼ teaspoon ground cinnamon
- 2 egg whites, lightly beaten, for brushing

1. FOR THE DOUGH: Process the flour, sugar, and salt in a food processor until combined. Add the butter and cream cheese and pulse until the mixture resembles coarse cornmeal, about ten 1-second pulses. Turn the mixture into a medium bowl.

2. Sprinkle 1 tablespoon water and the lemon juice over the mixture. Stir and press the dough together using a stiff rubber spatula until the dough sticks together. If the dough does not come together, stir in the remaining 1 tablespoon water until the dough forms large clumps and no dry flour remains. Turn the dough out onto the counter and flatten into a rough disk. Cut the disk into 6 equal pieces using a chef's knife. Flatten each piece into a 3-inch disk. Transfer the disks in a single layer to a flat dinner plate. Wrap the plate in plastic wrap and refrigerate for at least 30 minutes before rolling.

3. Remove the plate from the refrigerator and roll each piece between 2 pieces of lightly floured parchment paper to a 6-inch circle. (If the dough becomes soft and/or sticky, return it to the refrigerator until firm.) Remove and discard the top pieces of parchment paper. Stack the rounds on the plate with the parchment between each layer. Wrap the plate in plastic wrap and refrigerate while preparing the fruit.

4. FOR THE FILLING: Adjust two oven racks to the upper-middle and lower-middle positions and heat the oven to 400 degrees. Toss the apples with the lemon juice, ¼ cup of the sugar, and cinnamon. Arrange the parchment-lined dough rounds in a single layer on the counter. Following the photos, arrange about 1 cup of the apple slices, thick edges out, in a circular mound on each dough round, leaving a 1-inch border.

5. Fold the edges of the dough over the fruit. With cupped hands, gently press the dough to the filling, reinforcing the shape and compacting the apples. Slide 3 tartlets, still on top of the parchment, onto each of 2 baking sheets.

6. Bake until pale golden brown, about 15 minutes. Brush the surface of the crusts with the beaten egg whites and sprinkle the apples evenly with the remaining 2 tablespoons sugar. Return to the oven, rotating the baking sheets, and bake until the crust is deep golden brown and the apples are tender, about 15 minutes longer. Cool the tartlets on the baking sheets for 5 minutes, then transfer to a wire rack and cool until warm or room temperature before serving.

WHERE THINGS CAN GO WRONG: The amounts of cream cheese and butter used in this dough make it soft and delicate. For easiest handling, make sure that these ingredients are cold and that your kitchen is cool.

WHAT YOU CAN DO AHEAD OF TIME: The tartlets can be cooled completely, wrapped tightly in plastic wrap, and stored at room temperature for up to 2 days. The disks of dough can be wrapped tightly in plastic wrap and refrigerated for up to 2 days, or frozen for up to 1 month. Thaw frozen dough in the refrigerator. Before rolling, let the dough stand at room temperature for 15 minutes to soften.

NOTES FROM THE TEST KITCHEN

THE RIGHT SLICE
It is important to slice the apples thin (about ¼ inch) so that they cook all the way through during the relatively short baking time.

DOUBLE UP
To make 12 tartlets, double all of the ingredients, preparing the dough in two batches and baking the tartlets in two batches.

MAKING INDIVIDUAL TARTLETS

1. Arrange the apple slices in an even circle over the dough, leaving a 1-inch border.

2. Fill in the center with additional slices, lending support to the circular wall of apples.

3. Fold the outer edge of dough snugly inward over the apples and cup with your hands to compress and shape.

4. Grasping the parchment edges, transfer each tartlet to a baking sheet.

ITALIAN-STYLE
FIG-WALNUT TART

SERVES 8 TO 10

WHAT MAKES THIS A BEST RECIPE: Fig Newtons aside, dried figs aren't very popular in the United States, though we can think of a dozen Italian baked goods in which they play a starring role. Here we created a recipe for our favorite such confection, one that combines figs with crunchy walnuts in a sticky, citrus-scented paste slathered thick across a crisp, leavened crust. Unlike American pie or tart doughs, this tart's dough, called *pasta frolla*, is sweet and flavorful. Containing whole eggs, butter, and sugar, the pastry is good enough to eat on its own. To add lightness and puffiness to the crust, we also added baking powder to our dough, along with lemon zest and vanilla for flavor. Finally, a moderate amount of sugar boosted the crust's overall flavor. For the filling, we found that most markets carry three types of dried figs: Turkish, Calimyrna (a California-grown variety of Turkish Smyrna figs), and Mission. After trying each, we most preferred the softer, silkier texture of the Turkish or its close cousin, Calimyrna. We roughly chopped the figs, and then simmered them in water spiked with brandy and orange zest until tender before stirring in the walnuts. An added bonus: Unlike other pastry doughs, pasta frolla cooks through before it fully browns, which meant we could abandon the step of prebaking the crust altogether.

DOUGH

1–2 tablespoons water
1 large egg
1 teaspoon vanilla extract
1⅓ cups (about 6⅔ ounces) unbleached all-purpose flour
⅓ cup (about 2⅓ ounces) sugar
1¼ teaspoons baking powder
¼ teaspoon salt
   Finely grated zest of 1 lemon
7 tablespoons unsalted butter, cut into ¼-inch pieces and chilled

FILLING

1 pound dried Turkish or Calimyrna figs, stems removed and fruit chopped coarse
¼ cup (1¾ ounces) sugar
½ cup brandy
1 cup water
   Grated zest of 1 orange
1 cup walnuts, chopped coarse
   Confectioners' sugar for dusting

1. FOR THE DOUGH: Whisk 1 tablespoon water, egg, and vanilla together in a small bowl. Process the flour, sugar, baking powder, salt, and lemon zest in a food processor until combined. Add the butter and pulse until the mixture resembles coarse cornmeal, about seven 1-second pulses. With the machine running, add the egg mixture and process until the liquid ingredients are incorporated. Squeeze a handful of the dough; if it forms a moist ball, no more water is necessary. If the mixture is crumbly and dry, add the remaining 1 tablespoon water and process until just incorporated. Turn the dough out onto the counter and gently knead into a cohesive dough, about 30 seconds. Flatten the dough into a 5-inch disk. Wrap the disk in plastic wrap and refrigerate for at least 1 hour before rolling.

2. Remove the disk of dough from the refrigerator and roll it out on a lightly floured surface or between 2 lightly floured sheets of parchment paper or plastic wrap (or 4 small sheets together to form 2 large sheets) to a 13-inch circle about ¼ inch thick. (If the dough becomes soft and/or sticky, return it to the refrigerator until firm.) Following the photos on page 274, transfer the dough to a 10-inch tart pan with a removable bottom. Working around the circumference of the pan, ease the dough into the pan by gently lifting the edge of the dough with one hand while pressing it into the pan bottom with the other hand. Press the dough against the fluted sides of the pan, patching breaks or cracks if necessary. (If some sections of the edge are too thin, reinforce them by folding any excess dough back on itself.) Run a rolling pin over the top of the tart pan to remove excess dough. Set the dough-lined tart pan on a baking sheet or large plate and freeze for 30 minutes.

3. FOR THE FILLING: Meanwhile, bring the figs, sugar, brandy, and water to a simmer in a medium saucepan over medium heat. Simmer, stirring occasionally, until the liquid evaporates and the figs are very soft, about

10 minutes. Stir in the orange zest and walnuts and cool to room temperature.

4. Adjust an oven rack to the middle position and heat the oven to 325 degrees. Scrape the cooled fig and nut filling mixture into the chilled tart shell and smooth with a spatula. Bake until the edges of the tart are lightly browned, 25 to 30 minutes.

5. Transfer the tart to a wire rack to cool for 5 minutes, remove the outer ring of the pan, and cool completely, at least 3 hours. When ready to serve, dust with confectioners' sugar. Cut into wedges and serve.

WHERE THINGS CAN GO WRONG: Don't add too much water to this dough. Begin with just one tablespoon, process the dough, then test it by squeezing a handful to see if it comes together, and add more water if necessary. To avoid overworking the dough, finish kneading it by hand. If you process the dough in a food processor until it comes together into a ball, the baked crust will be tough and overly crisp, not flaky and biscuit-like, which is the desired texture.

WHAT YOU CAN DO AHEAD OF TIME: The tart can be cooled completely, wrapped tightly in plastic wrap, and refrigerated for up to 2 days. When ready to serve, dust with confectioners' sugar. The dough can be pressed into the pie plate, wrapped tightly in plastic wrap, and refrigerated for up to 2 days, or frozen for up to 1 month. The disk of dough can be wrapped tightly in plastic wrap and refrigerated for up to 2 days, or frozen for up to 1 month. Thaw frozen dough in the refrigerator. Before rolling, let the dough stand at room temperature for 15 minutes to soften.

NOTES FROM THE TEST KITCHEN

TART PANS

Tart pans can be divided into three basic categories based on materials: tinned steel (the classic choice), nonstick, and everything else—ranging from heavy ceramic to floppy silicone. Tarts baked in the tinned steel pan performed better than the rest. They browned evenly and released effortlessly. So for buttery tart pastry, stick with tinned steel pans like this one sold by **Kaiser Tinplate**.

HOW TO FIT TART DOUGH INTO THE PAN

1. After rolling out the dough, wrap it loosely around the rolling pin, and unroll it over a 10-inch tart pan with a removable bottom.

2. Lifting the edges of the dough, gently ease the dough into the pan.

3. Press the dough into the fluted sides of the pan and into the corners, forming a small seam.

4. If any part of the edge is too thin, reinforce it by folding some of the excess dough that overhangs the tart pan back on itself.

5. Run the rolling pin over the top of the tart pan to remove any excess dough and make a clean edge.

6. The finished edge should be ¼ inch thick. If it is too thick, press some of the dough up over the edge of the pan and trim it away.

PEACH CRUMBLE

SERVES 4

WHAT MAKES THIS A BEST RECIPE: There's a fundamental problem with peach crumble: the peaches. Few fruits are as finicky in flavor or texture, and some recipes try to address these problems by adjusting the amounts of sugar and thickener to suit the fruit's ripeness, resulting in a sticky puddle of mushy fruit buried beneath a gloppy beige crust. In our opinion, peach crumble should consist of fresh-tasting, lightly sweetened peaches topped with a buttery, crisp, nutty-tasting crumble. For this recipe, we peeled the peaches and sliced them ¾ inch thick so they held their shape in the oven, then we tossed them with sugar and allowed them to macerate for half an hour. The sugar drew off a fair amount of surprisingly mild-flavored juice, effectively minimizing the juices and maximizing the peaches' inherent sweetness. The peaches required no additional sugar after the maceration (though we did add back a little of the sweet "juice," in which we dissolved the thickener), but they did need a little help flavorwise. Warm spices like cinnamon and nutmeg were common in the recipes we found, and tasters approved of just a pinch of each. Salt helped define the flavors, as did a substantial splash of lemon juice. As for thickener, a little cornstarch barely bound the juices and gave the fruit a glossy sheen. To get the topping evenly browned (without overcooking the fruit), we cooked it separately in the oven until crisp, and then married it to the filling and cooked the whole dish just until the fruit bubbled about the edges.

FILLING

- 3½   pounds ripe but firm peaches (6 to 7 medium), peeled, pitted, and cut into ¾-inch-thick slices
- ⅓   cup (2⅓ ounces) granulated sugar
- 3–5   teaspoons fresh lemon juice (see note on page 277)

- 1¼   teaspoons cornstarch
  Pinch salt
  Pinch ground cinnamon
  Pinch ground nutmeg

TOPPING

- 1   cup (5 ounces) unbleached all-purpose flour
- ¼   cup (1¾ ounces) plus 1 tablespoon granulated sugar
- ¼   cup (1¾ ounces) packed light or dark brown sugar
- 2   teaspoons vanilla extract
- ⅛   teaspoon salt
- 6   tablespoons unsalted butter, cut into 6 pieces and softened
- ½   cup sliced almonds

1. FOR THE FILLING: Adjust two oven racks to the middle and lowest positions and heat the oven to 350 degrees. Gently toss the peaches and sugar in a large bowl; let stand for 30 minutes, tossing several times. Drain the peaches in a colander set over a large bowl. Whisk ¼ cup of the drained peach juice, lemon juice, cornstarch, salt, cinnamon, and nutmeg together in a small bowl; discard the excess peach juice. Toss the juice mixture with the peaches and transfer to an 8-inch-square glass baking dish.

2. FOR THE TOPPING: Meanwhile, pulse the flour, sugars (reserving 1 tablespoon of the granulated sugar), vanilla, and salt in a food processor until combined, about five 1-second pulses. Add the butter and half of the nuts and process until the mixture clumps together into large, crumbly balls, about 30 seconds, scraping down the sides of the bowl as needed. Sprinkle the remaining nuts over the mixture and combine with two quick pulses. Transfer the mixture to a parchment-lined baking sheet and spread into an even layer (the mixture should break up into roughly ½-inch chunks with some smaller, loose bits). Bake on the middle rack until the chunks are lightly browned and firm, 18 to 22 minutes.

3. TO ASSEMBLE: Grasping the edges of the parchment paper, slide the topping over the peaches and spread into an even layer. Sprinkle the remaining 1 tablespoon sugar over the top, increase the oven temperature to

375 degrees, and bake on the lowest rack until well browned and the fruit is bubbling around the edges, 25 to 35 minutes. Cool on a wire rack until warm, at least 15 minutes, before serving.

WHERE THINGS CAN GO WRONG: Do not add the lemon juice in step 1 until you taste the peaches. The amount you add will depend on their sweetness.

WHAT YOU CAN DO AHEAD OF TIME: The topping can be baked, cooled, and stored in an airtight container at room temperature for up to 3 days.

NOTES FROM THE TEST KITCHEN

OVERHAULING HO-HUM PEACHES

For our recipe, we took a few extra steps to eliminate the common problem of bland peaches and soggy topping in peach crumble.

1. MACERATE: Macerating the fruit in sugar and draining off the excess juices help to concentrate the peach flavor.

2. SEPARATE: Baking the topping separately before sliding it onto the fruit filling keeps it crumbly and crisp.

USING FROZEN PEACHES

If ripe peaches are unavailable, you can substitute five 10-ounce bags of frozen peaches, thawed overnight in the refrigerator.

SERRATED FRUIT PEELERS

After serrated peelers arrived on the market, we all but renounced our usual fruit-peeling tricks (including blanching it briefly in boiling water to loosen the skin). Similar to regular vegetable peelers, these specialized gadgets (with miniature serrations) make quick work of separating tough, thin skin from delicate fruit such as ripe peaches and tomatoes. But which brand is best? Less-than-stellar blades plagued a few of our models, and the extra force required left our hands sticky when we skinned peaches with these peelers. Sharp blades, by contrast, seemed to do most of the work for you. We liked the nonslip handle of **Oxo's Good Grips Serrated Peeler** (left), $6.99, which performed almost as well as our favorite— the **Messermeister Serrated Swivel Peeler** (right), $5.50. This peeler dazzled testers with its supremely sharp blade, which was eminently gentle, even on the ripest peach in the crate.

TRANSFERRING THE BAKED CRUMBLE

1. After the crumble topping is baked, lift the short sides of the parchment paper. (The crumble will break apart into uneven ½- to ¾-inch pieces.)

2. Slide the broken crumble pieces off the parchment and over the top of the peaches.

TROPICAL CARROT CAKE

SERVES 12

WHAT MAKES THIS A BEST RECIPE: Falling somewhere between health food and decadent dessert, carrot cake was the cake to make during the 1960s. And it wasn't long before cooks came up with variations like chocolate, banana, and our favorite, tropical carrot cake. Building on the warm flavors of traditional carrot cake, this tropical version adds coconut, pineapple, and warm spices. We set out to make a light, moist cake with big hits of coconut and pineapple. We intensified the flavor of the coconut by grinding it with both white and brown sugar in the food processor. Since we were looking for concentrated pineapple flavor, it made sense to try frozen pineapple juice concentrate; we mixed the concentrate with pureed frozen pineapple and cooked it down with a little cornstarch to evaporate excess moisture. We added this homemade pudding to the cake batter in place of much of the oil. A plain cream cheese frosting was good, but we wanted to add another layer of tropical flavors. Since we had some extra pudding mixture, we tried incorporating it into the cream cheese frosting; it worked like a charm. To put this dessert over the top, we toasted coconut and pressed it into the sides and on top of the cake. Now our light, full-flavored carrot cake both looked and tasted as if it were enjoying a nice vacation in the tropics.

PUDDING

- 1 pound frozen pineapple chunks, thawed
- ½ cup frozen pineapple juice concentrate, thawed
- 6 tablespoons cornstarch

CAKE

- 2½ cups (12½ ounces) unbleached all-purpose flour
- 4 teaspoons pumpkin pie spice
- 1 tablespoon baking powder
- ¾ teaspoon ground ginger
- ½ teaspoon salt
- 5 carrots, peeled and cut into 1-inch chunks

- 1 cup (2⅔ ounces) sweetened shredded coconut
- 1¼ cups (8¾ ounces) granulated sugar
- ½ cup (3½ ounces) packed light brown sugar
- 4 large eggs
- 1½ cups vegetable oil

FROSTING

- 12 tablespoons (1½ sticks) unsalted butter, softened
- 3 cups (12 ounces) confectioners' sugar
  Pinch salt
- 16 ounces cream cheese, cut into 8 pieces and softened
- 3 cups (8 ounces) sweetened shredded coconut, toasted

1. FOR THE PUDDING: Process the pineapple chunks and concentrate in a food processor until smooth. Transfer to a medium saucepan and whisk in the cornstarch. Simmer over medium heat, stirring constantly, until thickened, about 2 minutes. Transfer to a bowl and refrigerate, with plastic wrap pressed flush against its surface, until cold, at least 1½ hours.

2. FOR THE CAKE: Adjust an oven rack to the middle position and heat the oven to 350 degrees. Lightly coat two 9-inch cake pans with vegetable oil spray, then line the bottoms with parchment paper.

3. Whisk the flour, pumpkin pie spice, baking powder, ginger, and salt together in a large bowl. Process the carrots in a food processor until finely ground. Transfer to a large bowl and wipe the processor bowl dry. Process the coconut with the granulated sugar until the coconut is finely chopped. Add the brown sugar and eggs and blend until the mixture is smooth, about 1 minute. With the machine running, slowly pour in the oil and process until combined. Transfer the mixture to the bowl with the carrots. Stir in the flour mixture and ¾ cup of the pudding.

4. Divide the batter evenly between the prepared cake pans and smooth with a spatula. Bake until a toothpick inserted into the centers comes out clean, 30 to 35 minutes, rotating the cake pans halfway through baking. Cool the cakes in the pans for 10 minutes, then invert onto a greased wire rack; peel off and discard the parchment rounds. Invert the cakes again and cool completely before assembling, about 2 hours.

5. FOR THE FROSTING: With an electric mixer, beat the butter, confectioners' sugar, and salt on medium-high

speed in a large bowl until fluffy, about 3 minutes, scraping down the sides of the bowl as needed. Add the cream cheese, 1 piece at a time, and beat until incorporated, about 30 seconds. Beat in the remaining 1 cup pineapple pudding. (The mixture will appear slightly grainy.) Refrigerate until ready to use.

6. TO ASSEMBLE: Place one cake layer on a cake plate or cardboard round. Spread 2 cups of the frosting evenly across the top of the cake with a spatula. Place the second cake layer on top, then spread the remaining frosting evenly over the top and sides of the cake. Refrigerate for 15 minutes. Sprinkle the toasted coconut on top and press into the sides of the cake. Serve.

WHAT YOU CAN DO AHEAD OF TIME: The cakes can be cooled completely (unfrosted), wrapped tightly in plastic wrap, and frozen for up to 1 month. Thaw the cakes, still wrapped, at room temperature, then remove the plastic wrap and frost.

NOTES FROM THE TEST KITCHEN

HOW TO TOAST COCONUT
Toasting coconut brings out its tropical flavor. To toast, spread it in an even layer on a rimmed baking sheet and bake in a 325-degree oven, stirring often, until golden brown, 5 to 10 minutes.

GREAT DISCOVERIES

THE PROOF IS IN THE PUDDING
When developing my recipe for Tropical Carrot Cake, I had a hard time getting enough pineapple flavor into the cake. After many tests, I found success by making a pineapple pudding. I pureed thawed frozen pineapple, reinforced its flavor with thawed frozen pineapple concentrate, and cooked the mixture down with cornstarch to thicken it to a pudding-like consistency. I added the pudding to the cake and I knew I was onto something when, after 20 minutes in the oven, the test kitchen was filled with the aroma of pineapple. A little pineapple pudding remained, and I stirred it into the cream cheese frosting. Tasters lined up to help me try this fluffy cake, and then they came back for seconds.

DIANE UNGER | TEST COOK, *COOK'S COUNTRY*

CRANBERRY-APPLE CRISP
SERVES 8 TO 10

WHAT MAKES THIS A BEST RECIPE: The problem with cranberry-apple crisp is getting the right balance of flavors and textures—the cranberries can taste too sour, plus the apples bake unevenly, and the topping never lives up to the name "crisp." To get the right cranberry flavor in our crisp, we cooked fresh cranberries with sugar and a little water until they burst and thickened into a homemade sauce. We then added the mixture to diced apples (Granny Smith and Braeburns were tasters' favorite) and dried cranberries (which added concentrated cranberry flavor and a nice textural contrast), and topped the fruit with the classic combination of butter, flour, sugar, cinnamon, and oats. After an hour and a half in the oven, when the fruit juices started to bubble up, we had a winner. The scarlet filling looked and tasted packed with cranberry flavor. Adding some tapioca to the filling (better than either flour or cornstarch) helped to thicken the fruit juices. The only problem was that the crisp was taking nearly 90 minutes to bake. Any less time and the apples were too firm, but in 90 minutes the topping turned almost as hard as a stale granola bar. Since we were already dirtying a pot to make the cranberry sauce, we thought we'd use the same pot to jump-start the apples on the stovetop. Just five minutes of stovetop cooking was all it took to reduce the baking time from 90 to 30 minutes. The apples now cooked evenly in the baking pan, and the topping was no longer a dark, hard shell.

TOPPING

- ¾ cup (3¾ ounces) unbleached all-purpose flour
- ½ cup (3½ ounces) packed light brown sugar
- ½ cup (3½ ounces) granulated sugar
- 1 teaspoon ground cinnamon
- 12 tablespoons (1½ sticks) unsalted butter, cut into ½-inch pieces and chilled
- ¾ cup (2¼ ounces) old-fashioned rolled oats

FILLING

  1   **pound fresh or frozen cranberries (about 4 cups)**

1¼ **cups (8¾ ounces) granulated sugar**

 ¼ **cup water**

2½ **pounds Granny Smith apples (about 5 medium), peeled, cored, and cut into ½-inch pieces**

2½ **pounds Braeburn or Golden Delicious apples (about 5 medium), peeled, cored, and cut into ½-inch pieces**

  1   **cup dried sweetened cranberries**

  3   **tablespoons Minute tapioca**

1. FOR THE TOPPING: Adjust an oven rack to the middle position and heat the oven to 400 degrees. Pulse the flour, sugars, cinnamon, and butter in a food processor until the mixture resembles coarse crumbs, about ten 1-second pulses. Turn the mixture into a medium bowl and stir in the oats. Pinch the mixture with your fingers to create peanut-sized clumps; refrigerate.

2. FOR THE FILLING: Simmer the fresh or frozen cranberries, ¾ cup of the sugar, and water in a large Dutch oven over medium-high heat until jam-like, about 10 minutes. Transfer the mixture to a bowl; set aside. Add the apples, the remaining ½ cup sugar, and dried cranberries to the Dutch oven and cook over medium-high heat until the apples begin to release their juices, about 5 minutes.

3. Off the heat, stir the cranberry mixture and tapioca into the apple mixture. Pour into a 13 by 9-inch glass baking dish set on a rimmed baking sheet and smooth with a spatula.

4. TO ASSEMBLE: Scatter the chilled topping evenly over the filling and bake until the juices are bubbling and the topping is deep golden brown, about 30 minutes. (If the topping is browning too quickly, loosely cover with a piece of aluminum foil.) Cool on a wire rack for about 10 minutes before serving.

WHERE THINGS CAN GO WRONG: Make sure that the butter is chilled before making the topping. If the butter is too soft, the mixture will form a paste in the food processor and the topping will not be craggy and crisp.

WHAT YOU CAN DO AHEAD OF TIME: After pinching the topping into small clumps in step 1, you can transfer it to a zipper-lock bag and refrigerate it for up to 5 days, or freeze it for up to 1 month. The filling can be cooked up to 2 days ahead; transfer to the baking dish, cool to room temperature, wrap tightly in plastic wrap, and refrigerate. To bake, sprinkle the chilled topping evenly over the chilled filling, loosely cover with foil, and bake for 20 minutes. Uncover and bake until the juices are bubbling and the topping is deep golden brown, 15 to 20 minutes longer.

NOTES FROM THE TEST KITCHEN

TWO CRANBERRIES ARE BETTER THAN ONE

To pack cranberry flavor into our crisp, we cook fresh or frozen berries to a jammy consistency, then add chewy dried cranberries for texture and sweetness.

FRESH CRANBERRIES   **DRIED CRANBERRIES**

CRISP ESSENTIALS

1. Cook the cranberries, sugar, and water until the mixture is thick and jammy.

2. Mound the topping in the center of the pan, then use your fingers to rake the topping out toward the edges of the pan.

STRAWBERRY POKE CAKE

SERVES 12

WHAT MAKES THIS A BEST RECIPE: This recipe for strawberry poke cake, with its bright red streaks of strawberry gelatin and tender white cake, has a moist texture and a novel appearance. We took the original recipe, invented by Kraft Kitchens in 1969 as a vehicle to increase strawberry Jell-O sales, and improved upon it. The original cake recipe has exactly three ingredients: strawberry Jell-O, boxed white cake mix, and whipped cream. For our version, we made the cake from scratch and baked it longer than we normally do, which produced a slightly drier texture that could better withstand the gelatin without getting soggy. For big strawberry flavor, we cooked frozen strawberries with orange juice and sugar, and then strained out the solids and mixed the liquid with strawberry gelatin. We then poured this berry packed liquid over the cake and refrigerated it until it set up. For extra strawberry flavor, we pulsed the solids and 2 tablespoons of sugar to a jam-like consistency in the food processor and spread the mixture on top of the cake. The final touch to our cake was sweetened whipped cream.

CAKE

- 12 tablespoons (1½ sticks) unsalted butter, softened, plus more for the pan
- 2¼ cups (11¼ ounces) unbleached all-purpose flour, plus more for the pan
- 4 teaspoons baking powder
- 1 teaspoon salt
- 1 cup milk
- 6 large egg whites
- 2 teaspoons vanilla extract
- 1¾ cups (12¼ ounces) sugar

SYRUP AND TOPPING

- 4 cups frozen strawberries
- 6 tablespoons sugar
- 2 tablespoons orange juice
- ½ cup water
- 2 tablespoons strawberry-flavored gelatin
- 2 cups heavy cream

1. FOR THE CAKE: Adjust an oven rack to the middle position and heat the oven to 350 degrees. Grease and flour a 13 by 9-inch baking pan. Whisk the flour, baking powder, and salt together in a large bowl. Whisk the milk, egg whites, and vanilla together in a medium bowl.

2. With an electric mixer, beat the butter and sugar on medium-high speed in a large bowl until fluffy, about 2 minutes, scraping down the sides of the bowl as needed. Add half of the flour mixture and beat on medium-low speed until combined, about 30 seconds. Add half of the milk mixture and beat on low speed until combined, about 30 seconds. Repeat with the remaining flour and milk mixtures. Using a rubber spatula, give the batter a final stir. Scrape into the prepared pan and smooth with a spatula. Bake until a toothpick inserted into the center comes out clean, about 35 minutes, rotating the cake pan halfway through baking. Cool the cake completely in the pan on a wire rack, at least 1 hour.

3. FOR THE SYRUP AND TOPPING: Cook 3 cups of the strawberries, 2 tablespoons of the sugar, juice, and water in a medium saucepan over medium-low heat, covered, until the strawberries are softened, about 10 minutes. Pour through a fine-mesh strainer into a large bowl, reserving the solids. Whisk the gelatin into the liquid and cool to room temperature, at least 20 minutes.

4. Meanwhile, following the photos on page 284 and using a skewer, poke about 50 holes in the top of the cooled cake. Slowly pour the cooled liquid evenly over the top of the cake. Wrap tightly in plastic wrap and refrigerate until the gelatin is set, at least 3 hours or up to 2 days.

5. Pulse the reserved strained strawberries, 2 tablespoons of the sugar, and the remaining 1 cup strawberries in a food processor until the mixture resembles strawberry jam. Spread the strawberry mixture evenly over the cake. With an electric mixer, beat the cream and the remaining 2 tablespoons sugar on medium-high speed in a large bowl until soft peaks form. Spread the cream over the strawberries. Cut the cake into squares and serve.

WHERE THINGS CAN GO WRONG: Don't worry if the top of the cake looks slightly overbaked—the prolonged cooking time keeps the crumb from becoming too soggy after the strawberry syrup is poured on top.

WHAT YOU CAN DO AHEAD OF TIME: The cake with the fruit layer can be wrapped tightly in plastic wrap and refrigerated for up to 2 days. The cake can be cooled completely in step 2, wrapped in plastic wrap, and stored at room temperature for up to 2 days.

NOTES FROM THE TEST KITCHEN

PERFECTING THE POKE
Finding the right poking device wasn't as simple as you might think. Toothpicks were too small, and straws, handles of wooden spoons, pencils, and fingers were too big. A wooden skewer finally did the trick. But simply poking didn't create a large enough hole for the liquid to seep into. In order to create deep lines of red color against the white crumb, we had to poke and then twist the skewer to really separate the crumb.

1. Using a skewer, poke about 50 holes all over the top (do not poke all the way through to the bottom). Twist the skewer to make the holes slightly bigger.

2. Slowly pour the cooled gelatin mixture evenly over the entire surface of the cake.

RED VELVET CAKE
SERVES 12

WHAT MAKES THIS A BEST RECIPE: Frosted and uncut, it looks like any other cake. But cut—and bite—into our Red Velvet Cake and you'll know you're experiencing something special. Beyond its shocking color, there's something more to red velvet cake—an extra-tender cake and fluffy cream cheese frosting. Our research revealed that red cakes are actually nothing new. A faint red color is the by-product of a chemical reaction between vinegar and/or buttermilk and cocoa powder. Red cakes—with names like red devil cake and oxblood cake—date back to the late nineteenth century. Over time, the naturally occurring faint red color was augmented, first by beets (a common ingredient during the sugar rationing of World War II) and then by red food coloring (the standard choice in most recipes published since the 1950s). During the 1960s, the recipe appeared in countless newspapers, which sourced this cake in the Deep South, the Pacific Northwest, and even Canada. The best-known version of this recipe appeared in James Beard's 1972 classic, *American Cookery.* First we tried a few recipes using beets, but no one liked their vegetal flavor. After several tests, it was clear that food coloring was a must and there was no use trying to skimp on it; anything less than 2 tablespoons yielded a cake that was more pink than red. As for cocoa powder, we found that 2 tablespoons produced the best color and gave the cake a pleasant (but mild) cocoa flavor. To make the color uniform throughout the cake, we found it best to make a paste with the food coloring and cocoa powder before adding it to the batter. To top it off, tasters loved the contrast in color and flavor that a sweet, tangy, white cream cheese frosting gave the cake.

CAKE

12 tablespoons (1½ sticks) unsalted butter, softened, plus more for the pans

2¼ cups (11¼ ounces) unbleached all-purpose flour, plus more for the pans

1½ teaspoons baking soda

      Pinch salt
 1   cup buttermilk
 1   tablespoon white vinegar
 1   teaspoon vanilla extract
 2   large eggs
 2   tablespoons natural cocoa powder (see note)
 2   tablespoons (one 1-ounce bottle) red food coloring
1½   cups (10½ ounces) granulated sugar

FROSTING
 16   tablespoons (2 sticks) unsalted butter, softened
 4   cups (16 ounces) confectioners' sugar
      Pinch salt
 16   ounces cream cheese, cut into 8 pieces and softened
1½   teaspoons vanilla extract

1. FOR THE CAKE: Adjust an oven rack to the middle position and heat the oven to 350 degrees. Grease and flour two 9-inch cake pans. Whisk the flour, baking soda, and salt together in a medium bowl. Whisk the buttermilk, vinegar, vanilla, and eggs together in a medium bowl. Mix the cocoa and food coloring together in a small bowl until a smooth paste forms.

2. With an electric mixer, beat the butter and granulated sugar on medium-high speed in a large bowl until fluffy, about 3 minutes, scraping down the sides of the bowl as needed. Add one-third of flour mixture and beat on medium-low speed until just incorporated, about 30 seconds. Add half of the buttermilk mixture and beat on low speed until combined, about 30 seconds. Scrape down the sides of the bowl. Repeat, ending with the flour mixture. Scrape down the sides of the bowl, add the cocoa mixture, then mix on medium speed until completely incorporated, about 30 seconds. Using a rubber spatula, give the batter a final stir.

3. Divide the batter evenly between the prepared cake pans and smooth with a spatula. Bake until a toothpick inserted into the centers comes out clean, about 25 minutes, rotating the cake pans halfway through baking. Cool the cakes in the pans for 10 minutes, then turn out onto a wire rack to cool completely, at least 1 hour.

4. FOR THE FROSTING: With an electric mixer, beat the butter, confectioners' sugar, and salt on medium-high speed in a large bowl until fluffy, about 3 minutes, scraping down the sides of the bowl as needed. Add the

cream cheese, 1 piece at a time, and beat until incorporated, about 30 seconds. Beat in the vanilla. Refrigerate until ready to use.

5. TO ASSEMBLE: Place one cake layer on a cake plate or cardboard round. Spread 2 cups of the frosting evenly across the top of the cake with a spatula. Place the second cake layer on top, then spread the remaining frosting evenly over the top and sides of the cake. Serve.

WHERE THINGS CAN GO WRONG: This recipe must be prepared with natural cocoa powder. Dutch-processed cocoa will not yield the proper color or rise.

WHAT YOU CAN DO AHEAD OF TIME: The cakes can be cooled completely (unfrosted), wrapped tightly in plastic wrap, and frozen for up to 1 month. Thaw the cakes, still wrapped, at room temperature, then remove the plastic wrap and frost.

NOTES FROM THE TEST KITCHEN

TO DYE FOR
We prefer liquid food coloring to gel or paste colors; the liquid is much easier to incorporate and better distributes the cocoa powder. Look for the large bottle of McCormick Red Food Color (found alongside the flavorings and extracts in most supermarkets) so you won't have to buy the multi-pack and be left, as we were, with dozens of bottles of blue, green, and yellow coloring.

THE BEST ROUND CAKE PAN
A good all-purpose cake pan should have straight, tall sides (at least 2 inches high). We tested 8 pans that fit this description. All of the pans were passable, but the nonstick pans stood out. The dark coating on these pans promotes better browning than shiny surfaces and yields more attractive cakes. The **Chicago Metallic Professional Lifetime Non-Stick** ($14.95) was testers' top choice, and it is well suited to a wide range of cakes.

ITALIAN ALMOND CAKE

SERVES 8 TO 10

WHAT MAKES THIS A BEST RECIPE: This simple Italian-style almond cake is one of our favorite desserts. It is as good plain as it is topped with fresh berries and whipped cream or lightly sweetened mascarpone. We have tasted a whole range of almond cakes, from sweet and sticky confections to those with a dry, crumbly crumb and almond flavor that is barely discernible or overly artificial (from too much almond extract). This recipe produces a rustic cake with a pound cake–like crumb and only a slightly sweetened almond flavor. What sets this recipe apart from all others is that its flavor comes from almonds, not almond extract. To bring out the nutty richness of the almonds, we toasted them lightly until fragrant. Then it was a matter of how much flour to add so as not to sacrifice the cake's singular base of almond flour. Tasters liked the ratio of ¾ cup cake flour to 3½ cups almonds (ground fine in a food processor). Baking powder gave our cake the lift and texture it needed, and three eggs gave the cake good structure with a light spring and tender crumb. Milk enriched the batter. We like to eat this cake warm, but it is also memorable at room temperature.

3½ cups (about 14 ounces) blanched, slivered almonds, toasted and cooled
1¼ cups (8¾ ounces) sugar
    Pinch salt
¾   cup (3 ounces) cake flour
½   teaspoon baking powder
8   tablespoons (1 stick) unsalted butter, at room temperature
3   large eggs, at room temperature
½   cup whole milk

1. Adjust an oven rack to the middle position and heat the oven to 350 degrees. Lightly coat a 9-inch springform pan with vegetable oil spray, then line the bottom with parchment paper.

2. Process the almonds, ½ cup of the sugar, and salt in a food processor until very finely ground with a texture that resembles flour, 10 to 15 seconds. Add the flour and baking powder and pulse to incorporate, about 5 pulses; set aside.

3. With an electric mixer, beat the butter and remaining ¾ cup sugar on medium-high speed in a large bowl until fluffy, about 3 minutes, scraping down the sides of the bowl as needed. Add the eggs, 1 at a time, beating briefly after each addition to incorporate, about 1 minute. Add the ground almond mixture and beat until just incorporated, about 30 seconds. Add the milk and beat until just incorporated, about 30 seconds more.

4. Scrape the batter into the prepared pan and smooth with a spatula. Bake until the cake is puffed and golden on top and a toothpick inserted into the center comes out clean, 30 to 40 minutes, rotating the pan halfway through baking.

5. Cool the cake in the pan for 15 minutes, then remove the sides of the pan and let the cake cool to room temperature, about 2 hours, before removing the cake pan bottom. Serve warm or at room temperature.

WHERE THINGS CAN GO WRONG: Low-fat and nonfat milk cannot be substituted for the whole milk. Over-toasting the almonds will result in a cake with a dry, crumbly texture.

WHAT YOU CAN DO AHEAD OF TIME: The cake can be cooled completely, wrapped tightly in plastic wrap, and stored at room temperature for up to 5 days, or frozen for up to 1 month. If frozen, let the cake thaw completely at room temperature, 2 to 4 hours, then serve warm. To heat, warm the cake on a baking sheet in a 350-degree oven for 10 to 15 minutes.

LEMON LAYER CAKE
SERVES 10 TO 12

WHAT MAKES THIS A BEST RECIPE: Special occasions deserve an exceptional dessert, and nothing fits the bill better than this lemon layer cake, with its tangy, creamy lemon filling, tender, delicate cake, and sweet, fluffy frosting. The cake layer is a white butter cake: nicely flavored by butter yet lighter than the yellow cake due to the use of egg whites only (no yolks), with a fine crumb and texture. For the lemon filling, we made a smooth and creamy lemon curd, a combination of sugar, lemon juice, butter, and eggs cooked together until it reaches the consistency of custard. We also found that a little gelatin did a beautiful job of firming up the curd without marring its lush texture or changing its intense flavor. We were determined to find something lighter than buttercream for the icing, and we landed on an old-fashioned classic: seven-minute icing. This pure white icing is exceptionally light and glossy, and tasters found it to be an ideal topping for our delicate cake. To improve on the classic, we cut back on the sugar (by a quarter), added a squeeze of lemon juice, and used an electric mixer to do the work for us. Finally, we added a spoonful of corn syrup to the icing, which lent an impressive luster. With swirling peaks of white icing, this light, lemony cake is fashionable enough for any special occasion.

LEMON CURD FILLING

- 1 teaspoon unflavored gelatin
- 1 cup juice from 6 lemons
- 1½ cups (10½ ounces) sugar
- ⅛ teaspoon salt
- 4 large eggs, plus 6 large egg yolks (reserve egg whites for the cake)
- 8 tablespoons (1 stick) unsalted butter, cut into ½-inch cubes and frozen

CAKE

- 12 tablespoons (1½ sticks) unsalted butter, cut into 12 pieces, softened but still cool, plus more for the pans
- 2¼ cups (9 ounces) cake flour, plus more for the pans
- 1 cup whole milk, at room temperature
- 6 large egg whites, at room temperature, reserved from filling
- 2 teaspoons vanilla extract
- 1¾ cups (12¼ ounces) sugar
- 4 teaspoons baking powder
- 1 teaspoon salt

ICING

- 2 large egg whites
- 1 cup (7 ounces) sugar
- ¼ cup water
- 1 tablespoon fresh lemon juice
- 1 tablespoon light corn syrup

1. FOR THE FILLING: Sprinkle the gelatin over 1 tablespoon of the lemon juice in a small bowl. Cook the remaining lemon juice, sugar, and salt in a medium nonreactive saucepan over medium heat until the sugar dissolves and the mixture is hot but not boiling, about 2 minutes. Whisk the eggs and yolks together in a large nonreactive bowl. Whisking vigorously, slowly add the hot lemon-sugar mixture to the eggs. Return the mixture to the saucepan and cook over medium-low heat, stirring constantly, until the mixture registers 170 degrees on an instant-read thermometer and is thick enough to leave a trail when a spatula is scraped along the pan bottom, 4 to 6 minutes. Remove the pan from the heat and stir in the gelatin mixture until dissolved. Stir in the butter. Pour through a fine-mesh strainer into a clean nonreactive bowl and refrigerate, with plastic wrap pressed flush against its surface, until firm enough to spread, at least 4 hours.

2. FOR THE CAKE: Adjust an oven rack to the middle position and heat the oven to 350 degrees. Grease and flour two 9-inch cake pans and line the bottoms with parchment paper. Whisk the milk, egg whites, and vanilla together in a medium bowl.

3. Whisk the flour, sugar, baking powder, and salt together in a large bowl until combined. With an electric mixer on low speed, add the butter, one piece at a time, and beat until the mixture resembles moist crumbs. Add all but ½ cup of the milk mixture, increase the speed to medium, and beat until pale and fluffy, about 2 minutes. Turn the mixer to low speed and add the remaining ½ cup milk mixture, then increase to medium speed and beat for 30 seconds. Scrape down the sides of the bowl; mix at medium speed for 20 seconds. Divide the batter evenly between the prepared cake pans and smooth with a spatula.

4. Bake until a toothpick inserted into the centers comes out clean, 23 to 25 minutes, rotating the cake pans halfway through baking. Cool the cakes in the pans for 10 minutes, then invert onto a greased wire rack; peel off and discard the parchment rounds. Invert the cakes again and cool completely before assembling, about 2 hours.

5. TO ASSEMBLE: Using a large serrated knife, cut each cake into two even layers. Place the bottom of one cake layer on a cake plate or cardboard round. Spread 1 cup of the lemon filling evenly across the top of the cake with a spatula, leaving a ½-inch border around the edge. Replace the top cake layer, then spread 1 more cup of the filling on top. Place the bottom half of the second cake layer on top, then spread the remaining 1 cup filling on top. Place the last cake layer on top. Smooth out any filling that has leaked from the sides of the cake. Wrap in plastic wrap and refrigerate while making the icing.

6. FOR THE ICING: Combine all the ingredients in a large heatproof bowl; set the bowl over a medium saucepan containing 1 inch of simmering water, and stir constantly until the mixture registers 160 degrees on an instant-read thermometer, 5 to 10 minutes. Remove the bowl from the heat and with an electric mixer on medium speed, beat until soft peaks form, about 5 minutes. Increase the speed to medium-high and beat until stiff peaks form and the mixture has cooled to room temperature, about 5 minutes more. Spread the frosting evenly over the top and sides of the cake. Serve.

WHAT YOU CAN DO AHEAD OF TIME: The cakes can be cooled completely (unfrosted), wrapped tightly in plastic wrap, and frozen for up to 1 month. Thaw the cakes, still wrapped, at room temperature, then remove the plastic wrap and frost. The filling can be refrigerated in an airtight container for up to 1 day. Fold it with a rubber spatula to loosen and recombine it before spreading it onto the cake layers.

NOTES FROM THE TEST KITCHEN

SEVEN-MINUTE MAGIC
Along with its fluffy texture and glossy sheen, seven-minute icing offers the fringe benefit of retaining its volume for at least three days. What makes the egg whites in this old-fashioned recipe more stable than egg whites whipped for a mousse or a soufflé? Beating raw egg whites and sugar temporarily relaxes the tightly wound egg proteins, allowing air to be trapped inside the resulting matrix. The foam this produces is impermanent, however, and will begin to deflate soon after being whipped. Cooking the egg whites and sugar to 160 degrees causes the coiled egg proteins to permanently relax. When the warm mixture is then whipped, the egg proteins remain unraveled as they cool, forming a stable network that traps sugar and water. So the icing stays shiny, airy, and smooth long enough for you to enjoy the entire cake.

NO HEAT = WEAK FOAM
After just 30 minutes, the foam made by whipping raw egg whites with sugar and other ingredients has lost most of its volume.

HEAT = STABLE FOAM
After 24 hours, the foam made by heating the egg whites with sugar and other ingredients and then whipping still holds its volume.

CHOCOLATE BLACKOUT CAKE

SERVES 10 TO 12

WHAT MAKES THIS A BEST RECIPE: Mention Ebinger's to most Brooklynites over the age of forty and you'll see a sparkle of nostalgia in their eyes. Bring up Chocolate Blackout Cake and you might actually see a tear or two. When the Brooklyn-based chain of bakeries closed its doors, the borough went into mourning. On that fateful day, August 27, 1972, the *New York Times* ran a story titled, "Tears Replace the Coffee Cakes." Of all the lost Ebinger's recipes, none has received more attention in the past thirty-five years than its Chocolate Blackout Cake, which marries fudgy, dark chocolate layers with a rich, creamy chocolate pudding that acts as both filling and frosting. But what really sets this cake apart is its signature shaggy coating of chocolate cake crumbs. Blackout Cake got its name from the blackout drills performed by the Civilian Defense Corps during World War II. When the navy sent its ships to sea from the Brooklyn Navy Yard, the streets of the borough were "blacked out" to avoid silhouetting the battleships against the cityscapes of Brooklyn and Manhattan. The cake was so named because of its darkly chocolate—practically black—appearance. According to some, the crumbled cake crumbs on top are reminiscent of a city skyline. Ebinger's original recipe was never published, leaving cookbook authors and Brooklyn grandmothers to rely on their taste buds to reproduce "authentic" versions. After much testing and streamlining, we came up with our own version. We focused our testing on creating a simple cake with big chocolate flavor. We found the best results by using Dutch-processed cocoa powder bloomed in melted butter and combined with buttermilk, which carried its flavor through the cake; brewed coffee further enhanced the nuances of the cocoa. We did try adding melted chocolate to the batter but that made the cake dense and gummy. We also found that we could make the batter entirely in a saucepan on the stovetop, avoiding dirtying all the dishes usually required when making a layer cake.

PUDDING

1¼	cups (8¾ ounces) granulated sugar
6	ounces unsweetened chocolate, chopped
2	cups half-and-half
1	cup whole milk
¼	cup cornstarch
½	teaspoon salt
2	teaspoons vanilla extract

CAKE

8	tablespoons (1 stick) unsalted butter, plus more for the pans
1½	cups (7½ ounces) unbleached all-purpose flour, plus more for the pans
2	teaspoons baking powder
½	teaspoon baking soda
½	teaspoon salt
¾	cup (2¼ ounces) Dutch-processed cocoa powder
1	cup brewed coffee
1	cup buttermilk
1	cup (7 ounces) packed light brown sugar
1	cup (7 ounces) granulated sugar
2	large eggs
1	teaspoon vanilla extract

1. FOR THE PUDDING: Cook the granulated sugar, chocolate, half-and-half, milk, cornstarch, and salt in a large saucepan over medium heat, whisking constantly, until the chocolate is melted and the mixture begins to bubble, 2 to 4 minutes. Stir in the vanilla. Transfer the pudding to a large bowl and refrigerate, with plastic wrap pressed flush against its surface, until cold and set, at least 4 hours or up to 1 day.

2. FOR THE CAKE: Adjust an oven rack to the middle position and heat the oven to 325 degrees. Grease and flour two 8-inch cake pans. Whisk the flour, baking powder, baking soda, and salt together in a medium bowl. Melt the butter in a large saucepan over medium heat. Stir in the cocoa and cook until fragrant, about 1 minute. Off the heat, whisk in the coffee, buttermilk, and sugars until dissolved. Whisk in the eggs and vanilla, then slowly whisk in the flour mixture. Divide the batter evenly between the prepared cake pans and smooth with a spatula.

3. Bake until a toothpick inserted into the centers comes out clean, 30 to 35 minutes, rotating the cake pans halfway through baking. Cool the cakes in the pans for

15 minutes, then invert onto a wire rack. Cool the cakes to room temperature before frosting, at least 1 hour.

4. TO ASSEMBLE: Using a large serrated knife, slice each cake into two even layers. Following the photos, crumble one cake layer into medium crumbs and set aside. Place one cake layer on a cake plate or cardboard round. Spread 1 cup of the pudding over the cake layer and top with another layer. Repeat with 1 cup more pudding and the last cake layer. Spread the remaining pudding evenly over the top and sides of the cake. Sprinkle the cake crumbs evenly over the top and sides of cake, pressing lightly to adhere the crumbs. Serve.

WHERE THINGS CAN GO WRONG: Be sure to give the pudding and the cake enough time to cool or you'll end up with runny pudding and gummy cake.

WHAT YOU CAN DO AHEAD OF TIME: The cakes can be cooled completely (unfrosted), wrapped tightly in plastic wrap, and frozen for up to 1 month. Thaw the cakes, still wrapped, at room temperature, then remove the plastic wrap and frost.

NOTES FROM THE TEST KITCHEN

HOW TO ASSEMBLE BLACKOUT CAKE

1. Using your hands, crumble one cake layer into medium-sized crumbs.

2. Spread the pudding all over the top and sides of the cake.

3. Sprinkle the reserved cake crumbs all over the top and sides of the cake, then use your hands to gently press the crumbs into the pudding.

HOT FUDGE PUDDING CAKE
SERVES 6 TO 8

WHAT MAKES THIS A BEST RECIPE: Served warm with a scoop of vanilla ice cream, hot fudge pudding cake has got to be one of the most soul-satisfying desserts. Unfortunately, most recipes for hot fudge pudding cake read like recipes for disaster. You mix flour, sugar, cocoa powder, baking powder, milk, and oil by hand—much like a brownie batter. Once the batter is scraped into the pan, the fun starts. A mixture of cocoa powder and sugar is sprinkled over the top, and then boiling water is poured into the pan. The "batter" goes into the oven—no stirring allowed—looking like a mess. But as it bakes, the water, cocoa, and sugar bubble and brew and—as if by magic—form a chocolate sauce while the cake rises to the top. The result is a chewy, brownie-like cake saturated with pockets of pudding-style chocolate sauce. It's scooped out of the dish (not sliced like a regular cake) and usually gilded with a scoop of ice cream or a dollop of whipped cream that melts into the hot pudding. Although this might sound like chocolate heaven (chocolate cake and chocolate sauce!), this recipe isn't without problems. What looks deceptively rich and fudgy often has little chocolate flavor, and the cake layer can be hit or miss—it can easily get too dry or too wet in the center. Our goal was to develop a hot fudge pudding cake with the texture and flavor of a brownie and plenty of spoon-clinging pudding sauce dotted throughout. For fuller, rounder chocolate flavor, we switched from the natural cocoa powder used in most old-fashioned recipes to Dutch-processed cocoa, the European-style cocoa now available in American supermarkets. We also doubled the amount of cocoa in the batter. A big handful of semisweet chocolate chips added another layer of chocolate flavor and ensured plenty of gooey pockets in the baked cake. Trading flavorless vegetable oil for melted butter was another big improvement. For a more brownie-like texture, we added an egg yolk. We found that the success of the sauce depends on using the right ratio of boiling water, sugar, and cocoa. Too much

An unexpected technique turns regular pantry ingredients into a gooey, double-chocolate delight.

water (a common problem in the recipes we tested) and the sauce turned out thin and watery. We found that 1 cup of boiling water poured over ½ cup of sugar and ¼ cup of cocoa created a thick sauce with solid chocolate flavor. Our recipe has big chocolate flavor to match its gooey, fudgy appearance.

- 1 cup (7 ounces) sugar
- ½ cup (1½ ounces) Dutch-processed cocoa powder
- 1 cup (5 ounces) unbleached all-purpose flour
- 2 teaspoons baking powder
- ¼ teaspoon salt
- ½ cup milk
- 4 tablespoons (½ stick) unsalted butter, melted
- 1 large egg yolk
- 2 teaspoons vanilla extract
- ½ cup semisweet chocolate chips
- 1 cup boiling water
- Vanilla ice cream or whipped cream, for serving

1. Adjust an oven rack to the middle position and heat the oven to 350 degrees. Lightly coat an 8-inch square cake pan with vegetable oil spray. Whisk ½ cup of the sugar and ¼ cup of the cocoa in a small bowl.

2. Whisk the flour, the remaining ½ cup sugar, remaining ¼ cup cocoa, baking powder, and salt together in a large bowl. Whisk the milk, butter, egg yolk, and vanilla together in a medium bowl until smooth. Stir the milk mixture into the flour mixture until just combined. Fold in the chocolate chips (the batter will be stiff).

3. Scrape the batter into the prepared pan and smooth with a spatula. Sprinkle the reserved cocoa mixture evenly over the top. Carefully pour the boiling water over the cocoa. Do not stir.

4. Bake until the top of the cake looks crackled, the sauce is bubbling, and a toothpick inserted into the cakey area comes out with moist crumbs attached, about 25 minutes. Cool on a wire rack for about 10 minutes. To serve, scoop the warm cake into individual serving bowls and top with vanilla ice cream.

WHERE THINGS CAN GO WRONG: Do not overbake this cake or the pudding sauce will burn in the pan and the cake will be dry, not fudgy.

NOTES FROM THE TEST KITCHEN

IS IT DONE YET?
This highly unconventional cake breaks most of the usual rules, including how to judge when it's ready to come out of the oven.

1. When the top is crackled like a brownie and the sauce is bubbling up from the bottom, it's time to start testing for doneness. For the most accurate test, insert the toothpick close to the edge, where the cake is the firmest. (Don't insert the toothpick in the center, where the cake should be gooey.)

2. The toothpick should have large, moist crumbs attached. Check at least 2 spots to be sure you're not hitting a melted chocolate chip.

SOUR CREAM COFFEE CAKE

MAKES TWO 9-INCH CAKES, EACH SERVING 6

WHAT MAKES THIS A BEST RECIPE: A sour cream coffee cake with mounds of streusel topping is the king of coffee cakes. Not only does it taste rich and satisfying, but it is easy to make and can be served any time of day—not just at breakfast. And since you can hold the batter overnight in the fridge or freeze the batter for an anytime coffee cake, this simple recipe can be a lifesaver on busy mornings. The cake, made with all-purpose flour, white and dark brown sugar, eggs, butter, sour cream, baking powder, and baking soda, is a straightforward recipe that is sturdy enough to support the streusel topping. Three eggs produced a moist crumb just dense enough, and gave the cake a nice golden color. Crispy, crunchy, yet melt-in-your-mouth streusel requires a careful balance of sugar, flour, and butter; nuts and spices also warrant careful scrutiny. We liked the appearance and flavor from the combined use of granulated and light brown sugar. We also found that flour was necessary to keep the sugar in the streusel from melting or congealing in cement-like shards. Tasters unanimously agreed that nuts were needed, and pecans, almonds, and walnuts all tasted great. Cinnamon—and a hefty dose of it—was the only spice needed to lend warmth to the streusel's flavor.

STREUSEL

- ⅓ cup (2⅓ ounces) packed light brown sugar
- ⅓ cup (2⅓ ounces) granulated sugar
- ⅓ cup (1⅔ ounces) unbleached all-purpose flour
- 4 tablespoons (½ stick) unsalted butter, cut into ½ -inch pieces and chilled
- 1 tablespoon ground cinnamon
- 1 cup pecans, almonds, or walnuts, chopped

CAKE

- 3 cups (15 ounces) unbleached all-purpose flour
- 1 tablespoon baking powder
- 1 teaspoon baking soda
- 1 teaspoon ground cinnamon
- ¼ teaspoon salt
- 1¾ cups sour cream
- 1 cup (7 ounces) packed light brown sugar
- 1 cup (7 ounces) granulated sugar
- 3 large eggs
- 7 tablespoons unsalted butter, melted and cooled

1. FOR THE STREUSEL: Using your fingers, mix the sugars, flour, butter, and cinnamon together in a medium bowl until the mixture resembles coarse meal. Stir in the nuts and set aside.

2. FOR THE CAKE: Adjust an oven rack to the middle position and heat the oven to 350 degrees. Lightly coat two 9-inch cake pans with vegetable oil spray. Mix the flour, baking powder, baking soda, cinnamon, and salt together in a large bowl. Whisk the sour cream, sugars, eggs, and melted butter together in a medium bowl. Gently whisk the egg mixture into the flour mixture until smooth (do not overmix).

3. Scrape the batter into the prepared pans and smooth with a spatula. Sprinkle the streusel evenly over the top of both cakes.

4. Bake until the tops are golden and a toothpick inserted into the centers comes out with just a few crumbs attached, 25 to 30 minutes. Cool the cakes on a wire rack for 15 minutes before serving.

WHERE THINGS CAN GO WRONG: Do not try to bake all of the batter in one large cake pan because it will bake very unevenly.

WHAT YOU CAN DO AHEAD OF TIME: After sprinkling the streusel over the batter in step 3, the pans can be wrapped tightly in plastic wrap and refrigerated for up to 24 hours, or frozen for up to 1 month. (Do not thaw the frozen cakes before baking.) Bake as directed in step 4, increasing the baking time to 30 to 35 minutes if refrigerated, or 40 to 45 minutes if frozen.

SOUR CREAM COFFEE CAKE

INDIVIDUAL FALLEN CHOCOLATE CAKES
SERVES 8

WHAT MAKES THIS A BEST RECIPE: We love fallen chocolate cake because, despite its elegant appearance, it requires only a few ingredients *and* is very easy to make. This recipe yields an undercooked-in-the-center mound of intense, buttery chocolate cake, with an ethereal consistency. For the cake, we came up with a straightforward formula that consists of simply melting chocolate; beating whole eggs, sugar, and flavorings into a foam; and then folding the two together with a little flour for extra body. To mimic a restaurant dessert, we baked our cake in individual ramekins. Four hundred degrees was the best oven temperature, yielding a light, cake-like perimeter around a moist well of intense chocolate. And the best part of all: The batter can be poured into the ramekins, refrigerated, and then baked during dinner.

- 8 tablespoons (1 stick) unsalted butter, plus more for the ramekins
- 2 tablespoons unbleached all-purpose flour, plus more for the ramekins
- 8 ounces semisweet chocolate, chopped coarse
- ½ cup (3½ ounces) granulated sugar
- 4 large eggs plus 1 large egg yolk
- 1 teaspoon vanilla extract
- ¼ teaspoon salt

GARNISHES (OPTIONAL)
Confectioners' sugar or cocoa powder for dusting
Whipped cream for serving

1. Adjust an oven rack to the middle position and heat the oven to 400 degrees. Grease and flour eight 6-ounce ramekins or heatproof glass baking cups. Transfer the ramekins to a rimmed baking sheet. Meanwhile, melt the butter and chocolate in a medium heatproof bowl set over a pan of almost-simmering water, stirring occasionally, until smooth.

2. With an electric mixer, beat the granulated sugar, eggs, yolk, vanilla, and salt on high speed in a large bowl until the volume nearly triples, the color is very light, and the mixture drops from the beaters in a smooth, thick stream, 5 to 8 minutes. Scrape the egg mixture over the chocolate and butter mixture. Sprinkle the flour over the egg mixture, then gently fold until the mixture is uniformly colored. Ladle or pour the batter into the prepared ramekins.

3. Bake until the cakes have puffed about ½ inch above the rims of the ramekins, have a thin crust on top, and jiggle slightly at the center when the ramekins are shaken very gently, 12 to 13 minutes. Run a paring knife around the inside edges of the ramekins to loosen the cakes and invert onto serving plates; cool for 1 minute, then lift off the ramekins. Dust the cakes with confectioners' sugar, if using, and serve immediately with whipped cream, if using.

WHAT YOU CAN DO AHEAD OF TIME: The batter can be prepared through step 2, wrapped in plastic wrap, and refrigerated up to 8 hours. Return to room temperature for 30 minutes before baking.

NOTES FROM THE TEST KITCHEN
GETTING THE TEXTURE RIGHT

1. Although acceptable in a standard cake, this texture is too dry for this recipe.

2. Just a bit of uncooked batter should ooze out of the center when the cake is cut.

3. A puddle of uncooked batter flowing out of the cake's center is unappealing.

BLUEBERRY BOY BAIT

SERVES 12

This coffee cake has a crunchy cinnamon-sugar topping and is chock-full of sweet blueberries.

WHAT MAKES THIS A BEST RECIPE: After one bite of this moist and simple blueberry coffee cake, you'll be hooked. We found the source of this recipe in a 1954 edition of the *Chicago Tribune*. A fifteen-year-old girl named Adrienne (aka Renny) Powell of Chicago entered her dessert—Blueberry Boy Bait—in the junior division of the 1954 Pillsbury Grand National Baking Contest. She won second place, which included a $2,000 cash prize plus a promise to print her recipe in *Pillsbury's 5th Grand National Recipes Cookbook*. Renny named the cake (a family recipe) for the effect it had on teenage boys—one bite and they were hooked. For deeper flavor, we exchanged the shortening in the original recipe for butter and half of the granulated sugar for brown sugar. For more structure, we added an extra egg. And since this cake has "blueberry" in its name, we doubled the amount.

CAKE

- 16 tablespoons (2 sticks) unsalted butter, softened, plus more for the pan
- 2 cups (10 ounces) plus 1 teaspoon unbleached all-purpose flour, plus more for the pan
- 1 tablespoon baking powder
- 1 teaspoon salt
- ¾ cup (5¼ ounces) packed light brown sugar
- ½ cup (3½ ounces) granulated sugar
- 3 large eggs
- 1 cup whole milk
- ½ cup (2½ ounces) blueberries, fresh or frozen (see note)

TOPPING

- ½ cup (2½ ounces) blueberries, fresh or frozen (see note)
- ¼ cup (1¾ ounces) granulated sugar
- ½ teaspoon ground cinnamon

1. FOR THE CAKE: Adjust an oven rack to the middle position and heat the oven to 350 degrees. Grease and flour a 13 by 9-inch baking pan.

2. Whisk 2 cups of the flour, baking powder, and salt together in a medium bowl. With an electric mixer, beat the butter and sugars on medium-high speed in a large bowl until fluffy, about 3 minutes, scraping down the sides of the bowl as needed. Add the eggs, one at a time, beating until just incorporated. Reduce the speed to medium and beat in one-third of the flour mixture until incorporated; beat in half of the milk. Beat in half of the remaining flour mixture, then the remaining milk, and finally the remaining flour mixture. Toss the blueberries with the remaining 1 teaspoon flour, then gently fold into the batter. Scrape the batter into the prepared pan and smooth with a spatula.

3. FOR THE TOPPING: Scatter the blueberries over the top of the batter. Stir the granulated sugar and cinnamon together in a small bowl and sprinkle over the batter. Bake until a toothpick inserted into the center of the cake comes out clean, 45 to 50 minutes. Cool the cake in the pan for 20 minutes, then turn out and place on a serving platter or cutting board (topping side up). Cut into squares and serve warm or at room temperature.

WHERE THINGS CAN GO WRONG: If using frozen blueberries, do not let them thaw, as they will turn the batter a blue-green color.

WHAT YOU CAN DO AHEAD OF TIME: The cake can be stored in an airtight container at room temperature for up to 3 days.

CLASSIC POUND CAKE

MAKES ONE 9 BY 5-INCH LOAF

WHAT MAKES THIS A BEST RECIPE: Don't be fooled by its short ingredient list—pound cake is far from simple. More often than not, it bakes up heavy, squat, and dense. Pound cake recipes date back to the eighteenth century and originally called for a pound each of flour, sugar, butter, and eggs. But the historical recipes we've tried were too heavy and dense to please modern palates. For this recipe, we put an end to all the nonsense and retooled a classic recipe to make it more reliable. We found that giving the cake lift and a lighter crumb without the addition of a chemical leavener demands maximum aeration from the butter. After much trial and error, we realized that warm butter is too slack to aerate, so our recipe starts with chilly 60-degree butter. After the butter and sugar were properly creamed, we beat the eggs and added them very gradually, which produced a more voluminous batter and higher rise in the cake. It was time to add the flour, and we liked the more delicate crumb that cake flour produced. We found that sifting the flour over the batter (and folding it in by hand) lightened and fluffed the flour, making it easier to incorporate, which also reduced the risk of overworking the batter. We serve this cake on its own, but it is also great with fresh berries and whipped cream.

16 tablespoons (2 sticks) unsalted butter, cold, plus more for the pan

3 large eggs plus 3 large egg yolks

2 teaspoons vanilla extract

1¾ cups (7 ounces) cake flour, plus more for the pan

½ teaspoon salt

1¼ cups (8¾ ounces) sugar

1. Cut the butter into 1-tablespoon pieces and place in the bowl of a standing mixer; let stand at room temperature 20 to 30 minutes to soften slightly (the butter should reach no more than 60 degrees). Using a dinner fork, beat the eggs, egg yolks, and vanilla in a liquid measuring cup until combined. Let the egg mixture stand at room temperature until ready to use.

2. Adjust an oven rack to the middle position and heat the oven to 325 degrees. Grease and flour a 9 by 5-inch loaf pan.

3. In a standing mixer fitted with the flat beater, beat the butter and salt at medium-high speed until shiny, smooth, and creamy, 2 to 3 minutes, scraping the bottom and sides of the bowl once with a rubber spatula. Reduce the speed to medium; with the mixer running, gradually pour in the sugar (this should take about 60 seconds). Once all the sugar is added, increase the speed to medium-high and beat until the mixture is fluffy and almost white in color, 5 to 8 minutes, scraping the bottom and sides of the bowl once. With the mixer running at medium speed, gradually add the egg mixture in a slow, steady stream; this should take 60 to 90 seconds. Scrape the bottom and sides of the bowl; beat the mixture at medium-high speed until light and fluffy, 3 to 4 minutes (the mixture may look slightly broken). Remove the bowl from the mixer; scrape the bottom and sides.

4. In 3 additions, sift the flour over the butter/egg mixture; after each addition, fold gently with a rubber spatula until combined. Scrape along the bottom of the bowl to ensure that the batter is homogenous.

5. Transfer the batter to the prepared loaf pan and smooth the surface with a rubber spatula. Bake until golden brown and a wooden skewer inserted into the center of the cake comes out clean, about 70 to 80 minutes. Cool the cake in the pan on a wire rack for 15 minutes; invert the cake onto a wire rack, then turn the cake right side up. Cool the cake on a wire rack to room temperature, about 2 hours. Slice and serve.

WHERE THINGS CAN GO WRONG: This pound cake batter is so delicate that it will deflate if you add the eggs or flour too quickly. Add the eggs in a slow, steady stream, and be sure to sift the flour over the batter in three additions, folding after each addition with a spatula.

WHAT YOU CAN DO AHEAD OF TIME: The cake can be cooled completely, wrapped tightly in plastic wrap, and stored at room temperature for up to 3 days.

Pound cake has a simple ingredient list, but the mixing method requires precise attention to detail.

NOTES FROM THE TEST KITCHEN

OUR FAVORITE LOAF PAN

Seven years after applauding the Baker's Secret Non-Stick Loaf Pan as the best available choice, we wanted to see if anything new could best this bargain pan, which is available for $6 in supermarkets. Our primary concerns were the size of the pan and browning. Seven pound cakes, seven loaves of sandwich bread, and hours of baking later, we had a motley crew of baked goods and a new favorite loaf pan: the **Williams-Sonoma Goldtouch** ($19). The gold-colored nonstick surface yielded baked goods with a perfectly even, honeyed-copper crust.

SUCCESSFUL CREAMING

Cool butter and thorough mixing are essential to our pound cake recipe. We tried our recipe in four standing mixers and with four handheld mixers (all set to medium-high speed) and found that the creaming time varied from 5 to 8 minutes. These guidelines will help you determine when the butter is at the correct temperature and when the butter and sugar are properly creamed.

ROOM TEMPERATURE BUTTER
Room temperature butter (70 degrees) yields completely to pressure.

CHILLY BUTTER
Cool butter (60 degrees) yields slightly to pressure and will crack when pressed.

OVERCREAMED BATTER
Once the sugar has been incorporated, the butter temperature will rise to about 75 degrees. The batter will be very soft and look slick, shiny, and wet.

PERFECTLY CREAMED BATTER
Once the sugar has been incorporated, the butter temperature will rise to about 68 degrees. The batter will be light, fluffy, and off-white in color.

FLAT CAKE
The cake will be flat and dense.

DOMED CAKE
The cake will dome nicely.

NEW ORLEANS BOURBON BREAD PUDDING
WITH BOURBON SAUCE
SERVES 8 TO 10

WHAT MAKES THIS A BEST RECIPE: This recipe for bourbon bread pudding features a rich, scoopable custard that envelops the bread with a perfect balance of sweet spiciness and musky bourbon flavor. There's no doubt that it is an adult dessert. The history behind New Orleans's most famous dessert is as eclectic as the city itself. The basic custard and bread combination is of English origin. The bread—which in New Orleans is almost always a baguette—is from France. The addition of raisins to the custard can be credited to German settlers, while it was the Irish who infused the cream base with various liquors. The bourbon, of course, originally came from Kentucky traders. Our recipe is great because instead of cutting the bread into perfect cubes, we tore the baguette into ragged pieces for a more rustic look. We then toasted the pieces to a deep golden brown, which enriched their flavor and gave the bread a crispness that helped to prevent the finished dish from turning soggy. For a rich, caramel flavor, we used brown sugar (rather than the usual white sugar) to sweeten the custard, which in turn enhanced the bourbon. To make sure that our custard was creamy, not curdled, we replaced the traditional whole eggs with just egg yolks, lowered the oven temperature (to 300 degrees), and covered the baking dish with foil. As a finishing touch, we sprinkled cinnamon, sugar, and some butter over the top, which caramelized and formed a golden crust. And for a real taste of New Orleans, we drizzled servings of the pudding with a warm bourbon-based cream sauce.

BREAD PUDDING

- 6 tablespoons (¾ stick) unsalted butter, cubed and chilled, plus more for the pan
- 1 (18-to-20-inch) French baguette, torn into 1-inch pieces (10 cups)
- 1 cup golden raisins
- ¾ cup bourbon
- 3 cups heavy cream
- 1½ cups (10½ ounces) packed light brown sugar
- 1 cup whole milk
- 8 large egg yolks
- 1 tablespoon vanilla extract
- 1½ teaspoons ground cinnamon
- ¼ teaspoon ground nutmeg
- ¼ teaspoon salt
- 3 tablespoons granulated sugar

BOURBON SAUCE

- 1½ teaspoons cornstarch
- ¼ cup bourbon
- ¾ cup heavy cream
- 2 tablespoons granulated sugar
- 2 teaspoons unsalted butter, cut into small pieces
- Pinch salt

1. FOR THE BREAD PUDDING: Adjust an oven rack to the middle position and heat the oven to 450 degrees. Grease a 13 by 9-inch baking pan. Arrange the bread in a single layer on a baking sheet and bake until crisp and browned, about 12 minutes, turning the pieces over and rotating the baking sheet halfway through baking. Let the bread cool. Reduce the oven temperature to 300 degrees.

2. Meanwhile, heat the raisins with ½ cup of the bourbon in a small saucepan over medium-high heat until the bourbon begins to simmer, 2 to 3 minutes. Strain the mixture, reserving the bourbon and raisins separately.

3. Whisk the cream, brown sugar, milk, yolks, vanilla, 1 teaspoon of the cinnamon, nutmeg, and salt together in a large bowl. Whisk in the remaining ¼ cup bourbon

and the bourbon used to plump the raisins. Toss in the toasted bread until evenly coated. Let the mixture sit until the bread begins to absorb the custard, about 30 minutes, tossing occasionally. (If the majority of the bread is still hard when squeezed, soak for another 15 to 20 minutes.)

4. Pour half of the bread mixture into the prepared baking pan and sprinkle with half of the raisins. Pour the remaining bread mixture into the pan and sprinkle with the remaining raisins. Cover with foil and bake for 45 minutes.

5. Meanwhile, mix the granulated sugar and the remaining ½ teaspoon cinnamon in a small bowl. Using your fingers, cut the butter into the sugar mixture until the mixture is the size of small peas. Remove the foil from the pudding, sprinkle with the butter mixture, and bake, uncovered, until the custard is just set, 20 to 25 minutes. Increase the oven temperature to 450 degrees and bake until the top of the pudding forms a golden crust, about 2 minutes. Transfer the pudding to a wire rack and cool for at least 30 minutes or up to 2 hours.

6. FOR THE SAUCE: Meanwhile, whisk the cornstarch and 2 tablespoons of the bourbon together in a small bowl. Heat the cream and granulated sugar in a small saucepan over medium heat until the sugar dissolves. Whisk in the cornstarch mixture and bring to a boil. Reduce the heat to low and cook until the sauce thickens, 3 to 5 minutes. Off the heat, stir in the remaining 2 tablespoons bourbon, butter, and salt. Drizzle the warm sauce over the bread pudding before serving.

WHERE THINGS CAN GO WRONG: After soaking the bread in the custard for 30 minutes, if the majority of the bread is still hard when squeezed, be sure to soak it for another 15 to 20 minutes, or the bread cubes will be dry when baked.

WHAT YOU CAN DO AHEAD OF TIME: The sauce can be cooled completely and refrigerated in an airtight container for up to 5 days. Reheat in a small saucepan over medium-low heat.

NOTES FROM THE TEST KITCHEN

SECRETS TO NEW ORLEANS BOURBON BREAD PUDDING

1. Toasting the torn French baguette enhances its flavor and texture.

2. Soaking the bread for 30 minutes in the custard softens the bread without turning it soggy.

3. Covering the bread pudding with foil allows the custard to set without drying out.

4. Sprinkling the partially baked pudding with a sugary topping adds a crisp crust.

BLACK-BOTTOM CUPCAKES
MAKES 24 CUPCAKES

WHAT MAKES THIS A BEST RECIPE: Black-bottom cupcakes—with their near-black cake, moist, fudgy bottom, and creamy center of tangy cheesecake studded with mini chocolate chips—are our favorite. However, all too often they are greasy, slumped, and devoid of rich chocolate flavor. As for the cheesecake centers, they bake up dry, chalky, or completely separated from the cake in sunken craters. We love this recipe because it delivers a cake that has big chocolate flavor and is sturdy enough to support the cheesecake filling. The cake portion gets its dark color and chocolate flavor from cocoa. Our tasters much preferred the rounded flavor of Dutch-processed cocoa to natural cocoa. Adding a little sour cream to the batter accentuated the chocolate and added richness. Most recipes consist of cream cheese, sugar, and a whole egg, but the yolk lent an unappealing yellow hue and mealy texture when baked. Using two whites added moisture and helped the filling look better, but it also dulled the tang of the cream cheese. Since we were already using sour cream in the cake batter, we added some to the cheesecake filling, and it restored a needed tang. The inclusion of mini chocolate chips made our filling complete.

16	ounces cream cheese, at room temperature
1¾	cups (12¼ ounces) sugar
¾	teaspoon salt
2	large egg whites, at room temperature
2	tablespoons plus ¾ cup sour cream, at room temperature
⅓	cup miniature semisweet chocolate chips
1½	cups (7½ ounces) unbleached all-purpose flour
½	cup (1½ ounces) Dutch-processed cocoa powder
1¼	teaspoons baking soda
1⅓	cups water
8	tablespoons (1 stick) unsalted butter, melted and cooled slightly
1	teaspoon vanilla extract

1. Adjust two oven racks to the upper- and lower-middle positions and heat the oven to 400 degrees. Line 2

We add sour cream to both the chocolate and cheesecake components to bring out the best in each.

standard muffin tins with cupcake liners.

2. With an electric mixer, beat the cream cheese, ½ cup of the sugar, and ¼ teaspoon of the salt in a medium bowl on medium speed until smooth, about 30 seconds. Add the egg whites and 2 tablespoons of the sour cream and beat until combined, about 1 minute. Stir in the chocolate chips and set aside.

3. Whisk the remaining 1¼ cups sugar, the remaining ½ teaspoon salt, flour, cocoa, and baking soda together in a large bowl. Make a well in the center and whisk in the remaining ¾ cup sour cream, water, melted butter, and vanilla until just combined. Divide the batter evenly among the lined muffin cups and top each batter with 1 rounded tablespoon of the cream cheese mixture. Bake until the tops of the cupcakes just begin to crack, 23 to 25 minutes, rotating and switching the position of the muffin tins halfway through baking. Cool the cupcakes in the pans for 10 minutes, then transfer to a wire rack to cool completely. Serve.

WHERE THINGS CAN GO WRONG: Do not substitute regular chocolate chips for the miniature chips. Regular chips are much heavier and will sink to the bottom of the cupcakes.

WHAT YOU CAN DO AHEAD OF TIME: The cupcakes can be cooled completely and refrigerated in an airtight container for up to 2 days.

NEW YORK–STYLE CRUMB CAKE

NEW YORK–STYLE CRUMB CAKE

SERVES 8 TO 10

WHAT MAKES THIS A BEST RECIPE: Although crumb cake is not new on the baking scene, surprisingly few people can distinguish it from a regular streusel-topped coffee cake. This is because this quirky yet elegant cake has its origins deeply rooted in just one part of the United States, New York, where it arrived with the influx of German immigrants who came to the area in the late 1800s, their recipes for *Krummelkuchen* in hand. Some people associate crumb cake with Entenmann's, a Brooklyn bakery that has expanded into a national supermarket brand. Laden with shelf-stabilizing preservatives, this popular version of crumb cake doesn't do justice to the bakery-fresh original. Because we think everyone deserves a proper taste of this classic confection, we came up with a recipe to make at home—one that stands up to the legacy of authentic crumb cake. We started with the test kitchen's favorite yellow cake recipe, but we cut down on the butter and added buttermilk, which moistened the cake without making it greasy. The pièce de résistance of all crumb cakes is, of course, the crumb topping. We made the topping by combining sugar, brown sugar (for its butterscotchy flavor), and melted butter, with flour. When raw, the topping had a unified, dough-like consistency, which we broke apart with our fingers before sprinkling over the cake batter. These cohesive little nuggets held together when baked, giving our cake the quintessential crumb cake crumbs: sturdy on the outside, moist and tender on the inside. Just the right amount of cinnamon (¾ teaspoon) finished the crumbs off with some warm spice. Reducing the oven temperature, lengthening the baking time, and raising the oven rack to the upper-middle position gave the crumbs their irresistible golden edges. We had finally captured the essence of what made this cake a classic.

CRUMB TOPPING

- 8 tablespoons (1 stick) unsalted butter, melted and still warm
- ⅓ cup (2⅔ ounces) granulated sugar
- ⅓ cup (2⅔ ounces) packed dark brown sugar
- ¾ teaspoon ground cinnamon
- ⅛ teaspoon salt
- 1¾ cups (7 ounces) cake flour

CAKE

- 1¼ cups (5 ounces) cake flour (see note)
- ½ cup (3½ ounces) granulated sugar
- ¼ teaspoon baking soda
- ¼ teaspoon salt
- 6 tablespoons (¾ stick) unsalted butter, cut into 6 pieces, softened but still cool
- ⅓ cup buttermilk or plain low-fat yogurt
- 1 large egg plus 1 large yolk
- 1 teaspoon vanilla extract
  Confectioners' sugar for dusting

1. FOR THE TOPPING: Whisk the butter, sugars, cinnamon, and salt together in a medium bowl. Stir in the flour until the mixture resembles a thick, cohesive dough; set aside to cool to room temperature, 10 to 15 minutes.

2. FOR THE CAKE: Adjust an oven rack to the upper-middle position and heat the oven to 325 degrees. Line an 8-inch square baking pan with aluminum foil, allowing the extra foil to hang over the edges of the pan. Lightly coat the foil-lined pan with vegetable oil spray.

3. Whisk the flour, granulated sugar, baking soda, and salt in a large bowl until combined. With an electric mixer on low speed, add the butter, one piece at a time, beating until the mixture resembles moist crumbs, with no visible butter chunks remaining, 1 to 2 minutes. Add the buttermilk, egg, yolk, and vanilla and beat on medium-high speed until the batter is light and fluffy, about 1 minute, scraping down the sides of the bowl as needed.

4. Scrape the batter into the prepared pan and smooth with a spatula. Following the photos on page 306, break the crumb topping into large pea-sized pieces and spread in an even layer over the batter beginning with the edges and then working toward the center. Bake until the crumbs are golden and a skewer inserted into the center comes out clean, 35 to 40 minutes. Cool the cake in the pan on a wire rack for at least 30 minutes; remove from the baking pan by lifting the foil extensions. Dust with confectioners' sugar just before serving.

WHERE THINGS CAN GO WRONG: Don't be tempted to substitute all-purpose flour for the cake flour, as doing so will make a dry, tough cake. When topping the cake, take care not to push the crumbs into the batter.

WHAT YOU CAN DO AHEAD OF TIME: The cake can be cooled completely, wrapped tightly in plastic wrap, and stored at room temperature for up to 2 days. Dust with confectioners' sugar just before serving.

NOTES FROM THE TEST KITCHEN

YOU CAN DOUBLE IT
This recipe can be easily doubled and baked in a foil-lined and sprayed 13 by 9-inch baking pan. Increase the baking time to about 45 minutes.

DON'T BE TEMPTED

SUNKEN CAKE
If you use powdered buttermilk instead of the real thing, your crumb cake may sink as the batter will be thinner.

DRY CAKE
Using all-purpose flour instead of cake flour will make the cake crumb dry.

SECRETS TO BIGGER CRUMBS
Using both hands, break apart the crumb topping dough, rolling the broken dough between your thumb and forefinger to form crumbs about the size of large peas. Continue until all the dough has been broken down into crumbs. Sprinkle the crumbs evenly over the cake batter, breaking apart any larger chunks. Spread the crumbs from the outside of the cake toward the center so as not to make the center too heavy.

BREAKING THE DOUGH

PERFECT-SIZED CRUMBS

THE BEST SQUARE CAKE PAN
A square cake pan is a kitchen essential, but should you buy a glass, nonstick, or traditional metal model? We tested crumb cakes and corn bread in seven 8-inch pans to see how the various options performed. The **Williams-Sonoma Gold-touch** ($21) was our favorite. It produced evenly golden sides and bottoms on baked goods. This nonstick pan also yielded baked goods that stood a full 2 inches tall and sported straight (rather than flared) sides, making it easier to cut symmetrical pieces and to split cakes into two even layers.

CHOCOLATE POTS DE CRÈME

SERVES 8

WHAT MAKES THIS A BEST RECIPE: Chocolate pot de crème is the French version of chocolate pudding—rich, intensely chocolate, and with an irresistibly satiny texture. Think crème brûlée without the caramelized sugar crust but enriched with dark chocolate. Classically, pots de crème are made in petite lidded pots, but individual ramekins are the contemporary vessels. These rich chocolaty custards are served in small portions because more would be too much. Unfortunately, most recipes for pots de crème are finicky and laborious, requiring a hot water bath that threatens to splash the custards every time the pan is moved. In addition, the individual custards don't always cook at the same rate. Here in the test kitchen, we found a way to make this classic French dessert faster, simpler, and better. And we eliminated the need for any fussy equipment or a water bath—to make this recipe all you need is a saucepan and a spatula. We simply began by carefully heating egg yolks, sugar, and heavy cream until thickened, then poured the custard over chopped chocolate and let it sit until it melted. Then we combined the two. *C'est tout!* After pouring the chocolate mixture into pots or ramekins, we chilled the servings, making these a superb make-ahead dessert for a special occasion. Serve with whipped cream and garnish with a dusting of cocoa powder or chocolate shavings, if desired.

CUSTARD

- 10 ounces bittersweet chocolate (see note), chopped fine
- 1½ cups heavy cream
- ¾ cup half-and-half
- 5 large egg yolks
- 5 tablespoons sugar
- ¼ teaspoon salt
- 1 tablespoon vanilla extract
- ½ teaspoon instant espresso powder mixed with 1 tablespoon water

WHIPPED CREAM

- ½ cup heavy cream, chilled

Finish these rich custards with a dollop of whipped cream and a sprinkling of shaved bittersweet chocolate or a dusting of cocoa powder.

- 2 teaspoons sugar
- ½ teaspoon vanilla extract
  Cocoa powder for dusting (optional)
  Chocolate shavings for sprinkling (optional)

1. FOR THE CUSTARD: Place the chocolate in a medium heatproof bowl; set a fine-mesh strainer over the bowl.
2. Whisk the heavy cream, half-and-half, yolks, sugar, and salt together in a medium saucepan. Cook the mixture over medium-low heat, stirring constantly and scraping the bottom of the pot with a wooden spoon, until thickened and the custard registers 175 to 180 degrees on an instant-read thermometer, 8 to 12 minutes. Do not let the custard overcook. (See the photos on page 308.)
3. Immediately strain the custard into the bowl of chocolate. Let the mixture sit to melt the chocolate, about 5 minutes. Whisk gently until smooth, then whisk in the vanilla and espresso. Divide the mixture evenly among eight 5-ounce ramekins. Gently tap the ramekins against the counter to remove any air bubbles.
4. Cool the ramekins to room temperature, then cover with plastic wrap and refrigerate until chilled, at least 4 hours or up to 72 hours. Before serving, let stand at room temperature for 20 to 30 minutes.
5. FOR THE WHIPPED CREAM: With an electric mixer, beat the cream, sugar, and vanilla on medium-high speed in a large bowl until soft peaks form.
6. Spoon about 2 tablespoons of the whipped cream

over each custard and garnish with the cocoa or chocolate shavings, if using. Serve.

WHERE THINGS CAN GO WRONG: Be sure to cook the custard in step 2 over medium-low heat. If the custard overcooks or simmers, it will scorch on the bottom.

WHAT YOU CAN DO AHEAD OF TIME: The pots de crème can be cooled completely, wrapped in plastic wrap, and refrigerated for up to 3 days. Make the whipped cream just before serving.

NOTES FROM THE TEST KITCHEN

THE BEST CHOCOLATE FOR POTS DE CRÈME
We prefer pots de crème made with 60 percent cocoa bittersweet chocolate (our favorite brands are Ghirardelli, Callebaut, Valrhona, and El Rey), but 70 percent bittersweet chocolate can also be used. If using a 70 percent bittersweet chocolate (we like Lindt, El Rey, and Valrhona), reduce the amount of chocolate to 8 ounces.

WHEN IS THE CRÈME ANGLAISE READY?
An instant-read thermometer is the most reliable way to judge when crème anglaise has reached the proper temperature of 175 to 180 degrees. But you can also judge the progress of a custard sauce by its thickness. Dip a wooden spoon into the custard and run your finger across the back. (Yes, this old-fashioned method really does work.)

NOT YET. When the temperature registers between 165 and 170 degrees, the custard will still be thin, and a line drawn on the back of the spoon will not hold.

READY. When the temperature registers between 175 and 180 degrees, the custard will coat the spoon, and the line will maintain neat edges.

TOO FAR. When the temperature goes above 180 degrees, small chunks will become visible in the curdled custard.

BIG AND CHEWY LOW-FAT CHOCOLATE CHIP COOKIES
MAKES 1½ DOZEN COOKIES

WHAT MAKES THIS A BEST RECIPE: With this recipe, we created a low-fat chocolate chip cookie that doesn't look or taste like a diet cookie. This was not an easy task, when you consider that big and chewy bakery cookies, with huge amounts of chocolate chips, butter, and sugar, easily tip the scale at more than 200 calories and 8 grams of fat per cookie. When you remember that most "healthy" recipes use ingredients like applesauce, banana puree, molasses, and carob chips, it's pretty easy to understand why bakeries are still in business. The secret to our success was a homemade date puree, made from cooking and mashing dried dates. We replaced three-quarters of the butter in our favorite full-fat recipe with date puree and created a cookie with a rich, sweet flavor, with only a slight, almost unidentifiable hint of "fruitiness." While the slight hint of fruitiness from the dates wasn't unpleasant, we didn't want even a trace of "unusual" flavor in these cookies. Rather than taming the fruit flavor, we pumped up the butter flavor by melting and browning it. The nutty, concentrated flavor of the browned butter boosted the buttery flavor of the cookies, adding just enough richness to mask any remaining hints of date. And since this batter was so flavorful, we could now cut the full cup of chocolate chips (many recipes call for even more) back to just half a cup—and our cookies still tasted chocolaty. And with only 120 calories and 3 grams of fat, you can even have two.

- 1 cup water
- ¼ cup finely chopped pitted dates
- 3 tablespoons unsalted butter
- 2 cups (10 ounces) unbleached all-purpose flour
- ½ teaspoon baking soda
- ½ teaspoon salt
- 1¼ cups (8¾ ounces) packed light brown sugar
- 1 large egg
- 2 teaspoons vanilla extract
- ½ cup semisweet chocolate chips

1. Adjust an oven rack to the middle position and heat the oven to 325 degrees. Line 2 baking sheets with parchment paper.

2. Bring the water to a boil in a small saucepan over medium-high heat. Add the dates and simmer until tender and most of water has evaporated, about 20 minutes. Using a rubber spatula, press the dates through a fine-mesh strainer into a medium bowl. Scrape the dates remaining in the strainer into the bowl (you should have ¼ cup puree). Cook the butter in a small saucepan over medium heat until nutty brown, about 4 minutes. Let cool.

3. Whisk the flour, baking soda, and salt together in a medium bowl. With an electric mixer, beat the melted butter, brown sugar, and date puree on medium speed in a large bowl until blended. Add the egg and vanilla and continue to beat on medium speed until combined, scraping down the sides of the bowl as needed. Add the flour mixture and continue to beat on low speed until just combined. Reserve 2 tablespoons of the chips, then stir the remaining chips into the batter by hand.

4. Following the photos, and working with 2 tablespoons of dough at a time, roll the dough into balls. Pull each ball into two equal halves, creating jagged edges. Rotate the cookie halves so the jagged edges are facing up and press the two halves together at the base so they form a single ball. Place on the prepared baking sheets, spacing them about 2 inches apart, and press the remaining 2 tablespoons chips evenly over the cookies.

5. Bake the cookies, one sheet at a time, until the edges are light golden and the centers are soft and puffy, 15 to 18 minutes, rotating the baking sheet halfway through baking. Cool the cookies completely on the baking sheet. Bake the second batch of cookies while the first batch cools.

WHAT YOU CAN DO AHEAD OF TIME: The cookies can be cooled completely and stored in an airtight container at room temperature for up to 3 days.

NOTES FROM THE TEST KITCHEN

THE DATING GAME
Could we really cut the fat and calories of a typical chocolate chip cookie without sacrificing flavor and chew? Yes, thanks to the addition of pureed dates and a mere 3 tablespoons of browned butter.

DATES. Cooked, pureed dates add moisture and chew to our cookies.

BROWNED BUTTER. Browning the butter intensifies its flavor, so just a little butter can taste like a lot.

THE JAGGED EDGE
While browned butter and date puree gave us cookies that tasted every bit as good as regular chocolate chip cookies, they did have one effect we weren't crazy about—strange, shiny, smooth tops instead of the craggy tops we expect in chocolate chip cookies. To make sure that our low-fat cookies looked appealing, we found it necessary to perform a little assembly magic.

1. Roll 2 tablespoons of the dough into a ball. Hold the dough ball with the fingertips of both hands and pull it into two equal halves, creating jagged edges.

2. Rotate the cookie halves so that the jagged surfaces are facing up. Press the two halves together at their base so that they form a single ball.

3. Space the balls of dough, jagged side up, 2 inches apart on the prepared baking sheets.

FRENCH-STYLE MACAROONS

MAKES 20 SANDWICH COOKIES

WHAT MAKES THIS A BEST RECIPE: These light-as-air, meringue-y almond cookie sandwiches with a sweet cream filling will melt in your mouth. Originally created in Venice during the Renaissance, these cookies made their way to France, and today they are famous throughout the country. Once a rare find in the United States, macaroons have become increasingly popular, often appearing on a *petits-fours* tray (along with the bill) at many a fancy restaurant. To make them, a batter of almond flour, egg whites, and sugar is combined, then piped through a pastry bag onto a parchment paper–lined baking sheet and left to dry until a skin forms. (The step of allowing the batter to dry may seem a bit odd, but the skin that forms is crucial to ensuring a macaroon with an attractive, smooth surface.) After the cookies are baked and cooked, they are filled. The goal is to achieve a very light, crisp crust and moist, chewy interior. We found that five egg whites, whipped with granulated sugar and a pinch of cream of tartar for structure, yielded cookies that were light, yet moist. To make our cookies super-smooth, we took an extra step and processed the almond flour with confectioners' sugar in a food processor before incorporating the mixture into the whipped egg whites. Last but hardly least, a rich and creamy buttercream frosting served as our filling of choice. We had created a sandwich cookie with class.

COOKIES

- 3¾ **cups (15 ounces) almond flour (see page 313)**
- 3⅓ **cups (13⅓ ounces) confectioners' sugar**
- ⅛ **teaspoon salt**
- 5 **large egg whites, at room temperature**
  Pinch cream of tartar
- 5 **teaspoons granulated sugar**
- 1 **tablespoon vanilla extract**

BUTTERCREAM FILLING

- 2 **large eggs**
- ½ **cup (3½ ounces) granulated sugar**
- 1 **teaspoon vanilla extract**
  Pinch salt
- 16 **tablespoons (2 sticks) unsalted butter, cut into 8 pieces, softened but still cool**

1. FOR THE COOKIES: Line 2 baking sheets with parchment paper. Fit a large pastry bag with a ½-inch plain tip; set aside. Process half of the almond flour, confectioners' sugar, and the salt together in a food processor until the mixture is very finely ground, about 20 seconds. Transfer to a bowl and repeat with the remaining almond flour and confectioners' sugar; stir together and set aside.

2. With an electric mixer, beat the egg whites at medium-low speed in a large bowl until opaque and frothy, about 30 seconds. Add the cream of tartar, increase the speed to medium-high, and continue to beat until white, thick, voluminous, and the consistency of shaving cream, about 90 seconds. Slowly sprinkle in the granulated sugar and continue to beat until stiff peaks form and the sugar is incorporated, about 60 seconds.

3. Gently fold one-quarter of the almond flour mixture into the whites, followed by the vanilla. Gradually fold in the remaining almond mixture until a thick batter forms.

4. Fill the prepared pastry bag with the batter. Twisting the top of the bag to apply pressure, push the batter down toward the tip and pipe twenty 2-inch mounds on a prepared baking sheet, spacing the mounds about 1 inch apart. Use the back of a teaspoon or your finger dipped in a bowl of cold water to even out the shape and smooth the surface of the piped mounds. Repeat with the remaining batter and baking sheet. Let the cookies sit at room temperature until the tops are dry and a smooth skin has formed, 1 to 2 hours.

5. Adjust an oven rack to the middle position and heat the oven to 325 degrees. Bake the cookies, one sheet at a time, until lightly browned, about 20 minutes, rotating the baking sheet halfway through baking. Carefully slide the parchment paper with the cookies onto a wire rack

and cool completely. Bake the second batch of cookies while the first batch cools.

6. FOR THE FILLING: Combine the eggs, granulated sugar, vanilla, and salt in a large heatproof bowl; place the bowl over a pan of simmering water (do not let the bottom of the bowl touch the water). Whisking gently but constantly, heat the mixture until it is thin and foamy and registers 160 degrees on an instant-read thermometer.

7. Remove the bowl from the water. With an electric mixer, beat the egg mixture at medium-high speed until light, airy, and cooled to room temperature, about 5 minutes. Reduce the speed to medium and add the butter, 1 piece at a time (it may look curdled halfway through). Once all the butter is added, increase the speed to high and beat until light, fluffy, and thoroughly combined, about 1 minute.

8. TO ASSEMBLE: Spread about 1 tablespoon of the filling over the flat sides of half of the cooled cookies and gently cover with the flat sides of the remaining cookies to form sandwich cookies.

WHERE THINGS CAN GO WRONG: Allow the piped cookies to dry as directed in step 4—the skin that forms prevents the cookies from cracking in the oven. You should be able to portion all 40 cookies between 2 standard-sized baking sheets. If not, use 3 sheets. Note that however many sheets you use, you must bake only 1 sheet at a time for the cookies to bake evenly.

WHAT YOU CAN DO AHEAD OF TIME: The cookies (unfilled) can be stored in an airtight container at room temperature for up to 3 days, or frozen for up to 3 weeks. If frozen, let thaw at room temperature for 2 hours before filling. The buttercream filling can be refrigerated in an airtight container for up to 3 days.

NOTES FROM THE TEST KITCHEN

HOW TO MAKE ALMOND FLOUR

If you can't find almond flour (sold in well-stocked markets and specialty food stores), substitute 11 ounces of slivered almonds, and process to a fine flour in a food processor. Then process the almond flour with the confectioners' sugar in batches, as directed in step 1.

PIPING MACAROONS

1. Fill a large pastry bag with the batter and push the batter to the bottom of the bag using your hands or a spatula; twist the top of the bag to seal.

2. Pipe the batter in 2-inch mounds onto the parchment-lined baking sheets, spacing the mounds about 1 inch apart.

3. Use the back of a teaspoon or your finger dipped in cold water to even out the shape and smooth the surface of the piped mounds.

BROWN SUGAR COOKIES

MAKES 2 DOZEN COOKIES

WHAT MAKES THIS A BEST RECIPE: Inspired by a classic sugar cookie and the butterscotch, vanilla, and caramel flavors that brown sugar gives coffee cakes and other baked goods, we created a simple cookie that is chewy, with a crackling-crisp exterior and a big jolt of brown sugar flavor. Most sugar cookie recipes start by creaming softened butter with sugar until fluffy, beating in an egg or two, and then adding the dry ingredients (flour, baking powder, and salt). We used melted butter in our recipe, which helped us achieve the chewy texture we were after. Using dark brown sugar rather than light brown sugar allowed us to get more flavor from less sugar, which kept the cookies from being cloyingly sweet. Riffing off a classic sugar cookie technique, we rolled the dough balls in brown sugar cut with granulated sugar to produce the crackling exterior. One tablespoon of vanilla extract properly reinforced the brown sugar flavor, and a healthy dose of salt (½ teaspoon) balanced the sweetness and helped accentuate the more interesting flavor components in brown sugar. But our biggest success came from an unlikely refinement, browning the butter, which added a nutty flavor that complemented the rich brown sugar flavor.

14	tablespoons (1¾ sticks) unsalted butter
¼	cup (1¾ ounces) granulated sugar
2	cups (14 ounces) packed dark brown sugar
2	cups plus 2 tablespoons (about 10½ ounces) unbleached all-purpose flour
½	teaspoon baking soda
¼	teaspoon baking powder
½	teaspoon salt
1	large egg
1	large egg yolk
1	tablespoon vanilla extract

1. Adjust an oven rack to the middle position and heat the oven to 350 degrees. Line 2 baking sheets with parchment paper.

2. Heat 10 tablespoons of the butter in a 10-inch skillet over medium-high heat until melted, about 2 minutes. Continue to cook, swirling the pan constantly, until the butter is dark golden brown and has a nutty aroma, 1 to 3 minutes. Transfer the browned butter to a large heat-proof bowl. Stir the remaining 4 tablespoons butter into the hot butter to melt; set aside for 15 minutes.

3. Combine the granulated sugar and ¼ cup of the brown sugar in a shallow bowl; set aside. Whisk the flour, baking soda, and baking powder together in a medium bowl.

4. Stir the remaining 1¾ cups brown sugar and salt into the cooled butter until evenly combined. Scrape down the sides of the bowl. Add the egg, yolk, and vanilla and mix until fully incorporated, about 30 seconds. Scrape down the sides of the bowl. Add the flour mixture and mix until just combined, about 1 minute.

5. Working with 2 tablespoons of dough each time, roll the dough into 1½-inch balls. Working in batches, carefully roll the balls in the reserved sugar mixture and place them on the prepared baking sheets, spacing them about 2 inches apart.

6. Bake the cookies, one sheet at a time, until browned and still puffy and the edges have begun to set but the centers are still soft, 12 to 14 minutes, rotating the baking sheet halfway through baking. Do not overbake. (See the photo on page 316. The cookies will look raw between the cracks and seem underdone.)

7. Cool the cookies on the baking sheets for 5 minutes, then transfer to a wire rack and cool to room temperature. Bake the second batch of cookies while the first batch cools.

WHERE THINGS CAN GO WRONG: Avoid using a nonstick skillet to brown the butter. The dark color of the nonstick coating makes it difficult to gauge when the butter is sufficiently browned. Use fresh brown sugar, as older (read: harder and drier) brown sugar will make the cookies too dry. Do not overbake.

WHAT YOU CAN DO AHEAD OF TIME: The cookies can be cooled completely and stored in an airtight container at room temperature for up to 3 days.

NOTES FROM THE TEST KITCHEN

BUILDING BROWN SUGAR FLAVOR

Dark brown sugar was an obvious place to begin our efforts to create a cookie with a bold, nutty, butterscotch flavor. A whole tablespoon of vanilla helped, but everyone in the test kitchen was surprised at how much impact browning the butter had on the flavor of these cookies.

DARK BROWN SUGAR   **LOTS OF VANILLA**   **BROWNED BUTTER**

CHECKING DONENESS

Achieving the proper texture—crisp at the edges and chewy in the middle—is critical to this recipe. Because the cookies are so dark, it's hard to judge doneness by color. Instead, gently press halfway between the edge and center of the cookie. When it's done, it will form an indent with slight resistance. Check early and err on the side of underdone.

JOE FROGGERS

MAKES 2 DOZEN COOKIES

WHAT MAKES THIS A BEST RECIPE: These wonderful flat, oversized molasses-spice cookies are moist, salty, rum flavored, and, well—most unusual (and addictive). Joe Froggers date back more than 200 years to Black Joe's Tavern, located in Marblehead, Mass., a seaside town about 25 miles north of Boston. Looking for authentic recipes, we tested as many as we could find from Web sites, cookbooks, and magazines, but they baked up hard, with no warm and salty rum flavor. The Marblehead Museum and Historical Society recommended we consult *The Spirit of '76 Lives Here;* by Priscilla Sawyer Lord and Virginia Clegg Gamage (Chilton Book Company, 1971). The authors tell the story of Joseph Brown, a freed slave and Revolutionary War veteran who lived in Marblehead more than 200 years ago. Brown (known as "Old Black Joe") and his wife, Lucretia (affectionately known as Auntie Cresse), opened up Black Joe's Tavern in a part of Marblehead called Gingerbread Hill. Besides serving drinks (mostly rum), Joe and Auntie Cresse baked cookies: large, moist molasses and rum cookies made salty by the addition of Marblehead seawater. These cookies were popular sustenance on long fishing voyages, as they had no dairy to spoil and the combination of rum, molasses, and seawater kept them chewy for weeks. According to Samuel Roads Jr.'s *History and Traditions of Marblehead,* published in 1879, the funny name for these cookies referred to the lily pads (similar in size and shape to the cookies) and large croaking frogs that would fill the pond behind Joe's tavern. Thus the cookies became known as Joe Froggers. At Marblehead's Abbot Public Library, the librarians produced recipes from local news journals and town cookbooks, such as the *Marblehead, Massachusetts, Baptist Women's Fellowship* (1965). These recipes first stirred molasses together with baking soda. The reaction between the two made the mixture bubble and froth, leaving the soda with little leavening power. That, combined with the absence of egg, explained why the cookies are so flat. (The soda does contribute a deep, dark color.) We found that we needed to make some adjustments to the old recipes we found to arrive at just the right flavor and chewy texture. We doubled the amount of rum most recipes called for and halved the water. We weren't going to call for seawater (although we did test it), but dissolving 1½ teaspoons of salt into the rum and water worked fine. Some recipes called for shortening (Auntie Cresse most likely used lard), but butter tasted better. Our version of this old-fashioned American cookie won't stay fresh for weeks at sea like the original, but they are so salty, spicy, sweet, and chewy we're not sure that matters.

⅓ cup dark rum (such as Myers's)

1 tablespoon water

1½ teaspoons salt

3 cups (15 ounces) unbleached all-purpose flour, plus more for the counter

¾ teaspoon ground ginger

½ teaspoon ground allspice

¼ teaspoon ground nutmeg

⅛ teaspoon ground cloves

1 cup molasses (see note)

1 teaspoon baking soda

8 tablespoons (1 stick) unsalted butter, softened but still cool

1 cup (7 ounces) sugar

1. Stir the rum, water, and salt together in a small bowl until the salt dissolves. Whisk the flour, ginger, allspice, nutmeg, and cloves together in a medium bowl. Stir the molasses and baking soda together in medium bowl (the mixture will begin to bubble) and let sit until doubled in volume, about 15 minutes.

2. With an electric mixer, beat the butter and sugar on medium-high speed in a large bowl until fluffy, about 3 minutes, scraping down the sides of the bowl as needed. Reduce the speed to medium-low and gradually add the rum mixture. Add one-third of the flour mixture, beating on medium-low until just incorporated, followed by half of the molasses mixture, scraping down

the sides of the bowl as needed. Add half of the remaining flour mixture, followed by the remaining molasses mixture, and finally the remaining flour mixture. Wrap the bowl tightly in plastic wrap and refrigerate until stiff, at least 8 hours or up to 3 days.

3. Adjust two oven racks to the upper-middle and lower-middle positions and heat the oven to 375 degrees. Line 2 baking sheets with parchment paper. Working with half of the dough at a time on a heavily floured counter, roll the dough out to ¼-inch thickness. Using a 3½-inch round cookie cutter, cut out 12 cookies. Transfer 6 of the cookies to each baking sheet, spacing them 1½ inches apart.

4. Bake until set and just beginning to crack, about 8 minutes, rotating the baking sheets halfway through baking. Cool the cookies on the baking sheets for 10 minutes, then transfer to a wire rack to cool completely. Repeat with the remaining dough.

WHERE THINGS CAN GO WRONG: Place only 6 cookies on each baking sheet—they will spread. Use regular (not robust) molasses. Make sure to chill the dough for a full 8 hours or it will be too difficult to roll out.

WHAT YOU CAN DO AHEAD OF TIME: The cookies can be cooled completely and stored in an airtight container at room temperature for up to 1 week.

NOTES FROM THE TEST KITCHEN

GOOD REACTION
Molasses on its own is thick and sticky (left), but after baking soda is added it becomes light and frothy (right). This mixture gives the cookies a rich color and flavor.

KEY LIME BARS

MAKES SIXTEEN 2-INCH BARS

WHAT MAKES THIS A BEST RECIPE: This recipe for Key lime bars offers all the appealing qualities of Key lime pie but without the need for a fork. These bars are a brilliant pairing of rich and refreshing, sweet and tart, all in a buttery, crisp crumb crust. A graham cracker crust is traditional for a Key lime pie, but we swapped in animal cracker crumbs—their more neutral flavor placed the lime flavor squarely in the limelight. Whereas a pie crust can be tender and delicate, the crust for the bars needed sturdiness; this meant increasing the butter. Brown sugar outdid granulated because it gave the crust a slightly richer, rounder flavor. We made a firm, creamy, rich, finger-food-friendly filling by adding just 2 ounces of cream cheese to the traditional ingredients, sweetened condensed milk, lime juice, lime zest, and eggs. Half a cup of fresh lime juice and 1 tablespoon of grated lime zest was enough to make the lime flavor sparkle without scaring away those with low tartness thresholds and without thinning the filling. Some bar recipes include some sort of streusel or crunchy topping. We took a cue from the tropics and experimented with a toasted-coconut topping, which added a subtle textural contrast and more depth of flavor. The test kitchen was split over whether this topping was an improvement, so we left it optional.

CRUST

5 ounces animal crackers
3 tablespoons packed light or dark brown sugar
Pinch salt
4 tablespoons (½ stick) unsalted butter, melted and cooled slightly

FILLING

2 ounces cream cheese, at room temperature
1 tablespoon grated lime zest
Pinch salt

1 (14 ounce) can sweetened condensed milk
1 large egg yolk
½ cup Key lime or fresh lime juice (see page 320)

GARNISH (OPTIONAL)

¾ cup sweetened shredded coconut, toasted

1. Adjust an oven rack to the middle position and heat the oven to 325 degrees. Line an 8-inch square baking pan with aluminum foil, allowing the extra foil to hang over the edges of the pan (see page 321). Lightly coat the foil-lined pan with vegetable oil spray.

2. FOR THE CRUST: Process the animal crackers in a food processor until finely ground, about 10 seconds (you should have about 1¼ cups crumbs). Add the brown sugar and salt and pulse to combine. Drizzle the butter over the crumbs and pulse until the crumbs are evenly moistened with the butter, about ten 1-second pulses. Press the crumbs evenly into the bottom of the prepared pan. Bake until deep golden brown, 18 to 20 minutes. Cool the crust on a wire rack while making the filling. Do not turn off the oven.

3. FOR THE FILLING: While the crust cools, combine the cream cheese, zest, and salt in a medium bowl. Add the condensed milk and whisk until incorporated and no lumps of cream cheese remain; whisk in the yolk. Add the lime juice and whisk gently until incorporated (the mixture will thicken slightly).

4. TO ASSEMBLE: Pour the filling into the cooled crust and smooth with a spatula. Bake until set and the edges begin to pull away slightly from the sides, 15 to 20 minutes. Cool to room temperature on a wire rack, 1 to 2 hours. Cover with foil and refrigerate until thoroughly chilled, at least 2 hours.

5. Loosen the edges with a paring knife and remove from the baking pan by lifting the foil extensions. Using a chef's knife, cut into 16 squares. Sprinkle with the toasted coconut, if using.

WHERE THINGS CAN GO WRONG: Do not use bottled lime juice, or the filling will have an off-flavor. Grate the zest from the limes before juicing them, avoiding the bitter white pith that lies just beneath the outermost skin.

WHAT YOU CAN DO AHEAD OF TIME: The bars can be refrigerated in an airtight container for up to 2 days. (The crust will soften slightly.) Let the bars stand at room temperature about 15 minutes before serving.

NOTES FROM THE TEST KITCHEN

YOU CAN DOUBLE IT
The recipe can be doubled and baked in a 13 by 9-inch baking pan; increase the baking times by a minute or two.

ARE KEY LIMES REALLY KEY?
As their name suggests, Key lime bars are traditionally made from Key limes—a tiny, yellowish variety that grows only in tropical locales (like the Florida Keys, from which they got their name). Key lime aficionados herald the fruit's "distinctive" flavor and fragrance compared with conventional Persian limes. Our tasters were split over which variety made the better bar. The deciding factor may be the amount of work involved: To get the half cup of lime juice called for in our bar recipe, we had to squeeze three Persian limes. With the Key limes, it took almost 20! Both Key lime juice and regular lime juice are sold presqueezed in shelf-stable bottles, and we wondered whether these would do in a pinch. The short answer? No way. The four brands we tried were at best "bracingly bitter," and, in some cases, "just plain rancid." What's more, many baking recipes (including ours) call for the addition of zest—a tough proposition with a glass bottle.

KEY LIMES
Subtle tartness, skimpy yield

REGULAR LIMES
Bracing tartness, generous yield

BOTTLED CONCENTRATE
Convenience at a bitter price

PECAN BARS
MAKES 24 BARS

WHAT MAKES THIS A BEST RECIPE: We love this recipe for pecan bars because they pack all the best attributes of pie—buttery crust, gooey filling, and nutty topping—into individual, bite-sized bar cookies. Most pecan bar recipes use a shortbread crust, which we improved upon by adding ground pecans. We found that for the richest flavor and best texture, it was necessary to prebake the crust until it was just beginning to brown before adding the pecan filling, which offers the perfect balance of sweetness and gooeyness. To boost its flavor, we added a substantial amount of vanilla extract along with bourbon or rum. The liquor cut through the sweetness and intensified the flavor of the nuts. We toasted the pecans, the star of the show, to improve their flavor, and then chopped them coarse, making the squares visually appealing and easy to eat. These bars are packed with serious pecan flavor.

CRUST
- 1 cup (5 ounces) unbleached all-purpose flour
- ⅓ cup (2⅓ ounces) packed light brown sugar
- ¼ cup pecans, toasted and chopped coarse
- 1 teaspoon salt
- ¼ teaspoon baking powder
- 6 tablespoons (¾ stick) unsalted butter, cut into ½-inch pieces and chilled

PECAN FILLING
- ½ cup (3½ ounces) packed light brown sugar
- ⅓ cup light corn syrup
- 4 tablespoons (½ stick) unsalted butter, melted
- 1 tablespoon bourbon or dark rum
- 2 teaspoons vanilla extract
- ½ teaspoon salt
- 1 large egg, lightly beaten
- 2 cups pecans, toasted and chopped coarse

With pecans in the crust and on top of the filling, these sturdy and flavorful bars are like mini, portable pecan pies.

1. FOR THE CRUST: Adjust an oven rack to the middle position and heat the oven to 350 degrees. Line a 9-inch square baking pan with aluminum foil, allowing the extra foil to hang over the edges of the pan. Lightly coat the foil-lined pan with vegetable oil spray.

2. Process the flour, brown sugar, pecans, salt, and baking powder in a food processor until the mixture resembles coarse cornmeal, about five 1-second pulses. Add the butter and pulse until the mixture resembles sand, about eight 1-second pulses. Pat the mixture evenly into the prepared pan and bake until the crust is light brown and springs back when touched, about 20 minutes.

3. FOR THE FILLING: While the crust bakes, whisk the brown sugar, corn syrup, melted butter, bourbon, vanilla, and salt together in a medium bowl. Whisk in the egg until incorporated.

4. Pour the filling on top of the hot crust and sprinkle the pecans evenly over the top. Bake until the top is brown and cracks start to form across the surface, 22 to 25 minutes, rotating the pan halfway through baking. Cool to room temperature on a wire rack, 1 to 2 hours; remove from the baking pan by lifting the foil extensions. Using a chef's knife, cut into 24 bars.

WHAT YOU CAN DO AHEAD OF TIME: The bars can be cooled completely and stored in an airtight container for up to 5 days.

NOTES FROM THE TEST KITCHEN

ALL ABOUT NUTS
Toasting nuts helps release their essential oils, bringing out their full flavor and aroma. Toast the nuts in a skillet (without any oil) over medium heat, shaking the pan occasionally to prevent scorching, until they begin to darken slightly in color, generally 3 to 5 minutes.

MAKING A FOIL SLING
With their gooey fillings and high sugar content, brownies and bar cookies can be nearly impossible to remove from their baking pans—no matter how well the pan is greased. After baking countless batches, we finally found a method that works every time. Lining the pan with an aluminum foil or parchment paper "sling" before baking prevents any casualties. Once cooled, the bar cookies can be lifted easily from the pan, transferred to a cutting board, and cut into tidy squares or bars.

1. Fold two long sheets of aluminum foil so that they are as wide as the baking pan (if the pan is rectangular, the two sheets will be different sizes). Lay the sheets of foil in the pan, perpendicular to one another, with the extra hanging over the edges of the pan.

2. Push the foil flat into the corners and up the sides of the pan. Try to iron out any wrinkles in the foil, laying it flush to the pan. Spray the sides and bottom of the pan with vegetable oil spray before adding the batter.

3. After the bars or brownies have baked and cooled, use the foil sling to transfer them to a cutting board before cutting into squares or bars.

SEVEN-LAYER BARS

MAKES 45 BARS

WHAT MAKES THIS A BEST RECIPE: With layers of chocolate chips, coconut, and nuts piled high over a buttery graham cracker crust, these seven-layer bars are irresistible. The best thing about them is that there's no batter or dough to make—just layer pantry staples into a baking pan and wait for the oven to transform a jumble of ingredients into a chewy, crispy, sweet bar cookie. We prebaked the crust to give it the crisp texture that we were looking for. We also experimented with ingredients to boost flavor in the crust and finally hit upon the solution: toffee bits. Their buttery, salty flavor gave the crust real personality.

To improve their flavor and texture, we pre-toasted the coconut and nuts. Rice Krispies lent welcome crunch and lightness. To emphasize the chocolate flavor, we added a layer of milk chocolate, melted right over the hot crust, in addition to the usual chocolate chips. For us, the best part of this recipe is the rich butterscotch flavor and chewy texture added by the sweetened condensed milk. To remedy the sandy, dry texture of the original recipe, why not use more than one can? We found that two full cans created a rich, moist, candy-like bar cookie with plenty of chew and great caramel flavor.

1	cup toffee bits (such as Heath)
12	whole graham crackers
8	tablespoons (1 stick) unsalted butter, melted
8	ounces milk chocolate, chopped coarse
1	cup Rice Krispies
1	cup pecans, toasted and chopped coarse
1	cup semisweet chocolate chips
1	cup sweetened flaked coconut, toasted
2	(14-ounce) cans sweetened condensed milk
1	tablespoon vanilla extract

Toffee bits add flavor to these old-fashioned bars while Rice Krispies provide a welcome crunch.

1. Adjust an oven rack to the middle position and heat the oven to 350 degrees. Line a 13 by 9-inch baking pan with aluminum foil, allowing the extra foil to hang over the edges of the pan (see page 321). Lightly coat the foil-lined pan with vegetable oil spray.

2. Process the toffee bits in a food processor until finely ground, about 30 seconds. Add the graham crackers and process until finely ground. Transfer the mixture to a bowl and stir in the melted butter. Press the crumbs evenly into the bottom of the prepared pan. Bake until beginning to brown, about 10 minutes.

3. Remove the pan from the oven, sprinkle the crust with the milk chocolate, and allow the chocolate to soften, about 2 minutes. Using a spatula, spread the chocolate into an even layer. Scatter the Rice Krispies over the chocolate, pressing to adhere. Add layers of pecans, chocolate chips, and coconut, in that order, pressing each layer to adhere. Combine the condensed milk and vanilla in a small bowl and pour over the coconut.

4. Bake until golden brown, 25 to 30 minutes. Cool to room temperature on a wire rack, about 2 hours. Remove from the baking pan by lifting the foil extensions. Using a chef's knife, cut into 45 squares.

WHAT YOU CAN DO AHEAD OF TIME: The bars can be cooled completely and stored in an airtight container at room temperature for up to 3 days.

15-MINUTE CHOCOLATE WALNUT FUDGE

MAKES ABOUT 2½ POUNDS

WHAT MAKES THIS A BEST RECIPE: In our quest to develop the best recipe for chocolate fudge, we tested dozens of recipes, most of which simply never set up or were more like a candy bar than fudge. We finally achieved the melt-in-your-mouth creaminess and rich chocolate flavor that we were after using sweetened condensed milk and a combination of semisweet and unsweetened chocolates. The unsweetened chocolate lessened the sugary intensity of the fudge while leaving the approachable flavor of semisweet chocolate intact. The secret to our recipe was to add ½ teaspoon of baking soda, which made our fudge drier and firmer, without imparting any off-flavors. To make our fudge seem lighter and counterbalance the chocolate, we stirred chopped walnuts into the mix before pouring it into a baking dish and refrigerating it until set. An added bonus: Our final recipe takes just 15 minutes to prepare.

16 ounces semisweet chocolate, chopped fine
2 ounces unsweetened chocolate, chopped fine
½ teaspoon baking soda
⅛ teaspoon salt
1 (14-ounce) can sweetened condensed milk
1 tablespoon vanilla extract
1 cup coarsely chopped walnuts

1. Line an 8-inch square baking pan with aluminum foil, allowing the extra foil to hang over the edges of the pan (see page 321). Lightly coat the foil-lined pan with vegetable oil spray.

2. Toss the chocolates, baking soda, and salt in a medium heatproof bowl until the baking soda is evenly distributed. Stir in the condensed milk and vanilla. Set the bowl over a 4-quart saucepan containing 2 cups of simmering water. Stir with a rubber spatula until the chocolate is almost fully melted and a few small pieces remain, 2 to 4 minutes.

3. Remove the bowl from the heat and continue to stir until the chocolate is fully melted and the mixture is smooth, about 2 minutes. Stir in the walnuts. Transfer the fudge to the prepared pan and spread in an even layer with a spatula. Refrigerate until set, about 2 hours. Remove from the baking pan by lifting the foil extensions. Using a chef's knife, cut into squares.

WHERE THINGS CAN GO WRONG: Don't be tempted to make this fudge without the walnuts; they are crucial to the texture. Make sure to remove the fudge from the double boiler before the chocolate is fully melted. If the chocolate stays in the double boiler too long, there is the possibility of the chocolate separating and producing a fudge that is greasy.

WHAT YOU CAN DO AHEAD OF TIME: The fudge can be wrapped tightly in plastic wrap and stored in a cool place for up to 2 weeks, or frozen for up to 3 months. (This fudge will change texture and become drier the longer it is stored.) If freezing, do not cut the fudge into squares; thaw at room temperature, then cut.

NOTES FROM THE TEST KITCHEN

THE BEST CHOCOLATE FOR FUDGE
The quality of the chocolate used will affect the flavor and texture of the fudge. We prefer Ghirardelli semisweet and unsweetened chocolate in this recipe.

TO MAKE A DOUBLE BATCH
Double the amounts of all the ingredients and use a 13 by 9-inch pan. In step 2, use a large heatproof bowl and a Dutch oven containing 4 cups simmering water.

THREE KEY INGREDIENTS TO QUICK, RELIABLE FUDGE

SWEETENED CONDENSED MILK
Takes the place of the traditional sugar syrup.

BAKING SODA
Increases the pH of the fudge and makes the texture firmer.

UNSWEETENED CHOCOLATE
Adds intensity and tames excessive sweetness.

GREAT DISCOVERIES

BAKING SODA SAVES THE DAY

I love the slightly grainy but melt-in-your-mouth creaminess of traditional fudge, but for my foolproof 15-minute fudge recipe, I had a difficult time achieving the right balance using only sweetened condensed milk and chocolate—the texture was soft, dense, and more like frosting than fudge. I needed to find a way to change the fudge's texture; it needed to be firmer and lighter. The only moisture in the recipe was in the sweetened condensed milk, and I figured that cooking off some of this liquid would make the fudge drier and firmer. Unfortunately, simmering sweetened condensed milk proved highly problematic; it easily stuck to the bottom of the pan and burned—not exactly what I had in mind for a foolproof recipe. I was at a loss for how to make my fudge firmer and lighter. And that's when inspiration struck. If I couldn't remove moisture, maybe I could change the texture of my fudge by adding another ingredient. Chemical leaveners have the potential to change the texture of cakes and cookies, so maybe they would work their magic on fudge. I chose baking soda, which reacts with acidic ingredients (everything from buttermilk and lemon juice to chocolate) to produce carbon dioxide and thus lighten and lift baked goods. Starting with one-quarter teaspoon, I mixed baking soda with the chocolates before melting this mixture with the milk. Something was clearly happening: The fudge was becoming drier and less waxy, and it had a more traditional texture. After some research, I discovered that the baking soda was not only reacting with the acids in the chocolate but also altering the pH of the fudge. The proteins in the milk and chocolate are sensitive to changes in pH, losing their ability to retain moisture as the pH increases. One-half teaspoon of baking soda made my fudge drier and firmer without imparting any off-flavors.

DAVID PAZMIÑO | TEST COOK, *COOK'S ILLUSTRATED*

BEST-EVER HOT COCOA MIX
MAKES ABOUT 20 SERVINGS

WHAT MAKES THIS A BEST RECIPE: For this recipe, several unlikely ingredients create an instant cocoa mix that's rich and chocolaty—and ready in less than five minutes. When we were kids, a steaming mug of hot cocoa could turn a snowstorm into sunshine. Now that we're older, watery hot cocoa and dehydrated mini marshmallows just don't have the same effect. Now we make a big batch of our homemade mix to keep in the cupboard, ready whenever a craving for hot cocoa hits. For our hot cocoa, we preferred the mild but honest chocolate flavor of Dutch-processed cocoa (cocoa powder that has been treated with an alkali to neutralize some of its natural acidity) to the slightly bitter regular cocoa. To add sweetness, confectioners' sugar dissolved easily, and the cornstarch (which is added to confectioners' sugar to prevent clumping) thickened the hot cocoa, giving it a rich, smooth texture. Nonfat dry milk added a sweet dairy flavor, especially when we reconstituted the mix with hot milk rather than hot water. Our secret ingredient was white chocolate. In addition to providing a soft, creamy texture, the white chocolate married perfectly with the cocoa powder, pushing the chocolate flavor to new heights.

- 3   **cups nonfat dry milk**
- 2   **cups (8 ounces) confectioners' sugar**
- 1½ **cups (4½ ounces) Dutch-processed cocoa**
- 1½ **cups white chocolate chips**
- ¼   **teaspoon salt**

Combine the ingredients in a large bowl. Working in two batches, pulse the ingredients in a food processor until the chocolate is finely ground. To make hot cocoa, stir ⅓ cup of this mix into 1 cup of hot milk. Top with whipped cream or mini marshmallows.

WHAT YOU CAN DO AHEAD OF TIME: The cocoa mix can be stored in an airtight container at room temperature for up to 3 months.

CONVERSIONS

SOME SAY COOKING IS A SCIENCE AND AN ART.
We would say that geography has a hand in it, too. Flour milled in the United Kingdom and elsewhere will feel and taste different from flour milled in the United States. So we cannot promise that the loaf of bread you bake in Canada or England will taste the same as a loaf baked in the States, but we can offer guidelines for converting weights and measures. We also recommend that you rely on your instincts when making our recipes. Refer to the visual cues provided. If the bread dough hasn't "come together in a ball," as described, you may need to add more flour—even if the recipe doesn't tell you so. You be the judge. For more information on conversions and ingredient equivalents, visit our Web site at www.cooksillustrated.com and type "conversion chart" in the search box.

The recipes in this book were developed using standard U.S. measures following U.S. government guidelines. The charts below offer equivalents for U.S., metric, and Imperial (U.K.) measures. All conversions are approximate and have been rounded up or down to the nearest whole number. For example:

1 teaspoon	=	4.929 milliliters, rounded up to 5 milliliters
1 ounce	=	28.349 grams, rounded down to 28 grams

VOLUME CONVERSIONS

U.S.	METRIC
1 teaspoon	5 milliliters
2 teaspoons	10 milliliters
1 tablespoon	15 milliliters
2 tablespoons	30 milliliters
¼ cup	59 milliliters
⅓ cup	79 milliliters
½ cup	118 milliliters
¾ cup	177 milliliters
1 cup	237 milliliters
1¼ cups	296 milliliters
1½ cups	355 milliliters
2 cups	473 milliliters
2½ cups	592 milliliters
3 cups	710 milliliters
4 cups (1 quart)	0.946 liter
1.06 quarts	1 liter
4 quarts (1 gallon)	3.8 liters

WEIGHT CONVERSIONS

OUNCES	GRAMS
½	14
¾	21
1	28
1½	43
2	57
2½	71
3	85
3½	99
4	113
4½	128
5	142
6	170
7	198
8	227
9	255
10	283
12	340
16 (1 pound)	454

CONVERSIONS FOR INGREDIENTS COMMONLY USED IN BAKING

Baking is an exacting science. Because measuring by weight is far more accurate than measuring by volume, and thus more likely to achieve reliable results, in our recipes we provide ounce measures in addition to cup measures for many ingredients. Refer to the chart below to convert these measures into grams.

INGREDIENT	OUNCES	GRAMS
1 cup all-purpose flour*	5	142
1 cup whole wheat flour	5½	156
1 cup granulated (white) sugar	7	198
1 cup packed brown sugar (light or dark)	7	198
1 cup confectioners' sugar	4	113
1 cup cocoa powder	3	85
Butter†		
4 tablespoons (½ stick, or ¼ cup)	2	57
8 tablespoons (1 stick, or ½ cup)	4	113
16 tablespoons (2 sticks, or 1 cup)	8	227

*U.S. all-purpose flour, the most frequently used flour in this book, does not contain leaveners, as some European flours do. These leavened flours are called self-rising or self-raising. If you are using self-rising flour, take this into consideration before adding leavening to a recipe.
† In the United States, butter is sold both salted and unsalted. We generally recommend unsalted butter. If you are using salted butter, take this into consideration before adding salt to a recipe.

OVEN TEMPERATURES

FAHRENHEIT	CELSIUS	GAS MARK (IMPERIAL)
225	105	¼
250	120	½
275	130	1
300	150	2
325	165	3
350	180	4
375	190	5
400	200	6
425	220	7
450	230	8
475	245	9

CONVERTING TEMPERATURES FROM AN INSTANT-READ THERMOMETER

We include doneness temperatures in many of our recipes, such as those for poultry, meat, and bread. We recommend an instant-read thermometer for the job. Refer to the table above to convert Fahrenheit degrees to Celsius. Or, for temperatures not represented in the chart, use this simple formula:

Subtract 32 degrees from the Fahrenheit reading, then divide the result by 1.8 to find the Celsius reading.

EXAMPLE:
"Roast until the juice runs clear when the chicken is cut with a paring knife or the thickest part of the breast registers 160 degrees on an instant-read thermometer." To convert:

160° F − 32 = 128°
128° ÷ 1.8 = 71° C (rounded down from 71.11)

INDEX

A

Almond(s)
Cake, Italian, 287
flour, preparing, 313
French-Style Macaroons, 311–13, *312*
Picada, 50
Ring Coffee Cake, 110–12, *111*

Antipasto Pasta Salad, *122,* 141

Appetizers and starters
Ceviche, 239
Classic Cheddar Cheese Ball, 4, *5*
Cocktail Crab Cakes with Rémoulade Sauce,
    12–14, *13*
Crispy Polenta Triangles with Herbed Goat Cheese,
    10–11
French Onion and Bacon Tart, 20–22, *21*
German Pizza with Onion, Bacon, and Crème Fraîche,
    23–24
Hot Cheese Dip with Poblano and Chorizo, 6
Mini Beef and Cheese Empanadas, 14–16
Spicy Whipped Feta with Roasted Red Peppers, 7
Stuffed Mushrooms with Goat Cheese and Herb Stuffing,
    8, 9–10
The Ultimate Spicy Beef Nachos, 16–18, *17*
Zucchini Fritters, 19

Apple
-Cranberry Crisp, 280–81
Tartlets, Rustic Free-Form, 270–71

Artichokes, Tarragon, and Lemon, Creamy Baked Penne
    and Chicken with, 131–32

Arugula Salad with Grapes, Fennel, Gorgonzola, and
    Pecans, 30

Asian Cucumber Salad, Spicy, *26,* 27

Asparagus Omelet, 94

Authentic Beef Enchiladas, *168,* 169–70

B

Bacon
and Balsamic Vinegar, Roasted Glazed Turnips with, 63, *63*
and Cheddar, Creamy Cauliflower Casserole with, *56,* 73
Onion, and Crème Fraîche, German Pizza with, 23–24
and Onion Tart, French, 20–22, *21*
and Poached Egg, Frisée Salad with, 24–25

Baked Manicotti, *128,* 129–30

Baked Potatoes, 91

Baking powder, testing for freshness, 109

Bars
brownies, testing for doneness, 195
creating foil sling for pans, 321
Key Lime, 318–20, *319*
Pecan, 320–21
Seven-Layer, 322

Basil
Pasta Salad with Pesto, 140
Vinaigrette, Fresh, 31

Bean(s)
Black, Brazilian, with Ribs, Pork Tenderloin, and Sausage,
    46–47
Green, Casserole, *70,* 71–72
Green, Stir-Fried Sichuan, 60–62, *61*
green, trimming, 72
Indian-Style Curry with Potatoes, Cauliflower, Peas, and
    Chickpeas, 87–89, *88*
Slow-Cooker Lentil and Swiss Chard Stew, 53–54
The Ultimate Spicy Beef Nachos, 16–18, *17*

Beef
Brisket and Onions, Slow-Cooker, 167
chuck roast
    for best stew meat, 55
    Italian Pot Roast, *160,* 160–61
    Slow-Cooker Beef Stroganoff, 159
    Slow-Cooker Guinness Beef Stew, *34,* 54–55

Note: Page numbers *in italics* refer to color photographs.

Beef *(cont.)*
  ground
    Cincinnati Chili, *48*, 49
    From-the-Freezer Stuffed Peppers, 66–68, *67*
    Meatballs and Marinara, 136–38, *137*
    Mini Beef and Cheese Empanadas, 14–16
    30-Minute Meat Loaves, 148–49, *149*
    The Ultimate Spicy Beef Nachos, 16–18, *17*
    Well-Done Hamburgers, Charcoal-Grilled, 170–71
    Well-Done Hamburgers, Gas-Grilled, 171
  prime rib
    buying, 151
    Charcoal Grill-Roasted, *150*, 150–51
    foil "bone," creating, 151
    Gas Grill–Roasted, 151
  sirloin tips
    Philly Cheesesteaks, 172, *173*
    slicing thin, 172
  steak
    blade, trimming, 170
    Enchiladas, Authentic, *168*, 169–70
    Frites, 144–45
    and Potatoes, Charcoal-Grilled, with Blue Cheese Butter, 154–55, *155*
    and Potatoes, Gas-Grilled, with Blue Cheese Butter, 155
    sirloin, slicing, 154
    Skirt, Charcoal-Grilled, Fajitas, *152*, 153–54
    Skirt, Gas-Grilled, Fajitas, 154
    Slow-Cooker Italian Sunday Gravy, 138–39, *139*
  tenderloin
    Herb-Crusted, with Horseradish Cream Sauce, 146–48, *147*
    Roast, with Caramelized Onion and Mushroom Stuffing, 156–58, *157*
  tri-tip
    California-Style Barbecued, 162–64, *163*
    California-Style Barbecued, Gas-Grilled, 162
Beer
  Guinness, taste tests on, 55
  Slow-Cooker Guinness Beef Stew, *34*, 54–55
Bench scrapers, ratings of, 118
Berries
  Blueberry Boy Bait, 297
  Blueberry Streusel Muffins, 106–7, *107*
  Cranberry-Apple Crisp, 280–81
  Orange-Cranberry Rice Pilaf, 84, *85*
  Raspberry Chiffon Pie, 262–64, *263*
  Strawberry Poke Cake, *282*, 283–84
Best-Ever Hot Cocoa Mix, 325
Better Bran Muffins, *104*, 105–6
Big and Chewy Low-Fat Chocolate Chip Cookies, 308–10, *309*

Biscuits, Freezer, 113
Black-Bottom Cupcakes, 303
Blueberry Boy Bait, 297
Blueberry Streusel Muffins, 106–7, *107*
Boiled Potatoes, 91
Boning knives, ratings of, 258
Bourbon Bread Pudding, New Orleans, with Bourbon Sauce, 300–302, *301*
Bran Muffins, Better, *104*, 105–6
Brazilian Black Beans with Ribs, Pork Tenderloin, and Sausage, 46–47
Bread knives, ratings of, 258
Bread loaf pans, ratings of, 299
Bread(s)
  Almond Ring Coffee Cake, 110–12, *111*
  bread-making myths, 120
  bread-making techniques, 121
  Corn Dodgers, 119, *119*
  Double Corn Cornbread, 109
  Freezer Biscuits, 113
  hamburger buns, taste tests on, 171
  Olive-Rosemary, 116–18, *117*
  Pudding, New Orleans Bourbon, with Bourbon Sauce, 300–302, *301*
  testing for doneness, 195
  see also Muffins; Sandwiches; Stuffing; Tortillas
Broccoli
  Modern Chicken Divan, 204, *205*
Broiled Scallops with Creamy Mushroom Sauce, 249
Broth, vegetable, taste tests on, 54
Brownies, testing for doneness, 195
Brown Sugar Cookies, 314–16, *315*
Buns, hamburger, taste tests on, 171
Burgers
  Charcoal-Grilled Well-Done Hamburgers, 170–71
  Gas-Grilled Well-Done Hamburgers, 171
Butter, Herb, 144, 156–58, *157*

C

Cabbage
  Colcannon Soup, 41
Caesar Salad, Southwestern, 28, *29*
Cake pans
  round, ratings of, 286
  square, ratings of, 306

Cakes
  Almond, Italian, 287
  Almond Ring Coffee Cake, 110–12, *111*
  Black-Bottom Cupcakes, 303
  Blueberry Boy Bait, 297
  Carrot, Tropical, 278–80, *279*
  Chocolate Blackout, *260*, 291–92
  Fallen Chocolate, Individual, 296
  Lemon Layer, 288–90, *289*
  New York–Style Crumb, *304*, 305–6
  Pound, Classic, 298–99
  Red Velvet, 284–86, *285*
  Sour Cream Coffee Cake, 294, *295*
  Strawberry Poke, *282*, 283–84
  testing for doneness, 195

California-Style Barbecued Tri-Tip, 162–64, *163*

Capocollo, Salami, and Provolone, Stromboli with, 175–76

Carrot Cake, Tropical, 278–80, *279*

Carving boards, ratings of, 231

Casseroles
  Cauliflower, Creamy, with Bacon and Cheddar, *56*, 73
  Creamy Baked Penne and Chicken with Artichokes, Tarragon, and Lemon, 131–32
  Green Bean, *70*, 71–72
  King Ranch, *210*, 211
  Mashed Potato, 83
  Potato and Sausage Breakfast Popover, *100*, 101–2
  Zucchini and Tomato Tian, 59–60

Catfish in Salty-Sweet Caramel Sauce, 252

Cauliflower
  Casserole, Creamy, with Bacon and Cheddar, *56*, 73
  cutting, 73
  Potatoes, Peas, and Chickpeas, Indian-Style Curry with, 87–89, *88*
  Roasted, with Curry-Yogurt Sauce, *64*, 65

Cayenne pepper, 234

Ceviche, 239

Charcoal chimney starters, ratings of, 164

Charcoal-grilled recipes. *See* Grilled dishes

Chard, Swiss, and Lentil Stew, Slow-Cooker, 53–54

Cheddar Cheese
  Authentic Beef Enchiladas, *168*, 169–70
  and Bacon, Creamy Cauliflower Casserole with, *56*, 73
  Ball, Classic, 4, *5*
  Garlic Mashed Potatoes with Cheese, 82
  Mashed Potato Casserole, 83
  presliced, taste tests on, 171

Cheese
  Antipasto Pasta Salad, *122*, 141
  Arugula Salad with Grapes, Fennel, Gorgonzola, and Pecans, 30
  Asparagus Omelet, 94
  Baked Manicotti, *128*, 129–30
  Blue, Butter, Charcoal-Grilled Steak and Potatoes with, 154–55, *155*
  Cobb Chicken Salad, 214, *215*
  Creamy Baked Penne and Chicken with Artichokes, Tarragon, and Lemon, 131–32
  From-the-Freezer Stuffed Peppers, 66 68, *67*
  Garlicky Stuffed Baked Potatoes, 80–81, *81*
  Garlic Mashed Potatoes with, 82
  Monte Cristo Sandwiches, 114–16, *115*
  Philly Cheesesteaks, 172, *173*
  ricotta, taste tests on, 130
  Smoky Scalloped Potatoes, 77, *77*
  Soufflé, 102–3
  Stromboli with Salami, Capocollo, and Provolone, 175–76
  The Ultimate Spicy Beef Nachos, 16–18, *17*
  Zucchini and Tomato Tian, 59–60
  see also Cheddar Cheese; Cream cheese; Feta Cheese; Goat Cheese; Monterey Jack Cheese; Parmesan Cheese

Cheesecakes, testing for doneness, 195

Chef's knives, ratings of, 258

Cherry peppers, buying, 201

Chicken
  breasts
    bone-in, splitting, 201
    Cutlets, Parmesan-Crusted, 206
    Cutlets, Pecan-Crusted, 209
    Divan, Modern, 204, *205*
    Firecracker, *218*, 219–20
    Fricassee, Skillet Creole, 45
    Italian, with Sausage and Peppers, *196*, 200–201
    King Ranch Casserole, *210*, 211
    Marsala, 198, *199*
    and Penne, Creamy Baked, with Artichokes, Tarragon, and Lemon, 131–32
    Salad, Cobb, 214, *215*
    slicing thin, 40
    Soup, Thai-Style, 38–40, *39*
  pieces
    Barbecued, Classic, 224–26, *225*
    Barbecued, Classic, Gas-Grilled, 226
    Fried, Maryland, 212–13
    Picnic, Spice-Rubbed, 220–21
  thighs
    Latino-Style Chicken and Rice, 207–8
    Modern Coq au Vin, *202*, 202–3

Chicken *(cont.)*
  whole
    Butterflied Lemon, Charcoal-Grilled, 227–28, *229*
    Butterflied Lemon, Gas-Grilled, 228
    butterflying, 228
    Roast, with Root Vegetables, *216*, 216–17

Chickpeas, Potatoes, Cauliflower, and Peas, Indian-Style Curry with, 87–89, *88*

Chile(s)
  chipotle, about, 28
  chipotle, freezing, 28
  Firecracker Chicken, *218*, 219–20
  Hot Cheese Dip with Poblano and Chorizo, 6
  Hot Sauce, 46–47
  Peach-Habañero Chutney, 232
  Southwestern Caesar Salad, 28, *29*
  taming heat from, 201

Chili, Cincinnati, *48*, 49

Chili powder, taste tests on, 234

Chinese Barbecued Pork, *142*, 182–83

Chinese Sticky Ribs, 164–66, *165*

Chocolate
  Best-Ever Hot Cocoa Mix, 325
  Black-Bottom Cupcakes, 303
  Blackout Cake, *260*, 291–92
  Cakes, Individual Fallen, 296
  Chip Cookies, Big and Chewy Low-Fat, 308–10, *309*
  Hot Fudge Pudding Cake, 292–93
  Pots de Crème, 307–8
  Red Velvet Cake, 284–86, *285*
  Seven-Layer Bars, 322
  Walnut Fudge, 15-Minute, 323–25, *324*

Chorizo
  Mexican, about, 6
  and Poblano, Hot Cheese Dip with, 6
  Spanish, about, 6

Chutney, mango, taste tests on, 89

Chutney, Peach-Habañero, 232

Cider vinegar, taste tests on, 186

Cincinnati Chili, *48*, 49

Cinnamon, taste tests on, 234

Classic Barbecued Chicken, 224–26, *225*

Classic Cheddar Cheese Ball, 4, *5*

Classic Pound Cake, 298–99

Cleavers, ratings of, 258

Cloves, 234

Cobb Chicken Salad, 214, *215*

Cocktail Crab Cakes with Rémoulade Sauce, 12–14, *13*

Cocoa, Hot, Mix, Best-Ever, 325

Coconut
  milk, taste tests on, 40
  Seven-Layer Bars, 322
  Thai-Style Chicken Soup, 38–40, *39*
  Tropical Carrot Cake, 278–80, *279*

Coffee Cake
  Almond Ring, 110–12, *111*
  Blueberry Boy Bait, 297
  New York–Style Crumb Cake, *304*, 305–6
  Sour Cream, 294, *295*

Colanders, ratings of, 33

Colcannon Soup, 41

Cookies
  Brown Sugar, 314–16, *315*
  Chocolate Chip, Big and Chewy Low-Fat, 308–10, *309*
  Joe Froggers, 316–17
  testing for doneness, 195

Coriander, 234

Corn
  Double, Cornbread, 109
  Garden Fresh, 58, *58*
  removing from cob, 58

Cornbread, Double Corn, 109

Corn Dodgers, 119, *119*

Cornmeal
  Corn Dodgers, 119, *119*
  Double Corn Cornbread, 109

Crab
  Cakes, Cocktail, with Rémoulade Sauce, 12–14, *13*
  fresh, buying, 14

Cranberry
  -Apple Crisp, 280–81
  -Orange Rice Pilaf, 84, *85*

Cream cheese
  Black-Bottom Cupcakes, 303
  Red Velvet Cake, 284–86, *285*
  Tropical Carrot Cake, 278–80, *279*

Creamy Baked Penne and Chicken with Artichokes, Tarragon, and Lemon, 131–32

Creamy Cauliflower Casserole with Bacon and Cheddar, *56*, 73

Creole-Style Shrimp and Sausage Gumbo, 253–55, *254*

Crisp, Cranberry-Apple, 280–81

Crisp Iowa Skinny, 174

Crispy Polenta Triangles with Herbed Goat Cheese, 10–11

Crunchy Potato Wedges, 78–80, *79*

Cucumber(s)
English (hothouse), about, 27
Kirby, about, 27
removing seeds from, 27
Salad, Spicy Asian, *26*, 27

Cumin, taste tests on, 234

Cupcakes, Black-Bottom, 303

Curried dishes
Curry-Yogurt Sauce, *64*, 65
Indian-Style Curry with Potatoes, Cauliflower, Peas, and Chickpeas, 87–89, *88*
Thai-Style Chicken Soup, 38–40, *39*

Curry powder, taste tests on, 89, 234

Custards
Chocolate Pots de Crème, 307–8
testing for doneness, 195

Custard sauce, preparing, 308

D

Desserts
Best-Ever Hot Cocoa Mix, 325
Big and Chewy Low-Fat Chocolate Chip Cookies, 308–10, *309*
Brown Sugar Cookies, 314–16, *315*
Chocolate Pots de Crème, 307–8
Cranberry-Apple Crisp, 280–81
15-Minute Chocolate Walnut Fudge, 323–25, *324*
French-Style Macaroons, 311–13, *312*
Hot Fudge Pudding Cake, 292–93
Italian-Style Fig-Walnut Tart, *272*, 273–74
Joe Froggers, 316–17
Key Lime Bars, 318–20, *319*
New Orleans Bourbon Bread Pudding with Bourbon Sauce, 300–302, *301*
No-Fear Pie Crust, 264–65
Peach Crumble, 275–77, *276*
Pecan Bars, 320–21
Pumpkin-Praline Pie, *266*, 267–69
Raspberry Chiffon Pie, 262–64, *263*
Rustic Free-Form Apple Tartlets, 270–71
Seven-Layer Bars, 322
see also Cakes

Dips and spreads
Classic Cheddar Cheese Ball, 4, *5*
Hot Cheese Dip with Poblano and Chorizo, 6
Spicy Whipped Feta with Roasted Red Peppers, 7

Double Corn Cornbread, 109

Duck
breast, preparing for grilling, 233
breasts, buying, 233
Breasts, Charcoal-Grilled, with Peach-Habañero Chutney, 232–33
Breasts, Gas-Grilled, 233

Dutch ovens, ratings of, 49

E

Egg(s)
Asparagus Omelet, 94
Cheese Soufflé, 102–3
Fried, and Bread Crumbs, Spaghetti with, 124–26, *125*
Poached, and Bacon, Frisée Salad with, 24–25
poaching, tip for, 25
sizes, substitution chart, 95
whites, beating, 103

Electric knives, ratings of, 258

Empanadas, Mini Beef and Cheese, 14–16

Enchiladas, Authentic Beef, *168*, 169–70

Equipment, ratings of
bench scrapers, 118
box graters, 32
cake pans, round, 286
cake pans, square, 306
carving boards, 231
charcoal chimney starters, 164
colanders, 33
Dutch ovens, inexpensive, 49
garlic presses, 32
graters/zesters, 32
knives, 258
knife sharpeners, 214
ladles, 44
lasagna pans, 134
loaf pans, 299
mandolines, 60
measuring cups, 33
measuring spoons, 33
muffin tins, 108
pepper mills, 235

Equipment, ratings of *(cont.)*
  pie plates, 265
  pie servers, 264
  roasting racks, 217
  salad spinners, 33
  serrated fruit peelers, 277
  shears, kitchen, 32, 161
  skewers, metal, 242
  spatulas, heatproof rubber, 33
  spatulas, nonstick, 76
  spice grinders, 235
  spiders (wire skimmers), 145
  stockpots, 47
  strainers, fine-mesh, 32
  tart pans, 274
  thermometers, instant-read, 33, 194, 213
  thermometers, oven, 33
  tongs, 32
  vegetable peelers, 32
  waffle makers, 96
  whisks, 32
  wine openers, 203

F

Fajitas, Skirt Steak, Charcoal-Grilled, *152,* 153–54

Fajitas, Skirt Steak, Gas-Grilled, 154

Family-Style Shrimp Scampi, 250, *251*

Fennel, Grapes, Gorgonzola, and Pecans, Arugula Salad with, 30

Feta cheese
  buying, 7
  Spicy Whipped, with Roasted Red Peppers, 7
  Tomatoes, and Ouzo, Flambéed Shrimp with, 242–43
  Zucchini Fritters, 19

15-Minute Chocolate Walnut Fudge, 323–25, *324*

Fig-Walnut Tart, Italian-Style, *272,* 273–74

Firecracker Chicken, *218,* 219–20

Fish
  Catfish in Salty-Sweet Caramel Sauce, 252
  Ceviche, 239
  Salmon, Charcoal-Grilled Sweet and Saucy, *244,* 245–46
  Salmon, Gas-Grilled Sweet and Saucy, 245
  salmon fillets, skinning, 246
  Snapper, Charcoal-Grilled Blackened, 246–48, *247*
  Snapper, Gas-Grilled Blackened, 248
  testing for doneness, 194

Fish sauce, about, 40

Flambéing foods, 38

Flour, Manioc, Toasted, 46–47

Freezer Biscuits, 113

French Onion and Bacon Tart, 20–22, *21*

French-Style Macaroons, 311–13, *312*

Fresh Basil Vinaigrette, 31

Frisée Salad with Bacon and Poached Egg, 24–25

Fritters, Zucchini, 19

From-the-Freezer Stuffed Peppers, 66–68, *67*

Fruit
  citrus, zesting, 84
  Dried, Pecans, and Port, Stuffed Pork Chops with, 187–88, *189*
  see also specific fruits

Fruit peelers, ratings of, 277

Fudge, 15-Minute Chocolate Walnut, 323–25, *324*

G

Garden Fresh Corn, 58, *58*

Garlic
  flavoring recipes with, 44
  Garlicky Stuffed Baked Potatoes, 80–81, *81*
  Mashed Potatoes with Cheese, 82
  Potato Soup, 42–44, *43*
  presses, ratings of, 32

Gas-grilled recipes. *See* Grilled dishes

German Pizza with Onion, Bacon, and Crème Fraîche, 23–24

Ginger, peeling, 62

Gingerbread Muffins, 108

Goat Cheese
  Herbed, Crispy Polenta Triangles with, 10–11
  and Herb Stuffing, Stuffed Mushrooms with, *8,* 9–10
  Stuffed Plum Tomatoes, 68–69, *69*
  taste tests on, 11

Grains
  Better Bran Muffins, *104,* 105–6
  Corn Dodgers, 119, *119*
  Double Corn Cornbread, 109
  Multigrain Pancakes, 98–99, *99*
  see also Rice

Grapes, Fennel, Gorgonzola, and Pecans, Arugula Salad with, 30

Graters, box, ratings of, 32

Graters/zesters, ratings of, 32

Gravy, Slow-Cooker Italian Sunday, 138–39, *139*

Green Bean(s)

Casserole, *70,* 71–72

Stir-Fried Sichuan, 60–62, *61*

trimming, 72

Greens

Arugula Salad with Grapes, Fennel, Gorgonzola, and Pecans, 30

Frisée Salad with Bacon and Poached Egg, 24–25

measuring, 30

Slow-Cooker Lentil and Swiss Chard Stew, 53–54

Southwestern Caesar Salad, 28, *29*

Grilled dishes

California-Style Barbecued Tri-Tip, 162–64, *163*

Charcoal-Grilled Blackened Snapper, 246–48, *247*

Charcoal-Grilled Butterflied Lemon Chicken, 227–28, *229*

Charcoal-Grilled Duck Breasts with Peach-Habañero Chutney, 232–33

Charcoal-Grilled Lamb Chops with Near East Red Pepper Paste, *192,* 192–93

Charcoal-Grilled Lobsters, *236,* 256–57

Charcoal-Grilled Shrimp Skewers with Spicy Lemon-Garlic Sauce, 240–42, *241*

Charcoal-Grilled Skirt Steak Fajitas, *152,* 153–54

Charcoal-Grilled Steak and Potatoes with Blue Cheese Butter, 154–55, *155*

Charcoal-Grilled Sweet and Saucy Salmon, *244,* 245–46

Charcoal-Grilled Well-Done Hamburgers, 170–71

Charcoal Grill–Roasted Prime Rib, *150,* 150–51

Classic Barbecued Chicken, 224–26, *225*

Gas-Grilled Blackened Snapper, 248

Gas-Grilled Butterflied Lemon Chicken, 228

Gas-Grilled California-Style Barbecued Tri-Tip, 162

Gas-Grilled Classic Barbecued Chicken, 226

Gas-Grilled Duck Breasts, 233

Gas-Grilled Lamb Chops with Near East Red Pepper Paste, 193

Gas-Grilled Lexington-Style Pulled Pork, 186

Gas-Grilled Lobsters, 257

Gas-Grilled Roasted Turkey Breast, 224

Gas-Grilled Shrimp Skewers with Spicy Lemon-Garlic Sauce, 242

Gas-Grilled Skirt Steak Fajitas, 154

Gas-Grilled Steak and Potatoes with Blue Cheese Butter, 155

Gas-Grilled Sweet and Saucy Salmon, 245

Gas-Grilled Well-Done Hamburgers, 171

Gas Grill–Roasted Prime Rib, 151

Grill-Roasted Turkey Breast, 222–24, *223*

Lexington-Style Pulled Pork, *184,* 185–86

Gumbo, Creole-Style Shrimp and Sausage, 253–55, *254*

H

Ham

Monte Cristo Sandwiches, 114–16, *115*

Herb

Butter, 144, 156–58, *157*

-Crusted Beef Tenderloin with Horseradish Cream Sauce, 146–48, *147*

-Crusted Pork Loin, *179,* 179–80

Hoisin sauce, taste tests on, 183

Horseradish Cream Sauce, 146

Hot Cheese Dip with Poblano and Chorizo, 6

Hot Cocoa Mix, Best-Ever, 325

Hot Fudge Pudding Cake, 292–93

Hot Sauce, 46–47

I

Indian-Style Curry with Potatoes, Cauliflower, Peas, and Chickpeas, 87–89, *88*

Individual Fallen Chocolate Cakes, 296

Ingredients, tastings of

cheddar cheese, presliced, 171

coconut milk, 40

curry powder, 89

Dijon mustard, 31

goat cheese, 11

Guinness beer, 55

hamburger buns, 171

hoisin sauce, 183

ketchup, 226

lasagna noodles, no-boil, 130

mango chutney, 89

olive oil, extra-virgin, 7

peppercorns, black, 235

pumpkin, canned, 269

ricotta cheese, 130

soy sauce, 159

spices, 234

strawberry preserves, 116

tomatoes, crushed, canned, 138

tomatoes, whole, canned, 52

tomato paste, 127

tomato sauce, 170

tortilla chips, 18

vegetable broth, 54

vinegar, balsamic, 63

vinegar, cider, 186

vodka, 127

Italian Almond Cake, 287

Italian Chicken with Sausage and Peppers, *196*, 200–201

Italian Pot Roast, *160*, 160–61

Italian-Style Fig-Walnut Tart, *272*, 273–74

J

Joe Froggers, 316–17

K

Ketchup, taste tests on, 226

Key Lime Bars, 318–20, *319*

King Ranch Casserole, *210*, 211

Kitchen shears, ratings of, 32, 161

Kitchen tools, ratings of, 32–33

Knives
    essential, buying, 258
    holding and gripping, 259
    ratings of, 258
    sharpeners, ratings of, 214
    sharpening, 259

L

Ladles, ratings of, 44

Lamb
    Chops, Charcoal-Grilled, with Near East Red Pepper Paste, *192*, 192–93
    Chops, Gas-Grilled, with Near East Red Pepper Paste, 193

Lasagna
    Low-Fat Meaty, 132–34, *133*
    noodles, taste tests on, 130

Lasagna pans, ratings of, 134

Latino-Style Chicken and Rice, 207–8

Leeks
    Colcannon Soup, 41
    preparing and washing, 41

Lemon(s)
    Chicken, Butterflied, Charcoal-Grilled, 227–28, *229*
    Chicken, Butterflied, Gas-Grilled, 228
    Layer Cake, 288–90, *289*
    zesting, 84

Lentil and Swiss Chard Stew, Slow-Cooker, 53–54

Lexington-Style Pulled Pork, *184*, 185–86

Light and Crispy Waffles, 94–96, *97*

Lime(s)
    Key, about, 320
    Key, Bars, 318–20, *319*
    regular, about, 320

Loaf pans, ratings of, 299

Lobsters
    Charcoal-Grilled, *236*, 256–57
    Gas-Grilled, 257
    preparing for grilling, 257

Low-Fat Meaty Lasagna, 132–34, *133*

M

Macaroons, French-Style, 311–13, *312*

Main dishes
    meat
        Authentic Beef Enchiladas, *168*, 169–70
        Brazilian Black Beans with Ribs, Pork Tenderloin, and Sausage, 46–47
        California-Style Barbecued Tri-Tip, 162–64, *163*
        Charcoal-Grilled Lamb Chops with Near East Red Pepper Paste, *192*, 192–93
        Charcoal-Grilled Skirt Steak Fajitas, *152*, 153–54
        Charcoal-Grilled Steak and Potatoes with Blue Cheese Butter, 154–55, *155*
        Charcoal-Grilled Well-Done Hamburgers, 170–71
        Charcoal Grill–Roasted Prime Rib, *150*, 150–51
        Chinese Barbecued Pork, *142*, 182–83
        Chinese Sticky Ribs, 164–66, *165*
        Cincinnati Chili, *48*, 49
        Crisp Iowa Skinny, 174
        From-the-Freezer Stuffed Peppers, 66–68, *67*
        Gas-Grilled California-Style Barbecued Tri-Tip, 162
        Gas-Grilled Lamb Chops with Near East Red Pepper Paste, 193
        Gas-Grilled Lexington-Style Pulled Pork, 186
        Gas-Grilled Skirt Steak Fajitas, 154
        Gas-Grilled Steak and Potatoes with Blue Cheese Butter, 155
        Gas-Grilled Well-Done Hamburgers, 171
        Gas Grill–Roasted Prime Rib, 151
        Herb-Crusted Beef Tenderloin with Horseradish Cream Sauce, 146–48, *147*
        Herb-Crusted Pork Loin, *179*, 179–80
        Italian Pot Roast, *160*, 160–61
        Lexington-Style Pulled Pork, *184*, 185–86
        Philly Cheesesteaks, 172, *173*
        Pork Tenderloin Medallions with Apple-Cider Sauce, *190*, 190–91

Main dishes *(cont.)*

Roast Beef Tenderloin with Caramelized Onion and Mushroom Stuffing, 156–58, *157*

Slow-Cooker Beef Stroganoff, 159

Slow-Cooker Brisket and Onions, 167

Slow-Cooker Guinness Beef Stew, *34*, 54–55

Slow-Cooker Smothered Pork Chops, 176–78, *177*

Slow-Fried Shredded Pork, 181

Steak Frites, 144–45

Stromboli with Salami, Capocollo, and Provolone, 175–76

Stuffed Pork Chops with Port, Pecans, and Dried Fruit, 187–88, *189*

30-Minute Meat Loaves, 148–49, *149*

meatless

Indian-Style Curry with Potatoes, Cauliflower, Peas, and Chickpeas, 87–89, *88*

Slow-Cooker Lentil and Swiss Chard Stew, 53–54

pasta

Antipasto Pasta Salad, *122*, 141

Baked Manicotti, *128*, 129–30

Creamy Baked Penne and Chicken with Artichokes, Tarragon, and Lemon, 131–32

Low-Fat Meaty Lasagna, 132–34, *133*

Meatballs and Marinara, 136–38, *137*

Pasta Salad with Pesto, 140

Pasta with Fresh Tomato Sauce with Rosemary and Bacon, 135

Penne alla Vodka, 126–27, *127*

Slow-Cooker Italian Sunday Gravy, 138–39, *139*

Spaghetti with Fried Eggs and Bread Crumbs, 124–26, *125*

poultry

Charcoal-Grilled Butterflied Lemon Chicken, 227–28, *229*

Charcoal-Grilled Duck Breasts with Peach-Habañero Chutney, 232–33

Chicken Marsala, 198, *199*

Classic Barbecued Chicken, 224–26, *225*

Cobb Chicken Salad, 214, *215*

Firecracker Chicken, *218*, 219–20

Gas-Grilled Butterflied Lemon Chicken, 228

Gas-Grilled Classic Barbecued Chicken, 226

Gas-Grilled Duck Breasts, 233

Gas-Grilled Roasted Turkey Breast, 224

Grill-Roasted Turkey Breast, 222–24, *223*

Italian Chicken with Sausage and Peppers, *196*, 200–201

King Ranch Casserole, *210*, 211

Latino-Style Chicken and Rice, 207–8

Maryland Fried Chicken, 212–13

Modern Chicken Divan, 204, *205*

Modern Coq au Vin, *202*, 202–3

Parmesan-Crusted Chicken Cutlets, 206

Main dishes *(cont.)*

Pecan-Crusted Chicken Cutlets, 209

Roast Chicken with Root Vegetables, *216*, 216–17

Roast Salted Turkey, 230–31

Skillet Creole Chicken Fricassee, 45

Spice-Rubbed Picnic Chicken, 220–21

seafood

Broiled Scallops with Creamy Mushroom Sauce, 249

Catfish in Salty-Sweet Caramel Sauce, 252

Ceviche, 239

Charcoal-Grilled Blackened Snapper, 246–48, *247*

Charcoal-Grilled Lobsters, *236*, 256–57

Charcoal-Grilled Shrimp Skewers with Spicy Lemon-Garlic Sauce, 240–42, *241*

Charcoal-Grilled Sweet and Saucy Salmon, *244*, 245–46

Creole Style Shrimp and Sausage Gumbo, 253–55, *254*

Family-Style Shrimp Scampi, 250, *251*

Flambéed Shrimp with Tomatoes, Feta, and Ouzo, 242–43

Gas-Grilled Blackened Snapper, 248

Gas-Grilled Lobsters, 257

Gas-Grilled Shrimp Skewers with Spicy Lemon-Garlic Sauce, 242

Gas-Grilled Sweet and Saucy Salmon, 245

Mussels in White Wine with Parsley, 238

Spanish Shellfish Stew, 50–52, *51*

Mandolines, ratings of, 60

Mango chutney, taste tests on, 89

Manicotti, Baked, *128*, 129–30

Manioc Flour, Toasted, 46–47

Marinara Sauce, 136

Marsala wine, about, 198

Maryland Fried Chicken, 212–13

Mashed Potato Casserole, 83

Mashed Potatoes, 91

Mashed Potatoes, Garlic, with Cheese, 82

Measuring cups, ratings of, 33

Measuring spoons, ratings of, 33

Meat

Loaves, 30-Minute, 148–49, *149*

testing for doneness, 194

see also Beef; Lamb; Pork

Meatballs and Marinara, 136–38, *137*

Mini Beef and Cheese Empanadas, 14–16

Modern Chicken Divan, 204, *205*

Modern Coq au Vin, *202*, 202–3

Molasses

Joe Froggers, 316–17

Monte Cristo Sandwiches, 114–16, *115*

Monterey Jack cheese
Authentic Beef Enchiladas, *168,* 169–70
Hot Cheese Dip with Poblano and Chorizo, 6
King Ranch Casserole, *210,* 211
Mini Beef and Cheese Empanadas, 14–16

Muffins
Blueberry Streusel, 106–7, *107*
Bran, Better, *104,* 105–6
Gingerbread, 108
testing for doneness, 195

Muffin tins, ratings of, 108

Multigrain Pancakes, 98–99, *99*

Mushroom(s)
Antipasto Pasta Salad, *122,* 141
and Caramelized Onion Stuffing, Roast Beef Tenderloin
with, 156–58, *157*
Chicken Marsala, 198, *199*
cutting into quarters, 72
Green Bean Casserole, *70,* 71–72
Italian Pot Roast, *160,* 160–61
Low-Fat Meaty Lasagna, 132–34, *133*
Modern Coq au Vin, *202,* 202–3
portobello, removing gills from, 54
Sauce, Creamy, Broiled Scallops with, 249
Slow-Cooker Beef Stroganoff, 159
Slow-Cooker Lentil and Swiss Chard Stew, 53–54
Stuffed, with Goat Cheese and Herb Stuffing, *8,* 9–10
Thai Style Chicken Soup, 38–40, *39*

Mussels
buying and storing, 238
debearding, 52
Spanish Shellfish Stew, 50–52, *51*
in White Wine with Parsley, 238

Mustard, Dijon, taste tests on, 31

N

Nachos, Spicy Beef, The Ultimate, 16–18, *17*

New Orleans Bourbon Bread Pudding with Bourbon
Sauce, 300–302, *301*

New York–Style Crumb Cake, *304,* 305–6

No-Fear Pie Crust, 264–65

Nutmeg, 234

Nuts
15-Minute Chocolate Walnut Fudge, 323–25, *324*
Italian-Style Fig-Walnut Tart, *272,* 273–74
Sour Cream Coffee Cake, 294, *295*
toasting, 321
see also Almond(s); Pecan(s)

O

Olive oil, extra-virgin, taste tests on, 7

Olive-Rosemary Bread, 116–18, *117*

Omelet, Asparagus, 94

Onion(s)
Bacon, and Crème Fraîche, German Pizza with,
23–24
and Bacon Tart, French, 20–22, *21*
Brisket and, Slow-Cooker, 167
Caramelized, and Mushroom Stuffing, Roast Beef
Tenderloin with, 156–58, *157*
Green Bean Casserole, *70,* 71–72
slicing thin, 24

Orange-Cranberry Rice Pilaf, 84, *85*

Oranges, zesting, 84

Ouzo, about, 243

Oven-Baked Holiday Stuffing, 86

P

Pancakes, Multigrain, 98–99, *99*

Paprika, taste tests on, 234

Paring knives, ratings of, 258

Parmesan cheese
Baked Manicotti, *128,* 129–30
–Crusted Chicken Cutlets, 206
Modern Chicken Divan, 204, *205*
Pasta Salad with Pesto, 140
Southwestern Caesar Salad, 28, *29*

Pasta
Baked Manicotti, *128,* 129–30
cooking water, reserving, 126
Creamy Baked Penne and Chicken with Artichokes,
Tarragon, and Lemon, 131–32
with Fresh Tomato Sauce with Rosemary and Bacon,
135
Low-Fat Meaty Lasagna, 132–34, *133*
Meatballs and Marinara, 136–38, *137*
Penne alla Vodka, 126–27, *127*
Salad, Antipasto, *122,* 141
Salad with Pesto, 140
Slow-Cooker Italian Sunday Gravy, 138–39, *139*
Spaghetti with Fried Eggs and Bread Crumbs,
124–26, *125*

Pastries, testing for doneness, 195

Peach Crumble, 275–77, *276*

Peach-Habañero Chutney, 232

Peas, Potatoes, Cauliflower, and Chickpeas, Indian-Style Curry with, 87–89, *88*

Pecan(s)
Bars, 320–21
-Crusted Chicken Cutlets, 209
Dried Fruit, and Port, Stuffed Pork Chops with, 187–88, *189*
Grapes, Fennel, and Gorgonzola, Arugula Salad with, 30
Pumpkin-Praline Pie, *266,* 267–69
Seven-Layer Bars, 322

Penne alla Vodka, 126–27, *127*

Peppercorns
black pepper, taste tests on, 235
pepper mills, ratings of, 235
white pepper, about, 62, 235

Pepper(s)
Antipasto Pasta Salad, *122,* 141
Charcoal-Grilled Skirt Steak Fajitas, *152,* 153–54
cherry, buying, 201
Gas-Grilled Skirt Steak Fajitas, 154
preparing, 45
Red, Paste, Near East, Charcoal-Grilled Lamb Chops with, *192,* 192–93
Roasted Red, Spicy Whipped Feta with, 7
and Sausage, Italian Chicken with, *196,* 200–201
Stuffed, From-the-Freezer, 66–68, *67*
see also Chile(s)

Pesto, Pasta Salad with, 140

Philly Cheesesteaks, 172, *173*

Picada, 50

Pie Crust
blind-baking, 269
fitting dough into pie plate, 268
forming fluted edge, 265
No-Fear, 264–65

Pie plates, ratings of, 265

Pies
Pumpkin-Praline, *266,* 267–69
Raspberry Chiffon, 262–64, *263*
testing for doneness, 195

Pie servers, ratings of, 264

Pineapple
Tropical Carrot Cake, 278–80, *279*

Pizza, German, with Onion, Bacon, and Crème Fraîche, 23–24

Poblano and Chorizo, Hot Cheese Dip with, 6

Polenta Triangles, Crispy, with Herbed Goat Cheese, 10–11

Pork
chops
Smothered, Slow-Cooker, 176–78, *177*
Stuffed, with Port, Pecans, and Dried Fruit, 187–88, *189*
ground
Stir-Fried Sichuan Green Beans, 60–62, *61*
30-Minute Meat Loaves, 148–49, *149*
Loin, Herb-Crusted, *179,* 179–80
natural versus enhanced, 188
ribs
Chinese Sticky Ribs, 164–66, *165*
Slow-Cooker Italian Sunday Gravy, 138–39, *139*
spareribs membrane, removing, 166
shoulder roast
Chinese Barbecued, *142,* 182–83
cutting up, 183
Pulled, Lexington-Style, *184,* 185–86
Pulled, Lexington-Style, Gas-Grilled, 186
Slow-Fried, Shredded, 181
tenderloin
Crisp Iowa Skinny, 174
cutlets, preparing, 174
end pieces, creating medallion from, 191
Medallions with Apple-Cider Sauce, *190,* 190–91
Ribs, and Sausage, Brazilian Black Beans with, 46–47
see also Bacon; Ham; Sausage(s)

Potato(es)
Baked, 91
Boiled, 91
Cauliflower, Peas, and Chickpeas, Indian-Style Curry with, 87–89, *88*
Colcannon Soup, 41
cooking methods, 91
Garlic Soup, 42–44, *43*
green patches on, 90
Mashed, 91
Mashed, Casserole, 83
Mashed Garlic, with Cheese, 82
Roasted, 91
Roesti, 74–76, *75*
and Sausage Breakfast Popover Casserole, *100,* 101–2
Scalloped, Smoky, 77, *77*
Slow-Cooker Guinness Beef Stew, *34,* 54–55
starch content in, 90
and Steak, Charcoal-Grilled, with Blue Cheese Butter, 154–55, *155*
and Steak, Gas-Grilled, with Blue Cheese Butter, 155
Steak Frites, 144–45

Potato(es) *(cont.)*
  Stuffed Baked, Garlicky, 80–81, *81*
  varieties of, 90
  Wedges, Crunchy, 78–80, *79*

Pots de Crème, Chocolate, 307–8

Poultry
  testing for doneness, 194
  see also Chicken; Duck; Turkey

Pound Cake, Classic, 298–99

Pudding, Bread, New Orleans Bourbon, with Bourbon
  Sauce, 300–302, *301*

Puddings, testing for doneness, 195

Pumpkin, canned, taste tests on, 269

Pumpkin-Praline Pie, *266*, 267–69

Q

Quick BBQ Sauce, 224–26

R

Raisins
  Better Bran Muffins, *104*, 105–6
  New Orleans Bourbon Bread Pudding with Bourbon Sauce,
    300–302, *301*

Raspberry Chiffon Pie, 262–64, *263*

Red Velvet Cake, 284–86, *285*

Rémoulade Sauce, 12

Rice
  and Chicken, Latino-Style, 207–8
  From-the-Freezer Stuffed Peppers, 66–68, *67*
  Pilaf, Orange-Cranberry, 84, *85*
  varieties of, 84

Roast Beef Tenderloin with Caramelized Onion and
  Mushroom Stuffing, 156–58, *157*

Roast Chicken with Root Vegetables, *216*, 216–17

Roasted Cauliflower with Curry-Yogurt Sauce, *64*, 65

Roasted Glazed Turnips with Bacon and Balsamic Vinegar,
  63, *63*

Roasted Potatoes, 91

Roasting racks, ratings of, 217

Roast Salted Turkey, 230–31

Roesti, Potato, 74–76, *75*

Rosemary-Olive Bread, 116–18, *117*

Rustic Free-Form Apple Tartlets, 270–71

S

Saffron, 234

Salad dressing. *See* Vinaigrette

Salads
  Arugula, with Grapes, Fennel, Gorgonzola, and Pecans,
    30
  Caesar, Southwestern, 28, *29*
  Chicken, Cobb, 214, *215*
  Cucumber, Spicy Asian, *26*, 27
  Frisée, with Bacon and Poached Egg, 24–25
  Pasta, Antipasto, *122*, 141
  Pasta, with Pesto, 140

Salad spinners, ratings of, 33

Salami, Capocollo, and Provolone, Stromboli with,
  175–76

Salmon
  fillets, skinning, 246
  Sweet and Saucy, Charcoal-Grilled,
    244, 245–46
  Sweet and Saucy, Gas-Grilled, 245

Salsa, 18

Sandwiches
  Cobb Chicken Salad, 214, *215*
  Crisp Iowa Skinny, 174
  Monte Cristo, 114–16, *115*
  Philly Cheesesteaks, 172, *173*
  see also Burgers

Sauces
  BBQ, Quick, 224–26
  Curry-Yogurt, *64*, 65
  custard, preparing, 308
  Horseradish Cream, 146
  Hot, 46–47
  Marinara, 136
  Rémoulade, 12
  Slow-Cooker Italian Sunday Gravy,
    138–39, *139*
  Tomato, 129

Sausage(s)
  Antipasto Pasta Salad, *122*, 141
  chorizo, types of, 6
  From-the-Freezer Stuffed Peppers, 66–68, *67*
  Hot Cheese Dip with Poblano and Chorizo, 6
  Meatballs and Marinara, 136–38, *137*
  and Peppers, Italian Chicken with, *196*, 200–201
  Pork Tenderloin, and Ribs, Brazilian Black Beans with,
    46–47
  and Potato Breakfast Popover Casserole, *100*, 101–2
  and Shrimp Gumbo, Creole-Style, 253–55, *254*
  Skillet Creole Chicken Fricassee, 45

Sausage(s) *(cont.)*
Slow-Cooker Italian Sunday Gravy, 138–39, *139*
Stromboli with Salami, Capocollo, and Provolone, 175–76

Scallops
Broiled, with Creamy Mushroom Sauce, 249
buying, 249
Ceviche, 239
preparing, 52
Spanish Shellfish Stew, 50–52, *51*

Seafood. *See* Fish; Shellfish

Serrated fruit peelers, ratings of, 277

Seven-Layer Bars, 322

Shellfish
Ceviche, 239
Crab Cakes, Cocktail, with Rémoulade Sauce, 12–14, *13*
lobster, preparing for grilling, 257
Lobsters, Charcoal-Grilled, *236,* 256–57
Lobsters, Gas-Grilled, 257
mussels, buying and storing, 238
mussels, debearding, 52, 238
Mussels in White Wine with Parsley, 238
Scallops, Broiled, with Creamy Mushroom Sauce, 249
scallops, buying, 249
scallops, preparing, 52
Stew, Spanish, 50–52, *51*
see also Shrimp

Shrimp
Bisque, 36–38, *37*
buying, 243
Ceviche, 239
deveining, 250
Flambéed, with Tomatoes, Feta, and Ouzo, 242–43
and Sausage Gumbo, Creole-Style, 253–55, *254*
Scampi, Family-Style, 250, *251*
Skewers, Charcoal-Grilled, with Spicy Lemon-Garlic Sauce, 240–42, *241*
Skewers, Gas-Grilled, with Spicy Lemon-Garlic Sauce, 242
Spanish Shellfish Stew, 50–52, *51*

Sichuan Green Beans, Stir-Fried, 60–62, *61*

Side dishes
Cauliflower, Roasted, with Curry-Yogurt Sauce, *64,* 65
Cauliflower Casserole, Creamy, with Bacon and Cheddar, *56,* 73
Corn, Garden Fresh, 58, *58*
Green Bean Casserole, *70,* 71–72
Green Beans, Stir-Fried Sichuan, 60–62, *61*
Indian-Style Curry with Potatoes, Cauliflower, Peas, and Chickpeas, 87–89, *88*

Side dishes *(cont.)*
Orange-Cranberry Rice Pilaf, 84, *85*
Oven-Baked Holiday Stuffing, 86
potato(es)
Baked, 91
Boiled, 91
Garlicky Stuffed Baked, 80–81, *81*
Garlic Mashed, with Cheese, 82
Mashed, 91
Mashed Potato Casserole, 83
Roasted, 91
Roesti, 74–76, *75*
Smoky Scalloped, 77, *77*
Wedges, Crunchy, 78–80, *79*
Tomatoes, Plum, Stuffed, 68–69, *69*
Turnips, Roasted Glazed, with Bacon and Balsamic Vinegar, 63, *63*
Zucchini and Tomato Tian, 59–60

Skewers, ratings of, 242

Skillet Creole Chicken Fricassee, 45

Slicing/carving knives, ratings of, 258

Slow-cooker dishes
Slow-Cooker Beef Stroganoff, 159
Slow-Cooker Brisket and Onions, 167
Slow-Cooker Guinness Beef Stew, *34,* 54–55
Slow-Cooker Italian Sunday Gravy, 138–39, *139*
Slow-Cooker Lentil and Swiss Chard Stew, 53–54
Slow-Cooker Smothered Pork Chops, 176–78, *177*

Slow-Fried Shredded Pork, 181

Smoky Scalloped Potatoes, 77, *77*

Snapper, Blackened, Charcoal-Grilled, 246–48, *247*

Snapper, Blackened, Gas-Grilled, 248

Soufflé, Cheese, 102–3

Soufflé dishes, buying, 103

Soups
Chicken, Thai-Style, 38–40, *39*
Colcannon, 41
Potato Garlic, 42–44, *43*
Shrimp Bisque, 36–38, *37*
see also Stews

Sour Cream Coffee Cake, 294, *295*

Southwestern Caesar Salad, 28, *29*

Soy sauce, taste tests on, 159

Spaghetti with Fried Eggs and Bread Crumbs, 124–26, *125*

Spanish Shellfish Stew, 50–52, *51*

Spatulas, heatproof rubber, ratings of, 33

Spatulas, nonstick, ratings of, 76

Spice grinders, cleaning, 235

Spice grinders, ratings of, 235

Spice-Rubbed Picnic Chicken, 220–21

Spices 101, 234–35
  blooming, 235
  buying and storing, 235
  taste tests on, 234
  toasting, 235

Spicy Asian Cucumber Salad, *26*, 27

Spicy Whipped Feta with Roasted Red Peppers, 7

Spiders (wire skimmers), ratings of, 145

Squash
  canned pumpkin, taste tests on, 269
  Garden Fresh Corn, 58, *58*
  grating and squeezing dry, 19
  Pumpkin-Praline Pie, *266*, 267–69
  Zucchini and Tomato Tian, 59–60
  Zucchini Fritters, 19

Steak Frites, 144–45

Stews
  beef, best cuts for, 55
  Brazilian Black Beans with Ribs, Pork Tenderloin, and Sausage, 46–47
  Creole-Style Shrimp and Sausage Gumbo, 253–55, *254*
  Guinness Beef, Slow-Cooker, *34*, 54–55
  Indian-Style Curry with Potatoes, Cauliflower, Peas, and Chickpeas, 87–89, *88*
  Lentil and Swiss Chard, Slow-Cooker, 53–54
  Modern Coq au Vin, *202*, 202–3
  Shellfish, Spanish, 50–52, *51*

Stir-Fried Sichuan Green Beans, 60–62, *61*

Stockpots, ratings of, 47

Strainers, fine-mesh, ratings of, 32

Strawberry Poke Cake, *282*, 283–84

Strawberry preserves, taste tests on, 116

Stroganoff, Beef, Slow-Cooker, 159

Stromboli with Salami, Capocollo, and Provolone, 175–76

Stuffed Mushrooms with Goat Cheese and Herb Stuffing, *8*, 9–10

Stuffed Pork Chops with Port, Pecans, and Dried Fruit, 187–88, *189*

Stuffing, Holiday, Oven-Baked, 86

T

Tarts
  dough, patting into pan, 22, 274
  Fig-Walnut, Italian-Style, *272*, 273–74
  German Pizza with Onion, Bacon, and Crème Fraîche, 23–24
  Onion and Bacon, French, 20–22, *21*
  Rustic Free-Form Apple Tartlets, 270–71
  tart pans, ratings of, 274

Techniques
  almond flour, preparing, 313
  baked goods, testing for doneness, 195
  baking powder, testing for freshness, 109
  beef blade steaks, trimming, 170
  beef sirloin tips, slicing thin, 172
  beef skirt steak, slicing, 154
  bell peppers, preparing, 45
  bread making at a glance, 121
  cauliflower, cutting, 73
  chicken, butterflying, 228
  chicken breast, bone-in, splitting, 201
  chicken breasts, slicing thin, 40
  chipotle chiles, freezing, 28
  corn, removing from cob, 58
  corn tortillas, freezing, 170
  cucumbers, seeding, 27
  custard sauce, preparing, 308
  duck breast, preparing for grilling, 233
  eggs, poaching, 25
  egg whites, beating, 103
  fish, testing for doneness, 194
  flambéing foods, 38
  foil prime rib "bone," creating, 151
  foil sling for bar cookies, creating, 321
  fruit, citrus, zesting, 84
  ginger, peeling, 62
  green beans, trimming, 72
  greens, measuring, 30
  leeks, preparing and washing, 41
  lobster, preparing for grilling, 257
  meat, testing for doneness, 194
  mushrooms, cutting into quarters, 72
  mushrooms, removing gills from, 54
  mussels, debearding, 52
  nuts, toasting, 321
  onions, slicing thin, 24
  pasta water, reserving, 126
  pie crust, blind-baking, 269
  pie crust edges, forming, 265
  pie dough, fitting into pie plate, 268
  pork butt, cutting up, 183
  pork cutlets, preparing, 174